SHAKESPEAREAN PLAYHOUSES

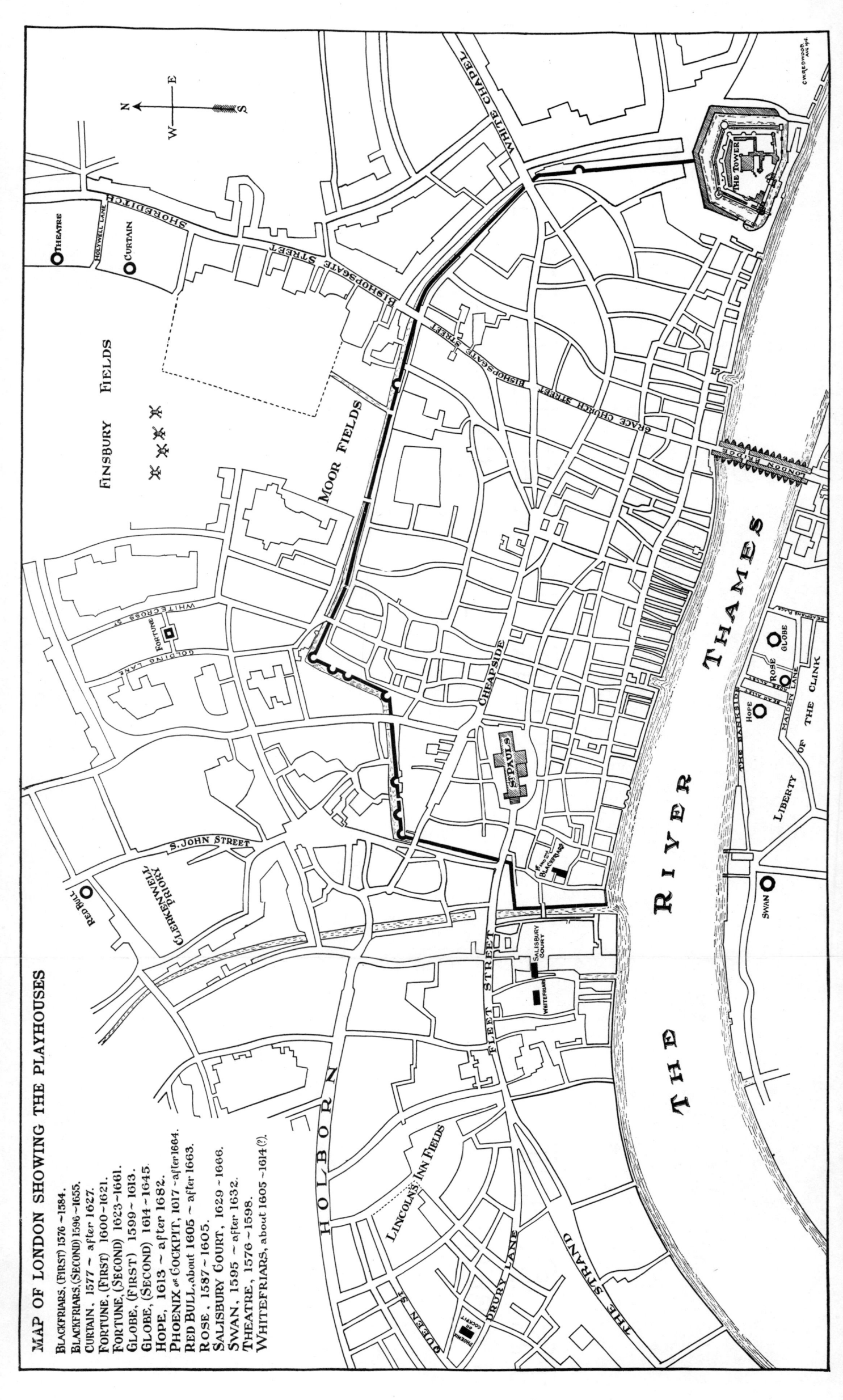

Shakespearean Playhouses

A HISTORY OF ENGLISH THEATRES *from the* BEGINNINGS *to the* RESTORATION

By JOSEPH QUINCY ADAMS
Cornell University

Gloucester, Mass.
PETER SMITH
1960

COPYRIGHT, 1917, BY
JOSEPH QUINCY ADAMS
REPRINTED, 1960,
BY PERMISSION OF
HOUGHTON MIFFLIN CO.

TO

LANE COOPER

IN GRATITUDE AND ESTEEM

PREFACE

THE method of dramatic representation in the time of Shakespeare has long received close study. Among those who have more recently devoted their energies to the subject may be mentioned W. J. Lawrence, T. S. Graves, G. F. Reynolds, V. E. Albright, A. H. Thorndike, and B. Neuendorff, each of whom has embodied the results of his investigations in one or more noteworthy volumes. But the history of the playhouses themselves, a topic equally important, has not hitherto been attempted. If we omit the brief notices of the theatres in Edmond Malone's *The Plays and Poems of William Shakespeare* (1790) and John Payne Collier's *The History of English Dramatic Poetry* (1831), the sole book dealing even in part with the topic is T. F. Ordish's *The Early London Theatres in the Fields*. This book, however, though good for its time, was written a quarter of a century ago, before most of the documents relating to early theatrical history were discovered, and it discusses only six playhouses. The present volume takes advantage of all the materials made available by the industry of later scholars, and records the history of seventeen regular, and five temporary or projected, theatres. The book is throughout the result of a first-hand examination of original sources, and represents an independent interpretation of the historical evidences. As a consequence of this, as well as of a comparison (now for the first time possible) of the detailed records of the several playhouses, many conclusions long held by scholars have been set aside. I have made no systematic attempt to point out the cases in which I depart from previously accepted opinions, for the scholar will discover them for himself; but I believe I have never thus departed without being aware of it, and without having carefully weighed the entire evidence. Sometimes the evidence has been too voluminous or complex for detailed presentation; in these instances I have had to content myself with reference by footnotes to the more significant documents bearing on the point.

In a task involving so many details I cannot hope to have escaped errors — errors due not only to oversight, but also to the limitations of my knowledge or to mistaken interpretation. For such I can offer no excuse, though I may request from my readers the same degree of tolerance which I have tried to show other laborers in the field. In reproducing old documents I have as a rule modernized the spelling and the punctuation, for in a work of this character there seems to be no advantage in preserving the accidents and perversities of early scribes and printers. I have also consistently altered the dates when the Old Style conflicted with our present usage.

PREFACE

I desire especially to record my indebtedness to the researches of Professor C. W. Wallace, the extent of whose services to the study of the Tudor-Stuart drama has not yet been generally realized, and has sometimes been grudgingly acknowledged; and to the labors of Mr. E. K. Chambers and Mr. W. W. Greg, who, in the *Collections* of The Malone Society, and elsewhere, have rendered accessible a wealth of important material dealing with the early history of the stage.

Finally, I desire to express my gratitude to Mr. Hamilton Bell and the editor of *The Architectural Record* for permission to reproduce the illustration and description of Inigo Jones's plan of the Cockpit; to the Governors of Dulwich College for permission to reproduce three portraits from the Dulwich Picture Gallery, one of which, that of Joan Alleyn, has not previously been reproduced; to Mr. C. W. Redwood, formerly technical artist at Cornell University, for expert assistance in making the large map of London showing the sites of the playhouses, and for other help generously rendered; and to my colleagues, Professor Lane Cooper and Professor Clark S. Northup, for their kindness in reading the proofs.

JOSEPH QUINCY ADAMS

ITHACA, NEW YORK

CONTENTS

I.	THE INN-YARDS	1
II.	THE HOSTILITY OF THE CITY	18
III.	THE THEATRE	27
IV.	THE CURTAIN	75
V.	THE FIRST BLACKFRIARS	91
VI.	ST. PAUL'S	111
VII.	THE BANKSIDE AND THE BEAR GARDEN	119
VIII.	NEWINGTON BUTTS	134
IX.	THE ROSE	142
X.	THE SWAN	161
XI.	THE SECOND BLACKFRIARS	182
XII.	THE GLOBE	234
XIII.	THE FORTUNE	267
XIV.	THE RED BULL	294
XV.	WHITEFRIARS	310
XVI.	THE HOPE	324
XVII.	ROSSETER'S BLACKFRIARS, OR PORTER'S HALL	342
XVIII.	THE PHŒNIX, OR COCKPIT IN DRURY LANE	348
XIX.	SALISBURY COURT	368
XX.	THE COCKPIT-IN-COURT, OR THEATRE ROYAL AT WHITEHALL	384
XXI.	MISCELLANEOUS: WOLF'S THEATRE IN NIGHTINGALE LANE; THE PROJECTED "AMPHITHEATRE"; OGILBY'S DUBLIN THEATRE; THE FRENCH PLAYERS' TEMPORARY THEATRE IN DRURY LANE; DAVENANT'S PROJECTED THEATRE IN FLEET STREET	410
	BIBLIOGRAPHY	433
	MAPS AND VIEWS OF LONDON	457
	INDEX	461

ILLUSTRATIONS

MAP OF LONDON SHOWING THE PLAYHOUSES *Frontispiece*	
AN INN-YARD	4
MAP OF LONDON SHOWING THE INN-PLAYHOUSES	9
THE SITE OF THE FIRST PLAYHOUSES	27
THE SITE OF THE FIRST PLAYHOUSES	31
A PLAN OF BURBAGE'S HOLYWELL PROPERTY	33
THE SITE OF THE CURTAIN PLAYHOUSE	79
BLACKFRIARS MONASTERY	93
THE SITE OF THE TWO BLACKFRIARS PLAYHOUSES	94
A PLAN OF FARRANT'S PLAYHOUSE	97
THE BANKSIDE	120
THE BANKSIDE	121
THE BEAR- AND BULL-BAITING RINGS	123
THE BEAR GARDEN	127
THE BEAR GARDEN AND THE ROSE	147
THE BEAR GARDEN AND THE ROSE	149
JOAN WOODWARD ALLEYN	152
THE MANOR OF PARIS GARDEN AND THE SWAN PLAYHOUSE	163
THE SWAN PLAYHOUSE	165
THE INTERIOR OF THE SWAN PLAYHOUSE	169
PLAN ILLUSTRATING THE SECOND BLACKFRIARS PLAYHOUSE	187
REMAINS OF BLACKFRIARS	196
RICHARD BURBAGE	234
WILLIAM SHAKESPEARE	238

ILLUSTRATIONS

A Plan of the Globe Property	242
The Bear Garden, the Rose, and the First Globe	245
The Bear Garden, the Rose, and the First Globe	246
The First Globe	248
The First Globe	253
Merian's View of London	256
The Second Globe	260
The Traditional Site of the Globe	262
The Site of the Fortune Playhouse	270
The Fortune Playhouse?	278
Edward Alleyn	282
The Site of the Red Bull Playhouse	294
A Plan of Whitefriars	312
Michael Drayton	314
The Sites of the Whitefriars and the Salisbury Court Playhouses	318
The Hope Playhouse, or Second Bear Garden	326
The Hope Playhouse, or Second Bear Garden	331
The Site of the Cockpit in Drury Lane	350
A Plan of the Salisbury Court Property	371
The Cockpit at Whitehall	390
Inigo Jones's Plans for the Cockpit-in-Court	396
Fisher's Survey of Whitehall showing the Cockpit-in-Court	398
The Theatro Olympico at Vicenza	399
The Cockpit-in-Court	407

SHAKESPEAREAN PLAYHOUSES

Shakespearean Playhouses

CHAPTER I

THE INN-YARDS

BEFORE the building of regular playhouses the itinerant troupes of actors were accustomed, except when received into private homes, to give their performances in any place that chance provided, such as open street-squares, barns, town-halls, moot-courts, schoolhouses, churches, and — most frequently of all, perhaps — the yards of inns. These yards, especially those of carriers' inns, were admirably suited to dramatic representations, consisting as they did of a large open court surrounded by two or more galleries. Many examples of such inn-yards are still to be seen in various parts of England; a picture of the famous White Hart, in Southwark, is given opposite page 4 by way of illustration. In the yard a temporary platform — a few boards, it may be, set on barrel-heads [1] — could be erected for a stage; in the adjacent stables a dressing-room could be provided for the actors; the rabble — always the larger and

---

[1] "Thou shalt not need to travel with thy pumps full of gravel any more, after a blind jade and a hamper, and stalk upon boards and barrel-heads." (*Poetaster*, III, i.)

more enthusiastic part of the audience — could be accommodated with standing-room about the stage; while the more aristocratic members of the audience could be comfortably seated in the galleries overhead. Thus a ready-made and very serviceable theatre was always at the command of the players; and it seems to have been frequently made use of from the very beginning of professionalism in acting.

One of the earliest extant moralities, *Mankind*, acted by strollers in the latter half of the fifteenth century, gives us an interesting glimpse of an inn-yard performance. The opening speech makes distinct reference to the two classes of the audience described above as occupying the galleries and the yard:

> O ye sovereigns that sit, and ye brothers that stand right up.

The "brothers," indeed, seem to have stood up so closely about the stage that the actors had great difficulty in passing to and from their dressing-room. Thus, Nowadays leaves the stage with the request:

> Make space, sirs, let me go out!

New Gyse enters with the threat:

> Out of my way, sirs, for dread of a beating!

While Nought, with even less respect, shouts:

> Avaunt, knaves! Let me go by!

Language such as this would hardly be appropriate if addressed to the "sovereigns" who sat in the galleries above; but, as addressed to the "brothers," it probably served to create a general feeling of good nature. And a feeling of good nature was desirable, for the actors were facing the difficult problem of inducing the audience to pay for its entertainment.

This problem they met by taking advantage of the most thrilling moment of the plot. The Vice and his wicked though jolly companions, having wholly failed to overcome the hero, Mankind, decide to call to their assistance no less a person than the great Devil himself; and accordingly they summon him with a "Walsingham wystyle." Immediately he roars in the dressing-room, and shouts:

> I come, with my legs under me!

There is a flash of powder, and an explosion of fireworks, while the eager spectators crane their necks to view the entrance of this "abhomynabull" personage. But nothing appears; and in the expectant silence that follows the actors calmly announce a collection of money, facetiously making the appearance of the Devil dependent on the liberality of the audience:

> *New Gyse.* Now ghostly to our purpose, worshipful sovereigns,
> We intend to gather money, if it please your negligence.
> For a man with a head that of great omnipotence —

Nowadays [*interrupting*]. Keep your tale, in goodness, I
  pray you, good brother!
    [*Addressing the audience, and pointing towards the
    dressing-room, where the Devil roars again.*]
He is a worshipful man, sirs, saving your reverence.
He loveth no groats, nor pence, or two-pence;
Give us red royals, if ye will see his abominable presence.
  New Gyse. Not so! Ye that may not pay the one, pay
  the other.

And with such phrases as "God bless you, master," "Ye will not say nay," "Let us go by," "Do them all pay," "Well mote ye fare," they pass through the audience gathering their groats, pence, and twopence; after which they remount the stage, fetch in the Devil, and continue their play without further interruption.

In the smaller towns the itinerant players might, through a letter of recommendation from their noble patron, or through the good-will of some local dignitary, secure the use of the town-hall, of the schoolhouse, or even of the village church. In such buildings, of course, they could give their performances more advantageously, for they could place money-takers at the doors, and exact adequate payment from all who entered. In the great city of London, however, the players were necessarily forced to make use almost entirely of public inn-yards — an arrangement which, we may well believe, they found far from satisfactory. Not being masters of the inns, they were merely tolerated; they had to content themselves with has-

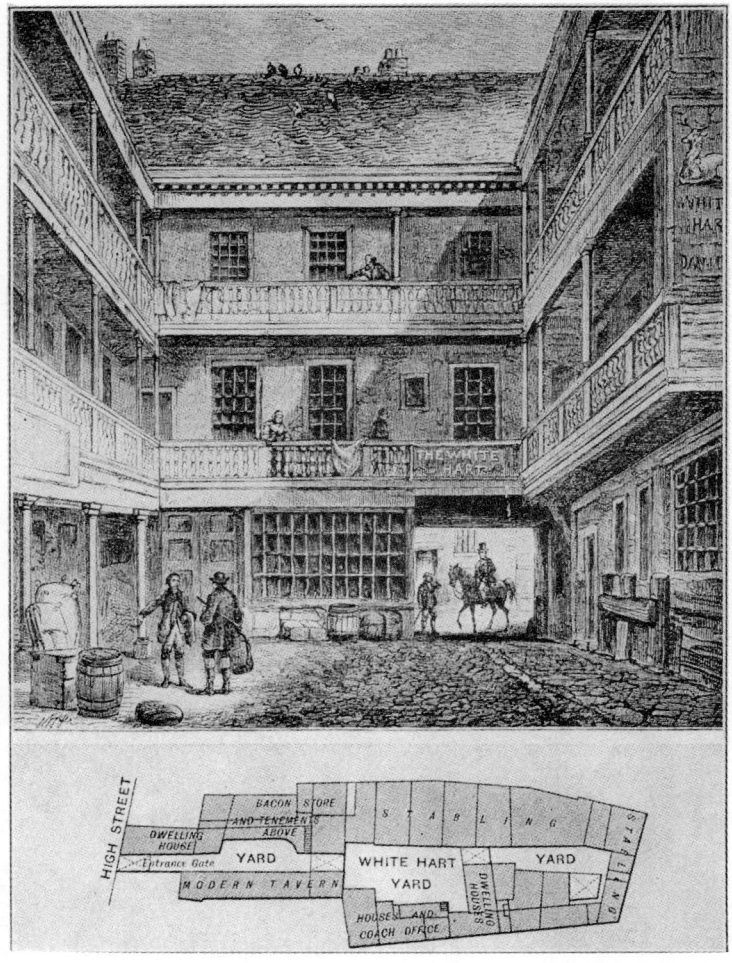

AN INN-YARD

The famous White Hart, in Southwark. The ground-plan shows the arrangement of a carriers' inn with the stabling below; the guest rooms were on the upper floors.

THE INN-YARDS

tily provided and inadequate stage facilities; and, worst of all, for their recompense they had to trust to a hat collection, at best a poor means of securing money. Often too, no doubt, they could not get the use of a given inn-yard when they most needed it, as on holidays and festive occasions; and at all times they had to leave the public in uncertainty as to where or when plays were to be seen. Their street parade, with the noise of trumpets and drums, might gather a motley crowd for the yard, but in so large a place as London it was inadequate for advertisement among the better classes. And as the troupes of the city increased in wealth and dignity, and as the playgoing public grew in size and importance, the old makeshift arrangement became more and more unsatisfactory.

At last the unsatisfactory situation was relieved by the specific dedication of certain large inns to dramatic purposes; that is, the proprietors of certain inns found it to their advantage to subordinate their ordinary business to the urgent demands of the actors and the playgoing public. Accordingly they erected in their yards permanent stages adequately equipped for dramatic representations, constructed in their galleries wooden benches to accommodate as many spectators as possible, and were ready to let the use of their buildings to the actors on an agreement by which the proprietor shared with the troupe in the "takings" at the door. Thus there came into existence a number of inn-playhouses, where the actors, as masters of the place, could make themselves quite at home, and where the public without special notification could be sure of always finding dramatic entertainment.

Richard Flecknoe, in his *Discourse of the English Stage* (1664), goes so far as to dignify these reconstructed inns with the name "theatres." At first, says he, the players acted "without any certain theatres or set companions, till about the beginning of Queen Elizabeth's reign they began here to assemble into companies, and set up theatres, first in the city (as in the inn-yards of the Cross Keys and Bull in Grace and Bishop's Gate Street at this day to be seen), till that fanatic spirit [i.e., Puritanism], which then began with the stage and after ended with the throne, banished them thence into the suburbs" — that is, into Shoreditch and the Bankside, where, outside the jurisdiction of the puritanical city fathers, they erected their first regular playhouses.

The "banishment" referred to by Flecknoe was the Order of the Common Council issued on December 6, 1574. This famous document described public acting as then taking place "in great inns, having chambers and secret places adjoining to their open stages and galleries"; and it ordered that henceforth "no inn-keeper, tavern-keeper, nor other person whatsoever within the liberties

THE INN-YARDS

of this city shall openly show, or play, nor cause or suffer to be openly showed or played within the house yard or any other place within the liberties of this city, any play," etc.

How many inns were let on special occasions for dramatic purposes we cannot say; but there were five "great inns," more famous than the rest, which were regularly used by the best London troupes. Thus Howes, in his continuation of Stow's *Annals* (p. 1004), in attempting to give a list of the playhouses which had been erected "within London and the suburbs," begins with the statement, "Five inns, or common osteryes, turned to playhouses." These five were the Bell and the Cross Keys, hard by each other in Gracechurch Street, the Bull, in Bishopsgate Street, the Bell Savage, on Ludgate Hill, and the Boar's Head, in Whitechapel Street without Aldgate.[1]

Although Flecknoe referred to the Order of the Common Council as a "banishment," it did not actually drive the players from the city. They were able, through the intervention of the Privy Council, and on the old excuse of rehearsing plays

---

[1] All historians of the drama have confused this great carriers' inn with the Boar's Head in Eastcheap made famous by Falstaff. The error seems to have come from the *Analytical Index of the Remembrancia*, which (p. 355) incorrectly catalogues the letter of March 31, 1602, as referring to the "Boar's Head in Eastcheap." The letter itself, however, when examined, gives no indication whatever of Eastcheap, and other evidence shows conclusively that the inn was situated in Whitechapel just outside of Aldgate.

for the Queen's entertainment, to occupy the inns for a large part of each year.[1] John Stockwood, in a sermon preached at Paul's Cross, August 24, 1578, bitterly complains of the "eight ordinary places" used regularly for plays, referring, it seems, to the five inns and the three playhouses — the Theatre, Curtain, and Blackfriars — recently opened to the public.

Richard Reulidge, in *A Monster Lately Found Out and Discovered* (1628), writes that "soon after 1580" the authorities of London received permission from Queen Elizabeth and her Privy Council "to thrust the players out of the city, and to pull down all playhouses and dicing-houses within their liberties: which accordingly was effected; and the playhouses in Gracious Street [i.e., the Bell and the Cross Keys], Bishopsgate Street [i.e., the Bull], that nigh Paul's [i.e., Paul's singing school?], that on Ludgate Hill [i.e., the Bell Savage], and the Whitefriars [2] were quite put down and suppressed by the care of these religious senators."

Yet, in spite of what Reulidge says, these five inns continued to be used by the players for many

---

[1] See especially *The Acts of the Privy Council* and *The Remembrancia* of the City of London.

[2] There is some error here. The city had no jurisdiction over Whitefriars, or Blackfriars either; but there was a playhouse in Blackfriars at the time, and it was suppressed in 1584, though not by the city authorities. Possibly Reulidge should have written "Whitechapel."

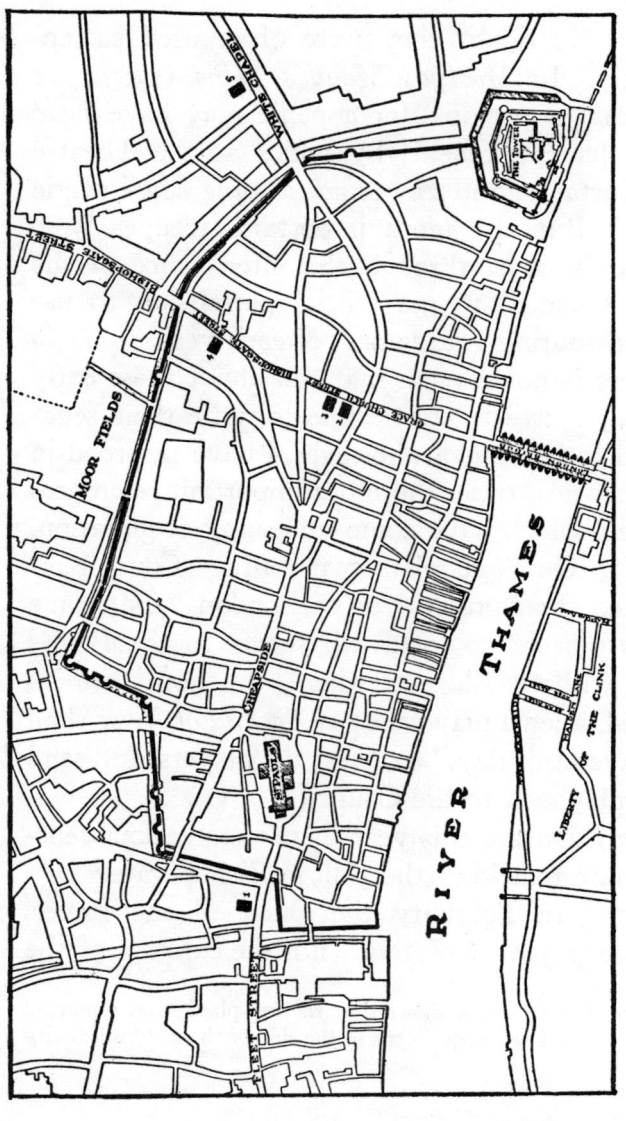

MAP OF LONDON SHOWING THE INN-PLAYHOUSES

1. The Bell Savage; 2. The Cross Keys; 3. The Bell; 4. The Bull; 5. The Boar's Head.

years.¹ No doubt they were often used surreptitiously. In *Martin's Month's Mind* (1589), we read that a person "for a penie may have farre better [entertainment] by oddes at the Theatre and Curtaine, and *any blind playing house* everie day."² But the more important troupes were commonly able, through the interference of the Privy Council, to get official permission to use the inns during a large part of each year.

There is not enough material about these early inn-playhouses to enable one to write their separate histories. Below, however, I have recorded in chronological order the more important references to them which have come under my observation.

1557. On September 5 the Privy Council instructed the Lord Mayor of London "that some of his officers do forthwith repair to the Boar's Head without Aldgate, where, the Lords are informed, a lewd play called *A Sackful of News* shall be played this day," to arrest the players, and send their playbook to the Council.³

1573. During this year there were various fencing contests held at the Bull in Bishopsgate.⁴

1577. In February the Office of the Revels made a payment of 10*d*. "ffor the cariadge of the

---

¹ *The Remembrancia* shows that the inn-playhouses remained for many years as sharp thorns in the side of the puritanical city fathers.
² Grosart, *Nash*, I, 179.
³ Dasent, *Acts of the Privy Council*, VI, 168.
⁴ W. Rendle, *The Inns of Old Southwark*, p. 235.

THE INN-YARDS

parts of ye well counterfeit from the Bell in gracious strete to St. Johns, to be performed for the play of *Cutwell*." [1]

1579. On June 23 James Burbage was arrested for the sum of £5 13*d*. "as he came down Gracious Street towards the Cross Keys there to a play." The name of the proprietor of this inn-playhouse is preserved in one of the interrogatories connected with the case: "Item. Whether did you, John Hynde, about xiii years past, in *anno* 1579, the xxiii of June, about two of the clock in the afternoon, send the sheriff's officer unto the Cross Keys in Gratious Street, being then the dwelling house of Richard Ibotson, citizen and brewer of London," etc.[2] Nothing more, I believe, is known of this person.

1579. Stephen Gosson, in *The Schoole of Abuse*, writes favorably of "the two prose books played at the Bell Savage, where you shall find never a word without wit, never a line without pith, never a letter placed in vain; the *Jew* and *Ptolome*, shown at the Bull . . . neither with amorous gesture wounding the eye, nor with slovenly talk hurting the ears of the chast hearers." [3]

---

[1] A. Feuillerat, *Documents Relating to the Office of the Revels in the Time of Queen Elizabeth*, p. 277.

[2] Burbage *v.* Brayne, printed in C. W. Wallace, *The First London Theatre*, pp. 82, 90. Whether Burbage was going to the Cross Keys as a spectator or as an actor is not indicated; but the presumption is that he was then playing at the inn, although he was proprietor of the Theatre.

[3] Arber's *English Reprints*, p. 40.

1582. On July 1 the Earl of Warwick wrote to the Lord Mayor requesting the city authorities to "give license to my servant, John David, this bearer, to play his profest prizes in his science and profession of defence at the Bull in Bishopsgate, or some other convenient place to be assigned within the liberties of London." The Lord Mayor refused to allow David to give his fencing contest "in an inn, which was somewhat too close for infection, and appointed him to play in an open place of the Leaden Hall," which, it may be added, was near the Bull.[1]

1583. William Rendle, in *The Inns of Old Southwark*, p. 235, states that in this year "Tarleton, Wilson, and others note the stay of the plague, and ask leave to play at the Bull in Bishopsgate, or the Bell in Gracechurch Street," citing as his authority merely "City MS." The Privy Council on November 26, 1583, addressed to the Lord Mayor a letter requesting "that Her Majesty's Players [i.e., Tarleton, Wilson, etc.] may be suffered to play within the liberties as heretofore they have done."[2] And on November 28 the Lord Mayor issued to them a license to play "at the sign of the Bull in Bishopsgate Street, and the sign of the Bell in Gracious Street, and nowhere else within this City."[3]

[1] See The Malone Society's *Collections*, I, 55–57.
[2] See *The Remembrancia*, in The Malone Society's *Collections*, I, 66.
[3] C. W. Wallace, *The First London Theatre*, p. 11.

1587. "James Cranydge played his master's prize the 21 of November, 1587, at the Bellsavage without Ludgate, at iiij sundry kinds of weapons. ... There played with him nine masters." [1]

Before 1588. In *Tarlton's Jests* [2] we find a number of references to that famous actor's pleasantries in the London inns used by the Queen's Players. It is impossible to date these exactly, but Tarleton became a member of the Queen's Players in 1583, and he died in 1588.

At the Bull in Bishops-gate-street, where the Queen's Players oftentimes played, Tarleton coming on the stage, one from the gallery threw a pippin at him.

There was one Banks, in the time of Tarleton, who served the Earl of Essex, and had a horse of strange qualities; and being at the Cross Keys in Gracious Street getting money with him, as he was mightily resorted to. Tarleton then, with his fellows playing at the Bell by, came into the Cross Keys, amongst many people, to see fashions.

At the Bull at Bishops-gate was a play of Henry the Fifth.

---

[1] *MS. Sloane*, 2530, f. 6–7, quoted by J. O. Halliwell in his edition of *Tarlton's Jests*, p. xi. The Bell Savage seems to have been especially patronized by fencers. George Silver, in his *Paradoxe of Defence* (1599), tells how he and his brother once challenged two Italian fencers to a contest "to be played at the Bell Savage upon the scaffold, when he that went in his fight faster back than he ought, should be in danger to break his neck off the scaffold."

[2] First printed in 1611; reprinted by J. O. Halliwell for The Shakespeare Society in 1844.

14   SHAKESPEAREAN PLAYHOUSES

The several "jests" which follow these introductory sentences indicate that the inn-yards differed in no essential way from the early public playhouses.

1588. "John Mathews played his master's prize the 31 day of January, 1588, at the Bell Savage without Ludgate." [1]

1589. In November Lord Burghley directed the Lord Mayor to "give order for the stay of all plays within the city." In reply the Lord Mayor wrote:

> According to which your Lordship's good pleasure, I presently sent for such players as I could hear of; so as there appeared yesterday before me the Lord Strange's Players, to whom I specially gave in charge and required them in Her Majesty's name to forbear playing until further order might be given for their allowance in that respect. Whereupon the Lord Admiral's Players very dutifully obeyed; but the others, in very contemptuous manner departing from me, went to the Cross Keys and played that afternoon.[2]

1594. On October 8, Henry, Lord Hunsdon, the Lord Chamberlain and the patron of Shakespeare's company, wrote to the Lord Mayor:

---

[1] *MS. Sloane*, 2530, f. 6–7, quoted by Halliwell in his edition of *Tarlton's Jests*, p. xi. There is some difficulty with the date. One of the "masters" before whom the prize was played was "Rycharde Tarlton," whom Halliwell takes to be the famous actor of that name; but Tarleton the actor died on September 3, 1588. Probably Halliwell in transcribing the manuscript silently modernized the date from the Old Style.

[2] *Lansdowne MSS.* 60, quoted by Collier, *History of English Dramatic Poetry* (1879), I, 265.

THE INN-YARDS

After my hearty commendations. Where my now company of players have been accustomed for the better exercise of their quality, and for the service of Her Majesty if need so require, to play this winter time within the city at the Cross Keys in Gracious Street, these are to require and pray your Lordship (the time being such as, thanks to God, there is now no danger of the sickness) to permit and suffer them so to do.[1]

By such devices as this the players were usually able to secure permission to act "within the city" during the disagreeable months of the winter when the large playhouses in the suburbs were difficult of access.

1594. Anthony Bacon, the elder brother of Francis, came to lodge in Bishopsgate Street. This fact very much disturbed his good mother, who feared lest his servants might be corrupted by the plays to be seen at the Bull near by.[2]

1596. William Lambarde, in his *Perambulation of Kent*,[3] observes that none of those who go "to Paris Garden, the Bell Savage, or Theatre, to behold bear-baiting, interludes, or fence play, can account of any pleasant spectacle unless they first pay one penny at the gate, another at the entry of the scaffold, and the third for a quiet standing."

[1] *The Remembrancia*, The Malone Society's *Collections*, I, 73.
[2] See W. Rendle, *The Inns of Old Southwark*, p. 236.
[3] The passage does not appear in the earlier edition of 1576, though it was probably written shortly after the erection of the Theatre in the autumn of 1576.

1602. On March 31 the Privy Council wrote to the Lord Mayor that the players of the Earl of Oxford and of the Earl of Worcester had been "joined by agreement together in one company, to whom, upon notice of Her Majesty's pleasure, at the suit of the Earl of Oxford, toleration hath been thought meet to be granted." The letter concludes:

And as the other companies that are allowed, namely of me the Lord Admiral, and the Lord Chamberlain, be appointed their certain houses, and one and no more to each company, so we do straightly require that this third company be likewise [appointed] to one place. And because we are informed the house called the Boar's Head is the place they have especially used and do best like of, we do pray and require you that the said house, namely the Boar's Head, may be assigned unto them.[1]

That the strong Oxford-Worcester combination should prefer the Boar's Head to the Curtain or the Rose Playhouse,[2] indicates that the inn-yard was not only large, but also well-equipped for acting.

1604. In a draft of a license to be issued to Queen Anne's Company, those players are allowed to act "as well within their now usual houses, called the Curtain and the Boar's Head, within our County of Middlesex, as in any other playhouse not used by others."[3]

---

[1] *The Remembrancia*, The Malone Society's *Collections*, I, 85.
[2] They had to use the Rose nevertheless; see page 158.
[3] The Malone Society's *Collections*, I, 265.

THE INN-YARDS

In 1608 the Boar's Head seems to have been occupied by the newly organized Prince Charles's Company. In William Kelly's extracts from the payments of the city of Leicester we find the entry: "Itm. Given to the Prince's Players, of Whitechapel, London, xx *s*."

In 1664, as Flecknoe tells us, the Cross Keys and the Bull still gave evidence of their former use as playhouses; perhaps even then they were occasionally let for fencing and other contests. In 1666 the great fire completely destroyed the Bell, the Cross Keys, and the Bell Savage; the Bull, however, escaped, and enjoyed a prosperous career for many years after. Samuel Pepys was numbered among its patrons, and writers of the Restoration make frequent reference to it. What became of the Boar's Head without Aldgate I am unable to learn; its memory, however, is perpetuated to-day in Boar's Head Yard, between Middlesex Street and Goulston Street, Whitechapel.

CHAPTER II

THE HOSTILITY OF THE CITY

AS the actors rapidly increased in number and importance, and as Londoners flocked in ever larger crowds to witness plays, the animosity of two forces was aroused, Puritanism and Civic Government, — forces which opposed the drama for different reasons, but with almost equal fervor. And when in the course of time the Governors of the city themselves became Puritans, the combined animosity thus produced was sufficient to drive the players out of London into the suburbs.

The Puritans attacked the drama as contrary to Holy Writ, as destructive of religion, and as a menace to public morality. Against plays, players, and playgoers they waged in pulpit and pamphlet a warfare characterized by the most intense fanaticism. The charges they made — of ungodliness, idolatrousness, lewdness, profanity, evil practices, enormities, and "abuses" of all kinds — are far too numerous to be noted here; they are interesting chiefly for their unreasonableness and for the violence with which they were urged.

And, after all, however much the Puritans might rage, they were helpless; authority to restrain acting was vested in the Lord Mayor, his brethren

THE HOSTILITY OF THE CITY

the Aldermen, and the Common Council. The attitude of these city officials towards the drama was unmistakable: they had no more love for the actors than had the Puritans. They found that "plays and players" gave them more trouble than anything else in the entire administration of municipal affairs. The dedication of certain "great inns" to the use of actors and to the entertainment of the pleasure-loving element of the city created new and serious problems for those charged with the preservation of civic law and order. The presence in these inns of private rooms adjoining the yard and balconies gave opportunity for immorality, gambling, fleecing, and various other "evil practices" — an opportunity which, if we may believe the Common Council, was not wasted. Moreover, the proprietors of these inns made a large share of their profits from the beer, ale, and other drinks dispensed to the crowds before, during, and after performances (the proprietor of the Cross Keys, it will be recalled, was described as "citizen and brewer of London"); and the resultant intemperance among "such as frequented the said plays, being the ordinary place of meeting for all vagrant persons, and masterless men that hang about the city, theeves, horse-stealers, whoremongers, cozeners, cony-catching persons, practicers of treason, and such other like,"[1] led

---

[1] So the Lord Mayor characterized playgoers; see *The Remembrancia*, in The Malone Society's *Collections*, I, 75.

to drunkenness, frays, bloodshed, and often to general disorder. Sometimes, as we know, turbulent apprentices and other factions met by appointment at plays for the sole purpose of starting riots or breaking open jails. "Upon Whitsunday," writes the Recorder to Lord Burghley, "by reason no plays were the same day, all the city was quiet." [1]

Trouble of an entirely different kind arose when in the hot months of the summer the plague was threatening. The meeting together at plays of "great multitudes of the basest sort of people" served to spread the infection throughout the city more quickly and effectively than could anything else. On such occasions it was exceedingly difficult for the municipal authorities to control the actors, who were at best a stubborn and unruly lot; and often the pestilence had secured a full start before acting could be suppressed.

These troubles, and others which cannot here be mentioned, made one of the Lord Mayors exclaim in despair: "The Politique State and Government of this City by no one thing is so greatly annoyed and disquieted as by players and plays, and the disorders which follow thereupon." [2]

This annoyance, serious enough in itself, was aggravated by the fact that most of the troupes

[1] The Malone Society's *Collections*, I, 164.
[2] *The Remembrancia*, in The Malone Society's *Collections*, I, 69.

THE HOSTILITY OF THE CITY

were under the patronage of great noblemen, and some were even high in favor with the Queen. As a result, the attempts on the part of the Lord Mayor and his Aldermen to regulate the players were often interfered with by other or higher authority. Sometimes it was a particular nobleman, whose request was not to be ignored, who intervened in behalf of his troupe; most often, however, it was the Privy Council, representing the Queen and the nobility in general, which championed the cause of the actors and countermanded the decrees of the Lord Mayor and his brethren. One of the most notable things in the City's *Remembrancia* is this long conflict of authority between the Common Council and the Privy Council over actors and acting.

In 1573 the situation seems to have approached a crisis. The Lord Mayor had become strongly puritanical, and in his efforts to suppress "stage-plays" was placing more and more obstacles in the way of the actors. The temper of the Mayor is revealed in two entries in the records of the Privy Council. On July 13, 1573, the Lords of the Council sent a letter to him requesting him "to permit liberty to certain Italian players"; six days later they sent a second letter, repeating the request, and "marveling that he did it not at their first request." [1] His continued efforts to suppress the drama finally led the troupes to appeal for re-

[1] Dasent, *Acts of the Privy Council*, VIII, 131, 132.

lief to the Privy Council. On March 22, 1574, the Lords of the Council dispatched "a letter to the Lord Mayor to advertise their Lordships what causes he hath to restrain plays." His answer has not been preserved, but that he persisted in his hostility to the drama is indicated by the fact that in May the Queen openly took sides with the players. To the Earl of Leicester's troupe she issued a special royal license, authorizing them to act "as well within our city of London and liberties of the same, as also within the liberties and freedoms of any our cities, towns, boroughs, etc., whatsoever"; and to the mayors and other officers she gave strict orders not to interfere with such performances: "Willing and commanding you, and every of you, as ye tender our pleasure, to permit and suffer them herein without any your lets, hindrances, or molestation during the term aforesaid, any act, statute, proclamation, or commandment heretofore made, or hereafter to be made, to the contrary notwithstanding."

This license was a direct challenge to the authority of the Lord Mayor. He dared not answer it as directly; but on December 6, 1574, he secured from the Common Council the passage of an ordinance which placed such heavy restrictions upon acting as virtually to nullify the license issued by the Queen, and to regain for the Mayor complete control of the drama within the city. The Preamble of this remarkable ordinance

THE HOSTILITY OF THE CITY

clearly reveals the puritanical character of the City Government:

Whereas heretofore sundry great disorders and inconveniences have been found to ensue to this city by the inordinate haunting of great multitudes of people, specially youths, to plays, interludes, and shews: namely, occasion of frays and quarrels; evil practises of incontinency in great inns having chambers and secret places adjoining to their open stages and galleries; inveigling and alluring of maids, specially orphans and good citizens' children under age, to privy and unmeet contracts; the publishing of unchaste, uncomly, and unshamefaced speeches and doings; withdrawing of the Queen's Majesty's subjects from divine service on Sundays and holy days, at which times such plays were chiefly used; unthrifty waste of the money of the poor and fond persons; sundry robberies by picking and cutting of purses; uttering of popular, busy, and seditious matters; and many other corruptions of youth, and other enormities; besides that also sundry slaughters and maimings of the Queen's subjects have happened by ruins of scaffolds, frames, and stages, and by engines, weapons, and powder used in plays. And whereas in time of God's visitation by the plague such assemblies of the people in throng and press have been very dangerous for spreading of infection. . . . And for that the Lord Mayor and his brethren the Aldermen, together with the grave and discreet citizens in the Common Council assembled, do doubt and fear lest upon God's merciful withdrawing his hand of sickness from us (which God grant), the people, specially the meaner and most unruly sort, should with sudden forgetting of His visitation, without fear of God's wrath, and without due respect of the good and politique means that He hath ordained for the preservation of common weals and peoples in health and good order, return to the undue use of such enormities, to the great offense of God. . . .[1]

The restrictions on playing imposed by the ordinance may be briefly summarized:

1. Only such plays should be acted as were free from all unchastity, seditiousness, and "uncomely matter."

2. Before being acted all plays should be "first perused and allowed in such order and form, and by such persons as by the Lord Mayor and Court of Aldermen for the time being shall be appointed."

3. Inns or other buildings used for acting, and their proprietors, should both be licensed by the Lord Mayor and the Aldermen.

4. The proprietors of such buildings should be "bound to the Chamberlain of London" by a sufficient bond to guarantee "the keeping of good order, and avoiding of" the inconveniences noted in the Preamble.

5. No plays should be given during the time of sickness, or during any inhibition ordered at any time by the city authorities.

6. No plays should be given during "any usual time of divine service," and no persons should be

---

[1] For the complete document see W. C. Hazlitt, *The English Drama and Stage*, p. 27.

THE HOSTILITY OF THE CITY

admitted into playing places until after divine services were over.

7. The proprietors of such places should pay towards the support of the poor a sum to be agreed upon by the city authorities.

In order, however, to avoid trouble with the Queen, or those noblemen who were accustomed to have plays given in their homes for the private entertainment of themselves and their guests, the Common Council added, rather grudgingly, the following proviso:

Provided alway that this act (otherwise than touching the publishing of unchaste, seditious, and unmeet matters) shall not extend to any plays, interludes, comedies, tragedies, or shews to be played or shewed in the private house, dwelling, or lodging of any nobleman, citizen, or gentleman, which shall or will then have the same there so played or shewed in his presence for the festivity of any marriage, assembly of friends, or other like cause, without public or common collections of money of the auditory or beholders thereof.

Such regulations if strictly enforced would prove very annoying to the players. But, as the Common Council itself informs us, "these orders were not then observed." The troupes continued to play in the city, protected against any violent action on the part of the municipal authorities by the known favor of the Queen and the frequent interference of the Privy Council. This state of affairs was not, of course, comfortable for the actors;

but it was by no means desperate, and for several years after the passage of the ordinance of 1574 they continued without serious interruption to occupy their inn-playhouses.

The long-continued hostility of the city authorities, however, of which the ordinance of 1574 was an ominous expression, led more or less directly to the construction of special buildings devoted to plays and situated beyond the jurisdiction of the Common Council. As the Reverend John Stockwood, in *A Sermon Preached at Paules Crosse, 1578*, indignantly puts it:

> Have we not *houses of purpose*, built with great charges for the maintenance of plays, and that *without the liberties*, as who would say "*There, let them say what they will say, we will play!*"

Thus came into existence playhouses; and with them dawned a new era in the history of the English drama.

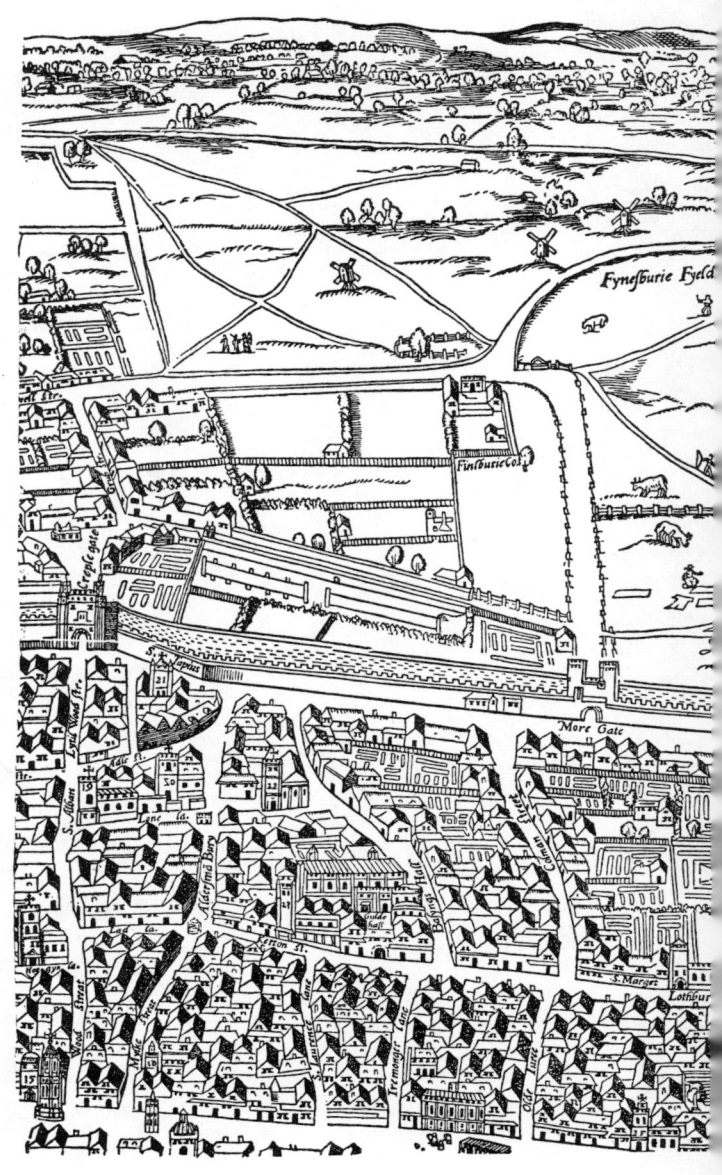

THE SITE OF
Finsbury Field and Holywell. The man walking fr
(From Agas's *Map of London*, r

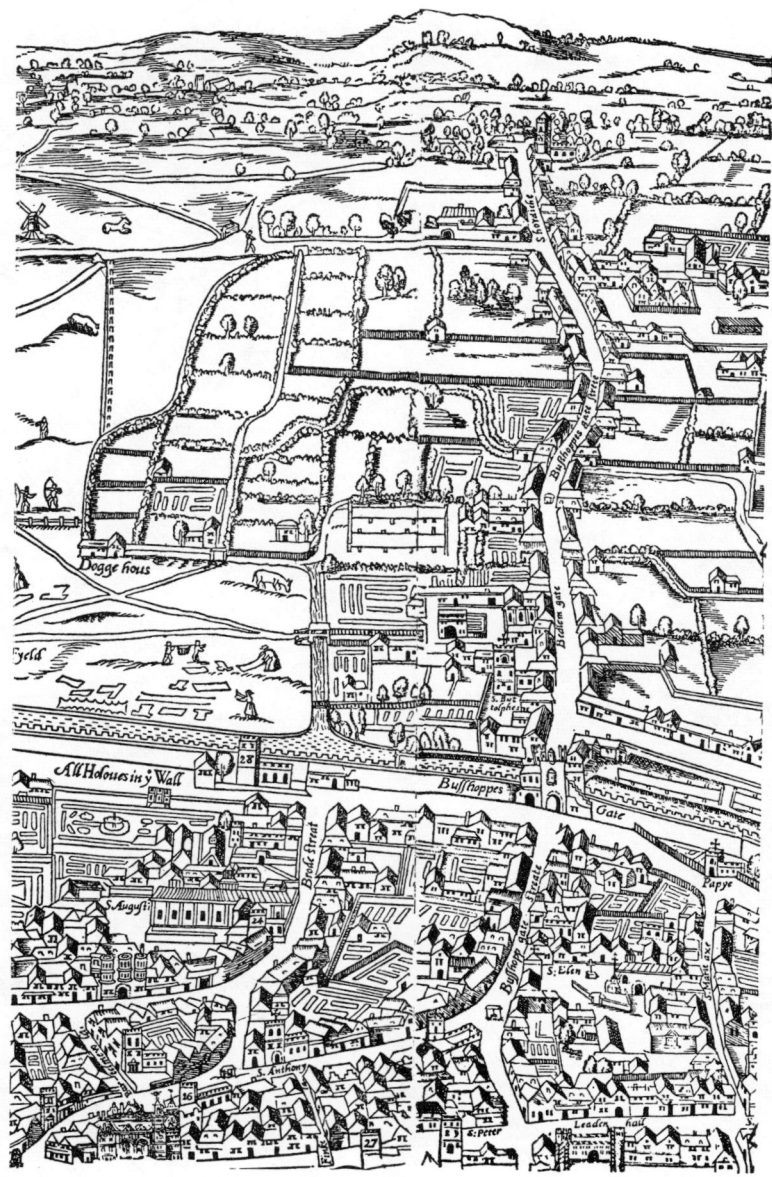

FIRST PLAYHOUSES
Field towards Shoreditch is just entering Holywell Lane.
ting the city as it was about 1560.)

CHAPTER III
THE THEATRE

THE hostility of the city to the drama was unquestionably the main cause of the erection of the first playhouse; yet combined with this were two other important causes, usually overlooked. The first was the need of a building specially designed to meet the requirements of the players and of the public, a need yearly growing more urgent as plays became more complex, acting developed into a finer art, and audiences increased in dignity as well as in size. The second and the more immediate cause was the appearance of a man with business insight enough to see that such a building would pay. The first playhouse, we should remember, was not erected by a troupe of actors, but by a money-seeking individual.[1] Although he was himself an actor, and the manager of a troupe, he did not, it seems, take the troupe into his confidence. In complete independence of any theatrical organization he pro-

---

[1] I emphasize this point because the opposite is the accepted opinion. We find it expressed in *The Cambridge History of English Literature*, VI, 431, as follows: "Certain players, finding the city obdurate, and unwilling to submit to its severe regulations, began to look about them for some means of carrying on their business out of reach of the mayor's authority," etc.

ceeded with the erection of his building as a private speculation; and, we are told, he dreamed of the "continual great profit and commodity through plays that should be used there every week."

This man, "the first builder of playhouses," — and, it might have been added, the pioneer in a new field of business, — was James Burbage, originally, as we are told by one who knew him well, "by occupation a joiner; and reaping but a small living by the same, gave it over and became a common player in plays."[1] As an actor he was more successful, for as early as 1572 we find him at the head of Leicester's excellent troupe.

Having in 1575 conceived the notion of erecting a building specially designed for dramatic entertainments, he was at once confronted with the problem of a suitable location. Two conditions narrowed his choice: first, the site had to be outside the jurisdiction of the Common Council; secondly, it had to be as near as possible to the city.

No doubt he at once thought of the two suburbs that were specially devoted to recreation, the Bankside to the south, and Finsbury Field to the north of the city. The Bankside had for many years been associated in the minds of Londoners with "sports and pastimes." Thither the citizens were accustomed to go to witness bear-baiting

---

[1] Deposition by Robert Myles, 1592, printed in Wallace's *The First London Theatre*, p. 141.

and bull-baiting, to practice archery, and to engage in various athletic sports. Thither, too, for many years the actors had gone to present their plays. In 1545 King Henry VIII had issued a proclamation against vagabonds, ruffians, idle persons, and common players,[1] in which he referred to their "fashions commonly used at the Bank." The Bankside, however, was associated with the lowest and most vicious pleasures of London, for here were situated the stews, bordering the river's edge. Since the players were at this time subject to the bitterest attacks from the London preachers, Burbage wisely decided not to erect the first permanent home of the drama in a locality already a common target for puritan invective.

The second locality, Finsbury Field, had nearly all the advantages, and none of the disadvantages, of the Bankside. Since 1315 the Field had been in the possession of the city,[2] and had been used as a public playground, where families could hold picnics, falconers could fly their hawks, archers could exercise their sport, and the militia on holidays could drill with all "the pomp and circumstance of glorious war." In short, the Field was eminently respectable, was accessible to the city, and was definitely associated with the idea of en-

[1] See page 134.
[2] See *The Remembrancia*, p. 274; Stow, *Survey*. The Corporation of London held the manor on lease from St. Paul's Cathedral until 1867.

tertainment. The locality, therefore, was almost ideal for the purpose Burbage had in mind.[1]

The new playhouse, of course, could not be erected in the Field itself, which was under the control of the city; but just to the east of the Field certain vacant land, part of the dissolved Priory of Holywell, offered a site in every way suitable to the purpose. The Holywell property, at the dissolution of the Priory, had passed under the jurisdiction of the Crown, and hence the Lord Mayor and the Aldermen could not enforce municipal ordinances there. Moreover, it was distant from the city wall not much more than half a mile. The old conventual church had been demolished, the Priory buildings had been converted into residences, and the land near the Shoreditch highway had been built up with numerous houses. The land next to the Field, however, was for the most part undeveloped. It contained some dilapidated tenements, a few old barns formerly belonging to the Priory, and small garden plots, conspicuous objects in the early maps.

Burbage learned that a large portion of this land lying next to the Field was in the possession of a well-to-do gentleman named Gyles Alleyn,[2] and

[1] Doubtless, too, Burbage was influenced in his choice by the fact that he had already made his home in the Liberty of Shoreditch, near Finsbury Field.

[2] For a detailed history of the property from the year 1128, and for the changes in the ownership of Alleyn's portion after the dissolution, see Braines, *Holywell Priory*.

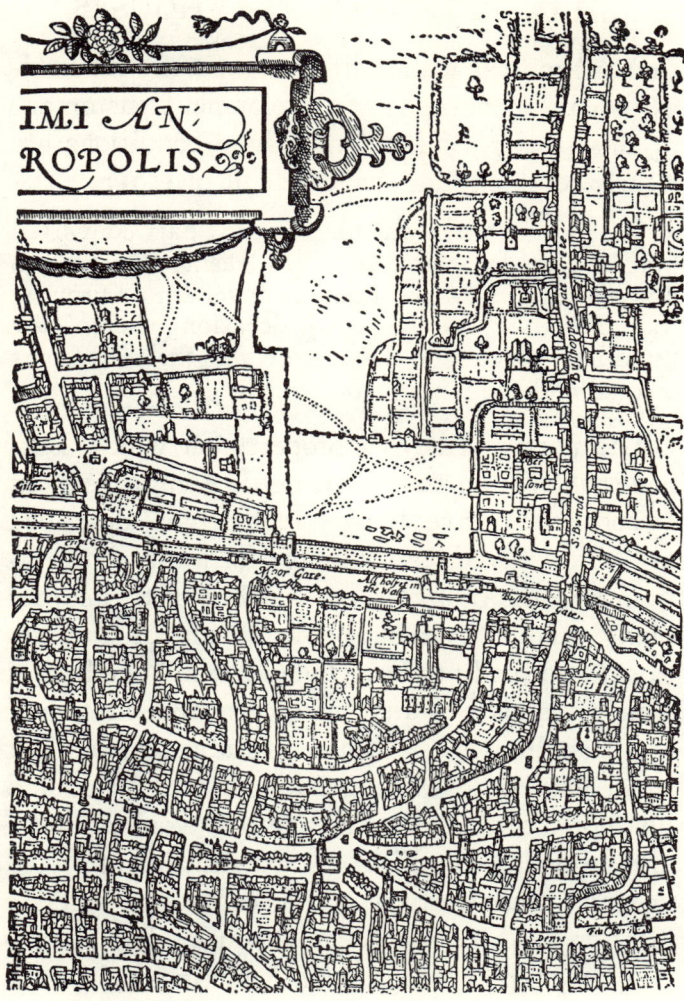

THE SITE OF THE FIRST PLAYHOUSES

Finsbury Field lies to the north (beyond Moor Field, the small rectangular space next to the city wall), and the Holywell Property lies to the right of Finsbury Field, between the Field and the highway. Holywell Lane divides the garden plots; the Theatre was erected just to the north, and the Curtain just to the south of this lane, facing the Field. (From the *Map of London* by Braun and Hogenbergius representing the city as it was in 1554–1558.)

that Alleyn was willing to lease a part of his holding on the conditions of development customary in this section of London. These conditions are clearly revealed in a chancery suit of 1591:

> The ground there was for the most part converted first into garden plots, and then leasing the same to diverse tenants caused them to covenant or promise to build upon the same, by occasion whereof the buildings which are there were for the most part erected and the rents increased.[1]

The part of Alleyn's property on which Burbage had his eye was in sore need of improvement. It consisted of five "paltry tenements," described as "old, decayed, and ruinated for want of reparation, and the best of them was but of two stories high," and a long barn "very ruinous and decayed and ready to have fallen down," one half of which was used as a storage-room, the other half as a slaughter-house. Three of the tenements had small gardens extending back to the Field, and just north of the barn was a bit of "void ground," also adjoining the Field. It was this bit of "void ground" that Burbage had selected as a suitable location for his proposed playhouse. The accompanying map of the property [2] will make clear the position of this "void ground" and of the barns and

---

[1] Halliwell-Phillipps, *Outlines*, I, 365. The suit concerns the Curtain property, somewhat south of the Alleyn property, but a part of the Priory.

[2] I have based this map in large measure on the documents presented by Braines in his excellent pamphlet, *Holywell Priory*.

A PLAN OF BURBAGE'S HOLYWELL PROPERTY

Based on the lease, and on the miscellaneous documents printed by Halliwell-Phillipps and by Braines. The "common sewer" is now marked by **Curtain Road**, and the "ditch from the horse-pond" by **New Inn Yard**.

tenements about it. Moreover, it will serve to indicate the exact site of the Theatre. If one will bear in mind the fact that in the London of to-day Curtain Road marks the eastern boundary of Finsbury Field, and New Inn Yard cuts off the lower half of the Great Barn, he will be able to place Burbage's structure within a few yards.[1]

The property is carefully described in the lease — quoted below — which Burbage secured from Alleyn, but the reader will need to refer to the map in order to follow with ease the several paragraphs of description:[2]

All those two houses or tenements, with appurtenances, which at the time of the said former demise made were in the several tenures or occupations of Joan Harrison, widow, and John Dragon.

And also all that house or tenement with the appurtenances, together with the garden ground lying behind part of the same, being then likewise in the occupation of William Gardiner; which said garden plot doth extend in breadth from a great stone wall there which doth enclose part of the garden then or lately being in the occupation of the said Gyles, unto the garden there then in the occupation of Edwin Colefox, weaver, and in length from the same

[1] For proof see Braines, *op. cit.*

[2] The original lease may be found incorporated in Alleyn *v.* Street, Coram Rege, 1599–1600, printed in full by Wallace, *The First London Theatre*, pp. 163–80, and again in Alleyn *v.* Burbage, Queen's Bench, 1602, Wallace, *op. cit.*, pp. 267–75. The lease, I think, was in English not Latin, and hence is more correctly given in the first document; in the second document the scrivener has translated it into Latin. The lease is also given in part on page 187.

THE THEATRE

house or tenement unto a brick wall there next unto the fields commonly called Finsbury Fields.

And also all that house or tenement, with the appurtenances, at the time of the said former demise made called or known by the name of the Mill-house; together with the garden ground lying behind part of the same, also at the time of the said former demise made being in the tenure or occupation of the aforesaid Edwin Colefox, or of his assigns; which said garden ground doth extend in length from the same house or tenement unto the aforesaid brick wall next unto the aforesaid Fields.

And also all those three upper rooms, with the appurtenances, next adjoining to the aforesaid Millhouse, also being at the time of the said former demise made in the occupation of Thomas Dancaster, shoemaker, or of his assigns; and also all the nether rooms, with the appurtenances, lying under the same three upper rooms, and next adjoining also to the aforesaid house or tenement called the Millhouse, then also being in the several tenures or occupations of Alice Dotridge, widow, and Richard Brockenbury, or of their assigns; together with the garden ground lying behind the same, extending in length from the same nether rooms down unto the aforesaid brick wall next unto the aforesaid Fields, and then or late being also in the tenure or occupation of the aforesaid Alice Dotridge.

And also so much of the ground and soil lying and being afore all the tenements or houses before granted, as extendeth in length from the outward part of the aforesaid tenements being at the time of the making of the said former demise in the occupation of the aforesaid Joan Harrison and John Dragon, unto a pond there being next unto the barn or stable then in the occupation of the right honorable the Earl of Rutland or of his assigns, and in breadth from the aforesaid tenement or Mill-house to the midst of the well being afore the same tenements.

And also all that Great Barn, with the appurtenances, at the time of the making of the said former demise made being in the several occupations of Hugh Richards, innholder, and Robert Stoughton, butcher; and also a little piece of ground then inclosed with a pale and next adjoining to the aforesaid barn, and then or late before that in the occupation of the said Robert Stoughton; together also with all the ground and soil lying and being between the said nether rooms last before expressed, and the aforesaid Great Barn, and the aforesaid pond; that is to say, extending in length from the aforesaid pond unto a ditch beyond the brick wall next the aforesaid Fields.

And also the said Gyles Alleyn and Sara his wife do by these presents demise, grant, and to farm lett unto the said James Burbage all the right, title, and interest which the said Gyles and Sara have or ought to have in or to all the grounds and soil lying between the aforesaid Great Barn and the barn being at the time of the said former demise in the occupation of the Earl of Rutland or of his assigns, extending in length from the aforesaid pond and from the aforesaid stable or barn then in the occupation of the aforesaid Earl of Rutland or of his assigns, down to the aforesaid brick wall next the aforesaid Fields.[1]

---

[1] This part of the property was claimed by the Earl of Rutland, and was being used by him. For a long time it was the subject of dispute. Ultimately, it seems, the Earl secured the title, as he had always had the use of the property. This probably explains why Burbage did not attempt to erect his playhouse there.

THE THEATRE

And also the said Gyles and Sara do by these presents demise, grant, and to farm lett to the said James all the said void ground lying and being betwixt the aforesaid ditch and the aforesaid brick wall, extending in length from the aforesaid [great stone] wall [1] which encloseth part of the aforesaid garden being at the time of the making of the said former demise or late before that in the occupation of the said Gyles Allen, unto the aforesaid barn then in the occupation of the aforesaid Earl or of his assigns.

The lease was formally signed on April 13, 1576, and Burbage entered into the possession of his property. Since the terms of the lease are important for an understanding of the subsequent history of the playhouse, I shall set these forth briefly:

First, the lease was to run for twenty-one years from April 13, 1576, at an annual rental of £14.

Secondly, Burbage was to spend before the expiration of ten years the sum of £200 in rebuild- and improving the decayed tenements.

Thirdly, in view of this expenditure of £200, Burbage was to have at the end of the ten years the right to renew the lease at the same rental of £14 a year for twenty-one years, thus making the lease good in all for thirty-one years:

And the said Gyles Alleyn and Sara his wife did thereby covenant with the said James Burbage that they should and would at any time within the ten

[1] The document by error reads "brick wall" but the mistake is obvious, and the second version of the lease does not repeat the error. This clause merely means that the ditch, not the brick wall, constituted the western boundary of the property.

years next ensuing at or upon the lawful request or demand of the said James Burbage make or cause to be made to the said James Burbage a new lease or grant like to the same presents for the term of one and twenty years more, to begin from the date of making the same lease, yielding therefor the rent reserved in the former indenture.[1]

Fourthly, it was agreed that at any time before the expiration of the lease, Burbage might take down and carry away to his own use any building that in the mean time he might have erected on the vacant ground for the purpose of a playhouse:

And farther, the said Gyles Alleyn and Sara his wife did covenant and grant to the said James Burbage that it should and might be lawful to the said James Burbage (in consideration of the imploying and bestowing the foresaid two hundred pounds in forme aforesaid) at any time or times before the end of the said term of one and twenty years, to have, take down, and carry away to his own proper use for ever all such buildings and other things as should be builded, erected, or set up in or upon the gardens and void grounds by the said James, either for a theatre or playing place, or for any other lawful use, without any stop, claim, let, trouble, or interruption of the said Gyles Alleyn and Sara his wife.[2]

Protected by these specific terms, Burbage proceeded to the erection of his playhouse. He must

[1] Quoted from Burbage *v.* Alleyn, Court of Requests, 1600, Wallace, *op. cit.*, p. 182. I have stripped the passage of some of its legal verbiage.
[2] Quoted from Burbage *v.* Alleyn, Court of Requests, 1600, Wallace, *op. cit.*, p. 182.

THE THEATRE

have had faith and abundant courage, for he was a poor man, quite unequal to the large expenditures called for by his plans. A person who had known him for many years, deposed in 1592 that "James Burbage was not at the time of the first beginning of the building of the premises worth above one hundred marks [1] in all his substance, for he and this deponent were familiarly acquainted long before that time and ever since." [2] We are not surprised to learn, therefore, that he was "constrained to borrow diverse sums of money," and that he actually pawned the lease itself to a money-lender.[3] Even so, without assistance, we are told, he "should never be able to build it, for it would cost five times as much as he was worth."

Fortunately he had a wealthy brother-in-law, John Brayne,[4] a London grocer, described as "worth five hundred pounds at the least, and by common fame worth a thousand marks." [5] In some way Brayne became interested in the new venture. Like Burbage, he believed that large profits would flow from such a novel undertaking; and as a result he readily agreed to share the expense of erecting and maintaining the building.

[1] That is, about £80.
[2] Wallace, *op. cit.*, p. 134; cf. p. 153.
[3] Wallace, *op. cit.*, p. 151. Cuthbert Burbage declared in 1635: "The Theatre he built with many hundred pounds taken up at interest." (Halliwell-Phillipps, *Outlines*, I, 317.)
[4] The name is often spelled "Braynes."
[5] Wallace, *op. cit.*, p. 109.

Years later members of the Brayne faction asserted that James Burbage "induced" his brother-in-law to venture upon the enterprise by unfairly representing the great profits to ensue;[1] but the evidence, I think, shows that Brayne eagerly sought the partnership. Burbage himself asserted in 1588 that Brayne "practiced to obtain some interest therein," and presumed "that he might easily compass the same by reason that he was natural brother"; and that he voluntarily offered to "bear and pay half the charges of the said building then bestowed and thereafter to be bestowed" in order "that he might have the moiety[2] of the above named Theatre."[3] As a further inducement, so the Burbages asserted, he promised that "for that he had no children," the moiety at his death should go to the children of James Burbage, "whose advancement he then seemed greatly to tender."

Whatever caused Brayne to interest himself in the venture, he quickly became fired with such hopes of great gain that he not only spent upon the building all the money he could gather or borrow, but sold his stock of groceries for £146, disposed of his house for £100, even pawned his clothes, and put his all into the new structure. The spirit in which he worked to make the venture a success, and the personal sacrifices that he

---

[1] See Wallace, *op. cit.*, pp. 139 *seq.*
[2] That is, half-interest.   [3] Wallace, *op. cit.*, p. 40.

THE THEATRE

and his wife made, fully deserve the quotation here of two legal depositions bearing on the subject:

This deponent, being servant, in Bucklersbury, aforesaid, to one Robert Kenningham, grocer, in which street the said John Brayne dwelled also, and of the same trade, he, the said Brayne, at the time he joined with the said James Burbage in the aforesaid lease, was reputed among his neighbors to be worth one thousand pounds at the least, and that after he had joined with the said Burbage in the matter of the building of the said Theatre, he began to slack his own trade, and gave himself to the building thereof, and the chief care thereof he took upon him, and hired workmen of all sorts for that purpose, bought timber and all other things belonging thereunto, and paid all. So as, in this deponent's conscience, he bestowed thereupon for his owne part the sum of one thousand marks at the least, in so much as his affection was given so greatly to the finishing thereof, in hope of great wealth and profit during their lease, that at the last he was driven to sell to this deponent's father his lease of the house wherein he dwelled for £100, and to this deponent all such wares as he had left and all that belonged thereunto remaining in the same, for the sum of £146 and odd money, whereof this deponent did pay for him to one Kymbre, an ironmonger in London, for iron work which the said Brayne bestowed upon the said Theatre, the sum of £40. And afterwards the said Brayne took the matter of the said building so upon him as he was driven to borrow money to supply the same, saying to this deponent that his brother Burbage was not able to help the same, and that he found not towards it above the value of fifty pounds, some part in mony and the rest in stuff.[1]

In reading the next deposition, one should bear in mind the fact that the deponent, Robert Myles, was closely identified with the Brayne faction, and was, therefore, a bitter enemy to the Burbages. Yet his testimony, though prejudiced, gives us a vivid picture of Brayne's activity in the building of the Theatre:

So the said John Brayne made a great sum of money of purpose and intent to go to the building of the said playhouse, and thereupon did provide timber and other stuff needful for the building thereof, and hired carpenters and plasterers for the same purpose, and paid the workmen continually. So as he for his part laid out of his own purse and what upon credit about the same to the sum of £600 or £700 at the least. And in the same time, seeing the said James Burbage nothing able either of himself or by his credit to contribute any like sum towards the building thereof, being then to be finished or else to be lost that had been bestowed upon it already, the said Brayne was driven to sell his house he dwelled in in Bucklersbury, and all his stock that was left, and give up his trade, yea in the end to pawn and sell both his own garments and his wife's, and to run in debt to many for money, to finish the said playhouse, and so to employ himself only upon that matter, and all whatsoever he could make, to his utter undoing, for he saieth that in the latter end of the finishing thereof, the said Brayne and his wife, the now complainants, were driven to labor in

[1] Wallace, *op. cit.*, p. 136.

THE THEATRE

the said work for saving of some of the charge in place of two laborers, whereas the said James Burbage went about his own business, and at sometimes when he did take upon him to do some thing in the said work, he would be and was allowed a workman's hire as other the workman there had.[1]

The last fling at Burbage is quite gratuitous; yet it is probably true that the main costs of erecting the playhouse fell upon the shoulders of Brayne. The evidence is contradictory; some persons assert that Burbage paid half the cost of the building,[2] others that Brayne paid nearly all,[3] and still others content themselves with saying that Brayne paid considerably more than half. The last statement may be accepted as true. The assertion of Gyles Alleyn in 1601, that the Theatre was "erected at the costs and charges of one Brayne and not of the said James Burbage, to the value of one thousand marks," [4] is doubtless incorrect; more correct is the assertion of Robert Myles, executor of the Widow Brayne's will, in 1597: "The said John Brayne did join with the said James [Burbage] in the building aforesaid, and did expend thereupon greater sums than the said James, that is to say, at least five or six hundred

---

[1] Brayne *v.* Burbage, 1592. Printed in full by Wallace, *op cit.* p. 141.
[2] Wallace, *op. cit.*, pp. 213, 217, 263, 265, *et al.*
[3] Wallace, *op. cit.*, pp. 137, 141, 142, 148, 153.
[4] Alleyn *v.* Burbage, Star Chamber Proceedings, 1601–02; printed by Wallace, *op. cit.*, p. 277.

pounds."[1] Since there is evidence that the playhouse ultimately cost about £700,[2] we might hazard the guess that of this sum Brayne furnished about £500,[3] and Burbage about £200. To equalize the expenditure it was later agreed that "the said Brayne should take and receive all the rents and profits of the said Theatre to his own use until he should be answered such sums of money which he had laid out for and upon the same Theatre more than the said Burbage had done."[4]

But if Burbage at the outset was "nothing able to contribute any" great sum of ready money towards the building of the first playhouse, he did contribute other things equally if not more important. In the first place, he conceived the idea, and he carried it as far towards realization as his means allowed. In the second place, he planned the building — its stage as well as its auditorium — to meet the special demands of the actors and the comfort of the audience. This called for bold originality and for ingenuity of a high order, for, it must be remembered, he had no model to study — he was designing the first structure of its kind in England.[5] For this task

[1] Myles *v.* Burbage and Alleyn, 1597; printed by Wallace, *op. cit.*, p. 159; cf. pp. 263, 106, 152.
[2] See Wallace, *op. cit.*, p. 277.
[3] This agrees with the claim of Brayne's widow.
[4] Wallace, *op. cit.*, p. 120.
[5] Mr. E. K. Chambers (*The Mediaeval Stage*, I, 383, note 2; II, 190, note 4) calls attention to a "theatre" belonging to the city of Essex as early as 1548. Possibly the Latin document he cites

THE THEATRE

he was well prepared. In the first place, he was an actor of experience; in the second place, he was the manager of one of the most important troupes in England; and, in the third place, he was by training and early practice a carpenter and builder. In other words, he had exact knowledge of what was needed, and the practical skill to meet those needs.

The building that he designed and erected he named — as by virtue of priority he had a right to do — "The Theatre."

Of the Theatre, unfortunately, we have no pictorial representation, and no formal description, so that our knowledge of its size, shape, and general arrangement must be derived from scattered and miscellaneous sources. That the building was large we may feel sure; the cost of its erection indicates as much. The Fortune, one of

---

referred to an amphitheatre of some sort near the city which was used for dramatic performances; at any rate "in theatro" does not necessarily imply the existence of a playhouse (cf., for example, *op. cit.*, I, 81–82). There is also a reference (quoted by Chambers, *op. cit.*, II, 191, note 1, from *Norfolk Archæology*, XI, 336) to a "game-house" built by the corporation of Yarmouth in 1538 for dramatic performances. What kind of house this was we do not know, but the corporation leased it for other purposes, with the proviso that it should be available "at all such times as any interludes or plays should be ministered or played." Howes, in his continuation of Stow's *Annals* (1631), p. 1004, declares that before Burbage's time he "neither knew, heard, nor read of any such theatres, set stages, or playhouses as have been purposely built, within man's memory"; and Cuthbert Burbage confidently asserted that his father "was the first builder of playhouses" — an assertion which, I think, cannot well be denied.

the largest and handsomest of the later playhouses, cost only £520, and the Hope, also very large, cost £360. The Theatre, therefore, built at a cost of £700, could not have been small. It is commonly referred to, even so late as 1601, as "the great house called the Theatre," and the author of *Skialetheia* (1598) applied to it the significant adjective "vast." Burbage, no doubt, had learned from his experience as manager of a troupe the pecuniary advantage of having an auditorium large enough to receive all who might come. Exactly how many people his building could accommodate we cannot say. The Reverend John Stockwood, in 1578, exclaims bitterly: "Will not a filthy play, with the blast of a trumpet, sooner call thither a thousand than an hour's tolling of the bell bring to the sermon a hundred?"[1] And Fleetwood, the City Recorder, in describing a quarrel which took place in 1584 "at Theatre door," states that "near a thousand people" quickly assembled when the quarrel began.

In shape the building was probably polygonal, or circular. I see no good reason for supposing that it was square; Johannes de Witt referred to it as an "amphitheatre," and the Curtain, erected the following year in imitation, was probably polygonal.[2] It was built of timber, and its exterior,

---

[1] The rest of his speech indicates that he had the Theatre in mind. The passage, of course, is rhetorical.

[2] One cannot be absolutely sure, yet the whole history of early playhouses indicates that the Theatre was polygonal (or circu-

no doubt, was — as in the case of subsequent playhouses — of lime and plaster. The interior consisted of three galleries surrounding an open space called the "yard." The German traveler, Samuel Kiechel, who visited London in the autumn of 1585, described the playhouses — i.e., the Theatre and the Curtain — as "singular [*sonderbare*] houses, which are so constructed that they have about three galleries, one above the other."[1] And Stephen Gosson, in *Plays Confuted* (*c.* 1581) writes: "In the playhouses at London, it is the fashion for youths to go first into the yard, and to carry their eye through every gallery; then, like unto ravens, where they spy the carrion, thither they fly, and press as near to the fairest as they can." The "yard" was unroofed, and all persons there had to stand during the entire performance. The galleries, however, were protected by a roof, were divided into "rooms," and were provided for the most part with seats. Gyles Alleyn inserted in the lease he granted to Burbage the following condition:

And further, that it shall or may [be] lawful for the said Gyles and for his wife and family, upon lawful request therefor made to the said James Burbage, his executors or assigns, to enter or come into

lar) in shape. The only reason for suspecting that it might have been square, doubtfully presented by T. S. Graves in "The Shape of the First London Theatre" (*The South Atlantic Quarterly*, July, 1914), seems to me to deserve no serious consideration.

[1] Quoted by W. B. Rye, *England as Seen by Foreigners*, p. 88.

the premises, and there in some one of the upper rooms to have such convenient place to sit or stand to see such plays as shall be there played, freely without anything therefor paying.[1]

The stage was a platform, projecting into the yard, with a tiring-house at the rear, and a balcony overhead. The details of the stage, no doubt, were subject to alteration as experience suggested, for its materials were of wood, and histrionic and dramatic art were both undergoing rapid development.[2] The furnishings and decorations, as in the case of modern playhouses, seem to have been ornate. Thus T[homas] W[hite], in *A Sermon Preached at Pawles Crosse, on Sunday the Thirde of November, 1577*, exclaims: "Behold the sumptuous Theatre houses, a continual monument of London's prodigality"; John Stockwood, in *A Sermon Preached at Paules Cross, 1578*, refers to it as "the gorgeous playing place erected in the Fields"; and Gabriel Harvey could think of no more appropriate epithet for it than "painted" — "painted theatres," "painted stage."

The building was doubtless used for dramatic performances in the autumn of 1576, although it was not completed until later; John Grigges, one of the carpenters, deposed that Burbage and

---

[1] Wallace, *op. cit.*, p. 177.

[2] There is no reason whatever to suppose, with Ordish, Mantzius, Lawrence, and others, that the stage of the Theatre was removable; for although the building was frequently used by fencers, tumblers, etc., it was never, so far as I can discover, used for animal-baiting.

THE THEATRE

Brayne "finished the same with the help of the profits that grew by plays used there before it was fully finished." [1] Access to the playhouse was had chiefly by way of Finsbury Field and a passage made by Burbage through the brick wall mentioned in the lease.[2]

The terms under which the owners let it to the actors were simple: the actors retained as their share the pennies paid at the outer doors for general admission, and the proprietors received as their share the money paid for seats or standings in the galleries.[3] Cuthbert Burbage states in 1635: "The players that lived in those first times had only the profits arising from the doors, but now the players receive all the comings in at the doors to themselves, and half the galleries." [4]

Before the expiration of two years, or in the early summer of 1578, Burbage and Brayne began to quarrel about the division of the money which fell to their share. Brayne apparently thought that he should at once be indemnified for all the money he had expended on the playhouse in excess of Burbage; and he accused Burbage of "indirect dealing"—there were even whispers of "a secret key" to the "common box" in which the

---

[1] Wallace, *op. cit.*, p. 135.
[2] For depositions to this effect see Halliwell-Phillipps, *Outlines*, 1, 350 ff.
[3] I suspect that the same terms were made with the actors by the proprietors of the inn-playhouses.
[4] Halliwell-Phillipps, *Outlines*, 1, 317.

money was kept.[1] Finally they agreed to "submit themselves to the order and arbitrament of certain persons for the pacification thereof," and together they went to the shop of a notary public to sign a bond agreeing to abide by the decision of the arbitrators. There they "fell a reasoning together," in the course of which Brayne asserted that he had disbursed in the Theatre "three times at the least as much more as the sum then disbursed by the said James Burbage." In the end Brayne unwisely hinted at "ill dealing" on the part of Burbage, whereupon "Burbage did there strike him with his fist, and so they went together by the ears, in so much," says the notary, "that this deponent could hardly part them." After they were parted, they signed a bond of £200 to abide by the decision of the arbitrators. The arbitrators, John Hill and Richard Turnor, "men of great honesty and credit," held their sessions "in the Temple church," whither they summoned witnesses. Finally, on July 12, 1578, after "having thoroughly heard" both sides, they awarded that the profits from the Theatre should be used first to pay the debts upon the building, then to pay Brayne the money he had expended in excess of Burbage, and thereafter to be shared "in divident equally between them."[2] These conditions,

[1] Wallace, *op. cit.*, pp. 142, 148.
[2] For the history of this quarrel, and for other details of the award see Wallace, *op. cit.*, pp. 102, 119, 138, 142, 143, 148, 152.

THE THEATRE

however, were not observed, and the failure to observe them led to much subsequent discord.

The arbitrators also decided that "if occasion should move them [Burbage and Brayne] to borrow any sum of money for the payment of their debts owing for any necessary use and thing concerning the said Theatre, that then the said James Burbage and the said John Brayne should *join* in pawning or mortgageing of their estate and interest of and in the same."[1] An occasion for borrowing money soon arose. So on September 26, 1579, the two partners mortgaged the Theatre to John Hide for the sum of £125 8s. 11d. At the end of a year, by non-payment, they forfeited the mortgage, and the legal title to the property passed to Hide. It seems, however, that because of some special clause in the mortgage Hide was unable to expel Burbage and Brayne, or to dispose of the property to others. Hence he took no steps to seize the Theatre; but he constantly annoyed the occupants by arrest and otherwise. This unfortunate transference of the title to Hide was the cause of serious quarreling between the Burbages and the Braynes, and finally led to much litigation.

In 1582 a more immediate disaster threatened the owners of the Theatre. One Edmund Peckham laid claim to the land on which the playhouse had been built, and brought suit against Alleyn for recovery. More than that, Peckham tried to

---

[1] Wallace, *op. cit.*, p. 103.

take actual possession of the playhouse, so that Burbage "was fain to find men at his own charge to keep the possession thereof from the said Peckham and his servants," and was even "once in danger of his own life by keeping possession thereof." As a result of this state of affairs, Burbage "was much disturbed and troubled in his possession of the Theatre, and could not quietly and peaceably enjoy the same. And therefore the players forsook the said Theatre, to his great loss."[1] In order to reimburse himself in some measure for this loss Burbage retained £30 of the rental due to Alleyn. The act led to a bitter quarrel with Alleyn, and figured conspicuously in the subsequent litigation that came near overwhelming the Theatre.

In 1585 Burbage, having spent the stipulated £200 in repairing and rebuilding the tenements on the premises, sought to renew the lease, according to the original agreement, for the extended period of twenty-one years. On November 20, 1585, he engaged three skilled workmen to view the buildings and estimate the sum he had disbursed in improvements. They signed a formal statement to the effect that in their opinion at least £220 had been thus expended on the premises. Burbage then "tendered unto the said Alleyn a new lease devised by his counsel, ready written and engrossed, with labels and wax thereunto affixed, agreeable to the covenant." But Alleyn

[1] See Wallace, *op. cit.*, pp. 201, 239, 240, 242.

refused to sign the document. He maintained that the new lease was not a verbatim copy of the old lease, that £200 had not been expended on the buildings, and that Burbage was a bad tenant and owed him rent. In reality, Alleyn wanted to extort a larger rental than £14 for the property, which had greatly increased in value.

On July 18, 1586, Burbage engaged six men, all expert laborers, to view the buildings again and estimate the cost of the improvements. They expressed the opinion in writing that Burbage had expended at least £240 in developing the property.[1] Still Alleyn refused to sign an extension of the lease. His conduct must have been very exasperating to the owner of the Theatre. Cuthbert Burbage tells us that his father "did often in gentle manner solicit and require the said Gyles Alleyn for making a new lease of the said premises according to the purporte and effect of the said covenant." But invariably Alleyn found some excuse for delay.

The death of Brayne, in August, 1586, led John Hide, who by reason of the defaulted mortgage was legally the owner of the Theatre, to redouble his efforts to collect his debt. He "gave it out in speech that he had set over and assigned the said lease and bonds to one George Clough, his . . . father-in-law (but in truth he did not so)," and "the said Clough, his father-in-law, did go about

[1] Wallace, *op. cit.*, pp. 229, 234, 228, 233.

to put the said defendant [Burbage] out of the Theatre, or at least did threaten to put him out." As we have seen, there was a clause in the mortgage which prevented Hide from ejecting Burbage;[1] yet Clough was able to make so much trouble, "divers and sundry times" visiting the Theatre, that at last Burbage undertook to settle the debt out of the profits of the playhouse. As Robert Myles deposed in 1592, Burbage allowed the widow of Brayne for "a certain time to take and receive the one-half of the profits of the galleries of the said Theatre ... then on a sudden he would not suffer her to receive any more of the profits there, saying that he must take and receive all till he had paid the debts. And then she was constrained, as his servant, to gather the money and to deliver it unto him."[2]

For some reason, however, the debt was not settled, and Hide continued his futile demands. Several times Burbage offered to pay the sum in full if the title of the Theatre were made over to his son Cuthbert Burbage; and Brayne's widow made similar offers in an endeavor to gain the entire property for herself. But Hide, who seems to have been an honest man, always declared that since Burbage and Brayne "did jointly mortgage it unto him" he was honor-bound to assign the property back to Burbage and the widow of Brayne jointly. So matters stood for a while.

[1] Wallace, *op. cit.*, p. 55.   [2] *Ibid.*, p. 105.

At last, however, in 1589, Hide declared that "since he had forborne his money so long, he could do it no more, so as they that came first should have it of him." Thereupon Cuthbert Burbage came bringing not only the money in hand, but also a letter from his master and patron, Walter Cape, gentleman usher to the Lord High Treasurer, requesting Hide to make over the Theatre to Cuthbert, and promising in return to assist Hide with the Lord Treasurer when occasion arose. Under this pressure, Hide accepted full payment of his mortgage, and made over the title of the property to Cuthbert Burbage. Thus Brayne's widow was legally excluded from any share in the ownership of the Theatre. Myles deposed, in 1592, that henceforth Burbage "would not suffer her to meddle in the premises, but thrust her out of all."

This led at once to a suit, in which Robert Myles acted for the widow. He received an order from the Court of Chancery in her favor, and armed with this, and accompanied by two other persons, he came on November 16, 1590, to Burbage's "dwelling house near the Theatre," called to the door Cuthbert Burbage, and in "rude and exclamable sort" demanded "the moiety of the said Theatre." James Burbage "being within the house, hearing a noise at the door, went to the door, and there found his son, the said Cuthbert, and the said Myles speaking loud together." Words were bandied, until finally Burbage, "dared by the same Myles with great threats and words that he would do this and could do that," lost his temper, and threatened to beat Myles off the ground.[1]

Next the widow, attended by Robert Myles and others, visited the home of the Burbages "to require them to perform the said award" of the court. They were met by James Burbage's wife, who "charged them to go out of her grounds, or else she would make her son break their knaves' heads." Aroused by this noise, "James Burbage, her husband, looking out a window upon them, called the complainant [Widow Brayne] murdering whore, and ... the others villaines, rascals, and knaves." And when Mistress Brayne spoke of the order of the court, "he cryed unto her, 'Go, go. A cart, a cart for you! I will obey no such order, nor I care not for any such orders, and therefore it were best for you and your companions to be packing betimes, for if my son [Cuthbert] come he will thump you hence!'" Just then Cuthbert did "come home, and in very hot sort bid them get thence, or else he would set them forwards, saying 'I care for no such order. The Chancery shall not give away what I have paid for.'" And so, after "great and horrible oathes" by James Burbage and his son, the widow and her attendants "went their ways."[2]

Receiving thus no satisfaction from these visits

---
[1] Wallace, *op. cit.*, pp. 57, 60, 62.   [2] *Ibid.*, p. 121.

THE THEATRE

to the home of James Burbage, the widow and Robert Myles came several times to the Theatre, bearing the order of the court in their hands; but each time they were railed upon and driven out. Finally, the widow, with her ever-faithful adjutant Robert Myles, his son Ralph, and his business partner, Nicholas Bishop, went "to the Theatre upon a play-day to stand at the door that goeth up to the galleries of the said Theatre to take and receive for the use of the said Margaret half of the money that should be given to come up into the said gallery." In the Theatre they were met by Richard Burbage, then about nineteen years old, and his mother, who "fell upon the said Robert Myles and beat him with a broom staff, calling him murdering knave." When Myles's partner, Bishop, ventured to protest at this contemptuous treatment of the order of the court, "the said Richard Burbage," so Bishop deposed, "scornfully and disdainfully playing with this deponent's nose, said that if he dealt in the matter, he would beat him also, and did challenge the field of him at that time." One of the actors then coming in, John Alleyn — brother of the immortal Edward Alleyn — "found the foresaid Richard Burbage, the youngest son of the said James Burbage, there with a broom staff in his hand; of whom when this deponent Alleyn asked what stir was there, he answered in laughing phrase how they came for a moiety, 'But,' quod he (holding up the said broom staff) 'I have, I think, delivered him a moiety with this, and sent them packing.'" Alleyn thereupon warned the Burbages that Myles could bring an action of assault and battery against them. "'Tush,' quod the father, 'no, I warrant you; but where my son hath now beat him hence, my sons, if they will be ruled by me, shall at their next coming provide charged pistols, with powder and hempseed, to shoot them in the legs.'"[1]

But if the Burbages could laugh at the efforts of Myles and the widow to secure a moiety of the Theatre from Cuthbert, they were seriously troubled by the continued refusal of Gyles Alleyn to renew the lease. James Burbage many times urged his landlord to fulfill the original agreement, but in vain. At last, Alleyn, "according to his own will and discretion, did cause a draft of a lease to be drawn, wherein were inserted many unreasonable covenants." The new conditions imposed by Alleyn were: (1) that Burbage should pay a rental of £24 instead of £14 a year; (2) that he should use the Theatre as a place for acting for only five years after the expiration of the original twenty-one-year lease, and should then convert the building to other uses; (3) that he should ultimately leave the building in the possession of Alleyn.[2] The first and third conditions, though unjust, Burbage was willing to accept, but the

[1] Wallace, *op. cit.*, pp. 63, 97, 100, 101, 114.
[2] See Wallace, *op. cit.*, pp. 195, 212, 216, 250, 258, *et al.*

second condition — that he should cease to use the Theatre for plays — he "utterly refused" to consider.

Finally, perceiving that it was useless to deal further with Alleyn, he made plans to secure a new playhouse in the district of Blackfriars, a district which, although within the city walls, was not under the jurisdiction of the city authorities. He purchased there the old Blackfriars refectory for £600, and then at great expense made the refectory into a playhouse. But certain influential noblemen and others living near by protested against this, and the Privy Council ordered that the building should not be used as a public playhouse. All this belongs mainly to the history of the Second Blackfriars Playhouse, and for further details the reader is referred to the chapter dealing with that theatre.

Shortly after the order of the Privy Council cited above, Burbage died, just two months before the expiration of his lease from Alleyn; and the Theatre with all its troubles passed to his son Cuthbert. By every means in his power Cuthbert sought to induce Alleyn to renew the lease: "Your said subject was thereof possessed, and being so possessed, your said servant did often require the said Alleyn and Sara his wife to make unto him the said new lease of the premises, according to the agreement of the said indenture." Cuthbert's importunity in the matter is clearly set forth in a deposition by Henry Johnson, one of Alleyn's tenants. It was Alleyn's custom to come to London at each of the four pay terms of the year, and stop at the George Inn in Shoreditch to receive his rents; and on such occasions Johnson often observed Cuthbert's entreaties with Alleyn. In his deposition he says that he "knoweth that the said complainant [Cuthbert Burbage] hath many times labored and entreated the defendant [Gyles Alleyn] to make him a new lease of the premises in question, for this deponent sayeth that many times when the defendant hath come up to London to receive his rents, he, this deponent, hath been with him paying him certain rent; and then he hath seen the plaintiff with his landlord, paying his rent likewise; and then, finding opportunity, the plaintiff would be intreating the defendant to make him a new lease of the premises in question; and sayeth that it is at least three years since [i.e., in 1597] he, this deponent, first heard the plaintiff labor and entreat the defendant for a new lease."[1] Cuthbert tells us that Alleyn did not positively refuse to renew the lease, "but for some causes, which he feigned, did defer the same from time to time, but yet gave hope to your subject, and affirmed that he would make him such a lease."[2]

Cuthbert's anxiety in this matter is explained by the fact that the old lease gave him the right

[1] Wallace, *op. cit.*, p. 246. [2] *Ibid.*, p. 184.

THE THEATRE

to tear down the Theatre and carry away the timber and other materials to his own use, provided he did so before the expiration of the twenty-one years. Yet, relying on Alleyn's promises to renew the lease, he "did forbear to pull downe and carry away the timber and stuff employed for the said Theatre and playing-house at the end of the said first term of one and twenty years." A failure to renew the lease would mean, of course, the loss of the building.

Alleyn, though deferring to sign a new lease, allowed Burbage to continue in possession of the property at "the old rent of £14." Yet the Theatre seems not to have been used for plays after the original lease expired.[1] The Lord Chamberlain's Company, which had been occupying the Theatre, and of which Richard Burbage was the chief actor, had moved to the Curtain; and the author of *Skialetheia*, printed in 1598, refers to the old playhouse as empty: "But see, yonder, one, like the unfrequented Theatre, walks in dark silence and vast solitude."[2]

To Cuthbert Burbage such a state of affairs

---

[1] The lease expired on April 13, 1597; on July 28 the Privy Council closed all playhouses until November. The references to the Theatre in *The Remembrancia* (see The Malone Society's *Collections*, I, 78) do not necessarily imply that the building was then actually used by the players.

[2] The same fact is revealed in the author's remark, "If my dispose persuade me to a play, I'le to the Rose or Curtain," for at this time only the Chamberlain's Men and the Admiral's Men were allowed to play.

was intolerable, and on September 29, 1598, he made a new appeal to Alleyn. Alleyn proffered a lease already drawn up, but Cuthbert would not "accept thereof" because of the "very unreasonable covenants therein contained."[1]

Shortly after this fruitless interview, or late in 1598, Gyles Alleyn resolved to take advantage of the fact that Cuthbert Burbage had not removed the Theatre before the expiration of the first twenty-one years. He contended that since Cuthbert had "suffered the same there to continue till the expiration of the said term ... the right and interest of the said Theatre was both in law and conscience absolutely vested" now in himself; accordingly he planned "to pull down the same, and to convert the wood and timber thereof to some better use for the benefit" of himself.[2]

But, unfortunately for Alleyn, Cuthbert Burbage "got intelligence" of this purpose, and at once set himself to the task of saving his property. He and his brother Richard, the great actor, took into their confidence the chief members of the Lord Chamberlain's Company, then performing at the Curtain Playhouse, namely William Shakespeare, John Heminges, Augustine Phillips, Thomas Pope, and William Kempe. These men agreed to form with the Burbages a syndicate to finance the erection of a new playhouse. The two Burbages agreed to bear one-half the expense, including the

[1] Wallace, *op. cit.*, pp. 216, 249. [2] *Ibid.*, pp. 277, 288.

THE THEATRE 63

timber and other materials of the old Theatre, and the five actors promised to supply the other half. Together they leased a suitable plot of land on the Bankside near Henslowe's Rose, the lease dating from December 25, 1598. These details having been arranged, it remained only for the Burbages to save their building from the covetousness of Alleyn.

On the night of December 28, 1598,[1] Alleyn being absent in the country, Cuthbert Burbage, his brother Richard, his friend William Smith, "of Waltham Cross, in the County of Hartford, gentleman," Peter Street, "cheefe carpenter," and twelve others described as "laborers such as wrought for wages," gathered at the Theatre and began to tear down the building. We learn that the widow of James Burbage "was there, and did see the doing thereof, and liked well of it";[2] and we may suspect that at some time during the day Shakespeare and the other actors were present as interested spectators.

The episode is thus vividly described by the indignant Gyles Allen:

The said Cuthbert Burbage, having intelligence of your subject's purpose herein, and unlawfully combining and confederating himself with the said Richard Burbage and one Peter Street, William Smith, and diverse other persons to the number of

---

[1] The date, January 20, 1599, seems to be an error.
[2] Wallace, *op. cit.*, p. 238.

twelve, to your subject unknown, did about the eight and twentieth day of December, in the one and fortieth year of your highness reign, and sithence your highness last and general pardon, by the confederacy aforesaid, riotously assembled themselves together, and then and there armed themselves with diverse and many unlawful and offensive weapons, as namely swords, daggers, bills, axes, and such like, and so armed did then repair unto the said Theatre, and then and there armed as aforesaid, in very riotous, outrageous, and forceable manner, and contrary to the laws of your highness realm, attempted to pull down the said Theatre. Whereupon, diverse of your subjects, servants and farmers, then going about in peaceable manner to procure them to desist from that unlawful enterprise, they, the said riotous persons aforesaid, notwithstanding procured then therein with great violence, not only then and there forcibly and riotously resisting your subjects, servants, and farmers, but also then and there pulling, breaking, and throwing down the said Theatre in very outrageous, violent, and riotous sort.[1]

The workmen, under the expert direction of Peter Street, carried the timber and other materials of the old Theatre to the tract of land on the Bankside recently leased by the new syndicate — as Gyles Alleyn puts it, "did then also in most forcible and riotous manner take and carry away from thence all the wood and timber thereof unto the Bankside, in the Parish of St. Mary

---

[1] Wallace, *op. cit.*, pp. 278–79. This document was discovered by J. O. Halliwell-Phillipps, who printed extracts in his *Outlines*. See also Ordish, *Early London Theatres*, pp. 75–76.

THE THEATRE

Overies, and there erected a new playhouse with the said timber and wood."

The playhouse thus erected was, of course, an entirely new structure. Nearly a quarter of a century had elapsed since James Burbage designed the old Theatre, during which time a great development had taken place both in histrionic art and in play writing; and, no doubt, many improvements were possible in the stage and in the auditorium to provide better facilities for the actors and greater comfort for the spectators. In designing such improvements the architect had the advice and help of the actors, including Shakespeare; and he succeeded in producing a playhouse that was a model of excellence. The name selected by the syndicate for their new building was "The Globe." For further details as to its construction, and for its subsequent history, the reader is referred to the chapter dealing with that building.

When Gyles Alleyn learned that the Burbages had demolished the Theatre and removed the timber to the Bankside, he was deeply incensed, not only at the loss of the building, but also, no doubt, at being completely outwitted. At once he instituted suit against Cuthbert Burbage; but he was so intemperate in his language and so reckless in his charges that he weakened his case. The suit dragged for a few years, was in part referred to Francis Bacon, and finally in the summer of 1601 was dismissed. Thus the history of the first

London playhouse, which is chiefly the history of quarrels and litigation, came to a close.

It is not possible now to indicate exactly the stay of the different troupes at the Theatre; the evidence is scattered and incomplete, and the inferences to be drawn are often uncertain.

When the building was opened in 1576, it was, no doubt, occupied by the Earl of Leicester's troupe, of which Burbage was the manager, and for which, presumably, the structure had been designed. Yet other troupes of players may also have been allowed to use the building — when Leicester's Men were touring the provinces, or, possibly, on days when Leicester's Men did not act. This arrangement lasted about six years.

In 1582 the use of the Theatre was interrupted by the interference of Peckham. For a long time the actors "could not enjoy the premises," and Burbage was forced to keep Peckham's servants out of the building with an armed guard night and day. As a result of this state of affairs, Leicester's troupe was dissolved; "many of the players," we are told, were driven away, and the rest "forsook the said Theatre." The last notice of these famous players is a record of their performance at Court on February 10, 1583.

Shortly after this, in March, 1583, Tilney, the Master of the Revels, organized under royal patronage a new company called the Queen's Men. For this purpose he selected twelve of the best

THE THEATRE

actors of the realm, including some of the members of Leicester's company.[1] The two best-known actors in the new organization were the Queen's favorite comedian, Richard Tarleton, the immortal "Lord of Mirth," and John Lanham, the leader and apparently the manager of the troupe. James Burbage, who may by this time, if not before, have retired from acting, was not included.

The newly organized Queen's Men in all probability occupied the Theatre which had been left vacant by the dissolution of Leicester's company. Mr. Wallace denies this, mainly on the evidence of a permit issued by the Lord Mayor, November 28, 1583, granting the Queen's Men the privilege of acting "at the sign of the Bull [Inn] in Bishopgate Street, and the sign of the Bell [Inn] in Gracious Street, and nowhere else within this city." But this permit, I think, lends scant support to Mr. Wallace's contention. The Lord Mayor had no authority to issue a license for the Queen's Men to play at the Theatre, for that structure was outside the jurisdiction of the city. The Privy Council itself, no doubt, had issued such a general license when the company was organized under royal patronage.[2] And now, ten months later, on

---

[1] For a list of the Queen's Men see Wallace, *op. cit.*, p. 11.

[2] Such a license would include also permission to act in the provinces. This latter was soon needed, for shortly after their organization the Queen's Men were driven by the plague to tour the provinces. They were in Cambridge on July 9, and probably returned to London shortly after. See Murray, *English Dramatic Companies*, I, 8.

November 26, 1583, the Council sends to the Lord Mayor a request "that Her Majesty's players may be suffered to play ... within the city and liberties *between this and shrovetide next*" [1] — in other words, during the winter season when access to the Theatre was difficult. It was customary for troupes to seek permission to act within the city during the winter months.[2] Thus the Queen's Men, in a petition written probably in the autumn of the following year, 1584, requested the Privy Council to dispatch "favorable letters unto the Lord Mayor of London to permit us to exercise within the city," and the Lord Mayor refused, with the significant remark that "if in winter ... the foulness of season do hinder the passage into the fields to play, the remedy is ill conceived to bring them into London." [3] Obviously the Queen's Men were seeking permission to play in the city only during the cold winter months; during the balmy spring, summer, and autumn months — for actors the best season of the year — they occupied their commodious playhouse in "the fields."

That this playhouse for a time, at least, was the Theatre is indicated by several bits of evi-

[1] The Malone Society's *Collections*, I, 66.
[2] Lord Hunsdon, on October 8, 1594, requested the Lord Mayor to permit the Chamberlain's Men "to play this winter time within the city at the Cross Keys in Gracious Street." See The Malone Society's *Collections*, I, 67.
[3] The Malone Society's *Collections*, I, 170, 172.

dence. Thus the author of *Martin's Month's Mind* (1589) speaks of "twittle-twattles that I had learned in ale-houses and at the Theatre of Lanham and his fellows." Again, Nash, in *Pierce Penniless* (1592), writes: "Tarleton at the Theatre made jests of him"; Harrington, in *The Metamorphosis of Ajax* (1596): "Which word was after admitted into the Theatre with great applause, by the mouth of Master Tarleton"; and the author of *Tarlton's Newes out of Purgatory* (c. 1589) represents Tarleton as connected with the Theatre. Now, unless Lanham, Tarleton, and their "fellows" usually or sometimes acted at the Theatre, it is hard to understand these and other similar passages.

The following episode tends to prove the same thing. On June 18, 1584, William Fleetwood, Recorder, wrote to Lord Burghley:[1]

Right honorable and my very good lord. Upon Whitsunday there was a very good sermon preached at the new churchyard near Bethelem, whereat my Lord Mayor was with his brethren; and by reason no plays were the same day, all the city was quiet. Upon Monday I was at the Court. . . . That night I returned to London and found all the wards full of watchers; the cause thereof was for that very near the Theatre or Curtain, at the time of the plays, there lay a prentice sleeping upon the grass; and one Challes, at Grostock, did turn upon the toe upon the belly of the same prentice. Whereupon the apprentice start up.

[1] The letter is printed in full in The Malone Society's *Collections*, I, 164.

In the altercation that followed, Challes remarked that "prentices were but the scum of the world." This led to a general rising of apprentices, and much disorder throughout the city. Fleetwood records the upshot thus:

> Upon Sunday my Lord [Mayor] sent two aldermen to the court for the suppressing and pulling down of the Theatre and Curtain. All the Lords [of the Privy Council] agreed thereunto saving my Lord Chamberlain and Mr. Vice-Chamberlain. But we obtained a letter to suppress them all. Upon the same night I sent for the Queen's Players [at the Theatre?] and my Lord Arundel's Players [at the Curtain?] and they all willingly obeyed the Lords's letters. The chiefest of Her Highness's Players advised me to send for the owner of the Theatre [James Burbage [1]], who was a stubborn fellow, and to bind him. I did so. He sent me word he was my Lord of Hundson's man, and that he would not come at me; but he would in the morning ride to my lord.

The natural inference from all this is that the Queen's Men and Lord Arundel's Men were then playing *outside the city* where they could be controlled only by "the Lords's Letters"; that the Queen's Men were occupying the Theatre, and that James Burbage was (as we know) not a mem-

---

[1] This could not have been Hide, as usually stated. Hide had nothing to do with the management of the Theatre, and was not "my Lord of Hunsdon's man." Hide's connection with the Theatre as sketched in this chapter shows the absurdity of such an interpretation of the document.

THE THEATRE 71

ber of that company, but merely stood to them in the relation of "owner of the Theatre."

What Burbage meant by calling himself "my Lord of Hunsdon's man" is not clear. Mr. Wallace contends that when Leicester's Men were dissolved, Burbage organized "around the remnants of Leicester's Company" a troupe under the patronage of Lord Hunsdon, and that this troupe, and not the Queen's Men, occupied the Theatre thereafter.[1] But we hear of Hunsdon's Men at Ludlow in July, 1582; and we find them presenting a play at Court on December 27, 1582. Since Leicester's troupe is recorded as acting at Court as late as February 10, 1583, it seems unlikely that Mr. Wallace's theory as to the origin of Hunsdon's Men is true. It may be, however, that after the dissolution of Leicester's Men, Burbage associated himself with Hunsdon's Men, and it may be that he allowed that relatively unimportant company to occupy the Theatre for a short time. Hunsdon's Men seem to have been mainly a traveling troupe; Mr. Murray states that notices of them "occur frequently in the provinces," but we hear almost nothing of them in London. Indeed, at the time of the trouble described by Fleetwood, Hunsdon's Men were in Bath.[2] If Burbage was a member of the troupe, he certainly did not accompany them on their extended tours;

[1] Wallace, *op. cit.*, p. 11.
[2] Murray, *English Dramatic Companies*, I, 321.

and when they played in London, if they used the Theatre, they must have used it jointly with the Queen's Men.

Late in 1585 the Theatre was affiliated with the adjacent Curtain. Burbage and Brayne made an agreement with the proprietor of that playhouse whereby the Curtain might be used "as an easore" [easer?] to the Theatre, and "the profits of the said two playhouses might for seven years space be in divident between them." This agreement, we know, was carried out, but whether it led to an exchange of companies, or what effect it had upon the players, we cannot say. Possibly to this period of joint management may be assigned the witticism of Dick Tarleton recorded as having been uttered "at the Curtain" where the Queen's Men were then playing.[1] It may even be that as one result of the affiliation of the two houses the Queen's Men were transferred to the Curtain.

In 1590, as we learn from the deposition of John Alleyn, the Theatre was being used by the Admiral's Men.[2] This excellent company had been formed early in 1589 by the separation of certain leading players from Worcester's Men, and it had probably occupied the Theatre since its organization. Its star actor, Edward Alleyn, was then at the height of his powers, and was producing with

---

[1] *Tarlton's Jests*, ed. by J. O. Halliwell, p. 16. Tarleton died in 1588.
[2] Wallace, *op. cit.*, pp. 101, 126.

THE THEATRE

great success Marlowe's splendid plays. We may suppose that the following passage refers to the performance of the Admiral's Men at the Theatre:

> He had a head of hair like one of my devils in *Dr. Faustus*, when the old Theatre crackt and frightened the audience.[1]

Late in 1590 the Admiral's Men seem to have been on bad terms with Burbage,[2] and when John Alleyn made his deposition, February 6, 1592, they had certainly left the Theatre. Mr. Greg, from entirely different evidence, has concluded that they were dispersed in 1591,[3] and this conclusion is borne out by the legal document cited above.

The next company that we can definitely associate with the Theatre was the famous Lord Chamberlain's Men. On April 16, 1594, Lord Strange, the Earl of Derby, died, and the chief members of his troupe — William Shakespeare, Richard Burbage, John Heminges, William Kempe, Thomas Pope, George Bryan, and Augustine Phillips — organized a new company under the patronage of the Lord Chamberlain. For ten days, in June, 1594, they acted at Newington Butts under the management of Philip Henslowe, then went, probably at once, to the Theatre, which they made their home until the Burbage lease of the prop-

---

[1] *The Black Booke*, 1604.   [2] Wallace, *op. cit.*, p. 101.
[3] Greg, *Henslowe's Diary*, II, 83. The Admiral's Men were reorganized in 1594, and occupied the Rose under Henslowe's management.

erty expired in the spring of 1597. Here, among other famous plays, they produced the original *Hamlet*, thus referred to by Lodge in *Wit's Miserie*, 1596:

He looks as pale as the visard of the ghost which cries so miserably at the Theatre, like an oyster-wife, "Hamlet, revenge!"

And here, too, they presented all of Shakespeare's early masterpieces.

Their connection with the building ceased in 1597 at the expiration of the Burbage lease; but their association with the proprietors of the Theatre was permanent. Their subsequent history, as also the history of the Burbage brothers, will be found in the chapters dealing with the Globe and the Second Blackfriars.[1]

[1] For other but unimportant references to the Theatre see The Malone Society's *Collections*, vol. 1: disorder at, October, 1577, p. 153; disorder at, on Sunday, April, 1580, p. 46; fencing allowed at, July, 1582, p. 57; fencing forbidden at, May, 1583, p. 62; to be closed during infection, May, 1583, p. 63; complaint against, by the Lord Mayor, September, 1594, p. 76. And see Halliwell-Phillipps, *Outlines*, 1, 363, for a special performance there by a "virgin," February 22, 1582.

CHAPTER IV
THE CURTAIN

ALTHOUGH James Burbage was, as his son asserted, "the first builder of playhouses," a second public playhouse followed hard on the Theatre, probably within twelve months. It was erected a short distance to the south of the Theatre, — that is, nearer the city, — and, like that building, it adjoined Finsbury Field.[1] To the two playhouses the audiences came trooping over the meadows, in "great multidudes," the Lord Mayor tells us; and the author of *Tarlton's Newes out of Purgatory* (*c.* 1589) describes their return to London thus: "With that I waked, and saw such concourse of people through the fields that I knew the play was done."[2]

The new playhouse derived its name from the Curtain estate, on which it was erected.[3] This estate was formerly the property of the Priory of Holywell, and was described in 1538 as "scituata et existentia extra portas ejusdem nuper monasterii prope pasturam dicte nuper Priorisse, vo-

---

[1] The site is probably marked by Curtain Court in Chasserau's survey of 1745, reproduced on page 79.

[2] Ed. by J. O. Halliwell, for The Shakespeare Society (1844), p. 105.

[3] The Rose and the Red Bull derived their names in a similar way from the estates on which they were erected.

catam *the Curteine*."[1] Why it was so called is not clear. The name may have been derived from some previous owner of the property; it may, as Collier thought, have come from some early association with the walls (*curtains*) or defenses of the city; or, it may have come, as Tomlins suggests, from the mediæval Latin *cortina*, meaning a court, a close, a farm enclosure.[2] Whatever its origin — the last explanation seems the most plausible — the interesting point is that it had no connection whatever with a stage curtain.

The building was probably opened to the London public in the summer or autumn of 1577. The first reference to it is found in T[homas] W[hite]'s *Sermon Preached at Pawles Crosse on Sunday the Thirde of November, 1577:* "Behold the sumptuous theatre houses, a continual monument of London's prodigality and folly";[3] and a reference to it by name appears in Northbrooke's *A Treatise*, licensed December, 1577: "Those places, also, which are made up and builded for such plays and interludes, as the Theatre and Curtain."[4]

[1] Halliwell-Phillipps, *Outlines*, I, 364.
[2] Tomlins, *Origin of the Curtain Theatre, and Mistakes Regarding It*, in The Shakespeare Society's Papers (1844), p. 29.
[3] J. D. Wilson, *The Cambridge History of English Literature*, VI, 435, says that this sermon was "delivered at Paul's cross on 9 December, 1576 and, apparently, repeated on 3 November in the following year." This is incorrect; White did preach a sermon at Paul's Cross on December 9, but not the sermon from which this quotation is drawn.
[4] Ed. by J. P. Collier, for The Shakespeare Society (1843), p. 85.

THE CURTAIN

Like the Theatre, the Curtain was a peculiarly shaped building, specially designed for acting; "those playhouses that are erected and built *only for such purposes* ... namely the Curtain and the Theatre," [1] writes the Privy Council; and the German traveler, Samuel Kiechel, who visited London in 1585, describes them as "*sonderbare*" structures. They are usually mentioned together, and in such a way as to suggest similarity of shape as well as of purpose. We may, I think, reasonably suppose that the Curtain was in all essential details a copy of Burbage's Theatre.[2] Presumably, then, it was polygonal (or circular) in shape,[3] was constructed of timber, and was finished on the outside with lime and plaster. The interior, as the evidence already cited in the chapter on the Theatre shows, consisted of three galleries surrounding an open yard. There was a platform projecting into the middle of the yard, with dressing-rooms at the rear, "heavens" overhead, and a flagpole rising above the "heavens." That some sign was displayed in front of the door is likely. Malone writes: "The original sign hung out at this playhouse (as Mr. Steevens has observed) was

[1] Dasent, *Acts of the Privy Council*, XXVII, 313.
[2] It seems, however, to have been smaller than the Theatre.
[3] Johannes de Witt describes the Theatre and the Curtain along with the Swan and the Rose as "amphitheatra" (see page 167). It is quite possible that Shakespeare refers to the Curtain in the Prologue to *Henry V* as "this wooden O," though the reference may be to the Globe.

the painting of a curtain striped."[1] Aubrey records that Ben Jonson "acted and wrote, but both ill, at the Green Curtain, a kind of nursery or obscure playhouse somewhere in the suburbs, I think towards Shoreditch or Clerkenwell."[2] By "at the Green Curtain" Aubrey means, of course, "at the sign of the Green Curtain"; but the evidence of Steevens and of Aubrey is too vague and uncertain to warrant any definite conclusions.

Of the early history of the Curtain we know little, mainly because it was not, like certain other playhouses, the subject of extensive litigation. We do not even know who planned and built it. The first evidence of its ownership appears fifteen years after its erection, in some legal documents connected with the Theatre.[3] In July, 1592, Henry Lanman, described as "of London, gentleman, of the age of 54 years," deposed: "That true it is about 7 years now shall be this next winter, they, the said Burbage and Brayne, having the profits of plays made at the Theatre, and this deponent having the profits of the plays done at the house called the Curtain near to the same, the said Burbage and Brayne, taking the Curtain as an esore[4] to their playhouse, did of

---

[1] Malone, *Variorum*, III, 54; cf. also Ellis, *The Parish of St. Leonard*.

[2] Did Steevens base his statement on this passage in Aubrey?

[3] Brayne *v.* Burbage, 1592, printed in full by Wallace, *The First London Theatre*, pp. 109–52. See especially pp. 126, 148.

[4] Easer?

THE CURTAIN

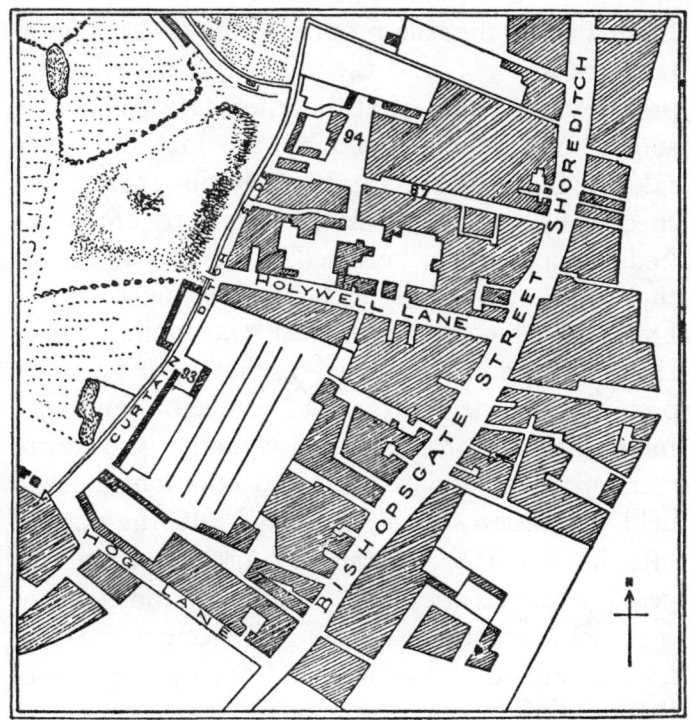

THE SITE OF THE CURTAIN PLAYHOUSE

From *An Actual Survey of the Parish of St. Leonard in Shoreditch, taken in the year 1745*, by Peter Chasserau, Surveyor. The key to the map gives "93" as Curtain Court, probably the site of the old playhouse; "87" as New Inn Yard, and "94" as Holywell Court, both interesting in connection with Burbage's Theatre. (Redrawn from the original for this volume.)

their own motion move this deponent that he would agree that the profits of the said two playhouses might for seven years space be in divident between them."[1]

From this statement it is evident that Henry

[1] Wallace, *op. cit.*, p. 148; cf. p. 126.

Lanman was the sole proprietor of the Curtain as far back as 1585, and the presumption is that his proprietorship was of still earlier date. This presumption is strengthened by the fact that in a sale of the Curtain estate early in 1582, he is specifically mentioned as having a tenure of an "edifice or building" erected in the Curtain Close, that is, that section of the estate next to the Field, on which the playhouse was built.[1] Since Lanman is not mentioned as having any other property on the estate, the "edifice or building" referred to was probably the playhouse. The document gives no indication as to how long he had held possession of the "edifice," but the date of sale, March, 1582, carries us back to within four years of the erection of the Curtain, and it seems reasonable to suppose, though of course we cannot be sure, that Lanman had been proprietor of the building from the very beginning.[2]

Certain records of the sale of the Curtain estate shortly before and shortly after the erection of the playhouse are preserved, but these throw very

[1] Tomlins, *op. cit.*, pp. 29-31.
[2] Of this Henry Lanman we know nothing beyond the facts here revealed. Possibly he was a brother of the distinguished actor John Lanman (the name is variously spelled Lanman, Laneman, Lenmann, Laneham, Laynman, Lanham), one of the chief members of Leicester's troupe, and one of the twelve men selected in 1583 to form the Queen's Men. But speculation of this sort is vain. It is to be hoped that in the future some student will investigate the life of this obscure theatrical manager, and trace his connection with the early history of the drama.

THE CURTAIN

little light upon the playhouse itself. We learn that on February 20, 1567, Lord Mountjoy and his wife sold the estate to Maurice Longe, clothworker, and his son William Longe, for the sum of £60; and that on August 23, 1571, Maurice Longe and his wife sold it to the then Lord Mayor, Sir William Allyn, for the sum of £200. In both documents the property is described in the same words: "All that house, tenement or lodge commonly called the *Curtain*, and all that parcel of ground and close, walled and enclosed with a brick wall on the west and north parts, called also the *Curtain Close*." The lodge here referred to, generally known as "Curtain House," was on, or very near, Holywell Lane;[1] the playhouse, as already stated, was erected in the close near the Field.[2]

How long Sir William Allyn held the property, or why it reverted to the Longe family, we do not know. But on March 18, 1582, we find William Longe, the son of "Maurice Longe, citizen and clothworker, of London, deceased," selling the same property, described in the same words, to one "Thomas Harberte, citizen and girdler, of London." In the meantime, of course, the playhouse had been erected, but no clear or direct

---

[1] Halliwell-Phillipps, *Outlines*, I, 365.
[2] The Privy Council on March 10, 1601, refers to it as "The Curtaine in Moorefeildes"; in ancient times, says Stow, Moorefields extended to Holywell. See Halliwell-Phillipps, *Outlines*, I, 364.

mention of the building is made in the deed of sale. Possibly it was included in the conventionally worded phrase: "and all and singular other messuages, tenements, edifices, and buildings, with all and singular their appurtenances, erected and builded upon the said close called the Curtain." [1] Among the persons named as holding tenures of the above-mentioned "edifices and buildings" in the close was Henry Lanman. It seems not improbable, therefore, that the Curtain, like the Theatre, was erected on leased ground.

It is impossible to give a connected history of the Curtain. Most of the references to it that we now possess are invectives in early puritanical writings, or bare mention, along with other playhouses, in letters or ordinances of the Privy Council and the Lord Mayor. Such references as these do not much help us in determining what companies successively occupied the building, or what varying fortunes marked its ownership and management. Yet a few scattered facts have sifted down to us, and these I have arranged in chronological order.

On the afternoon of April 6, 1580, an earthquake, especially severe in Holywell, shook the building during the performance of a play, and greatly frightened the audience. Munday says merely: "at the playhouses the people came running forth, surprised with great astonishment"; [2]

---

[1] Tomlins, *op. cit.*, p. 31.   [2] *View of Sundry Examples*, 1580.

but Stubbes, the Puritan, who saw in the event a "fearful judgment of God," writes with fervor: "The like judgment almost did the Lord show unto them a little before, being assembled at their theatres to see their bawdy interludes and other trumperies practised, for He caused the earth mightily to shake and quaver, as though all would have fallen down; whereat the people, sore amazed, some leapt down from the top of the turrets, pinnacles, and towers where they stood, to the ground, whereof some had their legs broke, some their arms, some their backs, some hurt one where, some another, and many score crushed and bruised."[1]

The disturbance at the Theatre and the Curtain in 1584, when one Challes "did turn upon the toe upon the belly of" an apprentice "sleeping upon the grass" in the Field near by, has been mentioned in the preceding chapter. If the interpretation of the facts there given is correct, Lord Arundel's Players were then occupying the Curtain.

In the winter of 1585 Lanman entered into his seven years' agreement with Burbage and Brayne by which the Theatre and the Curtain were placed under one management, and the profits shared "in divident between them." This agreement was faithfully kept by both parties, but there is no

---

[1] *The Anatomy of Abuses*, ed. F. J. Furnivall, New Shakspere Society, p. 180. For other descriptions of this earthquake see Halliwell-Phillipps, *Outlines*, 1, 369.

evidence that after the expiration of the seven years, in the winter of 1592, the affiliation was continued. What effect the arrangement had upon the companies of players occupying the two theatres we cannot now determine. To this period, however, I would assign the appearance of the Queen's Men at the Curtain.[1]

On July 28, 1597, as a result of the performance of Thomas Nashe's *The Isle of Dogs*, by Pembroke's Men at the Swan,[2] the Privy Council ordered the plucking down of "the Curtain and the Theatre."[3] The order, however, was not carried out, and in October plays were allowed again as before.

At this time the Lord Chamberlain's men were at the Curtain, having recently moved thither in consequence of the difficulties Cuthbert Burbage was having with Gyles Alleyn over the Theatre property. During the stay of the Chamberlain's Company, which numbered among its members William Shakespeare, Richard Burbage, William Kempe (who had succeeded Tarleton in popular favor as a clown), John Heminges, Thomas Pope, and Augustine Phillips, the playhouse probably attained its greatest distinction. Both Shakespeare and Jonson wrote plays for the troupe;

[1] *Tarlton's Jests*, ed. by J. O. Halliwell for the Shakespeare Society (1844), p. 16. For a discussion see the preceding chapter on the Theatre, p. 72.
[2] For details see the chapter on the Swan.
[3] Dasent, *Acts of the Privy Council*, XXVII, 313.

Romeo and Juliet, we are told, "won Curtain plaudities," as no doubt did many other of Shakespeare's early masterpieces; and Jonson's *Every Man in His Humour* created such enthusiasm here on its first performance as to make its author famous.[1]

In the summer of 1599 the Chamberlain's Men moved into their splendid new home, the Globe, on the Bankside, and the Curtain thus abandoned fell on hard times. Perhaps it was let occasionally to traveling troupes; in Jeaffreson's *Middlesex County Records*, under the date of March 11, 1600, is a notice of the arrest of one William Haukins "charged with a purse taken at a play at the Curtain." But shortly after, in April, 1600, when Henslowe and Alleyn began to erect their splendid new Fortune Playhouse, they were able to give the impression to Tilney, the Master of the Revels, and to the Privy Council, that the Curtain was to be torn down. Thus in the Council's warrant for the building of the Fortune, dated April 8, 1600, we read that "another house is [to be] pulled down instead of it"; [2] and when the Puritans later made vigorous protests against the erection of the Fortune, the Council defended itself by stating that "their Lordships have been informed by Edmund Tilney, Esquire, Her Ma-

[1] Marston, *The Scourge of Villainy* (1598); Bullen, *The Works of John Marston*, III, 372.
[2] Greg, *Henslowe Papers*, p. 52.

jesty's servant, and Master of the Revels, that the house now in hand to be built by the said Edward Alleyn is not intended to increase the number of the playhouses, but to be instead of another, namely the Curtain, which is either to be ruined and plucked down, or to be put to some other good use." [1]

All this talk of the Curtain's being plucked down or devoted to other uses suggests a contemplated change in the ownership or management of the building. We do not know when Lanman died (in 1592 he described himself as fifty-four years of age),[2] but we do know that at some date prior to 1603 the Curtain had passed into the hands of a syndicate. When this syndicate was organized, or who constituted its members, we cannot say. Thomas Pope, in his will, dated July 22, 1603, mentions his share "of, in, and to all that playhouse, with the appurtenances, called the Curtain"; [3] and John Underwood, in his will, dated October 4, 1624, mentions his "part or share . . . in the said playhouses called the Blackfriars, the Globe on the Bankside, and the Curtain." [4] It may be significant that both Pope and Underwood were sharers also in the Globe. Since,

---

[1] The Malone Society's *Collections*, 1, 82.
[2] Wallace, *op. cit.*, p. 148.
[3] J. P. Collier, *Lives of the Original Actors in Shakespeare's Plays*, p. 127. In exactly the same words Pope disposed of his share in the Globe.
[4] *Ibid.*, p. 230.

THE CURTAIN

however, further information is wanting, it is useless to speculate. We can only say that at some time after the period of Lanman's sole proprietorship, the Curtain passed into the hands of a group of sharers; and that after a discussion in 1600 of demolishing the building or devoting it to other uses, it entered upon a long and successful career.

On May 10, 1601, "the actors at the Curtain"[1] gave serious offense by representing on the stage persons "of good desert and quality, that are yet alive, under obscure manner, but yet in such sort as all the hearers may take notice both of the matter and the persons that are meant thereby." The Privy Council ordered the Justices of the Peace to examine into the case and to punish the offenders.[2]

Early in 1604 a draft of a royal patent for Queen Anne's Players — who had hitherto been under the patronage of Worcester[3] — gives those players permission to act "within their now usual houses, called the Curtain, and the Boar's Head."[4] On April 9, 1604, the Privy Council authorized the three companies of players that had been taken under royal patronage "to exercise their plays in their several and usual houses for that purpose,

---

[1] Possibly Derby's Men.
[2] See Dasent, *Acts of the Privy Council*, xxxi, 346.
[3] The company was formed by an amalgamation of Oxford's and Worcester's Men in 1602. See The Malone Society's *Collections*, i, 85.
[4] The Malone Society's *Collections*, i, 266.

and no other, viz., the Globe, scituate in Maiden Lane on the Bankside in the County of Surrey, the Fortune in Golding Lane, and the Curtain in Holywell."[1] The King's Men (the Burbage-Shakespeare troupe) occupied the Globe; Prince Henry's Men (the Henslowe-Alleyn troupe), the Fortune; and Queen Anne's Men, the Curtain.

But the Queen's Men were probably dissatisfied with the Curtain. It was small and antiquated, and it must have suffered by comparison with the more splendid Globe and Fortune. So the Queen's players had built for themselves a new and larger playhouse, called "The Red Bull." This was probably ready for occupancy in 1605, yet it is impossible to say exactly when the Queen's Men left the Curtain; their patent of April 15, 1609, gives them permission to act "within their now usual houses called the Red Bull, in Clerkenwell, and the Curtain in Holywell."[2] It may be that they retained control of the Curtain in order to prevent competition.

What company occupied the Curtain after Queen Anne's Men finally surrendered it is not clear. Mr. Murray is of the opinion that Prince Charles's Men moved into the Curtain "about December, 1609, or early in 1610."[3]

In 1613 "a company of young men" acted *The*

[1] Greg, *Henslowe Papers*, p. 61; Dasent, *Acts of the Privy Council*, xxxii, 511.
[2] The Malone Society's *Collections*, I, 270.
[3] *English Dramatic Companies*, I, 230.

THE CURTAIN

Hector of Germany "at the Red Bull and at the Curtain." Such plays, however, written and acted by amateurs, were not uncommon, and no significance can be attached to the event.

In 1622, as we learn from the Herbert Manuscripts, the Curtain was being occupied by Prince Charles's Servants.[1] In the same year the author of *Vox Graculi, or The Jack Daw's Prognostication for 1623*, refers to it thus: "If company come current to the Bull and Curtain, there will be more money gathered in one afternoon than will be given to Kingsland Spittle in a whole month; also, if at this time about the hours of four and five it wax cloudy and then rain downright, they shall sit dryer in the galleries than those who are the understanding men in the yard."

Prince Charles's Men did not remain long at the Curtain. At some date between June 10 and August 19, 1623, they moved to the larger and more handsome Red Bull.[2] After this, so far as I can discover, there is no evidence to connect the playhouse with dramatic performances. Malone, who presumably bases his statements on the now lost records of Herbert, says that shortly after the accession of King Charles I it "seems to have been used only by prize-fighters." [3]

The last mention of the Curtain is found in the

---

[1] Malone, *Variorum*, III, 59; cf. Chalmers's *Supplemental Apology*, p. 213, note y. Murray gives the date incorrectly as 1623.
[2] Murray, *English Dramatic Companies*, I, 237, note 1.
[3] Malone, *Variorum*, III, 54, note 2.

Middlesex County Records under the date February 21, 1627.[1] It is merely a passing reference to "the common shoare near the Curtain playhouse," yet it is significant as indicating that the building was then still standing. What ultimately became of it we do not know. For a time, however, its memory survived in Curtain Court (see page 79), and to-day its fame is perpetuated in Curtain Road.

[1] See Jeaffreson, *Middlesex County Records*, III, 164, from which the notice was quoted by Ordish, *Early London Theatres*, p. 106.

CHAPTER V

THE FIRST BLACKFRIARS

THE choir boys of the Chapel Royal, of Windsor, and of Paul's were all engaged in presenting dramatic entertainments before Queen Elizabeth. Each organization expected to be called upon one or more times a year — at Christmas, New Year's, and other like occasions — to furnish recreation to Her Majesty; and in return for its efforts each received a liberal "reward" in money. Richard Farrant, Master of the Windsor Chapel, was especially active in devising plays for the Queen's entertainment. But having a large family, he was poor in spite of his regular salary and the occasional "rewards" he received for the performances of his Boys at Court; and doubtless he often cast about in his mind for some way in which to increase his meagre income.

In the spring of 1576 James Burbage, having conceived the idea of a building devoted solely to plays, had leased a plot of ground for the purpose, and had begun the erection of the Theatre. By the autumn, no doubt, the building was nearing completion, if, indeed, it was not actually open to the public; and the experiment, we may suppose, was exciting much interest in the dramatic circles of London. It seems to have set Farrant to thinking. The professional actors, he observed, had one important advantage over the child actors: not only could they present their plays before the Queen and receive the usual court reward, but in addition they could present their plays before the public and thus reap a second and richer harvest. Since the child actors had, as a rule, more excellent plays than the professional troupes, and were better equipped with properties and costumes, and since they expended just as much energy in devising plays and in memorizing and rehearsing their parts, Farrant saw no reason why they, too, should not be allowed to perform before the public. This, he thought, might be done under the guise of rehearsals for the Court. Possibly the Queen might even wink at regular performances before the general public when she understood that this would train the Boys to be more skilful actors, would provide Her Majesty with more numerous and possibly more excellent plays, and would enable the Master and his assistants to live in greater comfort without affecting the royal purse.

For Farrant to build a playhouse specifically for the use of the Children was out of the question. In the first place, it would be too conspicuously a capitalization of the royal choristers for private gain; and in the second place, it would be far too hazardous a business venture for so poor

THE FIRST BLACKFRIARS

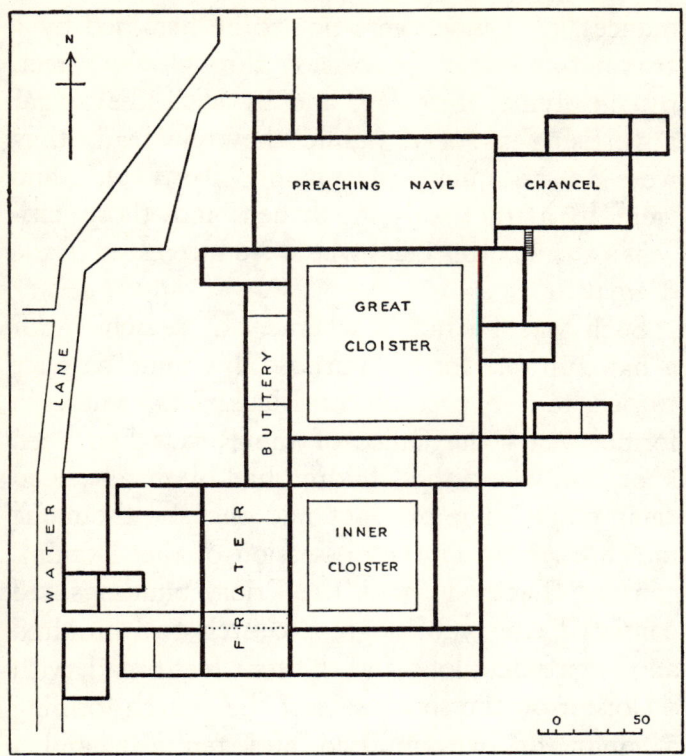

BLACKFRIARS MONASTERY

A plan of the various buildings as they appeared before the dissolution, based on the Loseley Manuscripts and other documents, surveys, and maps. The Buttery became Farrant's, the Frater Burbage's playhouse. (Drawn by the author.)

a man as he to undertake. The more sensible thing for him to do was to rent somewhere a large hall which could at small expense be converted into a place suitable for training the Children in their plays, and for the entertainment of select — possibly at first invited — audiences. The perfor-

94 SHAKESPEAREAN PLAYHOUSES

mances, of course, were not to be heralded by a trumpet-and-drum procession through the street, by the flying of a flag, and by such-like vulgar advertising as of a public show; instead, they were to be quiet, presumably "private," and were to attract only noblemen and those citizens of the better class who were interested in the drama.[1]

Such was Farrant's scheme. In searching for a hall suitable for his purpose, his mind at once turned to the precinct of Blackfriars, where in former years the Office of the Revels had been kept, and where the Children had often rehearsed their plays. The precinct had once, as the name indicates, been in the possession of the Dominican or "Black" Friars. The Priory buildings had consisted chiefly of a great church two hundred and twenty feet long and sixty-six feet broad, with a cloister on the south side of the church forming a square of one hundred and ten feet, and a smaller cloister to the south of this. At the dissolution of the religious orders, the property had passed into the possession of the Crown; hence, though within the city walls, it was not

---

[1] From this notion of privacy, I take it, arose the term "private" theatre as distinguished from "common" or "public" theatre. The interpretation of the term suggested by Mr. W. J. Lawrence, and approved by Mr. William Archer, namely, that it was a legal device to escape the city ordinance of 1574, cannot be accepted. The city had no jurisdiction over the precinct of Blackfriars, nor did Farrant live in the building.

THE SITES OF THE TWO BLACKFRIARS PLAYHOUSES

The smaller rectangle at the north represents the Buttery, later Farrant's playhouse; the larger rectangle represents the Frater, later Burbage's playhouse. (From Ogilby and Morgan's *Map of London*, 1677, the sites marked by the author.)

THE FIRST BLACKFRIARS 95

under the jurisdiction of the city authorities. Farrant probably did not anticipate any interference on the part of the Common Council with the royal choristers "practicing" their plays in order "to yield Her Majesty recreation and delight," yet the absolute certainty of being free from the adverse legislation of the London authorities was not to be ignored. Moreover, the precinct was now the home of many noblemen and wealthy gentlemen, and Farrant probably thought that, as one of the most fashionable residential districts in London, it was suitable for "private" performances to be given by members of Her Majesty's household.

In furthering his project he sought the counsel and aid of his "very friend" Sir Henry Neville, Lieutenant of Windsor, who, it is to be presumed, was interested in the Windsor Boys. It happened that Neville knew of exactly such rooms as were desired, rooms in the old monastery of Blackfriars which he himself had once leased as a residence, and which, he heard, were "to be let either presently, or very shortly." These rooms were in the southwestern corner of the monastery, on the upper floor of two adjoining buildings formerly used by the monks as a buttery and a frater. A history of the rooms up to the time of their use as a theatre may be briefly sketched.

In 1548 the buttery and frater, with certain other buildings, were let by King Edward to Sir

Thomas Cawarden, Master of the Revels; and in 1550 they were granted to him outright. In 1554 Cawarden sold the northern section of the buttery, fifty-two feet in length, to Lord Cobham, whose mansion it adjoined. The rest of the buttery, forty-six feet in length, and the frater, he converted into lodgings. Since the frater was of exceptional breadth — fifty-two feet on the outside, forty-six feet on the inside — he ran a partition through its length, dividing it into two parts. The section of the frater on the west of this partition he let to Sir Richard Frith; the section on the east, with the remainder of the buttery not sold to Lord Cobham, he let to Sir John Cheeke. It is with the Cheeke Lodgings that we are especially concerned.

About September, 1554, Cheeke went to travel abroad, and surrendered his rooms in the Blackfriars. Sir Thomas Cawarden thereupon made use of them "for the Office of the Queen's Majesty's Revells"; thus for a time the Cheeke Lodgings were intimately connected with dramatic activities. But at the death of Cawarden, in 1559, the Queen transferred the Office of the Revels to St. John's, and the Blackfriars property belonging to Cawarden passed into the possession of Sir William More.

In 1560 the new proprietor let the Cheeke Lodgings to Sir Henry Neville, with the addition of "a void piece of ground" eighteen feet wide

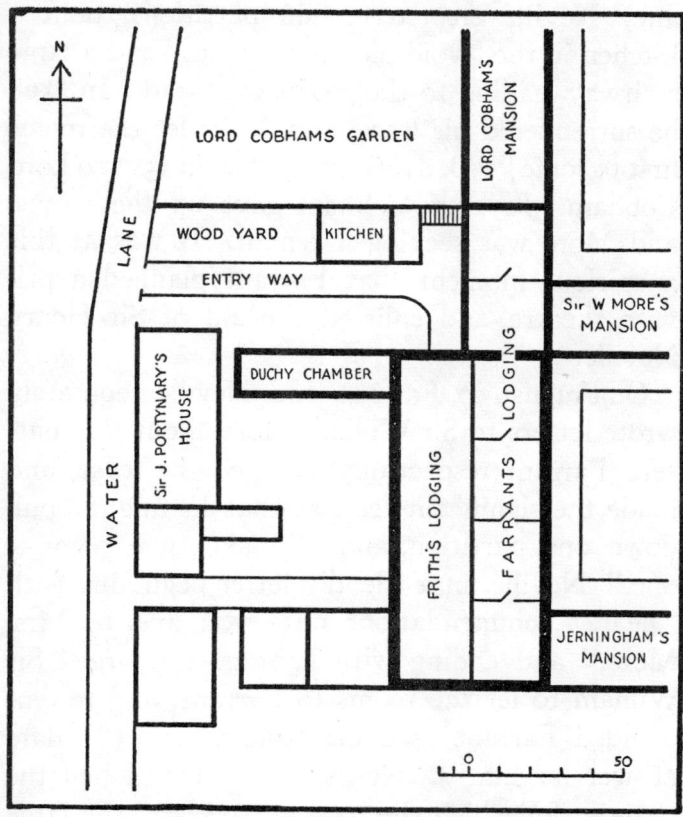

A PLAN OF FARRANT'S PLAYHOUSE

Frith's Lodging and the four southern rooms of Farrant's Lodging were on the upper floor of the Frater; the two northern rooms of Farrant's Lodging were on the upper floor of the Buttery. The playhouse was erected in the two rooms last mentioned.

98 SHAKESPEAREAN PLAYHOUSES

extending west to Water Lane.[1] During his tenancy Neville erected certain partitions, built a kitchen in the "void piece of ground," and a large stairway leading to the rooms overhead. In 1568 he surrendered his lease, and More let the rooms first to some "sylk dyers," and then in 1571 to Lord Cobham. In 1576 Cobham gave up the rooms, and More was seeking a tenant. It was at this auspicious moment that Farrant planned a private theatre, and enlisted the aid of Sir Henry Neville.

On August 27 Farrant and Neville separately wrote letters to Sir William More about the matter. Farrant respectfully solicited the lease, and made the significant request that he might "pull down one partition, and so make two rooms — one." Neville, in a friendly letter beginning with "hearty commendations unto you and to Mrs. More," and ending with light gossip, urged Sir William to let the rooms to Farrant, and recommended Farrant as a desirable tenant ("I dare answer for him"). Neither letter mentioned the purpose for which the rooms, especially the large room referred to by Farrant, were to be used; but More doubtless understood that the Windsor Children were to practice their plays there, with

[1] This was enclosed with brick walls, and the greater part used as a wood-yard. This yard was later purchased by James Burbage when he secured the frater for his playhouse. The kitchen, shed, and stairs, built on the eastern part, were sold to Cobham.

occasional private rehearsals. Largely as a result of Neville's recommendation, More decided to let the rooms to Farrant. The progress of the negotiations is marked by a letter from Farrant to More, dated September 17, 1576, requesting that there be granted him also a certain "little dark room," which he found would be useful.

The lease as finally signed describes the property thus:

> Sir William More hath demised, granted, and to ferm letten, and by these presents doth demise, grant, and to ferm let unto the said Richard Farrant all those his six upper chambers, lofts, lodgings, or rooms, lying together within the precinct of the late dissolved house or priory of the Blackfriars, otherwise called the friars preachers, in London; which said six upper chambers, lofts, lodgings, or rooms, were lately, amongst others, in the tenure and occupation of the right honourable Sir William Brooke, Knight, Lord Cobham; and do contain in length from the north end thereof to the south end of the same one hundred fifty and six foot and a half of assize; whereof two of the said six upper chambers, lofts, lodgings, or rooms in the north end of the premises, together with the breadth of the little room under granted, do contain in length forty [1] and six foot and a half, and from the east to the west part thereof in breadth twenty and five foot of assize; [2]

[1] By an error in the manuscript this reads "fifty"; but the rooms are often described and always as "forty-six" feet in length; moreover, the error is made obvious by the rest of the lease.

[2] The breadth is elsewhere given as twenty-six, and twenty-seven feet.

and the four other chambers, or rooms, residue of the said six upper chambers, do contain in length one hundred and ten foot, and in breadth from the east to the west part thereof twenty-two foot of assize. ... And also ... the great stairs lately erected and made by the said Sir Henry Neville upon part of the said void ground and way.

It was agreed that the lease should run for twenty-one years, and that the rental should be £14 per annum. But Sir William More, being a most careful and exacting landlord, with the interest of his adjacent lodgings to care for, inserted in the lease the following important proviso, which was destined to make trouble, and ultimately to wreck the theatre:

Provided also that the said Richard Farrant, his executors or assigns, or any of them, shall not in any wise demise, let, grant, assign, set over, or by any ways or means put away his or their interest or term of years, or any part of the same years, of or in the said premises before letten, or any part, parcel, or member thereof to any person, or persons, at any time hereafter during this present lease and term of twenty-one years, without the special license, consent, and agreement of the said Sir William More, his heirs and assigns, first had, and obtained in writing under his and their hands and seals.

The penalty affixed to a violation of this provision was the immediate forfeiture of the lease.

Apparently Farrant entered into possession of the rooms on September 29 [1] (although the formal

---

[1] The date from which the lease was made to run.

THE FIRST BLACKFRIARS

lease was not signed until December 20), and we may suppose that he at once set about converting the two upper rooms at the north end of the lodgings into a suitable theatre.[1] Naturally he took for his model the halls at Court in which the Children had been accustomed to act. First, we are told, he "pulled down partitions to make that place apt for that purpose"; next, he "spoiled" the windows — by which is meant, no doubt, that he stopped up the windows, for the performances were to be by candle-light. At one end of the hall he erected a platform to serve as a stage, and in the auditorium he placed benches or chairs. There was, presumably, no room for a gallery; if such had been erected, the indignant More would certainly have mentioned it in his bill of complaints.[2] Chandeliers over the stage, and, possibly, footlights, completed the necessary arrangements. For these alterations Farrant, we are told, became "greatly indebted," and he died three or four years later with the debt still unpaid.

[1] It is usually said that he converted the entire seven rooms into his theatre, but that seems highly unlikely. The northern section was 46 x 26 feet, the southern section 110 x 22 — absurd dimensions for an auditorium. Moreover, that Farrant originally planned to use only the northern section is indicated by his request to be allowed to "pull down one partition and so make two rooms — one." The portion not used for the playhouse he rented; in 1580, we are told, he let "two parcels thereof to two several persons."

[2] M. Feuillerat, I think, is wrong in supposing that there was a gallery. He deduces no proof for his contention, and the evidence is against him.

More complained that the alterations had put the rooms into a state of "great ruin," which meant, of course, from the point of view of a landlord desiring to let them again for residential purposes. Just how costly or how extensive the alterations were we cannot now determine; but we may reasonably conclude that Farrant made the hall not only "commodious for his purpose," but also attractive to the aristocratic audiences he intended to gather there to see his plays.

To reach the hall, playgoers had to come first into Water Lane, thence through "a way leading from the said way called Water Lane" to "a certain void ground" before the building. Here "upon part of the said void ground" they found a "great stairs, which said great stairs do serve and lead into" the upper rooms — or, as we may now say, Blackfriars Playhouse.[1]

Having thus provided a playhouse, Farrant next provided an adequate company of boy actors. To do this, he combined the Children of Windsor with the Children of the Chapel Royal, of which William Hunnis was master. What arrangement he made with Hunnis we do not know, but the Court records show that Farrant was regarded as the manager of the new organization; he is actually referred to in the payments as "Master of the

---

[1] There must have been two stairways leading to the upper rooms; I have assumed that playgoers used Neville's stairs to reach the theatre.

THE FIRST BLACKFRIARS

Children of Her Majesty's Chapel," and Hunnis's official connection with the Children is ignored.

Farrant may have been able to open his playhouse before the close of the year; or he may have first begun performances there in the early months of 1577. He would certainly be anxious to make use of the new play he was preparing for presentation at Court on Twelfth Day, January 6, 1577.

For four years, 1576–1580, the playhouse was operated without trouble. Sir William More, however, was not pleased at the success with which the actors were meeting. He asserted that when he made the lease he was given to understand that the building was to be used "only for the teaching of the Children of the Chapel" — with, no doubt, a few rehearsals to which certain persons would be *privately* invited. But, now, to his grief, he discovered that Farrant had "made it a continual house for plays." He asserted that the playhouse had become offensive to the precinct; and doubtless some complaints had been made to him, as landlord, by the more aristocratic inhabitants.[1] At any rate, he became anxious to regain possession of the building.

In the autumn of 1580 he saw an opportunity to break the lease and close the playhouse. Far-

---

[1] I suspect that the theatre gave greater offense to More himself than it did to any one else, for it adjoined his home, and the audience made use of the private passage which led from Water Lane to his mansion. Unquestionably he suffered worse than any one else both from the noise and the crowds.

rant made the mistake of letting "two parcels thereof to two severall persons" without first gaining the written consent of More, and at once More "charged him with forfeiture of his lease." But before More could "take remedy against him" Farrant died, November 30, 1580. More, however, "entered upon the house, and refused to receive any rent but conditionally."

By his will, proved March 1, 1581, Farrant left the lease of the Blackfriars to his widow, Anne Farrant. But she had no authority over the royal choristers, nor was she qualified to manage a company of actors, even if she had had the time to do so after caring for her "ten little ones." What use, if any, was made of the playhouse during the succeeding winter we do not know. The widow writes that she, "being a sole woman, unable of herself to use the said rooms to such purpose as her said husband late used them, nor having any need or occasion to occupy them to such commodity as would discharge the rents due for the said rooms in the bill alledged, nor being able to sustain, repair, and amend the said rooms," etc.;[1] the natural inference from which is that for a time the playhouse stood unused. The widow, of course, was anxious to sublet the building to some one who could make use of it as a playhouse; and on December 25, 1580, she addressed a letter to Sir William More asking his written permission

[1] Wallace, *The Evolution of the English Drama*, p. 163.

to make such a disposal of the lease. The letter has a pathetic interest that justifies its insertion here:

To the right worshipful Sir William More, Knight, at his house near Guilford, give these with speed.
Right worshipful Sir:
After my humble commendations, and my duty also remembered — where it hath pleased your worship to grant unto my husband in his life time one lease of your house within the Blackfriars, for the term of twenty-one years, with a proviso in the end thereof that he cannot neither let nor set the same without your worship's consent under your hand in writing. And now for that it hath pleased God to call my said husband unto His mercy, having left behind him the charge of ten small children upon my hand, and my husband besides greatly indebted, not having the revenue of one groat any way coming in, but by making the best I may of such things as he hath left behind him, to relieve my little ones. May it therefore please your worship, of your abundant clemency and accustomed goodness, to consider a poor widow's distressed estate, and for God's cause to comfort her with your worship's warrant under your hand to let and set the same to my best comodity during the term of years in the said lease contained, not doing any waste. In all which doing, I shall evermore most abundantly pray unto God for the preservation of your worship's long continuance. From Grenwich, the twenty-fifth of December,
By a poor and sorrowful widow,
ANNE FARRANT.[1]

[1] Wallace, *The Evolution of the English Drama*, p. 153.

Whether she secured in writing the permission she requested we do not know. Four years later More said that she did not. Possibly, however, she was orally given to understand that she might transfer the lease to her husband's former partner in the enterprise, William Hunnis.[1] Hunnis naturally was eager to make use of the building in preparation for the Christmas plays at Court. At some date before September 19, he secured the use of the playhouse on a temporary agreement with the widow; but in order to avoid any difficulty with More, he interviewed the latter, and presented a letter of recommendation from the Earl of Leicester. This letter has been preserved among Sir William's papers:

Sir William More:
Whereas my friend, Mr. Hunnis, this bearer, informeth me that he hath of late bought of Farrant's widow her lease of that house in Blackfriars which you made to her husband, deceased, and means there to practice the Queen's Children of the Chapel, being now in his charge, in like sort as his predecessor did, for the better training them to do Her Majesty's service; he is now a suitor to me to recommend him to your good favour — which I do very heartily, as one that I wish right well unto, and will give you thanks for any continuance or friendship you shall show him for the furtherance of this his honest request. And thus, with my hearty commen-

---

[1] More had "refused to accept any rent but conditionally." Probably he refused written consent to the sublease for the same reason.

THE FIRST BLACKFRIARS

dations, I wish you right heartily well to fare. From the Court, this nineteenth of September, 1581.
Your very friend,
R. LEICESTER.[1]

The result of this interview we do not know. But on December 20 following, the widow made a formal lease of the property to William Hunnis and John Newman, at a rental of £20 13s. 4d. a year, an increase of £6 13s. 4d. over the rental she had to pay More. She required of them a bond of £100 to guarantee their performance of all the covenants of the lease. Thereupon the theatre under Hunnis and Newman resumed its career — if, indeed, this had ever been seriously interrupted.

In the course of time, More's anxiety to recover possession of the hall seems to have increased. The quarterly payments were not promptly met by the widow, and the repairs on the building were not made to his satisfaction. Probably through fear of the increasing dissatisfaction on the part of More, Hunnis and Newman transferred their lease, in 1583, to a young Welsh scrivener, Henry Evans, who had become interested in dramatic affairs. This transfer of the lease without More's written consent was a second clear breach of the original contract, and it gave More exactly the opportunity he sought. Accordingly, he declared the original lease to Farrant void, and made a

[1] Wallace, *The Evolution of the English Drama*, p. 154.

new lease of the house "unto his own man, Thomas Smallpiece, to try the said Evans his right." But Evans, being a lawyer, knew how to take care of himself. He "demurred in law," and "kept the same in his hands with long delays."

The widow, alarmed at the prospect of losing her lease, brought suit, in December, 1583, against Hunnis and Newman separately for the forfeiture of their several bonds of £100, contending that they had not paid promptly according to their agreement, and had not kept the building in proper repair. Hunnis and Newman separately brought suit in the Court of Requests for relief against the widow's suits. Meanwhile More was demanding judgment against Evans. Hunnis, it seems, carried his troubles to the Court and there sought help. Queen Elizabeth could take no direct action, because Sir William More was a good friend of hers, who had entertained her in his home. But she might enlist the aid of one of her noblemen who were interested in the drama. However this was, the young Earl of Oxford, himself a playwright and the patron of a troupe of boy-actors, came to the rescue of the theatre. He bought the lease of the building from Evans, and undertook to reorganize its affairs. To Hunnis's twelve Children of the Chapel he added the Children of St. Paul's Cathedral, making thus a company of adequate size. He retained Hunnis, no doubt, as one of the trainers of the Boys, and he kept Evans as manager of the troupe. Moreover, shortly after the purchase, probably in June, 1583, he made a free gift of the lease to his private secretary, John Lyly, a young man who had recently won fame with the first English novel, *Euphues*. The object of this, like the preceding transfers of title, it seems, was to put as many legal blocks in the path of Sir William More as possible. More realized this, and complained specifically that "the title was posted from one to another"; yet he had firmly made up his mind to recover the property, and in spite of Oxford's interference, he instructed his "learned council" to "demand judgment."

Meanwhile the dramatic organization at Blackfriars continued under the direction of Hunnis, Evans, and Lyly, with the Earl of Oxford as patron. Not only was Lyly the proprietor of the theatre, but he attempted to supply it with the necessary plays. He had already shown his power to tell in effective prose a pleasing love romance. That power he now turned to the production of his first play, written in haste for the Christmas festivities. The play, *Alexander and Campaspe*, was presented before Her Majesty on January 1, 1584, and at Blackfriars, with great applause. Lyly's second play, *Sapho and Phao*, was produced at Court on March 3, following, and also at Blackfriars before the general public.

But at the Easter term, 1584, Sir William More got judgment in his favor. The widow begged Sir Francis Walsingham to intercede in her behalf, declaring that the loss of the lease "might be her utter undoing."[1] Walsingham sent the letter to More, and apparently urged a consideration of her case. More, however, refused to yield. He banished Lyly, Hunnis, Evans, and the Children from the "great upper hall," and reconverted the building into tenements.

[1] The letter is printed in full by Mr. Wallace in *The Evolution of the English Drama*, p. 158. Mr. Wallace, however, misdates it. It was not written until after More had "recovered it [the lease] against Evans."

CHAPTER VI
ST. PAUL'S

AS shown in the preceding chapter, not only were the Children of the Chapel Royal and of Windsor called upon to entertain the Queen with dramatic performances, but the Children of St. Paul's were also expected to amuse their sovereign on occasion. And following the example of the Children of the Chapel and of Windsor in giving performances before the public in Blackfriars, the Paul's Boys soon began to give such performances in a building near the Cathedral.[1] The building so employed was doubtless one of the structures owned by the Church. Burbage and Heminges refer to it as "the said house near St. Paul's Church."[2] Richard Flecknoe, in *A Discourse of the English Stage* (1664), places it "behind the Convocation-house in Paul's";[3] and Howes, in his continuation of Stow's *Annals* (1631), says that it was the "singing-school" of the Cathedral.[4] That the auditorium was small we may

---

[1] Murray, *English Dramatic Companies*, I, 325, erroneously says: "Their public place was, probably, from the first, the courtyard of St. Paul's Cathedral."

[2] Wallace, *Shakespeare and his London Associates*, p. 95.

[3] That is, in or near Pater Noster Row.

[4] *Annales, or A Generall Chronicle of England*, 1631, signature iiii 1, verso.

well believe. So was the stage. Certain speakers in the Induction to *What You Will*, acted at Paul's in 1600, say: "Let's place ourselves within the curtains, for, good faith, the stage is so very little, we shall wrong the general eye else very much." Both Fleay and Lawrence [1] contend that the building was "round, like the Globe," and as evidence they cite the Prologue to Marston's *Antonio's Revenge*, acted at Paul's in 1600, in which the phrases "within this round" and "within this ring" are applied to the theatre. The phrases, however, may have reference merely to the circular disposition of the benches about the stage. That high prices of admission to the little theatre were charged we learn from a marginal note in *Pappe with an Hatchet* (1589), which states that if a tragedy "be showed at Paul's, it will cost you four pence; at the Theatre two pence." [2] The Children, indeed, catered to a very select public. Persons who went thither were gentle by birth and by behavior as well; and playwrights, we are told, could always feel sure there of the "calm attention of a choice audience." [3] Lyly, in the Prologue to *Midas*, acted at Paul's in 1589, says: "Only this doth encourage us, that presenting our studies before *Gentlemen*,

---

[1] F. G. Fleay, *A Biographical Chronicle of the English Drama*, II, 76; W. J. Lawrence, *The Elizabethan Playhouse*, p. 17.

[2] R. W. Bond, *The Complete Works of John Lyly*, III, 408. Higher prices of admission were charged to all the private playhouses.

[3] John Marston, *Antonio's Revenge*, acted at Paul's in 1600.

ST. PAUL'S

though they receive an inward dislike, we shall not be hissed with an open disgrace." Things were quite otherwise in the public theatres of Shoreditch and the Bankside.

Under the direction of their master, Sebastian Westcott, the Boys acted before the public at least as early as 1578,[1] for in December of that year the Privy Council ordered the Lord Mayor to permit them to "exercise plays" within the city;[2] and Stephen Gosson, in his *Plays Confuted*, written soon afterwards, mentions *Cupid and Psyche* as having been recently "plaid at Paules."

Westcott died in 1582, and was succeeded by Thomas Gyles. Shortly after this we find the Children of Paul's acting publicly with the Children of the Chapel Royal at the little theatre in Blackfriars. For them John Lyly wrote his two earliest plays, *Campaspe* and *Sapho and Phao*, as the title-pages clearly state. But their stay at Blackfriars was short. When in 1584 Sir William More closed up the theatre there, they fell back upon their singing-school as the place for their public performances.

At the same time the Queen became greatly interested in promoting their dramatic activities. To their master, Thomas Gyles, she issued, in

---

[1] There is a record of a play by the Paul's Boys in 1527 before ambassadors from France, dealing with the heretic Luther; but exactly when they began to give public performances for money we do not know.

[2] Malone, *Variorum*, III, 432.

April, 1585, a special commission "to take up apt and meet children" wherever he could find them. It was customary for the Queen to issue such a commission to the masters of her two private chapels, but never before, or afterwards, had this power to impress children been conferred upon a person not directly connected with the royal choristers. Its issuance to Gyles in 1585 clearly indicates the Queen's interest in the Paul's Boys as actors, and her expectation of being frequently entertained by them. And to promote her plans still further, she appointed the successful playwright John Lyly as their vice-master, with the understanding, no doubt, that he was to keep them — and her — supplied with plays. This he did, for all his comedies, except the two just mentioned, were written for the Cathedral Children, and were acted by them at Court, and in their little theatre "behind the Convocation House."

Unfortunately under Lyly's leadership the Boys became involved in the bitter Martin Marprelate controversy, for which they were suppressed near the end of 1590. The printer of Lyly's *Endimion*, in 1591, says to the reader: "Since the plays in Paul's were dissolved, there are certain comedies come to my hands by chance, which were presented before Her Majesty at several times by the Children of Paul's."

Exactly how long the Children were restrained it is hard to determine. In 1596 Thomas Nash, in *Have*

ST. PAUL'S

With You to Saffron Walden, expressed a desire to see "the plays at Paul's up again." Mr. Wallace thinks they may have been allowed "up again" in 1598;[1] Fleay, in 1599 or 1600;[2] the evidence, however, points, I think, to the spring or early summer of 1600. The Children began, naturally, with old plays, "musty fopperies of antiquity"; the first, or one of the first, new plays they presented was Marston's *Jack Drum's Entertainment,* the date of which can be determined within narrow limits. References to Kempe's Morris, which was danced in February, 1600, as being still a common topic of conversation, and the entry of the play in the Stationers' Registers on September 8, 1600, point to the spring or early summer of 1600 as the date of composition. This makes very significant the following passage in the play referring to the Paul's Boys as just beginning to act again after their long inhibition:

    Sir Ed. I saw the Children of Paul's last night,
And troth they pleas'd me pretty, pretty well.
The Apes in time will do it handsomely.
    Plan. S'faith, I like the audience that frequenteth there
With much applause. A man shall not be choak't
With the stench of garlic, nor be pasted
To the barmy jacket of a beer-brewer.
    Bra. Ju. 'T is a good, gentle audience; and I hope the
        Boys
Will come one day into the Court of Requests.

---

[1] *The Children of the Chapel,* p. 153.
[2] *A Chronicle History of the London Stage,* p. 152.

Shortly after this the Boys were indeed called "into the Court of Requests," for on New Year's Day, 1601, they were summoned to present a play before Her Majesty.

Their master now was Edward Pierce, who had succeeded Thomas Gyles. In 1605 the experienced Edward Kirkham, driven from the management of the Blackfriars Theatre, became an assistant to Pierce in the management of Paul's. In this capacity we find him in 1606 receiving the payment for the two performances of the Boys at Court that year.[1]

Among the playwrights engaged by Pierce to write for Paul's were Marston, Middleton, Chapman, Dekker, Webster, and Beaumont; and, as a result, some of the most interesting dramas of the period were first acted on the small stage of the singing-school. Details in the history of the Children, however, are few. We find an occasional notice of their appearance at Court, but our record of them is mainly secured from the title-pages of their plays.

The last notice of a performance by them is as follows: "On the 30th of July, 1606, the youths of Paul's, commonly called the Children of Paul's, played before the two Kings [of England and of Denmark] a play called *Abuses*, containing both a comedy and a tragedy, at which

---

[1] Cunningham, *Extracts from the Accounts of the Revels*, p. xxxviii.

the Kings seemed to take great delight and be much pleased." [1]

The reason why the Children ceased to act is made clear in the lawsuit of Keysar *v.* Burbage *et al.*, recently discovered and printed by Mr. Wallace.[2] From this we learn that when Rosseter became manager of the Children of the Queen's Revels at the private playhouse of Whitefriars in 1609, he undertook to increase his profits by securing a monopoly both of child-acting and of private theatres. Blackfriars had been deserted, and the only other private theatre then in existence was Paul's. So Rosseter agreed to pay Pierce a dead rent of £20 a year to keep the Paul's playhouse closed:

> One Mr. Rosseter, a partner of the said complainant, dealt for and compounded with the said Mr. Pierce to the only benefit of him, the said Mr. Rosseter, the now complainant, the rest of their partners and Company [at the Whitefriars] . . . that thereby they might . . . advance their gains and profit to be had and made in their said house in the Whitefriars, that there might be a cessation of playing and plays to be acted in the said house near St. Paul's Church aforesaid, for which the said Rosseter compounded with the said Pierce to give him the said Pierce twenty pounds per annum.[3]

In this attempt to secure a monopoly in private playhouses Rosseter was foiled by the com-

---
[1] Nichols, *The Progresses of James*, IV, 1073.
[2] *Shakespeare and his London Associates*, p. 80.   [3] *Ibid.*, p. 95.

ing of Shakespeare's troupe to the Blackfriars; but the King's Men readily agreed to join in the payment of the dead rent to Pierce, for it was to their advantage also to eliminate competition.

The agreement which Rosseter secured from Pierce was binding "for one whole year"; whether it was renewed we do not know, but the Children never again acted in "their house near St. Paul's Church."

CHAPTER VII

THE BANKSIDE AND THE BEAR GARDEN

FROM time out of mind the suburb of London known as "the Bankside" — the term was loosely applied to all the region south of the river and west of the bridge — had been identified with sports and pastimes. On Sundays, holidays, and other festive occasions, the citizens, their wives, and their apprentices were accustomed to seek outdoor entertainment across the river, going thither in boats (of which there was an incredible number, converting "the silver sliding Thames" almost into a Venetian Grand Canal), or strolling on foot over old London Bridge. On the Bankside the visitors could find maypoles for dancing, butts for the practice of archery, and broad fields for athletic games; or, if so disposed, they could visit bull-baitings, bear-baitings, fairs, stage-plays, shows, motions, and other amusements of a similar sort.

Not all the attractions of the Bankside, however, were so innocent. For here, in a long row bordering the river's edge, were situated the famous stews of the city, licensed by authority of the Bishop of Winchester; and along with the stews, of course, such places as thrive in a district devoted to vice

—houses for gambling, for coney-catching, and for evil practices of various sorts. The less said of this feature of the Bankside the better.

More needs to be said of the bull- and bear-baiting, which probably constituted the chief amusement of the crowds from the city, and which was later closely associated with the drama and with playhouses. This sport, now surviving in the bull-fights of Spain and of certain Spanish-American countries, was in former times one of the most popular species of entertainment cultivated by the English. Even so early as 1174, William Fitz-Stephen, in his *Descriptio Nobilissimæ Ciuitatis Londoniæ*, under the heading *De Ludis*, records that the London citizens diverted themselves on holiday occasions with the baiting of beasts, when "strong horn-goring bulls, or immense bears, contend fiercely with dogs that are pitted against them."[1] In some towns the law required that bulls intended for the butcher-shop should first be baited for the amusement of the public before being led to the slaughter-house. Erasmus speaks of the "many herds of bears" which he saw in England "maintained for the purpose of baiting." The baiting was accomplished by tying the bulls or bears to stakes, or when possible releasing them in an amphitheatre, and pitting against them bull-dogs, bred through cen-

[1] "Pingues tauri cornupetæ, seu vrsi immanes, cum obiectis depugnant canibus."

THE BANKSIDE

Showing the Bear- and Bull-baiting Rings. (From the *Map of London* by Braun and Hogenbergius, representing the city in 1554–1558.)

THE BANKSIDE

This was the second district of London used for public playhouses. Notice the amphitheatres for animal-baiting. (From William Smith's MS. of the Description of England, c. 1580.)

BANKSIDE AND BEAR GARDEN

turies for strength and ferocity. Occasionally other animals, as ponies and apes, were brought into the fight, and the sport was varied in miscellaneous ways. Some of the animals, by unusual courage or success, endeared themselves to the heart of the sporting public. Harry Hunks, George Stone, and Sacarson were famous bears in Shakespeare's time; and the names of many of the "game bulls" and "mastiff dogs" became household words throughout London.

The home of this popular sport was the Bankside. The earliest extant map of Southwark,[1] drawn about 1542, shows in the very centre of High Street, just opposite London Bridge, a circular amphitheatre marked "The Bull Ring"; and doubtless there were other places along the river devoted to the same purpose. The baiting of bears was more closely identified with the Manor of Paris Garden,[2] that section of the Bank lying to the west of the Clink, over towards the marshes of Lambeth. The association of bear-baiting with this particular section was probably due to the fact that in early days the butchers of London used a part of the Manor of Paris Gar-

---

[1] The map is reproduced in facsimile by Rendle as a frontispiece to *Old Southwark and its People*.

[2] Or Parish Garden, possibly the more correct form. For the early history of the Manor see William Bray, *The History and Antiquities of the County of Surrey*, III, 530; Wallace, in *Englische Studien* (1911), XLIII, 341, note 3; Ordish, *Early London Theatres*, p. 125.

den for the disposal of their offal,[1] and the entrails and other refuse from the slaughtered beasts furnished cheap and abundant food for the bears and dogs. The Earl of Manchester wrote to the Lord Mayor and the Common Council, in 1664, that he had been informed by the master of His Majesty's Game of Bears and Bulls, and others, that "the Butcher's Company had formerly caused all their offal in Eastcheap and Newgate Market to be conveyed by the beadle of the Company unto two barrow houses, conveniently placed on the river side, for the provision and feeding of the King's Game of Bears."

At first, apparently, the baiting of bears was held in open places,[2] with the bear tied to a stake and the spectators crowding around, or at best standing on temporary scaffolds. But later, permanent amphitheatres were provided. In Braun and Hogenberg's *Map of London*, drawn between 1554 and 1558, and printed in 1572, we find two well-appointed amphitheatres, with stables and kennels attached, labeled respectively "The Bear

---

[1] Blount, in his *Glossographia* (1681), p. 473, says of Paris Garden: "So called from Robert de Paris, who had a house and garden there in Richard II.'s time; who by proclamation, ordained that the butchers of London should buy that garden for receipt of their garbage and entrails of beasts, to the end the city might not be annoyed thereby."

[2] See Gilpin's *Life of Cranmer* for a description of a bear-baiting before the King held on or near the river's edge. See also the proclamation of Henry VIII in 1546 against the stews, which implies the non-existence of regular amphitheatres.

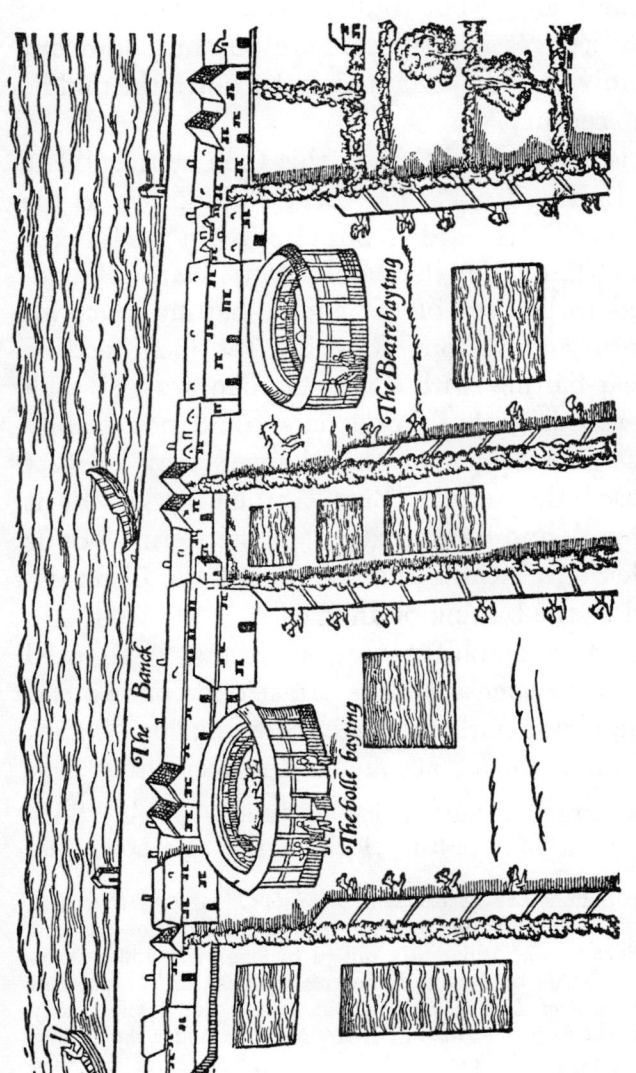

THE BEAR- AND BULL-BAITING RINGS. (From Agas's *Map of London*, representing the city as it was about 1560.)

These "rings" later gave place to the Bear Garden.

Baiting" and "The Bull Baiting." When these amphitheatres were erected we do not know, but probably they do not antedate by much the middle of the century.[1]

It is to be noted that at this time neither "The Bull Baiting" nor "The Bear Baiting" is in the Manor of Paris Garden, but close by in the Liberty of the Clink. Yet the name "Paris Garden" continued to be used of the animal-baiting place for a century and more. Possibly the identification of bear-baiting with Paris Garden was of such long standing that Londoners could not readily adjust themselves to the change; they at first confused the terms "Bear Garden" and "Paris Garden," and later extended the term "Paris Garden" to include that section of the Clink devoted to the baiting of animals.

The two amphitheatres, it seems, were used until 1583, when a serious catastrophe put an end to one if not both of them. Stow, in his *Annals*, gives the following account of the accident:

The same thirteenth day of January, being Sunday, about four of the clock in the afternoon, the

---

[1] Sir Sidney Lee (*Shakespeare's England*, II, 428) says that one of the amphitheatres was erected in 1526. I do not know his authority; he was apparently misled by one of Rendle's statements. Neither of the amphitheatres is shown in Wyngaerde's careful *Map of London* made about 1530–1540; possibly they are referred to in the *Diary* of Henry Machyn under the date of May 26, 1554. The old "Bull Ring" in High Street had then disappeared, and the baiting of bulls was henceforth more or less closely associated, as was natural, with the baiting of bears.

BANKSIDE AND BEAR GARDEN

old and underpropped scaffolds round about the Bear Garden, commonly called Paris Garden, on the south side of the river of Thamis over against the city of London, overcharged with people, fell suddenly down, whereby to the number of eight persons, men and women, were slain, and many others sore hurt and bruised to the shortening of their lives.[1]

Stubbes, the Puritan, writes in his more heightened style:

Upon the 13 day of January last, being the Saboth day, *Anno* 1583, the people, men, women, and children, both young and old, an infinite number, flocking to those infamous places where these wicked exercises are usually practised (for they have their courts, gardens, and yards for the same purpose), when they were all come together and mounted aloft upon their scaffolds and galleries, and in the midst of all their jolity and pastime, all the whole building (not one stick standing) fell down with a most wonderful and fearful confusion. So that either two or three hundred men, women, and children (by estimation), whereof seven were killed dead, some were wounded, some lamed, and otherwise bruised and crushed almost to death. Some had their brains dashed out, some their heads all to-squashed, some their legs broken, some their arms, some their backs, some their shoulders, some one hurt, some another.[2]

The building, which the Reverend John Field described as "old and rotten,"[3] was a complete

---

[1] Stow, *Annals* (ed. 1631), p. 696.
[2] Philip Stubbes, *The Anatomie of Abuses* (ed. Furnivall), p. 179.
[3] *A Godly Exhortation by Occasion of the Late Judgement of God, Shewed at Paris-Garden* (London, 1583). Another account of the disaster may be found in Vaughan's *Golden Grove* (1600).

ruin; "not a stick was left so high as the bear was fastened to." The Puritan preachers loudly denounced the unholy spectacles, pointing to the catastrophe as a clear warning from the Almighty; and the city authorities earnestly besought the Privy Council to put an end to such performances. Yet the owners of the building set to work at once, and soon had erected a new house, stronger and larger and more pretentious than before. The Lord Mayor, in some indignation, wrote to the Privy Council on July 3, 1583, that "the scaffolds are new builded, and the multitudes on the Saboth day called together in most excessive number." [1]

The New Bear Garden, octagonal in form, was probably modeled after the playhouses in Shoreditch, and made in all respects superior to the old amphitheatre which it supplanted.[2] We find that it was reckoned among the sights of the city, and was exhibited to distinguished foreign visitors. For example, when Sir Walter Raleigh undertook to entertain the French Ambassador, he carried him to view the monuments in Westminster Abbey and to see the new Bear Garden.

A picture of the building is to be seen in the Hon-

---

[1] The Malone Society's *Collections*, I, 65.
[2] What became of the other amphitheatre labeled "The Bull Baiting" I do not know. Stow, in his *Survey*, 1598, says: "Now to return to the west bank, there be two bear gardens, the old and new places, wherein be kept bears, bulls, and other beasts to be baited."

BANKSIDE AND BEAR GARDEN

THE BEAR GARDEN

From Visscher's *Map of London*, published in 1616, but representing the city as it was several years earlier.

dius *View of London*, 1610 (see page 149), and in the small inset views from the title-pages of Holland's *Herowlogia*, 1620, and Baker's *Chronicle*,

1643 (see page 147), all three of which probably go back to a view of London made between 1587 and 1597, and now lost. Another representation of the structure is to be seen in the Delaram portrait of King James, along with the Rose and the Globe (see opposite page 246). The best representation of the building, however, is in Visscher's *View of London* (see page 127), printed in 1616, but drawn several years earlier.[1]

Although we are not directly concerned with the history of the Bear Garden,[2] a few descriptions of "the royal game of bears, bulls, and dogs" drawn from contemporary sources will be of interest and of specific value for the discussion of the Hope Playhouse — itself both a bear garden and a theatre.

Robert Laneham, in his *Description of the Entertainment at Kenilworth* (1575), writes thus of a baiting of bears before the Queen:

> Well, syr, the Bearz wear brought foorth intoo the Coourt, the dogs set too them. . . . It was a Sport very pleazaunt of theez beastz; to see the bear with his pink nyez leering after hiz enemiez approoch, the nimbleness & wayt of ye dog to take his auauntage, and the fors & experiens of the bear agayn to auoyd

---

[1] For a fuller discussion of these various maps and views see pages 146, 248, and 328. Norden's map of 1594 (see page 147) merely indicates the site of the building.

[2] For such a history the reader is referred to Ordish, *Early London Theatres;* Greg, *Henslowe's Diary*, II, and *Henslowe Papers;* Young, *The History of Dulwich College;* Rendle, *The Bankside*, and *The Playhouses at Bankside*.

BANKSIDE AND BEAR GARDEN

the assauts: if he war bitten in one place, how he woold pynch in an oother to get free: that if he wear taken onez, then what shyft, with byting, with clawing, with rooring, tossing, & tumbling he woold woork to wynd hym self from them: and when he waz lose, to shake his earz tywse or thryse, wyth the blud and the slauer aboout his fiznomy, waz a matter of a goodly releef.

John Houghton, in his *Collection for Improvement of Husbandry and Trade*,[1] gives a vivid account of the baiting of the bull. He says:

The bull takes great care to watch his enemy, which is a mastiff dog (commonly used to the sport) with a short nose that his teeth may take the better hold; this dog, if right, will creep upon his belly that he may, if possible, get the bull by the nose; which the bull as carefully strives to defend by laying it close to the ground, where his horns are also ready to do what in them lies to toss the dog; and this is the true sport. But if more dogs than one come at once, or they are cowardly and come under his legs, he will, if he can, stamp their guts out. I believe I have seen a dog tossed by a bull thirty, if not forty foot high; and when they are tossed, either higher or lower, the men above strive to catch them on their shoulders, lest the fall might mischief the dogs. They commonly lay sand about that if they fall upon the ground it may be the easier. Notwithstanding this care a great many dogs are killed, more have their limbs broke, and some hold so fast that, by the bull's

---

[1] No. 108, August, 1694. Quoted by J. P. Malcolm, *Anecdotes of the Manners and Customs of London from the Roman Invasion of the Year 1700* (London, 1811), p. 433.

swinging them, their teeth are often broken out. . . . The true courage and art is to hold the bull by the nose 'till he roars, which a courageous bull scorns to do. . . . This is a sport the English much delight in; and not only the baser sort, but the greatest lords and ladies.

An attendant upon the Duke of Nexara, who visited England in 1544, wrote the following account of a bear-baiting witnessed in London:

In another part of the city we saw seven bears, some of them of great size. They were led out every day to an enclosure, where being tied with a long rope, large and intrepid dogs are thrown to them, in order that they may bite and make them furious. It is no bad sport to see them fight, and the assaults they give each other. To each of the large bears are matched three or four dogs, which sometimes get the better and sometimes are worsted, for besides the fierceness and great strength of the bears to defend themselves with their teeth, they hug the dogs with their paws so tightly, that, unless the masters came to assist them, they would be strangled by such soft embraces. Into the same place they brought a pony with an ape fastened on its back, and to see the animal kicking amongst the dogs, with the screams of the ape, beholding the curs hanging from the ears and neck of the pony, is very laughable.[1]

Orazio Busino, the chaplain of the Venetian Embassy in London, writes in his *Anglipotrida* (1618):

---

[1] The original manuscript of this narrative, in Spanish, is preserved in the British Museum. I quote the translation by Frederick Madden, in *Archæologia*, XIII, 354–55.

BANKSIDE AND BEAR GARDEN 131

The dogs are detached from the bear by inserting between the teeth . . . certain iron spattles with a wooden handle; whilst they take them off the bull (keeping at a greater distance) with certain flat iron hooks which they apply to the thighs or even to the neck of the dog, whose tail is simultaneously dexterously seized by another of these rufflers. The bull can hardly get at anybody, as he wears a collar round his neck with only fifteen feet of rope, which is fastened to a stake deeply planted in the middle of the theatre. Other rufflers are at hand with long poles to put under the dog so as to break his fall after he has been tossed by the bull; the tips of these [poles] are covered with thick leather to prevent them from disembowelling the dogs. The most spirited stroke is considered to be that of the dog who seizes the bull's lip, clinging to it and pinning the animal for some time; the second best hit is to seize the eyebrows; the third, but far inferior, consists in seizing the bull's ear.[1]

Paul Hentzner, the German traveler who visited London in 1598, wrote thus of the Bear Garden:

There is still another place, built in the form of a theatre, which serves for the baiting of bulls and bears; they are fastened behind, and then worried by great English bull-dogs, but not without great risk to the dogs, from the horns of the one, and the teeth of the other; and it sometimes happens they are killed upon the spot; fresh ones are immediately supplied in the places of those that are wounded or tired. To this entertainment there often follows that of whipping a blinded bear, which is performed by five or six men standing circularly with whips,

[1] *The Calendar of State Papers*, Venetian, xv, 258.

which they exercise upon him without any mercy, as he cannot escape from them because of his chain; he defends himself with all his force and skill, throwing down all who come within his reach, and are not active enough to get out of it, and tearing the whips out of their hands and breaking them.

The following passage is taken from the diary of the Duke of Wirtemberg (who visited London in 1592), "noted down daily in the most concise manner possible, at his Highness's gracious command, by his private secretary":[1]

On the 1st of September his Highness was shown in London the English dogs, of which there were about 120, all kept in the same enclosure, but each in separate kennel. In order to gratify his Highness, and at his desire, two bears and a bull were baited; at such times you can perceive the breed and mettle of the dogs, for although they receive serious injuries from the bears, and are caught by the horns of the bull and tossed into the air so as frequently to fall down again upon the horns, they do not give in, [but fasten on the bull so firmly] that one is obliged to pull them back by the tails and force open their jaws. Four dogs at once were set on the bull; they however could not gain any advantage over him, for he so artfully contrived to ward off their attacks that they could not well get at him; on the contrary, the bull served them very scurvily by striking and beating at them.

[1] The secretary was named Jacob Rathgeb, and the diary was published at Tübingen in 1602 with a long title beginning: *A True and Faithful Narrative of the Bathing Excursion which His Serene Highness*, etc. A translation will be found in Rye, *England as Seen by Foreigners*, pp. 3–53.

BANKSIDE AND BEAR GARDEN

The following is a letter from one William Faunte to Edward Alleyn, then proprietor of the Bear Garden, regarding the sale of some game bulls:

I understood by a man which came with two bears from the garden, that you have a desire to buy one of my bulls. I have three western bulls at this time, but I have had very ill luck with them, for one of them hath lost his horn to the quick, that I think he will never be able to fight again; that is my old Star of the West: he was a very easy bull. And my bull Bevis, he hath lost one of his eyes, but I think if you had him he would do you more hurt than good, for I protest I think he would either throw up your dogs into the lofts, or else ding out their brains against the grates.[1]

Finally, among the Alleyn papers of Dulwich College is an interesting bill, or advertisement, of an afternoon's performance at the Bear Garden:

To-morrow being Thursday shall be seen at the Bear Garden on the Bankside a great match played by the gamesters of Essex, who hath challenged all comers whatsoever to play five dogs at the single bear for five pounds, and also to weary a bull dead at the stake; and for your better content [you] shall have pleasant sport with the horse and ape and whipping of the blind bear. *Vivat Rex!*

In 1613 the Bear Garden was torn down, and a new and handsomer structure erected in its place. For the history of this building the reader is referred to the chapter on "The Hope."

---
[1] Collier, *The Alleyn Papers*, p. 31.

CHAPTER VIII
NEWINGTON BUTTS

THE Bankside, as the preceding chapter indicates, offered unusual attractions to the actors. It had, indeed, long been associated with the drama: in 1545 King Henry VIII, in a proclamation against vagabonds, players,[1] etc., noted their "fashions commonly used at the Bank, and such like naughty places, where they much haunt"; and in 1547 the Bishop of Winchester made complaint that at a time when he intended to have a dirge and mass for the late King, the actors in Southwark planned to exhibit "a solemn play, to try who shall have the most resort, they in game or I in earnest."[2] The players, therefore, were no strangers to "the Bank." And when later in the century the hostility of the Common Council drove them to seek homes in localities not under the jurisdiction of the city, the suburb across the river offered them a suitable refuge. For, although a large portion of Southwark was under the jurisdiction of London, certain parts were not,

[1] It is just possible — but, I think, improbable — that the term "common players" as used in this proclamation referred to gamblers. The term is regularly used in law to designate actors.
[2] *The Calendar of State Papers, Domestic, 1547,* February 5, p. 1; cf. Tytler's *Edward VI and Mary,* 1, 20.

NEWINGTON BUTTS

notably the Liberty of the Clink and the Manor of Paris Garden, two sections bordering the river's edge, and the district of Newington lying farther back to the southwest. In these places the actors could erect their houses and entertain the public without fear of the ordinances of the Corporation, and without danger of interruption by puritanical Lord Mayors.

Yet, as we have seen, the first public playhouses were erected not on the Bankside — a "naughty" place, — but near Finsbury Field to the north of the city; and the reasons which led to the selection of such a quiet and respectable district have been pointed out.[1] It was inevitable, however, that sooner or later a playhouse should make its appearance in the region to the south of the city. And at an early date — how early it is impossible to say, but probably not long after the erection of the Theatre and the Curtain — there appeared in Southwark a building specially devoted to the use of players. Whether it was a new structure modeled after the theatres of Shoreditch, or merely an old building converted into a playhouse, we cannot say. It seems to have been something more than an inn-yard fitted up for dramatic purposes, and yet something less than the "sumptuous theatre houses" erected "on purpose" for plays to the north of the city.

Whatever the building was, it was situated at

[1] See page 29.

Newington Butts (a place so called from the butts for archery anciently erected there), and, unfortunately, at a considerable distance from the river. Exactly how far playgoers from London had to walk to reach the theatre after crossing over the river we do not know; but the Privy Council speaks of "the tediousness of the way" thither,[1] and Stow notes that the parish church of Newington was "distant one mile from London Bridge." Further information about the building — its exact situation, its size, its exterior shape, its interior arrangement, and such-like details — is wholly lacking.

Nor are we much better off in regard to its ownership, management, and general history. This seems to be due to the fact that it was not intimately associated with any of the more important London troupes; and to the fact that after a few unsuccessful years it ceased to exist. Below I have recorded the few and scattered references which constitute our meagre knowledge of its history.

The first passage cited may refer to the playhouse at Newington Butts. It is an order of the Privy Council, May 13, 1580, thus summarized by the clerk:

A letter to the Justices of Peace of the County of Surrey, that whereas their Lordships do understand

---

[1] The Council again refers to the building in the phrase "in any of these remote places." (Dasent, *Acts of the Privy Council*, XII, 15.)

NEWINGTON BUTTS

that notwithstanding their late order given to the Lord Mayor to forbid all plays within and about the city until Michaelmas next for avoiding of infection, nevertheless certain players do play sundry days every week at Newington Butts in that part of Surrey without the jurisdiction of the said Lord Mayor, contrary to their Lordship's order; their Lordships require the Justices not only to inquire who they be that disobey their commandment in that behalf, and not only to forbid them expressly for playing in any of these remote places near unto the city until Michaelmas, but to have regard that within the precinct of Surrey none be permitted to play; if any do, to commit them and to advertise them, &c.[1]

The next passage clearly refers to "the theatre" at Newington Butts. On May 11, 1586, the Privy Council dispatched a letter to the Lord Mayor, which the clerk thus summarized:

A letter to the Lord Mayor: his Lordship is desired, according to his request made to their Lordships by his letters of the vii th of this present, to give order for the restraining of plays and interludes within and about the city of London, for the avoiding of infection feared to grow and increase this time of summer by the common assemblies of people at those places; and that their Lordships have taken the like order for the prohibiting of the use of plays at the theatre, and the other places about Newington, out of his charge.[2]

Chalmers[3] thought the word "theatre" was used of the Newington Playhouse, and for this

---

[1] Dasent, *Acts of the Privy Council*, XII, 15.   [2] *Ibid.*, XIV, 102.
[3] *Apology*, p. 403.

he was taken to task by Collier,[1] who says: "He confounds it with the playhouse emphatically called 'the Theatre' in Shoreditch; and on consulting the Register, we find that no such playhouse as the Newington Theatre is there spoken of." But Chalmers was right; for if we consult the "Registers" we find the following letter, dispatched to the Justices of Surrey on the very same day that the letter just quoted was sent to the Lord Mayor:

A letter to the Justices of Surrey, that according to such direction as hath been given by their Lordships to the Lord Mayor to restrain and inhibit the use of plays and interludes in public places in and about the City of London, in respect of the heat of the year now drawing on, for the avoiding of the infection like to grow and increase by the ordinary assemblies of the people to those places, they are also required in like sort to take order that the plays and assemblies of the people at the theatre or any other places about Newington be forthwith restrained and forborn as aforesaid, &c.[2]

The phrase, "the theatre or any other places about Newington," when addressed to the "Justices of the Peace of Surrey" could refer only to the Newington Butts Playhouse.

On June 23, 1592, because of a riot in Southwark, the Privy Council closed all the playhouses in and about London.[3] Shortly after this the Lord

---

[1] *History of English Dramatic Poetry* (1879), III, 131.
[2] Dasent, *Acts of the Privy Council*, XIV, 99.
[3] Greg, *Henslowe's Diary*, II, 50, 73.

Strange's Men, who were then occupying the Rose, petitioned the Council to be allowed to resume acting in their playhouse. The Council granted them instead permission to act three times a week at Newington Butts; but the players, not relishing this proposal, chose rather to travel in the provinces. Soon finding that they could not make their expenses in the country, they returned to London, and again appealed to the Privy Council to be allowed to perform at the Rose.[1] The warrant issued by the Council in reply to this second petition tells us for the first time something definite about the Newington Butts Theatre:

> To the Justices, Bailiffs, Constables, and Others to Whom it Shall Appertain:
> Whereas not long since, upon some considerations, we did restrain the Lord Strange his servants from playing at the Rose on the Bankside, and enjoyned them to play three days [a week] at Newington Butts; now forasmuch as we are satisfied that by reason of the tediousness of the way, and that of long time plays have not there been used on working days, and for that a number of poor watermen are thereby relieved, you shall permit and suffer them, or any other, there [at the Rose] to exercise themselves in such sort as they have done heretofore, and that the Rose may be at liberty without any restraint so long as it shall be free from infection, any commandment from us heretofore to the contrary notwithstanding.[2]

[1] Greg, *Henslowe Papers*, p. 42.   [2] *Ibid.*, pp. 43–44.

From this warrant we learn that so early as 1592 the Newington house was almost deserted, and that "of long time" plays had been given there only occasionally.

Two years later, on June 3, 1594, Henslowe sent the Admiral's and the Chamberlain's Men to play temporarily at the half-deserted old playhouse, probably in order to give opportunity for needed repairs at the Rose.[1] The section of his *Diary*, under the heading, "In the name of god Amen begininge at newington my Lord Admeralle men & my Lord Chamberlen men As followethe 1594," constitutes the fullest and clearest — and, one may add, the most illustrious — chapter in the history of this obscure building; for although it extends over only ten days, it tells us that Edward Alleyn, Richard Burbage, and William Shakespeare then trod the Newington stage, and it records the performance there of such plays as *The Jew of Malta*, *Andronicus*, *The Taming of a Shrew*, and *Hamlet*.

We next hear of the building near the end of the century: in 1599, says Mr. Wallace, it was "only a memory, as shown by a contemporary record to be published later."[2]

Two other references close the history. In *A Woman is a Weathercock*, III, iii, printed in 1612,

[1] There is no evidence that Henslowe owned the house at Newington; he might very well have rented it for this particular occasion.
[2] Wallace, *The First London Theatre*, p. 2.

NEWINGTON BUTTS

but written earlier, one of the actors exclaims of an insufferable pun: "O Newington Conceit!" The fact that this sneer is the only reference to the Newington Playhouse found in contemporary literature is a commentary on the low esteem in which the building was held by the Elizabethans, and its relative unimportance for the history of the drama.

The last notice is in Howe's continuation of Stow's *Annals* (1631).[1] After enumerating all the theatres built in London and the suburbs "within the space of three-score years," he adds vaguely, "besides one in former time at Newington Butts."

[1] Page 1004.

CHAPTER IX
THE ROSE

DOUBTLESS one reason for the obscure rôle which the theatre at Newington played in the history of the drama was "the tediousness of the way" thither. The Rose, the second theatre to make its appearance in Surrey, was much more conveniently situated with respect to the city, for it was erected in the Liberty of the Clink and very near the river's edge. As a result, it quickly attained popularity with London playgoers, and before the end of the century had caused the centre of dramatic activity to be shifted from Finsbury Field to the Bank.

The builder of the Rose was one Philip Henslowe, then, so far as our evidence goes, unknown to the dramatic world, but destined soon to become the greatest theatrical proprietor and manager of the Tudor-Stuart age. We find him living on the Bankside and in the Liberty of the Clink at least as early as 1577. At first, so we are told, he was "but a poor man," described as "servant ... unto one Mr. Woodward." Upon the death of his employer, Woodward, he married the widow, Agnes Woodward, and thus came into the possession of considerable property. "All his wealth

THE ROSE

came by her," swore the charwoman Joan Horton. This, however, simply means that Henslowe obtained his original capital by his marriage; for, although very illiterate, he was shrewd in handling money, and he quickly amassed "his wealth" through innumerable business ventures.

As one of these ventures, no doubt, he leased from the Parish of St. Mildred, on March 24, 1585, a small piece of property on the Bankside known as "The Little Rose." "Among the early surveys, 1 Edward VI," says Rendle, "we see that this was not merely a name — the place was a veritable Rose Garden." [1] At the time of the lease the property is described as consisting of a dwelling-house called "The Rose," "two gardens adjoining the same" consisting of "void ground," and at least one other small building. The dwelling-house Henslowe probably leased as a brothel — for this was the district of the stews; and the small building mentioned above, situated at the south end of one of the gardens, he let to a London grocer named John Cholmley, who used it "to keep victualing in." [2]

Not satisfied, however, with the income from

---

[1] W. Rendle, in *The Antiquarian Magazine and Bibliographer*, VIII, 60.

[2] For the earlier history of the Rose estate see Rendle, *The Bankside*, p. xv, and Greg, *Henslowe's Diary*, II, 43. "The plan of the Rose estate in the vestry of St. Mildred's Church in London marks the estate exactly, but not the precise site of the Rose Playhouse. The estate consisted of three rods, and was east of Rose Alley." (Rendle, *The Bankside*, p. xxx.)

these two buildings, Henslowe a year and a half later was planning to utilize a part of the "void ground" for the erection of a theatre. What interested him in the drama we do not know, but we may suppose that the same reason which led Burbage, Brayne, Lanman, and others to build playhouses influenced him, namely, the prospect of "great gains to ensue therefrom."[1]

For the site of his proposed playhouse he allotted a small parcel of ground ninety-four feet square and lying in the corner formed by Rose Alley and Maiden Lane (see page 245). Then he interested in the enterprise his tenant Cholmley, for, it seems, he did not wish to undertake so expensive and precarious a venture without sharing the risk with another. On January 10, 1587, he and Cholmley signed a formal deed of partnership, according to which the playhouse was to be erected at once and at the sole cost of Henslowe; Cholmley, however, was to have from the beginning a half-interest in the building, paying for his share by installments of £25 10s. a quarter for a period of eight years and three months.[2] The total sum to be paid by Cholmley, £816, possibly repre-

[1] Possibly the fact that Burbage had just secured control of the Curtain, and hence had a monopoly of playhouses, was one of the reasons for a new playhouse.
[2] The deed of partnership is preserved among the Henslowe papers at Dulwich College. For an abstract of the deed see Greg, *Henslowe Papers*, p. 2. Henslowe seems to have driven a good bargain with Cholmley.

THE ROSE

sents the estimated cost of the building and its full equipment, plus rental on the land.

The building is referred to in the deed of January 10 as "a playhouse now in framing and shortly to be erected and set up." Doubtless it was ready for occupancy early in the summer. That performances were given there before the close of the year is at least indicated by an order of the Privy Council dated October 29, 1587:

> A letter to the Justices of Surrey, that whereas the inhabitants of Southwark had complained unto their Lordships declaring that the order by their Lordships set down for the restraining of plays and interludes within that county on the Sabbath Days is not observed, and especially within the Liberty of the Clink, and in the Parish of St. Saviours . . .[1]

The Rose was in "the Liberty of the Clink and in the Parish of St. Saviours," and so far as we have any evidence it was the only place there devoted to plays. Moreover, a distinct reference to it by name appears in the Sewer Records in April, 1588, at which date the building is described as "new."[2]

In Norden's *Map of London* (1593), the Rose and the adjacent Bear Garden are correctly placed with respect to each other, but are crudely drawn (see page 147). The representation of both as circular — the Bear Garden, we know, was polygonal — was due merely to this crudeness; yet the Rose

---

[1] Dasent, *Acts of the Privy Council*, xv, 271.
[2] Discovered by Mr. Wallace and printed in the London *Times*, April 30, 1914.

seems to have been indeed circular in shape, "the Bankside's round-house" referred to in *Tom Tell Troth's Message*. The building is so pictured in the Hondius map of 1610 (see page 149), and in the inset maps on the title-pages of Holland's *Herowlogia*, 1620, and Baker's *Chronicle*, 1643 (see page 147), all three of which apparently go back to an early map of London now lost. The building is again pictured as circular, with the Bear Garden at the left and the Globe at the right, in the Delaram portrait of King James (opposite page 246).[1]

From Henslowe's *Diary* we learn that the playhouse was of timber, the exterior of lath and plaster, the roof of thatch; and that it had a yard, galleries, a stage, a tiring-house, heavens, and a flagpole. Thus it differed in no essential way from the playhouses already erected in Shoreditch or subsequently erected on the Bank.[2]

What troupes of actors used the Rose during the

[1] The circular building pictured in these maps has been widely heralded as the First Globe, but without reason; all the evidence shows that it was the Rose. For further discussion see the chapters dealing with the Bear Garden, the Globe, and the Hope. In the Merian *View*, issued in Frankfort in 1638, the Bear Garden and the Globe, each named, are shown conspicuously in the foreground; in the background is vaguely represented an unnamed playhouse polygonal in shape. This could not possibly be the Rose. Merian's *View* was a compilation from Visscher's *View* of 1616 and some other view of London not yet identified; it has no independent authority, and no value whatever so far as the Rose is concerned.

[2] If we may believe Johannes de Witt, the Rose was "more magnificent" than the theatres in Shoreditch. See page 167.

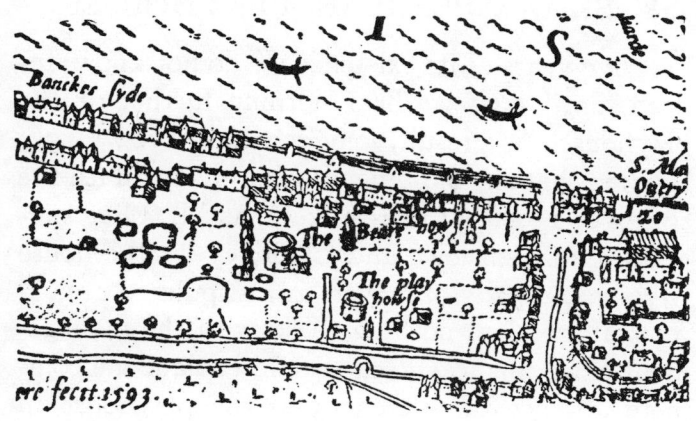

THE BEAR GARDEN AND THE ROSE

The upper view, from Norden's *Map of London*, 1593, shows the relative position of the Bear Garden and Rose. The lower view, an inset from the title-page of Baker's *Chronicle*, 1643, also shows the relative position, and gives a more detailed picture of the two structures. The Bear Garden is represented as polygonal, the Rose as circular.

first five years of its existence we do not know; indeed, until 1592 we hear nothing further of the playhouse. As a result, some scholars have wrongly inferred that the building was not erected until the spring of 1592.[1] It seems likely, as Mr. Greg suggests, that Henslowe and Cholmley let the house to some company of players at a stipulated annual rent, and so had nothing to do with the management of its finances. This would explain the complete absence of references to the playhouse in Henslowe's accounts.

During this obscure period of five years Cholmley disappears from the history of the Rose. It may be that he withdrew from the undertaking at the outset;[2] it may be that he failed to meet his payments, and so forfeited his moiety; or it may be that, becoming dissatisfied with his bargain, he sold out to Henslowe. Whatever the cause, his interest in the playhouse passed over to Henslowe, who appears henceforth as the sole proprietor.

In the spring of 1592 the building was in need of repairs, and Henslowe spent a large sum of money in thoroughly overhauling it.[3] The lathing and

[1] Ordish, *Early London Theatres*, p. 155; Mantzius, *A History of Theatrical Art*, p. 58. Mr. Wallace's discovery of a reference to the Rose in the Sewer Records for April, 1588, quite overthrows this hypothesis.

[2] This seems unlikely. At the beginning of Henslowe's *Diary* we find the scrawl "Chomley when" (Greg, *Henslowe's Diary* I, 217); this was written not earlier than 1592, and it shows that Cholmley was at that time in Henslowe's mind.

[3] Greg, *Henslowe's Diary*, I, 7.

THE BEAR GARDEN AND THE ROSE

A small inset view of London, from the map entitled "The Kingdome of Great Britaine and Ireland," printed in Speed's *Atlas* (1611). The map is dated 1610, but the inset view of London was copied, like the inset views to Baker's *Chronicle* (1643) and to Holland's *Heroologia* (1620), from a lost map of London drawn about 1589–1599.

plastering of the exterior were done over, the roof was re-thatched, new rafters were put in, and much heavy timber was used, indicating important structural alterations. In addition, the stage was painted, the lord's room and the tiring-house were provided with ceilings, a new flagpole was erected, and other improvements were introduced. Clearly an attempt was made to render the building not only stronger, but also more attractive in appearance and more modern in equipment.

The immediate occasion for these extensive alterations and repairs was the engagement of Lord Strange's Men to occupy the playhouse under Henslowe's management. This excellent troupe, with Edward Alleyn at its head, was perhaps the best company of actors then in London. It later became the Lord Chamberlain's Company, with which Shakespeare was identified; even at this early date, although documentary proof is lacking, he may have been numbered among its obscure members. The troupe opened the Rose on February 19, 1592, with a performance of Robert Greene's *Friar Bacon and Friar Bungay*, and followed this with many famous plays, such as *The Spanish Tragedy*, *The Jew of Malta*, *Orlando Furioso*, and *Henry VI*.[1]

The coming of Lord Strange's Men to the Rose led to a close friendship between Henslowe and Edward Alleyn, then twenty-six years of age, and

[1] For a list of their plays see Greg, *Henslowe's Diary*, 1, 13 ff.

THE ROSE

at the height of his fame as an actor, a friendship which was cemented in the autumn by Alleyn's marriage to Henslowe's stepdaughter (and only child) Joan Woodward. The two men, it seems, were thoroughly congenial, and their common interests led to the formation of a business partnership which soon became the most important single force in the theatrical life of the time.

Lord Strange's Men continued to act at the Rose from February 19 until June 23, 1592, when the Privy Council, because of a serious riot in Southwark, ordered the closing of all playhouses in and about London until Michaelmas following. Strange's Men very soon petitioned the Council to be allowed to reopen their playhouse; the Council, in reply, compromised by granting them permission to act three days a week at Newington Butts. This, however, did not please the actors, and they started on a tour of the provinces. In a short time, discovering that they could not pay their expenses on the road, they again petitioned for permission to open the Rose, complaining that "our company is great, and thereby our charge intolerable in traveling the country," and calling attention to the fact that "the use of our playhouse on the Bankside, by reason of the passage to and from the same by water, is a great relief to the poor watermen there."[1] The petition was accompanied by a supporting petition from the watermen asking the Council "for

[1] Greg, *Henslowe Papers*, p. 42.

God's sake and in the way of charity to respect us your poor watermen." As a result of these petitions the Council gave permission, probably late in August, 1592, for the reopening of the playhouse.[1] But before Strange's Men could take advantage of this permission, a severe outbreak of the plague caused a general inhibition of acting, and not until December 29, 1592, were they able to resume their performances at the Rose. A month later the plague broke out again with unusual severity, and on February 1, 1593, playing was again inhibited. The year rapidly developed into one of the worst plague-years in the history of the city; between ten and fifteen thousand persons died of the epidemic, and most of the London companies, including Strange's Men, went on an extended tour of the country.

Near the close of the year, and while Strange's Men were still traveling, the plague temporarily subsided, and Sussex's Men, who were then in London, secured the use of the Rose. They began to act there on December 27, 1593; but on February 6, 1594, the plague having again become threatening, acting was once more inhibited. This brief occupation of the Rose by Sussex's Men was notable only for the first performance of *Titus Andronicus*.[2]

[1] See Greg, *Henslowe Papers*, p. 43. For a general discussion of various problems involved, see Greg, *Henslowe's Diary*, II, 51-2.
[2] Greg, *Henslowe's Diary*, I, 16.

JOAN WOODWARD ALLEYN

The stepdaughter and only child of Philip Henslowe, whose marriage to the great actor Edward Alleyn led to the Henslowe-Alleyn theatrical enterprises. The portrait is here reproduced for the first time. (From the Dulwich Picture Gallery, by permission.)

At Easter, April 1, Strange's Men being still absent, Henslowe allowed the Rose to be used for eight days by "the Queen's Men and my Lord of Sussex's together." This second brief chapter in the long and varied history of the playhouse is interesting only for two performances of the old *King Leir*.[1]

As a result of the severe plague and the long continued inhibition of acting, there was a general confusion and subsequent reorganization of the various London troupes. The Admiral's Men, who had been dispersed in 1591, some joining Strange's Men, some going to travel in Germany, were brought together again; and Edward Alleyn, who had formerly been their leader, and who even after he became one of Strange's Men continued to describe himself as "servant to the right honorable the Lord Admiral,"[2] was induced to rejoin them. Alleyn thereupon brought them to the Rose, where they began to perform on May 14, 1594. After three days, however, they ceased, probably to allow Henslowe to make repairs or improvements on the building.

Strange's Men also had undergone reorganization. On April 16, 1594, they lost by death their patron, the Earl of Derby. Shortly afterwards they secured the patronage of the Lord Chamber-

---

[1] Greg, *Henslowe's Diary*, I, 17.
[2] He is so described, for example, in the warrant issued by the Privy Council on May 6, 1593, to Strange's Men.

lain, and before June 3, 1594, they had arrived in London and reported to their former manager, Henslowe.

At this time, apparently, the Rose was still undergoing repairs; so Henslowe sent both the Admiral's and the Chamberlain's Men to act at Newington Butts, where they remained from June 3 to June 13, 1594. On June 15 the Admiral's Men moved back to the Rose, which henceforth they occupied alone; and the Chamberlain's Men, thus robbed of their playhouse, went to the Theatre in Shoreditch.

During the period of Lent, 1595, Henslowe took occasion to make further repairs on his playhouse, putting in new pales, patching the exterior with new lath and plaster, repainting the woodwork, and otherwise furbishing up the building. The total cost of this work was £108 10s. And shortly after, as a part of these improvements, no doubt, he paid £7 2s. for "making the throne in the heavens."[1]

Near the close of July, 1597, Pembroke's Men at the Swan acted Nashe's satirical play, *The Isle of Dogs*, containing, it seems, a burlesque on certain persons high in authority. As a result the Privy Council on July 28 ordered all acting in and about London to cease until November 1, and all public playhouses to be plucked down and ruined.[2]

[1] Greg, *Henslowe's Diary*, I, 4.
[2] For the details of this episode see the chapter on the Swan.

THE ROSE

The latter part of the order, happily, was not put into effect, and on October 11 the Rose was allowed to open again. The Privy Council, however, punished the Swan and Pembroke's Company by ordering that only the Admiral's Men at the Rose and the Chamberlain's Men at the Curtain should henceforth be "allowed." As a consequence of this trouble with the authorities the best actors of Pembroke's Company joined the Admiral's Men under Henslowe. This explains the entry in the *Diary:* "In the name of God, amen. The xi of October began my Lord Admiral's and my Lord Pembroke's Men to play at my house, 1597." [1] The two companies were very soon amalgamated, and the strong troupe thus formed continued to act at the Rose under the name of the Admiral's Men.

The Chamberlain's Men, who in 1594 had been forced to surrender the Rose to the Admiral's Men and move to the Theatre, and who in 1597 had been driven from the Theatre to the Curtain, at last, in 1599, built for themselves a permanent home, the Globe, situated on the Bankside and close to the Rose. Henslowe's ancient structure [2] was eclipsed by this new and handsome building, "the glory of the Bank"; and the Admiral's Men, no doubt, felt themselves placed at a serious disad-

---

[1] Greg, *Henslowe's Diary*, I, 54.
[2] In January, 1600, the Earl of Nottingham refers to "the dangerous decay" of the Rose. See Greg, *Henslowe Papers*, p. 45; cf. p. 52.

vantage. As a result, in the spring of 1600, Henslowe and Alleyn began the erection of a splendid new playhouse, the Fortune, designed to surpass the Globe in magnificence, and to furnish a suitable and permanent home for the Admiral's Men. The building was situated in the suburb to the north of the city, far away from the Bankside and the Globe.

The erection of this handsome new playhouse led to violent outbursts from the Puritans, and vigorous protests from the city fathers. Accordingly the Privy Council on June 22, 1600, issued the following order: [1]

Whereas divers complaints have heretofore been made unto the Lords and other of Her Majesty's Privy Council of the manifold abuses and disorders that have grown and do continue by occasion of many houses erected and employed in and about London for common stage-plays; and now very lately by reason of some complaint exhibited by sundry persons against the building of the like house [the Fortune] in or near Golding Lane . . . the Lords and the rest of Her Majesty's Privy Council with one and full consent have ordered in manner and form as follows. First, that there shall be about the city two houses, and no more, allowed to serve for the use of the common stage-plays; of the which houses, one [the Globe] shall be in Surrey, in that place which is commonly called the Bankside, or thereabouts; and the other [the Fortune], in Middlesex.

This sealed the fate of the Rose.

[1] Dasent, *Acts of the Privy Council*, xxx, 395.

THE ROSE

In July the Admiral's Men had a reckoning with Henslowe, and prepared to abandon the Bankside. After they had gone, but before they had opened the Fortune, Henslowe, on October 28, 1600, let the Rose to Pembroke's Men for two days.[1] Possibly the troupe had secured special permission to use the playhouse for this limited time; possibly Henslowe thought that since the Fortune was not yet open to the public, no objection would be made. Of course, after the Admiral's Men opened the Fortune — in November or early in December, 1600 — the Rose, according to the order of the Privy Council just quoted, had to stand empty.

Its career, however, was not absolutely run. In the spring of 1602 Worcester's Men and Oxford's Men were "joined by agreement together in one company," and the Queen, "at the suit of the Earl of Oxford," ordered that this company be "allowed." Accordingly the Privy Council wrote to the Lord Mayor on March 31, 1602, informing him of the fact, and adding: "And as the other companies that are allowed, namely of me the Lord Admiral and the Lord Chamberlain, be appointed their certain houses, and one and no more to each company, so we do straightly require that this company be likewise [appointed] to one place. And because we are informed the house called the Boar's Head is the place they have especially used and do

[1] Greg, *Henslowe's Diary*, I, 131.

best like of, we do pray and require you that that said house, namely the Boar's Head, may be assigned unto them."[1] But the Lord Mayor seems to have opposed the use of the Boar's Head, and the upshot was that the Council gave permission for this "third company" to open the Rose. In Henslowe's *Diary*, we read: "Lent unto my Lord of Worcester's Players as followeth, beginning the 17 day of August, 1602."

This excellent company, destined to become the Queen's Company after the accession of King James, included such important actors as William Kempe, John Lowin, Christopher Beeston, John Duke, Robert Pallant, and Richard Perkins; and it employed such well-known playwrights as Thomas Heywood (the "prose Shakespeare," who was also one of the troupe), Henry Chettle, Thomas Dekker, John Day, Wentworth Smith, Richard Hathway, and John Webster. The company continued to act at the Rose until March 16, 1603, when it had a reckoning with Henslowe and left the playhouse.[2] In May, however, after the coming of King James, it returned to the Rose, and we find Henslowe opening a new account: "In the name of God, amen. Beginning to play again by the King's license, and laid out since for my Lord of

[1] *The Remembrancia*, II, 189; The Malone Society's *Collections*, I, 85.

[2] On March 19 the Privy Council formally ordered the suppression of all plays. This was five days before the death of Queen Elizabeth.

THE ROSE

Worcester's Men, as followeth, 1603, 9 of May." [1] Since only one entry follows, it is probable that the company did not remain long at the Rose. No doubt, the outbreak of the plague quickly drove them into the country; and on their return to London in the spring of 1604 they occupied the Boar's Head and the Curtain.

After this there is no evidence to connect the playhouse with dramatic performances.

Henslowe's lease of the Little Rose property, on which his playhouse stood, expired in 1605, and the Parish of St. Mildred's demanded an increase in rental. The following note in the *Diary* refers to a renewal of the lease:

Memorandum, that the 25 of June, 1603, I talked with Mr. Pope at the scrivener's shop where he lies,[2] concerning the taking of the lease anew of the little Rose, and he shewed me a writing betwixt the parish

---

[1] Greg, *Henslowe's Diary*, I, 190.

[2] Some scholars have supposed that this was Morgan Pope, a part owner of the Bear Garden; but he is last heard of in 1585, and by 1605 was probably dead. Mr. Greg is of the opinion that Thomas Pope, the well-known member of the King's Men at the Globe, is referred to. From this has been developed the theory that Pope, acting for the Globe players, had rented the Rose and closed it in order to prevent competition with the Globe on the Bankside. I believe, however, that the "Mr. Pope" here referred to was neither of these men, but merely the agent of the Parish of St. Mildred. It is said that he lived at a scrivener's shop. This could not apply to the actor Thomas Pope, for we learn from his will, made less than a month later, that he lived in a house of his own, furnished with plate and household goods, and cared for by a housekeeper; and with him lived Susan Gasquine, whom he had "brought up ever since she was born."

and himself which was to pay twenty pound a year rent,[1] and to bestow a hundred marks upon building, which I said I would rather pull down the playhouse than I would do so, and he bad me do, and said he gave me leave, and would bear me out, for it was in him to do it.[2]

Henslowe did not renew his lease of the property. On October 4, 1605, the Commissioners of the Sewers amerced him for the Rose, but return was made that it was then "out of his hands."[3] From a later entry in the Sewer Records, February 14, 1606, we learn that the new owner of the Rose was one Edward Box, of Bread Street, London. Box, it seems, either tore down the building, or converted it into tenements. The last reference to it in the Sewer Records is on April 25, 1606, when it is referred to as "the late playhouse."[4]

[1] The old rental was £7 a year.
[2] Greg, *Henslowe's Diary*, I, 178.
[3] Wallace in the London *Times*, April 30, 1914, p. 10. In view of these records it seems unnecessary to refute those persons who assert that the Rose was standing so late as 1622. I may add, however, that before Mr. Wallace published the Sewer Records I had successfully disposed of all the evidence which has been collected to show the existence of the Rose after 1605. The chief source of this error is a footnote by Malone in *Variorum*, III, 56; the source of Malone's error is probably to be seen in his footnote, *ibid.*, p. 66.
[4] For the tourist the memory of the old playhouse to-day lingers about Rose Alley on the Bank.

CHAPTER X
THE SWAN

THE Manor of Paris Garden,[1] situated on the Bankside just to the west of the Liberty of the Clink and to the east of the Lambeth marshes, had once been in the possession of the Monastery of Bermondsey. At the dissolution of the monasteries by Henry VIII, the property passed into the possession of the Crown; hence it was free from the jurisdiction of the Lord Mayor and Aldermen of London, and was on this account suitable for the erection of a playhouse. From the Crown the property passed through several hands, until finally, in 1589, the entire "lordship and manor of Paris Garden" was sold for £850 to Francis Langley, goldsmith and citizen of London.[2]

Langley had purchased the Manor as an investment, and was ready to make thereon such improvements as seemed to offer profitable returns. Burbage and Henslowe were reputed to be growing wealthy from their playhouses, and Langley was tempted to erect a similar building on his newly acquired property. Accordingly at some date before November, 1594, he secured a license to erect a

---

[1] Or "Parish Garden." See the note on page 121.
[2] The sale took the form of a lease for one thousand years.

theatre in Paris Garden. The license was promptly opposed by the Lord Mayor of London, who addressed to the Lord High Treasurer on November 3, 1594, the following letter:

> I understand that one Francis Langley . . . intendeth to erect a new stage or theatre (as they call it) for the exercising of plays upon the Bankside. And forasmuch as we find by daily experience the great inconvenience that groweth to this city and the government thereof by the said plays, I have emboldened myself to be an humble suitor to your good Lordship to be a means for us rather to suppress all such places built for that kind of exercise, than to erect any more of the same sort.[1]

The protest of the Lord Mayor, however, went unheeded, and Langley proceeded with the erection of his building. Presumably it was finished and ready for the actors in the earlier half of 1595.

The name given to the new playhouse was "The Swan." What caused Langley to adopt this name we do not know;[2] but we may suppose that it was suggested to him by the large number of swans which beautified the Thames. Foreigners on their first visit to London were usually very much impressed by the number and the beauty of these birds. Hentzner, in 1598, stated that the river "abounds in swans, swimming in flocks; the sight

[1] The Malone Society's *Collections*, I, 74–76.
[2] The swan was not uncommon as a sign, especially along the river; for example, it was the sign of one of the famous brothels on the Bankside, as Stow informs us.

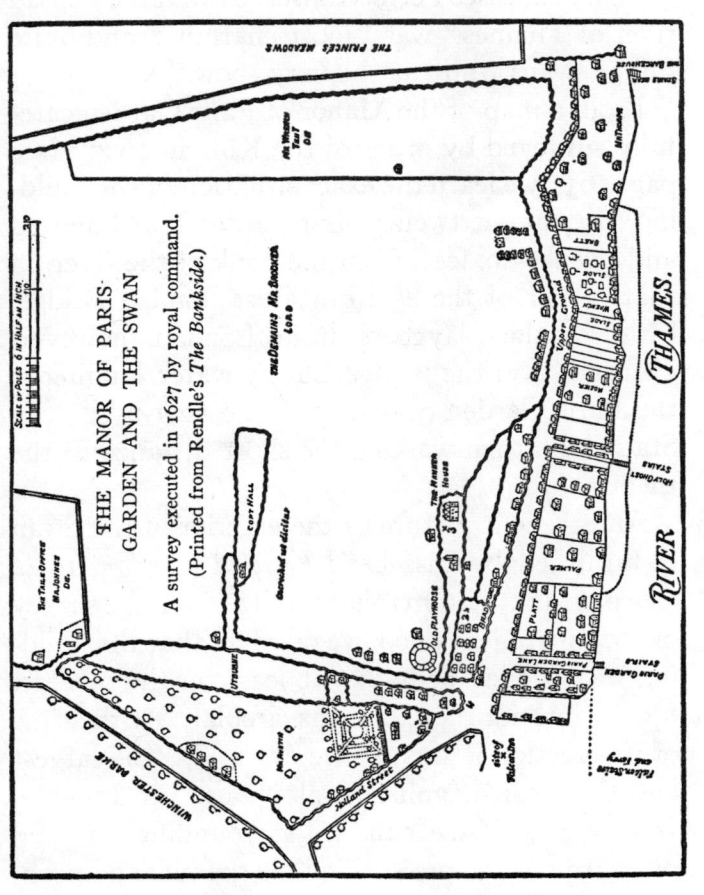

of them and their noise is vastly agreeable to the boats that meet them in their course"; and the Italian Francesco Ferretti observed that the "broad river of Thames" was "most charming, and quite full of swans white as the very snow." [1]

From a map of the Manor of Paris Garden carefully surveyed by order of the King in 1627 [2] (see page 163), we learn the exact situation of the building. It was set twenty-six poles, or four hundred and twenty-six feet, from the bank of the river, in that corner of the estate nearest London Bridge. Most of the playgoers from London, however, came not over the Bridge, but by water, landing at the Paris Garden Stairs, or at the near-by Falcon Stairs, and then walking the short distance to the theatre.

An excellent picture of the exterior of the Swan is furnished by Visscher's *View of London*, 1616, (see page 165). From this, as well as from the survey of 1627 just mentioned, we discover that the building was duodecahedral — at least on the outside, for the interior probably was circular. At the time of its erection it was, so we are told, "the largest and the most magnificent playhouse" in London. It contained three galleries surrounding an open pit, with a stage projecting into the pit; and probably it differed in no essential respect from the

---

[1] Quoted in Rye, *England as Seen by Foreigners*, p. 183.
[2] Reproduced by Rendle, *The Bankside, Southwark, and the Globe Playhouse*.

THE SWAN PLAYHOUSE
(From Visscher's *View of London*, 1616).

playhouses already built. In one point, however, it may have differed — although of this I cannot feel sure: it may have been provided with a stage that could be removed so as to allow the building to be used on occasions for animal-baiting. The De Witt drawing shows such a stage; and possibly Stow in his *Survey* (1598) gives evidence that the Swan was in early times employed for bear-baiting:

> And to begin at the west bank as afore, thus it followeth. On this bank is the bear gardens, in number twain; to wit, the old bear garden [i.e., the one built in 1583?] and the new [i.e., the Swan?], places wherein be kept bears, bulls, and other beasts, to be baited at stakes for pleasure; also mastiffs to bait them in several kennels are there nourished.[1]

Moreover, in 1613 Henslowe used the Swan as the model for the Hope, a building designed for both acting and animal-baiting. It should be noted, however, that in all documents the Swan is invariably referred to as a *playhouse*, and there is no evidence — beyond that cited above — to indicate that the building was ever employed for the baiting of bears and bulls.

In the summer of 1596 a Dutch traveler named Johannes de Witt, a priest of St. Mary's in Utrecht, visited London, and saw, as one of the most interesting sights of the city, a dramatic performance at the Swan. Later he communicated a description of the building to his friend Arend van Buchell,[2] who recorded the description in his commonplace-book,

---

[1] Stow's original manuscript (Harl. MSS., 544), quoted by Collier, *History of English Dramatic Poetry* (1879), III, 96, note 3. The text of the edition of 1598 differs very slightly.

[2] Apparently he allowed Van Buchell to transcribe the description and the rough pen-sketch from his notebook or traveler's diary.

THE SWAN

along with a crude and inexact drawing of the interior (see page 169), showing the stage, the three galleries, and the pit.[1] The description is headed: "Ex Observationibus Londinensibus Johannis de Witt." After a brief notice of St. Paul's, and a briefer reference to Westminster Cathedral, the traveler begins to describe what obviously interested him far more. I give below a translation of that portion relating to the playhouses:

There are four amphitheatres in London [the Theatre, Curtain, Rose, and Swan] of notable beauty, which from their diverse signs bear diverse names. In each of them a different play is daily exhibited to the populace. The two more magnificent of these are situated to the southward beyond the Thames, and from the signs suspended before them are called the Rose and the Swan. The two others are outside the city towards the north on the highway which issues through the Episcopal Gate, called in the vernacular Bishopgate.[2] There is also a fifth [the Bear Garden], but of dissimilar structure, devoted to the baiting of beasts, where are maintained in separate cages and enclosures many bears and dogs of stupendous size, which are kept for fighting, furnishing thereby a most delightful spectacle to men. Of all the theatres,[3] however, the largest and the most magnificent is that one of which the sign is a swan, called in the vernacular the Swan

[1] This interesting document was discovered by Dr. Karl T. Gaedertz, and published in full in *Zur Kenntnis der altenglischen Bühne* (Bremen, 1888).
[2] "Viâ quâ itur per Episcopalem portam vulgariter Biscopgate nuncupatam."
[3] "Theatrorum."

Theatre;[1] for it accommodates in its seats three thousand persons, and is built of a mass of flint stones (of which there is a prodigious supply in Britain),[2] and supported by wooden columns painted in such excellent imitation of marble that it is able to deceive even the most cunning. Since its form resembles that of a Roman work, I have made a sketch of it above.

Exactly when the Swan was opened to the public, or what troupes of actors first made use of it, we do not know. The visit of Johannes de Witt, however, shows that the playhouse was occupied in 1596; and this fact is confirmed by a statement in the lawsuit of Shaw *v.* Langley.[3] We may reasonably suppose that not only in 1596, but also in 1595 the building was used by the players.

Our definite history of the Swan, however, begins with 1597. In February of that year eight distinguished actors, among whom were Robert Shaw, Richard Jones, Gabriel Spencer, William

[1] "Id cuius intersignium est cygnus (vulgo te theatre off te cijn)." Mr. Wallace proposes to emend the last clause to read: "te theatre off te cijn off te Swan," thus making "cijn" mean "sign"; but is not this Flemish, and does not "cijn" mean "Swan"?

[2] It is commonly thought that De Witt was wrong in stating that the Swan was built of flint stones. Possibly the plaster exterior deceived him; or possibly in his memory he confused this detail of the building with the exterior of the church of St. Mary Overies, which was indeed built of "a mass of flint stones." On the other hand, the long life of the building after it had ceased to be of use might indicate that it was built of stones.

[3] Discovered by Mr. Wallace and printed in *Englische Studien* (1911), XLIII, 340–95. These documents have done much to clear up the history of the Swan and the Rose in the year 1597.

THE INTERIOR OF THE SWAN PLAYHOUSE
Sketched by Johannes de Witt in 1596.

Bird, and Thomas Downton, "servants to the right honorable the Earl of Pembroke," entered into negotiations with Langley, or, as the legal document puts it, "fell into conference with the said Langley for and about the hireing and taking a playhouse of the said Langley, situate in the old Paris Garden, in the Parish of St. Saviours, in the County of Surrey, commonly called and known by the name of the sign of the Swan." The result of this conference was that the members of Pembroke's Company [1] became each severally bound for the sum of £100 to play at the Swan for one year, beginning on February 21, 1597.

This troupe contained some of the best actors in London; and Langley, in anticipation of a successful year, "disbursed and laid out for making of the said house ready, and providing of apparel fit and necessary for their playing, the sum of £300 and upwards." Since he was at very little cost in making the Swan ready, "for the said house was then lately afore used to have plays in it," most of this sum went for the purchase of "sundry sort of rich attire and apparel for them to play withall."

Everything seems to have gone well until near the end of July, when the company presented *The Isle of Dogs*, a satirical play written in part by the

[1] I cannot agree with Mr. Wallace that Langley induced these players to desert Henslowe, secured for them the patronage of Pembroke, and thus was himself responsible for the organization of the Pembroke Company.

"young Juvenal" of the age, Thomas Nashe, and in part by certan "inferior players," chief of whom seems to have been Ben Jonson.[1] The play apparently attacked under a thin disguise some persons high in authority. The exact nature of the offense cannot now be determined, but Nashe himself informs us that "the troublesome stir which happened about it is a general rumour that hath filled all England,"[2] and the Queen herself seems to have been greatly angered. On July 28, 1597, the Privy Council sent a letter to the Justices of Middlesex and of Surrey informing them that Her Majesty "hath given direction that not only no plays shall be used within London or about the city or in any public place during this time of summer, but that also those playhouses that are erected and built only for such purposes shall be plucked down." Accordingly the Council ordered the Justices to see to it that "there be no more plays used in any public place within three miles of the city until Allhallows [i.e., November 1] next"; and, furthermore, to send for the owners of the various playhouses "and enjoin them by vertue hereof forthwith to pluck down quite the stages, galleries, and rooms that are made for people to stand in, and so to deface the

---

[1] For an account of *The Isle of Dogs* see E. K. Chambers, *Modern Language Review* (1909), IV, 407, 511; R. B. McKerrow, *The Works of Thomas Nashe*, v, 29; and especially the important article by Mr. Wallace in *Englische Studien* already referred to.
[2] *Nashes Lenten Stuffe* (1599), ed. McKerrow, III, 153.

same as they may not be employed again to such use." [1]

The Council, however, did not stop with this. It ordered the arrest of the authors of the play and also of the chief actors who took part in its performance. Nashe saved himself by precipitate flight, but his lodgings were searched and his private papers were turned over to the authorities. Robert Shaw and Gabriel Spencer, as leaders of the troupe, and Ben Jonson, as one of the "inferior players" who had a part in writing the play,[2] were thrown into prison. The rest of the company hurried into the country, their speed being indicated by the fact that we find them acting in Bristol before the end of July.

Some of these events are referred to in the following letter, addressed by the Privy Council "to Richard Topclyfe, Thomas Fowler, and Richard Skevington, esquires, Doctor Fletcher, and Mr. Wilbraham":

---

[1] Dasent, *Acts of the Privy Council*, XXVII, 313. Possibly the other public playhouses were suppressed along with the Swan in response to the petition presented to the Council on July 28, (i.e. on the same day) by the Lord Mayor and Aldermen requesting the "final suppressing of the said stage plays, as well at the Theatre, Curtain, and Bankside as in all other places in and about the city." See The Malone Society's *Collections*, I, 78.

[2] In a marginal gloss to *Nashes Lenten Stuffe* (1599), ed. McKerrow, III, 154, Nashe says: "I having begun but the induction and first act of it, the other four acts without my consent or the best guess of my drift or scope, by the players were supplied, which bred both their trouble and mine too."

THE SWAN

Upon information given us of a lewd play that was played in one of the playhouses on the Bankside, containing very seditious and slanderous matter, we caused some of the players [Robert Shaw, Gabriel Spencer, and Ben Jonson[1]] to be apprehended and committed to prison, whereof one of them [Ben Jonson] was not only an actor but a maker of part of the said play. Forasmuch as it is thought meet that the rest of the players or actors in that matter shall be apprehended to receive such punishment as their lewd and mutinous behaviour doth deserve, these shall be therefore to require you to examine those of the players that are committed (whose names are known to you, Mr. Topclyfe), what is become of the rest of their fellows that either had their parts in the devising of that seditious matter, or that were actors or players in the same, what copies they have given forth [2] of the said play, and to whom, and such other points as you shall think meet to be demanded of them, wherein you shall require them to deal truly, as they will look to receive any favour. We pray you also to peruse such papers as were found in Nashe his lodgings, which Ferrys, a messenger of the Chamber, shall deliver unto you, and to certify us the examinations you take.[3]

[1] The identity of the three players is revealed in an order of the Privy Council dated October 8, 1597: "A warrant to the Keeper of the Marshalsea to release Gabriel Spencer and Robert Shaw, stage-players, out of prison, who were of late committed to his custody. The like warrant for the releasing of Benjamin Jonson." Dasent, *Acts of the Privy Council*, xxviii, 33.)

[2] Such a copy was formerly preserved in a volume of miscellaneous manuscripts at Alnwick Castle, but has not come down to modern times. See F. J. Burgoyne, *Northumberland Manuscripts* (London, 1904).

[3] Dasent, *Acts of the Privy Council*, xxvii, 338.

This unfortunate occurrence destroyed Langley's dream of a successful year. It also destroyed the splendid Pembroke organization, for several of its chief members, even before the inhibition was raised, joined the Admiral's Men. On August 6 Richard Jones went to Henslowe and bound himself to play for two years at the Rose, and at the same time he bound his friend Robert Shaw, who was still in prison; on August 10 William Bird came and made a similar agreement; on October 6 Thomas Downton did likewise. Their leader, Gabriel Spencer, also probably had an understanding with Henslowe, although he signed no bond; and upon his release from the Marshalsea he joined his friends at the Rose.[1]

In the meantime the Queen's anger was abating, and the trouble was blowing over. The order to pluck down all the public playhouses was not taken seriously by the officers of the law, and Henslowe actually secured permission to reopen the Rose on October 11. The inhibition itself expired on November 1, but the Swan was singled out for further punishment. The Privy Council ordered that henceforth license should be granted to two companies only: namely, the Admiral's at the Rose, and the Chamberlain's at the Curtain. This meant, of course, the closing of the Swan.

[1] Langley sued these actors on their bond to him of £100 to play only at the Swan; see the documents printed by Mr. Wallace. Ben Jonson also joined Henslowe's forces at the Rose, as did Anthony and Humphrey Jeffes, who were doubtless members of the Pembroke Company.

THE SWAN 175

In spite of this order, however, the members of Pembroke's Company remaining after the chief actors had joined Henslowe, taking on recruits and organizing themselves into a company, began to act at the Swan without a license. For some time they continued unmolested, but at last the two licensed companies called the attention of the Privy Council to the fact, and on February 19, 1598, the Council issued the following order to the Master of the Revels and the Justices of both Middlesex and Surrey:

Whereas license hath been granted unto two companies of stage players retayned unto us, the Lord Admiral and Lord Chamberlain ... and whereas there is also a third company who of late (as we are informed) have by way of intrusion used likewise to play ... we have therefore thought good to require you upon receipt hereof to take order that the aforesaid third company may be suppressed, and none suffered hereafter to play but those two formerly named, belonging to us, the Lord Admiral and Lord Chamberlain.[1]

Thus, after February 19, 1598, the Swan stood empty, so far as plays were concerned, and we hear very little of it during the next few years. Indeed, it never again assumed an important part in the history of the drama.

In the summer of 1598 [2] it was used by Robert

[1] Dasent, *Acts of the Privy Council*, XXVIII, 327.
[2] After the order of February 19, when the "intruding company" was driven out, and before September 7 when Meres's *Palladis Tamia* was entered in the Stationers' Registers.

Wilson for a contest in extempore versification. Francis Meres, in his *Palladis Tamia,* writes: "And so is now our witty Wilson, who for learning and extemporall wit in this faculty is without compare or compeere, as, to his great and eternal commendations, he manifested in his challenge at the Swan on the Bankside."

On May 15, 1600, Peter Bromvill was licensed to use the Swan "to show his feats of activity at convenient times in that place without let or interruption." [1] The Privy Council in issuing the license observed that Bromvill "hath been recommended unto Her Majesty from her good brother the French King, and hath shewed some feats of great activity before Her Highness."

On June 22, 1600, the Privy Council "with one and full consent" ordered "that there shall be about the city two houses, and no more, allowed to serve for the use of the common stage plays; of the which houses, one [the Globe] shall be in Surrey ... and the other [the Fortune] in Middlesex." [2] This order in effect merely confirmed the order of 1598 which limited the companies to two, the Admiral's and the Chamberlain's.

Early in 1601 Langley died; and in January, 1602, his widow, as administratrix, sold the Manor of Paris Garden, including the Swan Playhouse, to Hugh Browker, a prothonotary of the Court of

---

[1] Dasent, *Acts of the Privy Council,* xxx, 327.
[2] *Ibid.,* 395.

THE SWAN

Common Pleas. The property remained in the possession of the Browker family until 1655.[1]

On November 6, 1602, the building was the scene of the famous hoax known as *England's Joy*, perpetrated upon the patriotic citizens of London by one Richard Vennar.[2] Vennar scattered hand-bills over the city announcing that at the Swan Playhouse, on Saturday, November 6, a company of "gentlemen and gentlewomen of account" would present with unusual magnificence a play entitled *England's Joy*, celebrating Queen Elizabeth. It was proposed to show the coronation of Elizabeth, the victory of the Armada, and various other events in the life of "England's Joy," with the following conclusion: "And so with music, both with voice and instruments, she is taken up into heaven; when presently appears a throne of blessed souls; and beneath, under the stage, set forth with strange fire-works, diverse black and damned souls, wonderfully described in their several torments."[3] The price of admission to the performance was to

[1] For this and other details as to the subsequent history of the property see Wallace, *Englische Studien*, XLIII, 342; Rendle, *The Antiquarian Magazine*, VII, 207; and cf. the map on page 163.

[2] Many writers, including Mr. Wallace, have confused this Richard Vennar with William Fennor, who later challenged Kendall to a contest of wit at the Fortune. For a correct account, see T. S. Graves, "Tricks of Elizabethan Showmen" (in *The South Atlantic Quarterly*, April, 1915, XIV) and "A Note on the Swan Theatre" (in *Modern Philology*, January, 1912, IX, 431).

[3] From the broadside printed in *The Harleian Miscellany*, X, 198. For a photographic facsimile, see Lawrence, *The Elizabethan Playhouse* (Second Series), p. 68.

be "two shillings, or eighteen pence at least." In spite of this unusually high price, an enormous audience, including a "great store of good company and many noblemen," passed into the building. Whereupon Vennar seized the money paid for admission, and showed his victims "a fair pair of heels." The members of the audience, when they found themselves thus duped, "revenged themselves upon the hangings, curtains, chairs, stools, walls, and whatsoever came in their way, very outrageously, and made great spoil." [1]

On February 8, 1603, John Manningham recorded in his *Diary:* "Turner and Dun, two famous fencers, playd their prizes this day at the Bankside, but Turner at last run Dun so far in the brain at the eye, that he fell down presently stone dead; a goodly sport in a Christian state, to see one man kill another!" The place where the contest was held is not specifically mentioned, but in all probability it was the Swan.[2]

For the next eight years all is silence, but we may suppose that the building was occasionally let for special entertainments such as those just enumerated.

[1] *Letters Written by John Chamberlain*, Camden Society (1861), p. 163; *The Calendar of State Papers, Domestic, 1601–1603*, p. 264. See also Manningham's *Diary*, pp. 82, 93.

[2] This seems to be the source of the statement by Mr. Wallace (*Englische Studien*, XLIII, 388), quoting Rendle (*The Antiquarian Magazine*, VII, 210): "In 1604, a man named Turner, in a contest for a prize at the Swan, was killed by a thrust in the eye." Rendle cites no authority for his statement.

THE SWAN

In 1611 Henslowe undertook to manage the Lady Elizabeth's Men, promising among other things to furnish them with a suitable playhouse. Having disposed of the Rose in 1605, he rented the Swan and established his company there. In 1613, however, he built the Hope, and transferred the Lady Elizabeth's Men thither.

The Swan seems thereafter to have been occupied for a time by Prince Charles's Men. But the history of this company and its intimate connection with the Lady Elizabeth's Company is too vague to admit of definite conclusions. So far as we can judge, the Prince's Men continued at the Swan until 1615, when Henslowe transferred them to the Hope.[1]

After 1615 the Swan was deserted for five years so far as any records show. But in 1621 the old playhouse seems to have been again used by the actors. The Overseers of the Poor in the Liberty of Paris Garden record in their Account Book: "Monday, April the 9th, 1621, received of the players £5 3s. 6d."[2] From this it is evident that in the spring of 1621 some company of players, the name of which has not yet been discovered, was occupy-

---

[1] These dates are in a measure verified by the records of the Overseers of the Poor for the Liberty of Paris Garden, printed by Mr. Wallace (*Englische Studien*, XLIII, 390, note 1). Mr. Wallace seems to labor under the impression that this chapter in the history of the Swan (1611–1615) was unknown before, but it was adequately treated by Fleay and later by Mr. Greg.

[2] Wallace, *op. cit.*, p. 390, note 1.

ing the Swan. Apparently, however, the company did not remain there long, for the Account Book records no payment the following year; nor, although it extends to the year 1671, does it again record any payments from actors at the Swan. There is, indeed, no evidence to connect the playhouse with dramatic performances after 1621.[1] In the map of 1627 it is represented as still standing, but is labeled "the *old* playhouse," and is not even named.

Five years later it is referred to in Nicolas Goodman's *Holland's Leaguer* (1632), a pamphlet celebrating one of the most notorious houses of ill fame on the Bankside.[2] Dona Britannica Hollandia, the proprietress of this house, is represented as having been much pleased with its situation:

Especially, and above all the rest, she was most taken with the report of three famous amphitheatres, which stood so near situated that her eye might take view of them from the lowest turret. One was the *Continent of the World* [i.e., the Globe], because half the year a world of beauties and brave spirits resorted unto it; the other was a building of excellent *Hope*, and though wild beasts and gladiators did most possess it, yet the gallants that came to behold

---

[1] Rendle quotes a license of 1623 for "T. B. and three assistants to make shows of Italian motions at the Princes Arms or the Swan." (*The Antiquarian Magazine*, 1885, VII, 211.) But this may be a reference to an inn rather than to the large playhouse.

[2] What seems to be a picture of this famous house may be seen in Merian's *View of London*, 1638 (see opposite page 256), with a turret, and standing just to the right of the Swan.

THE SWAN

those combats, though they were of a mixt society, yet were many noble worthies amongst them; the last which stood, and, as it were, shak'd hands with this fortress, being in times past as famous as any of the other, was now fallen to decay, and like a dying *Swanne*, hanging down her head, seemed to sing her own dirge.

This is the last that we hear of the playhouse, that was "in times past as famous as any of the other." What finally became of the building we do not know. It is not shown in Hollar's *View of London*, in 1647, and probably it had ceased to exist before the outbreak of the Civil War.

CHAPTER XI

THE SECOND BLACKFRIARS

IN 1596 Burbage's lease of the plot of ground on which he had erected the Theatre was drawing to a close, and all his efforts at a renewal had failed. The owner of the land, Gyles Alleyn, having, in spite of the terms of the original contract, refused to extend the lease until 1606, was craftily plotting for a substantial increase in the rental; moreover, having become puritanical in his attitude towards the drama, he was insisting that if the lease were renewed, the Theatre should be used as a playhouse for five years only, and then should either be torn down, or be converted into tenements. Burbage tentatively agreed to pay the increased rental, but, of course, he could not possibly agree to the second demand; and when all negotiations on this point proved futile, he realized that he must do something at once to meet the awkward situation.

In the twenty years that had elapsed since the erection of the Theatre and the Curtain in Holywell, the Bankside had been developed as a theatrical district, and the Rose and the Swan, not to mention the Bear Garden, had made the south side of the river the popular place for entertainments.

THE SECOND BLACKFRIARS 183

Naturally, therefore, any one contemplating the erection of a playhouse would immediately think of this locality. Burbage, however, was a man of ideas. He believed that he could improve on the Bankside as a site for his theatre. He remembered how, at the outset of his career as a theatrical manager, he had had to face competition with Richard Farrant who had opened a small "private" playhouse in Blackfriars. Although that building had not been used as a "public" playhouse, and had been closed up after a few years of sore tribulation, it had revealed to Burbage the possibilities of the Blackfriars precinct for theatrical purposes. In the first place, the precinct was not under the jurisdiction of the city, so that actors would not there be subject to the interference of the Lord Mayor and his Aldermen. As Stevens writes in his *History of Ancient Abbeys, Monasteries, etc.*: "All the inhabitants within it were subject to none but the King ... neither the Mayor, nor the sheriffs, nor any other officers of the City of London had the least jurisdiction or authority therein." Blackfriars, therefore, in this fundamental respect, was just as desirable a location for theatres as was Holywell to the north of the city, or the Bankside to the south. In the second place, Blackfriars had a decided advantage over those two suburban localities in that it was "scituated in the bosome of the Cittie," [1]

[1] The Petition of 1619, in The Malone Society's *Collections*, I, 93.

near St. Paul's Cathedral, the centre of London life, and hence was readily accessible to playgoers, even during the disagreeable winter season. In the third place, the locality was distinctly fashionable. To give some notion of the character of its inhabitants, I record below the names of a few of those who lived in or near the conventual buildings at various times after the dissolution: George Brooke, Lord Cobham; William Brooke, Lord Cobham, Lord Chamberlain of the Queen's Household; Henry Brooke, Lord Cobham, Lord Warden of the Cinque Ports; Sir Thomas Cheney, Treasurer of the Queen's Household, and Lord Warden of the Cinque Ports; Henry Carey, Lord Hunsdon, Lord Chamberlain of the Queen's Household; George Carey, Lord Hunsdon, who as Lord Chamberlain was the patron of Shakespeare's troupe; Sir Thomas Cawarden, Master of the Revels; Sir Henry Jerningham, Fee Chamberlain to the Queen's Highness; Sir Willam More, Chamberlain of the Exchequer; Lord Zanche; Sir John Portynary; Sir William Kingston; Sir Francis Bryan; Sir John Cheeke; Sir George Harper; Sir Philip Hoby, Lady Anne Gray; Sir Robert Kyrkham; Lady Perrin; Sir Christopher More; Sir Henry Neville; Sir Thomas Saunders; Sir Jerome Bowes; and Lady Jane Guildford.[1]

[1] It is true that poor people also, feather-dealers and such-like, lived in certain parts of Blackfriars, but this, of course, did not affect the reputation of the precinct as the residence of noblemen.

THE SECOND BLACKFRIARS 185

Obviously the locality was free from the odium which the public always associated with Shoreditch and the Bankside, the recognized homes of the London stews.[1]

Thus, a playhouse erected in the precinct of Blackfriars would escape all the grave disadvantages of situation which attached to the existing playhouses in the suburbs, and, on the other hand, would gain several very important advantages.

Burbage's originality, however, did not stop with the choice of Blackfriars as the site of his new theatre; he determined to improve on the form of building as well. The open-air structure which he had designed in 1576, and which had since been copied in all public theatres, had serious disadvantages in that it offered no protection from the weather. Burbage now resolved to provide a large "public" playhouse, fully roofed in, with the entire audience and the actors protected against the inclemency of the sky and the cold of winter. In short, his dream was of a theatre centrally located, comfortably heated, and, for its age, luxuriously appointed.

With characteristic energy and courage he at

---

[1] In Samuel Rowlands's *Humors Looking Glass* (1608), a rich country gull is represented as filling his pockets with money and coming to London. Here a servant "of the Newgate variety" shows him the sights of the city:

> Brought him to the Bankside where bears do dwell,
> And unto Shoreditch where the whores keep hell.

once set about the task of realizing this dream. He found in the Blackfriars precinct a large building which, he thought, would admirably serve his purpose. This building was none other than the old Frater of the Monastery, a structure one hundred and ten feet long and fifty-two feet wide, with stone walls three feet thick, and a flat roof covered with lead. From the Loseley documents, which M. Feuillerat has placed at the disposal of scholars,[1] we are now able to reconstruct the old Frater building, and to point out exactly that portion which was made into a playhouse.[2]

At the time of the dissolution, the top story consisted of a single large room known as the "Upper Frater," and also as the "Parliament Chamber" from the fact that the English Parliament met here on several occasions; here, also, was held the trial before Cardinals Campeggio and Wolsey for the divorce of the unhappy Queen Catherine and Henry VIII — a scene destined to be reënacted in the same building by Shakespeare and his fellows many years later. In 1550 the room was granted, with various other properties in Blackfriars, to Sir Thomas Cawarden.[3]

[1] *Blackfriars Records*, in The Malone Society's *Collections*, (1913).
[2] For a reconstruction of the Priory buildings and grounds, and for specific evidence of statements made in the following paragraphs, the reader is referred to J. Q. Adams, *The Conventual Buildings of Blackfriars, London*, in the University of North Carolina *Studies in Philology*, XIV, 64.
[3] Feuillerat, *Blackfriars Records*, pp. 7, 12.

THE SECOND BLACKFRIARS

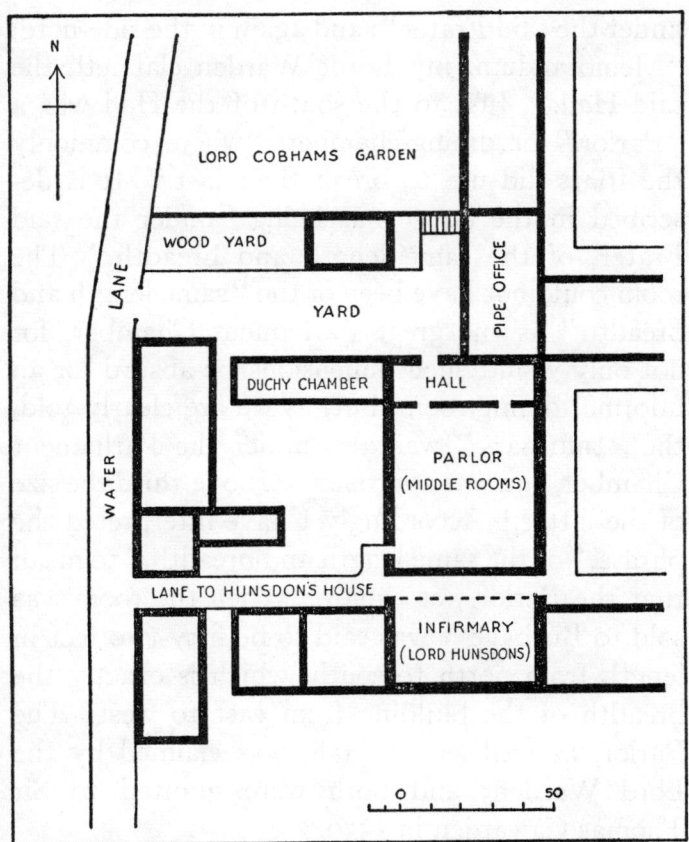

PLAN ILLUSTRATING THE SECOND BLACKFRIARS PLAYHOUSE

The Playhouse was made by combining the Hall and the Parlor.

The space below the Parliament Chamber was divided into three units. At the northern end was a "Hall" extending the width of the building. It is mentioned in the Survey [1] of 1548 as "a Hall...

[1] Feuillerat, *Blackfriars Records*, p. 7.

under the said Frater"; and again in the side-note: "Memorandum, my Lorde Warden claimeth the said Hall." Just to the south of the Hall was a "Parlor," or dining-chamber, "where commonly the friars did use to break their fast." It is described in the Survey as being "under the said Frater, of the same length and breadth." The room could not have been of the "same length and breadth" as the great Parliament Chamber, for not only would such dimensions be absurd for an informal dining-room, but, as we are clearly told, the "Infirmary" was also under the Parliament Chamber, and was approximately one-third the size of the latter.[1] Accordingly I have interpreted the phrase, "of the same length and breadth," to mean that the Parlor was square. When the room was sold to Burbage it was said to be fifty-two feet in length from north to south, which is exactly the breadth of the building from east to west. The Parlor, as well as the Hall, was claimed by the Lord Warden; and both were granted to Sir Thomas Cawarden in 1550.

South of the Parlor was the Infirmary, described as being "at the western corner of the Inner Cloister" (of which the Frater building constituted the western side), as being under the Parliament Chamber, and as being approximately one-third the size of the Parliament Chamber. The Infirmary seems to have been structurally distinct from

[1] Feuillerat, *Blackfriars Records*, pp. 105–06.

THE SECOND BLACKFRIARS

the Hall and Parlor.[1] It was three stories high, consisting of a "room beneath the Fermary," the Infirmary itself, a "room above the same";[2] while the Parliament Chamber, extending itself "over the room above the Fermary," constituted a fourth story. Furthermore, not only was the Infirmary a structural unit distinct from the Hall and the Parlor at the north, but it never belonged to Cawarden or More, and hence was not included in the sale to Burbage. It was granted in 1545 to Lady Mary Kingston,[3] from whom it passed to her son, Sir Henry Jerningham, then to Anthony Kempe, who later sold it to Lord Hunsdon;[4] and at the time the playhouse was built, the Infirmary was still in the occupation of Hunsdon.

At the northern end of the Frater building, and extending westward, was a narrow structure fifty feet in length, sixteen feet in breadth, and three stories in height, regarded as a "part of the frater parcel." The middle story, which was on the same level with the Parliament Chamber, was known as the "Duchy Chamber," possibly because of its use in connection with the sittings of Parliament, or with the meetings of the

---

[1] In all probability it was separated from the Hall and Parlor by a passage leading through the Infirmary into the Inner Cloister yard.
[2] One reason for the greater height may have been the slope of the ground towards the river; a second reason was the unusual height of the Parlor.
[3] Feuillerat, *Blackfriars Records*, p. 105.   [4] *Ibid.*, p. 124.

Privy Council there. The building was granted to Cawarden in 1550.[1]

Upon the death of Cawarden all his Blackfriars holdings passed into the possession of Sir William More. From More, in 1596, James Burbage purchased those sections of the Frater building which had originally been granted to Cawarden [2] — that is, all the Frater building except the Infirmary — for the sum of £600, in modern valuation about $25,000.[3] Evidently he had profited by Farrant's experience with More and by his own experience with Gyles Alleyn, and had determined to risk no more leases, but in the future to be his own landlord, cost what it might.

The properties which he thus secured were:

(1) The Parliament Chamber, extending over the Hall, Parlor, and Infirmary. This great chamber, it will be recalled, had previously been divided by Cawarden into the Frith and Cheeke Lodgings;[4] but now it was arranged as a single tenement of seven rooms, and was occupied by the eminent physician William de Lawne:[5] "All those seven

[1] Feuillerat, *Blackfriars Records*, p. 8.
[2] For the deed of sale see *ibid.*, p. 60.
[3] It should be observed, however, that Burbage paid only £100 down, and that he immediately mortgaged the property for more than £200. The playhouse was not free from debt until 1605. See Wallace, *The First London Theatre*, p. 23.
[4] The northern section of the Cheeke Lodging (a portion of the old Buttery) which had constituted Farrant's private theatre, and which was no real part of the Frater building, had been converted by More into the Pipe Office.
[5] A prosperous physician. His son was one of the illustrious

THE SECOND BLACKFRIARS

great upper rooms as they are now divided, being all upon one floor, and sometime being one great and entire room, with the roof over the same, covered with lead." Up into this tenement led a special pair of stairs which made it wholly independent of the rest of the building.

(2) The friar's "Parlor," now made into a tenement occupied by Thomas Bruskett, and called "the Middle Rooms, or Middle Stories" — possibly from the fact that it was the middle of three tenements, possibly from the fact that having two cellars under its northern end it was the middle of three stories. It is described as being fifty-two feet in length north and south, and thirty-seven feet in width. Why a strip of nine feet should have been detached on the eastern side is not clear; but that this strip was also included in the sale to Burbage is shown by later documents.

(3) The ancient "Hall" adjoining the "Parlor" on the north, and now made into two rooms. These rooms were combined with the ground floor of the Duchy Chamber building to constitute a tenement occupied by Peter Johnson: "All those two lower rooms now in the occupation of the said Peter Johnson, lying directly under part of the said seven great upper rooms." The dimensions are not

---

founders of the Society of Apothecaries, and one of its chief benefactors. His portrait may be seen to-day in Apothecaries' Hall. See C. R. B. Barrett, *The History of the Society of Apothecaries of London.*

given, but doubtless the two rooms together extended the entire width of the building and were approximately as broad as the Duchy Chamber building, with which they were united.

(4) The Duchy Chamber building "at the north end of the said seven great upper rooms, and at the west side thereof." At the time of the sale the ground floor of this building was occupied by Peter Johnson, who had also the Hall adjoining it on the west; the middle story was occupied by Charles Bradshaw; and the top story by Edward Merry.[1]

Out of this heterogeneous property Burbage was confronted with the problem of making a playhouse. Apparently he regarded the Parliament Chamber as too low, or too inaccessible for the purposes of a theatre; this part of his property, therefore, he kept as a lodging, and for many years it served as a dormitory for the child-actors. The Duchy Chamber building, being small and detached from the Frater building, he reserved also as a lodging.[2] In the Hall and the Parlor, however,

[1] Mr. Wallace's description of the building and the way in which it was converted into a playhouse (*The Children of the Chapel at Blackfriars*, pp. 37–41) is incorrect. For the various details cited above see the deed of sale to Burbage.

[2] This may have contained the two rooms in which Evans lived, and "the schoolhouse and the chamber over the same," which are described (see the documents in Fleay's *A Chronicle History of the London Stage*, p. 210 ff.) as being "severed from the said great hall." In another document this schoolhouse is described as "schola, anglice *schoolhouse*, ad borealem finem Aulæ prædictæ." (Wallace, *The Children of the Chapel at Blackfriars*, p. 40.)

THE SECOND BLACKFRIARS

he saw the possibility of a satisfactory auditorium. Let us therefore examine this section of the Frater building more in detail, and trace its history up to the time of the purchase.

The Parlor was described as "a great room, paved," and was said to have been "used and occupied by the friars themselves to their own proper use as a parlor to dine and sup in."[1] Sir John Portynary, whose house adjoined the Duchy Chamber, tells us that in 1550, when King Edward granted the Blackfriars property to Cawarden, "Sir Thomas Cawarden, knight, entered into the same house in the name of all that which the King had given him within the said friars, and made his lodging there; and about that time did invite this examinant and his wife to supper there, together with diverse other gentlemen; and they all supped together with the said Sir Thomas Cawarden, in the same room [the Parlor] where the said school of fence is now kept, and did there see a play."[2]

Later Cawarden leased the Parlor to a keeper of an ordinary: "One Woodman did hold the said house where the said school of fence is kept, and another house thereby of Sir Thomas Cawarden, and in the other room kept an ordinary table, and had his way to the same through the said house where the said school of fence is kept."[3]

[1] Feuillerat, *Blackfriars Records*, pp. 43, 47, 48.
[2] *Ibid.*, p. 52.   [3] *Ibid.*, p. 51.

In 1563 William Joyner established in the rooms the school of fence mentioned above, which was still flourishing in 1576.[1]

When in 1583 John Lyly became interested in the First Blackfriars Playhouse, he obtained a lease of the rooms, but it is not clear for what purpose. Later he sold the lease to Rocho Bonetti, the Italian fencing-master, who established there his famous school of fence.[2] In George Silver's *Paradoxes of Defence*, 1599, is a description of Bonetti's school, which will, I think, help us to reconstruct in our imagination the "great room, paved" which was destined to become Shakespeare's playhouse:

He caused to be fairely drawne and set round about the schoole all the Noblemen's and Gentlemen's Armes that were his schollers, and, hanging right under their Armes, their Rapiers, Daggers, Gloves of Male, and Gantlets. Also he had benches and stooles, the roome being verie large, for Gentlemen to sit about his schoole to behold his teaching.

He taught none commonly under twentie, fortie, fifty, or an hundred pounds. And because all things should be verie necessary for the Noblemen and Gentlemen, he had in his schoole a large square table, with a green carpet, done round with a verie brode rich fringe of gold; alwaies standing upon it a verie faire standish covered with crimson velvet, with inke, pens, pen-dust, and sealing-waxe, and quiers of verie excellent fine paper, gilded, readie for the Noblemen and Gentlemen (upon occasion) to write their letters, being then desirous to follow

---

[1] Feuillerat, *Blackfriars Records*, p. 121.   [2] *Ibid.*, p. 122.

THE SECOND BLACKFRIARS

their fight, to send their men to dispatch their businesse.

And to know how the time passed, he had in one corner of his Schoole, a Clocke, with a verie faire large diall; he had within that Schoole a roome the which he called his privie schoole, with manie weapons therein, where he did teach his schollers his secret fight, after he had perfectly taught them their rules. He was verie much loved in the Court.

We are further told by Silver that Bonetti took it upon himself "to hit anie Englishman with a thrust upon anie button." It is no wonder that Shakespeare ridiculed him in *Romeo and Juliet* as "the very butcher of a silk button," and laughed at his school and his fantastic fencing-terms:

Mercutio. Ah! the immortal "passado"! the "punto reverso"! the "hay"!
Benvolio. The what?
Mercutio. The pox of such antick, lisping, affecting fantasticoes! These new tuners of accents! — "By Jesu, a very good blade!"

At the date of the sale to Burbage, February 4, 1596, the fencing school of Bonetti, had become "those rooms and lodgings, with the kitchen thereunto adjoining, called the Middle Rooms or Middle Stories, late being in the tenure or occupation of Rocco Bonetti, and now being in the tenure or occupation of Thomas Bruskett, gentleman."

To make his playhouse Burbage removed all the partitions in the Middle Rooms, and restored the Parlor to its original form — a great room covering the entire breadth of the building, and extending fifty-two feet in length from north to south. To this he added the Hall at the north, which then existed as two rooms in the occupation of Peter Johnson. The Hall and Parlor when combined made an auditorium described as "per estimacionem in longitudine ab australe ad borealem partem eiusdem sexaginta et sex pedes assissæ sit plus sive minus, et in latitudine ab occidentale ad orientalem partem eiusdem quadraginto et sex pedes assissæ sit plus sive minus."[1] The forty-six feet of width corresponds to the interior width of the Frater building, for although it was fifty-two feet wide in outside measurement, the stone walls were three feet thick. The sixty-six feet of length probably represents the fifty-two feet of the Parlor plus the breadth of the Hall.

The ceiling of these two rooms must have been of unusual height. The Infirmary, which was below the Parliament Chamber at the south, was three stories high; and the windows of the Parlor, if we may believe Pierce the Ploughman, were "wrought as a chirche":

> An halle for an heygh kinge · an household to holden,
> With brode bordes abouten · y-benched well clene,
> With windowes of glas · wrought as a chirche.

As a result Burbage was able to construct within the auditorium at least two galleries,[2] after the

---

[1] Wallace, *The Children of the Chapel at Blackfriars*, p. 39, note 1.
[2] Mr. Wallace, *The Children of the Chapel at Blackfriars*, p. 42, quotes from the Epilogue to Marston's *The Dutch Courtesan*, acted at Blackfriars, "And now, my fine Heliconian gallants,

REMAINS OF BLACKFRIARS

This remnant of the old monastery was discovered in 1872 on the rebuilding of the offices of *The Times*. It illustrates the substantial character of the Blackfriars buildings, and may even be apart of the old Frater, for *The Times* occupies that portion of the monastery. The windows of the Frater, according to Pierce the Ploughman, were "wrought as a chirche." (From a painting in the Guildhall Museum.)

manner of the public theatres. The Parliament Chamber above was kept, as I have stated, for residential purposes. This is why the various legal documents almost invariably refer to the playhouse as "that great hall or room, with the rooms over the same." [1]

The main entrance to the playhouse was at the north, over the "great yard" which extended from the Pipe Office to Water Lane.[2] The stage was opposite this entrance, or at the southern end of the hall, as is shown by one of the documents printed by Mr. Wallace.[3] Since the building was not, like the other playhouses of London, open to the sky, the illumination was supplied by candles, hung in branches over the stage; as Gerschow noted, after visiting Blackfriars, "alle bey Lichte agiret, welches ein gross Ansehen macht." [4] The obvious advantage of artificial light for producing beautiful stage effects must have added not a little to the popularity of the Blackfriars Playhouse.

and you, my worshipful friends in the middle region," and adds that the "reference to 'the middle region' makes it clear there were three" galleries. Does it not, however, indicate that there were only two galleries?

[1] See the documents printed in Fleay's *A Chronicle History of the London Stage*, pp. 211, 215, 240, etc. Mr. Wallace, however (*The Children of the Chapel at Blackfriars*, p. 40 ff.), would have us believe that an additional story was added: "the roof was changed, and rooms, probably of the usual dormer sort, were built above." I am quite sure he is mistaken.

[2] Cf. Playhouse Yard in the London of to-day.

[3] *The Children of the Chapel at Blackfriars*, p. 43, note 3.

[4] *The Diary of the Duke of Stettin-Pomerania*, in *Transactions of the Royal Historical Society* (1892), VI, 26.

The cost of all the alterations and the equipment could hardly have been less than £300, so that the total cost of the property was at least £900, or in modern valuation approximately $35,000. Burbage's sons, in referring to the building years later, declared that their father had "made it into a playhouse with great charge."

"And," they added significantly, "with great trouble." The aristocratic inhabitants of the Blackfriars precinct did not welcome the appearance in their midst of a "public," or, as some more scornfully designated it, a "common," playhouse; and when they discovered the intentions of Burbage, they wrote a strong petition to the Privy Council against the undertaking. This petition, presented to the Council in November, 1596, I quote below in part:

To the right honorable the Lords and others of Her Majesty's most honorable Privy Council. — Humbly shewing and beseeching your honors, the inhabitants of the precinct of the Blackfriars, London, that whereas one Burbage hath lately bought certain rooms in the same precinct near adjoining unto the dwelling houses of the right honorable the Lord Chamberlaine [Lord Cobham] and the Lord of Hunsdon, which rooms the said Burbage is now altering, and meaneth very shortly to convert and turn the same into a common playhouse, which will grow to be a very great annoyance and trouble, not only to all the noblemen and gentlemen thereabout inhabiting, but also a general inconvenience to all the inhabitants of the same precinct, both by rea-

THE SECOND BLACKFRIARS 199

son of the great resort and gathering together of all manner of vagrant and lewd persons ... as also for that there hath not at any time heretofore been used any common playhouse within the same precinct, but that now all players being banished by the Lord Mayor from playing within the city ... they now think to plant themselves in liberties, etc.[1]

The first person to sign the petition was the Dowager Lady Elizabeth Russell; the second was none other than George Cary, Lord Hunsdon, at the time the patron of Burbage's company of actors.[2] It is not surprising, therefore, that as a result of this petition the Lords of the Privy Council (of which Lord Cobham was a conspicuous member) issued an order in which they "forbad the use of the said house for plays."[3] This order wrecked the plans of Burbage quite as effectively as did the stubbornness of Gyles Alleyn.

Possibly the mental distress Burbage suffered at the hands of the Privy Council and of Gyles Alleyn affected his health; at least he did not long survive this last sling of fortune. In February, 1597, just before the expiration of the Alleyn lease, he died, leaving the Theatre to his son Cuthbert, the bookseller, Blackfriars to his actor-son, Richard, the star of Shakespeare's troupe, and his troubles to

---

[1] For the full document see Halliwell-Phillipps, *Outlines*, I, 304. For the date, see The Malone Society's *Collections*, I, 91.
[2] Shortly after this he was appointed Lord Chamberlain, under which name his troupe was subsequently known.
[3] Petition of 1619, The Malone Society's *Collections*, I, 91.

both. With good reason Cuthbert declared many years later that the ultimate success of London theatres had "been purchased by the infinite cost and pains of the family of Burbages."

When later in 1597 the Lord Chamberlain's Players were forced to leave Cuthbert's Theatre, Richard Burbage was not able to establish them in his comfortable Blackfriars house; instead, they first went to the old Curtain in Shoreditch, and then, under the leadership of the Burbage sons, erected for themselves a brand-new home on the Bankside, called "The Globe."

The order of the Privy Council had summarily forbidden the use of Blackfriars as a "public" playhouse. Its proprietor, however, Richard Burbage, might take advantage of the precedent established in the days of Farrant, and let the building for use as a "private" theatre.[1] Exactly when he was first able to lease the building as a "private" house we do not know, for the history of the building between 1597 (when it was completed) and 1600 (when it was certainly occupied by the Children of the Chapel) is very indistinct. We have no definite evidence to connect the Chapel Children, or, indeed, any specific troupe, with Blackfriars during these years. Yet prior to 1600 the building seems to have been used for acting. Richard Bur-

---

[1] The constables and other officers in the Petition of 1619 say: "The owner of the said playhouse, doth under the name of a private house . . . convert the said house to a public playhouse." (The Malone Society's *Collections*, I, 91.)

THE SECOND BLACKFRIARS

bage himself seems to say so. In leasing the building to Evans, in 1600, he says that he considered "with himself that" Evans could not pay the rent "except the said Evans could erect and keep a company of playing-boys or others to play plays and interludes in the said playhouse in such sort *as before time had been there used.*"[1] Now, unless this refers to Farrant's management of the Chapel Boys in Blackfriars — nearly a quarter of a century earlier — it means that before 1600 some actors, presumably "playing-boys," had used Burbage's theatre. Moreover, there seems to be evidence to show that the troupe thus vaguely referred to was under the management of Evans; for, in referring to his lease of Blackfriars in 1600, Evans describes the playhouse as "then or late in the tenure or occupation of your said oratour."[2] What these vague references mean we cannot now with our limited knowledge determine. But there is not sufficient evidence to warrant the usual assumption that Evans and Giles had opened the Blackfriars with the Children of the Chapel in 1597.[3]

The known history of Blackfriars as a regular theatre may be said to begin in the autumn of 1600. On September 2 of that year, Henry Evans signed a lease of the playhouse for a period of twenty-one years, at an annual rental of £40. This interesting

[1] Fleay, *A Chronicle History of the London Stage*, p. 234.
[2] *Ibid.*, p. 211.
[3] This theory has been urged by Fleay, by Mr. Wallace in *The Children of the Chapel at Blackfriars*, and by others.

step on the part of Evans calls for a word of explanation as to his plans.

The Children of the Chapel Royal, who had attained such glory at Blackfriars during the Farrant-Hunnis-Evans-Oxford-Lyly régime, had thereafter sunk into dramatic insignificance. Since 1584, when Lyly was forced to give up his playhouse, they had not presented a play at Court. Probably they did not entirely cease to act, for they can be vaguely traced in the provinces during a part of this period; but their dramatic glory was almost wholly eclipsed. Evans, who had managed the Boys under Hunnis, Oxford, and Lyly, hoped now to reëstablish the Children of the Chapel at Blackfriars as they had been in his younger days. Like James Burbage, he was a man of ideas. His plan was to interest in his undertaking the Master of the Chapel, Nathaniel Giles, who had succeeded to the office at the death of Hunnis in 1597, and then to make practical use of the patent granted to the Masters of the Children to take up boys for Her Majesty's service. Such a patent, in the normal course of events, had been granted to Giles, as it had been to his predecessors. It read in part as follows:

Elizabeth, by the grace of God, &c., to all mayors, sheriffs, bailiffs, constables, and all other our officers, greeting. For that it is meet that our Chapel Royal should be furnished with well-singing children from time to time, we have, and by these pres-

THE SECOND BLACKFRIARS 203

ents do authorize our well-beloved servant, Nathaniel Giles, Master of our Children of our said Chapel, or his deputy, being by his bill subscribed and sealed, so authorized, and having this our present commission with him, to take such and so many children as he, or his sufficient deputy, shall think meet, in all cathedral, collegiate, parish churches, chapels, or any other place or places, as well within liberty as without, within this our realm of England, whatsoever they be.[1]

In such a commission Evans saw wonderful possibilities. He reasoned that since the Queen had forced upon the Chapel Children the twofold service of singing at royal worship and of acting plays for royal entertainment, this twofold service should be met by a twofold organization, the one part designed mainly to furnish sacred music, the other designed mainly to furnish plays. Such a dual organization, it seemed to him, was now more or less necessary, since the number of boy choristers in the Chapel Royal was limited to twelve, whereas the acting of plays demanded at least twice as many. Once the principle that the Chapel Royal should supply the Queen with plays was granted, the commission could be used to furnish the necessary actors; and the old fiction, established by Farrant and Hunnis, of using a "private" playhouse as a means of exercising or training the boys for Court service, would enable the promoters to give public

---

[1] The full commission is printed in Wallace, *The Children of the Chapel at Blackfriars*, p. 61.

performances and thus handsomely reimburse themselves for their trouble.

Such was Evans's scheme, based upon his former experience with the Children at Farrant's Blackfriars, and suggested, perhaps, by the existence of Burbage's Blackfriars now forbidden to the "common" players. He presented his scheme to Giles, the Master of the Children; and Giles, no doubt, presented it at Court; for he would hardly dare thus abuse the Queen's commission, or thus make a public spectacle of the royal choristers, without in some way first consulting Her Majesty, and securing at least her tacit consent. That Giles and Evans did secure royal permission to put their scheme into operation is certain, although the exact nature of this permission is not clear. Later, for misdemeanors on the part of the management, the Star Chamber ordered "that all assurances made to the said Evans concerning the said house, or plays, or interludes, should be utterly void, and to be delivered up to be cancelled." [1]

Armed with these written "assurances," and with the royal commission to take up children, Evans and Giles began to form their company. This explains the language used by Heminges and Burbage: "let the said playhouse unto Henry Evans . . . who intended then presently to erect or set up a company of boys." [2] Their method of

[1] Fleay, *A Chronicle History of the London Stage*, p. 248.
[2] *Ibid.*, p. 234. Note that Evans is not to "continue" a troupe there, as Fleay and Wallace believe, but to "erect" one.

THE SECOND BLACKFRIARS

recruiting players may best be told by Henry Clifton, in his complaint to the Queen:

> But so it is, most excellent Sovereign, that the said Nathaniel Giles, confederating himself with one James Robinson, Henry Evans, and others,[1] yet unto Your Majesty's said subject unknown how [many], by color of Your Majesty's said letters patents, and the trust by Your Highness thereby to him, the said Nathaniel Giles, committed, endeavoring, conspiring, and complotting how to oppress diverse of Your Majesty's humble and faithful subjects, and thereby to make unto themselves an unlawful gain and benefit, they, the said confederates, devised, conspired, and concluded, for their own corrupt gain and lucre, to erect, set up, furnish, and maintain a playhouse, or place in the Blackfriars, within Your Majesty's city of London; and to the end they might the better furnish their said plays and interludes with children, whom they thought most fittest to act and furnish the said plays, they, the said confederates, abusing the authority and trust by Your Highness to him, the said Nathaniel Giles, and his deputy or deputies, by Your Highness's said letters patents given and reposed, hath, sithence Your Majesty's last free and general pardon, most wrongfully, unduly, and unjustly taken diverse and several children from diverse and sundry schools of learning and other places, and apprentices to men of trade from their masters, no way fitting for Your Majesty's service in or for your Chapel Royal, but the children have so taken and employed in acting and furnishing of the said plays and interludes, so by them complotted and

[1] Possibly Robinson and the "others" were merely deputies.

agreed to be erected, furnished, and maintained, against the wills of the said children, their parents, tutors, masters, and governors, and to the no small grief and oppressions [of] Your Majesty's true and faithful subjects. Amongst which numbers, so by the persons aforesaid and their agents so unjustly taken, used and employed, they have unduly taken and so employed one John Chappell, a grammar school scholar of one Mr. Spykes School near Cripplegate, London; John Motteram, a grammar scholar in the free school at Westminster; Nathaniel Field, a scholar of a grammar school in London kept by one Mr. Monkaster;[1] Alvery Trussell, an apprentice to one Thomas Gyles; one Phillipp Pykman and [one] Thomas Grymes, apprentices to Richard and George Chambers; Salmon Pavy,[2] apprentice to one Peerce; being children no way able or fit for singing, nor by any the said confederates endeavoured to be taught to sing, but by them, the said confederates, abusively employed, as aforesaid, only in plays and interludes.[3]

In spite of the obvious animosity inspiring Clifton's words, we get from his complaint a clear notion of how Evans and Giles supplemented the Children of the Chapel proper with actors. In a short time they brought together at Blackfriars a remarkable troupe of boy-players, who, with Jonson and Chapman as their poets, began to astonish London. For, in spite of certain limitations, "the

[1] Field became later famous both as an actor and playwright. His portrait is preserved at Dulwich College.
[2] Salathiel Pavy, whose excellent acting is celebrated in Jonson's tender elegy, quoted in part below.
[3] Star Chamber Proceedings, printed in full by Fleay, *op. cit.*, p. 127.

THE SECOND BLACKFRIARS

children" could act with a charm and a grace that often made them more attractive than their grown-up rivals. Middleton advises the London gallant "to call in at the Blackfriars, where he should see a nest of boys able to ravish a man." [1] Jonson gives eloquent testimony to the power of little Salathiel Pavy to portray the character of old age:

> Years he numbered scarce thirteen
>   When Fates turned cruel,
> Yet three filled zodiacs had he been
>   The stage's jewel;
> And did act, what now we moan,
>   Old men so duly,
> As, sooth, the Parcae thought him one,
>   He played so truly.[2]

And Samuel Pepys records the effectiveness of a child-actor in the rôle of women: "One Kinaston, a boy, acted the Duke's sister, but made the loveliest lady that ever I saw in my life." [3]

Moreover, to expert acting these Boys of the Chapel Royal added the charms of vocal and instrumental music, for which many of them had been specially trained. The Duke of Stettin-Pomerania, who upon his grand tour of the European countries in 1602 attended a play at Blackfriars, bears eloquent testimony to the musical powers of the children: "For a whole hour before the play

[1] *Father Hubbard's Tales* (ed. Bullen, VIII, 77).
[2] Jonson, *Epigrams*, cxx, *An Epitaph on Salathiel Pavy, a Child of Queen Elizabeth's Chapel.*
[3] *Diary*, August 18, 1660.

begins, one listens to charming [*köstliche*] instrumental music played on organs, lutes, pandorins, mandolins, violins, and flutes; as, indeed, on this occasion, a boy sang *cum voce tremula* to the accompaniment of a bass-viol, so delightfully [*lieblich*] that, if the Nuns at Milan did not excel him, we had not heard his equal in our travels." [1] In addition, the Children were provided with splendid apparel — though not at the cost of the Queen, as Mr. Wallace contends.[2] Naturally they became popular. On January 6, 1601, they were summoned to Court to entertain Her Majesty — the first recorded performance of the Children of the Chapel at Court since the year 1584, when Sir William More closed the first Blackfriars.

Perhaps the most interesting testimony to the success of the Chapel Children in their new playhouse is that uttered by Shakespeare in *Hamlet* (1601), in which he speaks of the performances by the "little eyases" as a "late innovation." The success of the "innovation" had driven Shake-

---

[1] *The Diary of the Duke of Stettin-Pomerania*, printed in *Transactions of the Royal Historical Society* (1890). The diary was written by the Duke's tutor, Gerschow, at the express command of the Duke.

[2] It is hard to believe Mr. Wallace's novel theory that the Children of the Chapel were subsidized by Elizabeth, as presented in his otherwise valuable *The Children of the Chapel at Blackfriars*. Burbage and Heminges knew nothing of such a royal patronage at Blackfriars (see Fleay, *op. cit.*, p. 236), nor did Kirkham, the Yeoman of the Revels (*ibid.*, p. 248). Kirkham and his partners spent £600 on apparel, etc., according to Kirkham's statement.

speare and his troupe of grown-up actors to close the Globe and travel in the country, even though they had *Hamlet* as an attraction. The good-natured way in which Shakespeare treats the situation is worthy of special observation:

Ham. What players are they?
Ros. Even those you were wont to take delight in, the tragedians of the city.[1]
Ham. How chances it they travel? their residence, both in reputation and profit, was better both ways.[2]
Ros. I think their inhibition comes by means of the late innovation.
Ham. Do they hold the same estimation they did when I was in the city? are they so followed?
Ros. No, indeed, they are not!
Ham. How comes it? do they grow rusty?
Ros. Nay, their endeavour keeps in the wonted pace; but there is, sir, an aerie of children,[3] little eyases, that cry out on the top of question, and are most tyrannically clapped for 't. These are now the fashion, and so berattle the "common stages" — so they call them — that many wearing rapiers [i.e., gallants] are afraid of goosequills, and dare scarce come thither.
Ham. What! are they children? who maintains 'em? how are they escoted? Will they pursue the quality no longer than they can sing?

The passage ends with the question from Hamlet: "Do the boys carry it away?" which gives Rosencrantz an opportunity to pun on the sign of

---

[1] The Children were acting light comedies such as *Cynthia's Revels;* the Lord Chamberlain's Men were acting *Hamlet*.
[2] Shakespeare's troupe is known to have been traveling in the spring of 1601.
[3] Cf. Middleton's *Father Hubbard's Tales*, already quoted, "a nest of boys." Possibly the idea was suggested by the fact that the children were lodged and fed in the building.

the Globe Playhouse: "Ay, that they do, my lord; Hercules and his load, too."

Shortly after the great dramatist had penned these words, the management of Blackfriars met with disaster. The cause, however, went back to December 13, 1600, when Giles and Evans were gathering their players. In their overweening confidence they made a stupid blunder in "taking up" for their troupe the only son and heir of Henry Clifton, a well-to-do gentleman of Norfolk, who had come to London for the purpose of educating the boy. Clifton says in his complaint that Giles, Evans, and their confederates, "well knowing that your subject's said son had no manner of sight in song, nor skill in music," on the 13th day of December, 1600, did "waylay the said Thomas Clifton" as he was "walking quietly from your subject's said house towards the said school," and "with great force and violence did seize and surprise, and him with like force and violence did, to the great terror and hurt of him, the said Thomas Clifton, haul, pull, drag, and carry away to the said playhouse." As soon as the father learned of this, he hurried to the playhouse and "made request to have his said son released." But Giles and Evans "utterly and scornfully refused to do" this. Whereupon Clifton threatened to complain to the Privy Council. But Evans and Giles "in very scornful manner willed your said subject to complain to whom he would." Clifton suggested that "it was not fit that a gentle-

THE SECOND BLACKFRIARS

man of his sort should have his son and heir (and that his only son) to be so basely used." Giles and Evans "most arrogantly then and there answered that they had authority sufficient so to take any nobleman's son in this land"; and further to irritate the father, they immediately put into young Thomas's hand "a scroll of paper, containing part of one of their said plays or interludes, and him, the said Thomas Clifton, commanded to learn the same by heart," with the admonition that "if he did not obey the said Evans, he should be surely whipped." [1]

Clifton at once appealed to his friend, Sir John Fortescue, a member of the Privy Council, at whose order young Thomas was released and sent back to his studies. Apparently this ended the episode. But Clifton, nourishing his animosity, began to investigate the management of Blackfriars, and to collect evidence of similar abuses of the Queen's commission, with the object of making complaint to the Star Chamber. In October, 1601, Evans, it seems, learned of Clifton's purpose, for on the 21st of that month he deeded all his property to his son-in-law, Alexander Hawkins.[2] Clifton finally presented his complaint to the Star Chamber on December 15, 1601,[3] but his complaint was probably not acted on until early in 1602, for during the

[1] The full complaint is printed by Fleay, *op. cit.*, p. 127.
[2] *Ibid.*, pp. 244–45.
[3] Wallace, *The Children of the Chapel at Blackfriars*, p. 84, note 4.

Christmas holidays the Children were summoned as usual to present their play before the Queen.[1]

Shortly after this, however, the Star Chamber passed on Clifton's complaint. The decree itself is lost, but the following reference to it is made in a subsequent lawsuit: "The said Evans ... was censured by the right honorable Court of Star Chamber for his unorderly carriage and behaviour in taking up of gentlemen's children against their wills and to employ them for players, and for other misdemeanors in the said Decree contained; and further that all assurances made to the said Evans concerning the said house or plays or interludes

---

[1] On December 29, 1601, Sir Dudley Carleton wrote to his friend John Chamberlain: "The Queen dined this day privately at My Lord Chamberlain's. I came even now from the Blackfriars, where I saw her at the play with all her *candidæ auditrices*." From this it has been generally assumed that Elizabeth visited the playhouse in Blackfriars to see the Children act there; and Mr. Wallace, in his *The Children of the Chapel at Blackfriars*, pp. 26, 87, 95–97, lays great emphasis upon it to show that the Queen was directly responsible for establishing and managing the Children at Blackfriars. But the assumption that the Queen attended a performance at the Blackfriars Playhouse is, I think, unwarranted. The Lord Chamberlain at this time was Lord Hunsdon, who lived "in the Blackfriars." No doubt on this Christmas occasion he entertained the Queen with a great dinner, and after the dinner with a play given, not in a playhouse, but in his mansion. (Lord Cobham, who was formerly Lord Chamberlain, and who also lived in Blackfriars, had similarly entertained the Queen with plays "in Blackfriars"; cf. also The Malone Society's *Collections*, II, 52.) Furthermore, the actors on this occasion were probably not the Children of the Chapel, as Mr. Wallace thinks, but Lord Hunsdon's own troupe. Possibly one of Shakespeare's new plays (*Hamlet* ?) was then presented before the Queen for the first time.

THE SECOND BLACKFRIARS 213

should be utterly void, and to be delivered up to be canceled." [1] Doubtless the decree fell with equal force upon Giles and the others connected with the enterprise, for after the Star Chamber decree Giles and Robinson disappear from the management of the playhouse. Evans was forbidden to have any connection with plays there; and for a time, no doubt, the building was closed.

Evans, however, still held the lease, and was under the necessity of paying the rent as before. Then came forward Edward Kirkham, who, in his official capacity as Yeoman of the Revels, had become acquainted with the dramatic activities of the Children of the Chapel. He saw an opportunity to take over the Blackfriars venture now that Evans and probably Giles had been forbidden by the Star Chamber to have any connection with plays in that building. Having associated with him William Rastell, a merchant, and Thomas Kendall,[2] a haberdasher, he made overtures to Evans, the owner of the lease. Evans, however, was determined to retain a half-interest in the playhouse, and to evade the order of the Star Chamber by using his son-in-law, Alexander Hawkins, as his agent. Accordingly, on April 20, 1602, "Articles of Agreement" were signed between Evans and Hawkins on the one part, and Kirkham, Rastell, and

---

[1] Fleay, *op. cit.*, p. 248.
[2] We find in Henslowe's *Diary* a player named William Kendall, but we do not know that he was related to Thomas.

Kendall on the other part, whereby the latter were admitted to a half-interest in the playhouse and in the troupe of child-actors. Kirkham, Rastell, and Kendall agreed to pay one-half of the annual rent of £40,[1] to pay one-half of the repairs on the building, and in addition to spend £400 on apparel and furnishings for the troupe. Under this reorganization — with Evans as a secret partner — the Children continued to act with their customary success.

About a month later, however, Lord Hunsdon, the Lord Chamberlain, whose house adjoined Blackfriars, seems to have inquired into the affairs of the new organization.[2] What Kirkham told him led him to order Evans off the premises. Evans informs us that he was "commanded by his Lordship to avoid and leave the same; for fear of whose displeasure, the complainant [Evans] was forced to leave the country."[3] He felt it prudent to remain away from London "for a long space and time"; yet he "lost nothing," for "he left the said Alexander Hawkins to deal for him and to take such benefit of the said house as should belong unto him in his absence."[4]

If we may judge from the enthusiastic account given by the Duke of Stettin-Pomerania, who vis-

[1] The agreements remind one of the organization of the Globe. It seems clear that Kirkham, Rastell, and Kendall held their moiety in joint tenancy.
[2] Fleay, *op. cit.*, pp. 211–13; 216; 220.
[3] *Ibid.*, p. 220. [4] *Ibid.*, p. 217.

THE SECOND BLACKFRIARS 215

ited Blackfriars in the September following, the Children were just as effective under Kirkham's management as they had been under the management of Giles and Evans. It is to be noted, however, that Elizabeth did not again invite the Blackfriars troupe to the Court.

The death of the Queen in 1603 led to the closing of all playhouses. This was followed by a long attack of the plague, so that for many months Blackfriars was closed, and "by reason thereof no such profit and commodity was raised and made of and by the said playhouse as was hoped for." [1] Evans actually "treated" with Richard Burbage "about the surrendering and giving up the said lease," but Burbage declined to consider the matter.

Shortly after this the plague ceased, and acting, stimulated by King James's patronage, was resumed with fervor. The Blackfriars Company was reorganized under Edward Kirkham, Alexander Hawkins (acting for Evans), Thomas Kendall, and Robert Payne; and on February 4, 1604, it secured a royal patent to play under the title "The Children of the Queen's Revels." [2] According to this

[1] Fleay, *op. cit.*, p. 235.
[2] For the patent, commonly misdated January 30, see The Malone Society's *Collections*, 1, 267. Mr. Wallace, in *The Century Magazine* (September, 1910, p. 747), says that the company secured its patent "through the intercessions of the poet Samuel Daniel." It is true that the Children of Her Majesty's Royal Chamber of Bristol secured their patent in 1615 at the intercession of Daniel, but I know of no evidence that he intervened in behalf of the Blackfriars troupe.

patent, the poet Samuel Daniel was specially appointed to license their plays: "Provided always that no such plays or shows shall be presented before the said Queen our wife by the said Children, or by them anywhere publicly acted, but by the approbation and allowance of Samuel Daniel, whom her pleasure is to appoint for that purpose." At this time, too, or not long after, John Marston was allowed a share in the organization, and thus was retained as one of its regular playwrights.

The success of the new company is indicated by the fact that it was summoned to present a play at Court in February, 1604, and again two plays in January, 1605. Evans's activity in the management of the troupe in spite of the order of the Star Chamber is evident from the fact that the payment for the last two court performances was made directly to him.

In the spring of 1604 the company gave serious offense by acting Samuel Daniel's *Philotas*, which was supposed to relate to the unfortunate Earl of Essex; but the blame must have fallen largely on Daniel, who not only wrote the play, but also licensed its performance. He was summoned before the Privy Council to explain, and seems to have fully proved his innocence. Shortly after this he published the play with an apology affixed.[1]

The following year the Children gave much more

---

[1] A letter from Daniel to the Earl of Devonshire vindicating the play is printed in Grosart's *Daniel*, i, xxii.

serious offense by acting *Eastward Hoe*, a comedy in which Marston, Chapman, and Jonson collaborated. Not only did the play ridicule the Scots in general, and King James's creation of innumerable knights in particular, but one of the little actors was actually made, it seems, to mimic the royal brogue: "I ken the man weel; he is one of my thirty pound Knights." Marston escaped by timely flight, but Jonson and Chapman were arrested and lodged in jail, and were for a time in some danger of having their nostrils slit and their ears cropped. Both Chapman and Jonson asserted that they were wholly innocent, and Chapman openly put the blame of the offensive passages on Marston.[1] Marston, however, was beyond the reach of the King's wrath, so His Majesty punished instead the men in control of Blackfriars. It was discovered that the manager, Kirkham, had presented the play without securing the Lord Chamberlain's allowance. As a result, he and the others in charge of the Children were prohibited from any further connection with the playhouse. This doubtless explains the fact that Kirkham shortly after appears as one of the managers of Paul's Boys.[2] It explains, also, the following statement made by Evans in the course of one of the later legal documents: "After the King's most excellent Majesty, upon some mis-

[1] See Dobell, "Newly Discovered Documents," in *The Athenæum*, March 30, 1901.
[2] Cunningham, *Revels*, p. xxxviii.

demeanors committed in or about the plays there, *and specially upon the defendant's* [Kirkham's] *acts and doings there,* had prohibited that no plays should be more used there," etc.[1] Not only was Kirkham driven from the management of the troupe and the playhouse closed for a time, but the Children were denied the Queen's patronage. No longer were they allowed to use the high-sounding title "The Children of the Queen's Majesty's Revels"; instead, we find them described merely as "The Children of the Revels," or as "The Children of Blackfriars."[2]

For a time, no doubt, affairs at the playhouse were at a standstill. Evans again sought to surrender his lease to Burbage, but without success.[3] Marston, having escaped the wrath of the King by flight, decided to end his career as a playwright and turn country parson. It was shortly after this, in all probability, that he sold his share in the Blackfriars organization to one Robert Keysar, a goldsmith of London, for the sum of £100.[4]

Keysar, it seems, undertook to reopen the playhouse, and to continue the Children there at his own expense.[5] From the proprietors he rented the playhouse, the stock of apparel, the furnishings,

---

[1] Fleay, *op. cit.*, p. 221.
[2] Except carelessly, as when sometimes called "The Children of the Chapel."
[3] Wallace, *Shakespeare and his London Associates*, p. 82.
[4] *Ibid.*, pp. 81, 86, 89, 93.
[5] Wallace, *Shakespeare and his London Associates*, p. 80 ff.

THE SECOND BLACKFRIARS 219

and playbooks. This, I take it, explains the puzzling statement made by Kirkham some years later:

> This repliant [Kirkham] and his said partners [Rastell and Kendall] have had and received the sum of one hundred pounds per annum for their part and moiety in the premises without any manner of charges whatsoever [i.e., during Kirkham's management of the troupe prior to 1605].[1] And after that this replyant and his said partners had received the foresaid profits [i.e., after Kirkham and his partners had to give up the management of the Children in 1605], the said Children, which the said Evans in his answer affirmeth to be the Queen's Children [i.e., they are no longer the Queen's Children, for after 1605 they had been deprived of the Queen's patronage; but Kirkham was in error, for Evans with legal precision had referred to the company as 'The Queen's Majesty's Children of the Revels (for so it was often called)'] were masters themselves [i.e., their own managers], and this complainant and his said partners received of them, and of one Keysar who was interest with them, above the sum of one hundred and fifty pounds per annum only for the use of the said great hall, without all manner of charges, as this replyant will make it manifest to this honorable court.[2]

Under Keysar's management the Blackfriars troupe continued to act as the Children of the

---

[1] That is, £33, more or less, a share. We have documentary evidence to show that a share in the Red Bull produced £30, and a share in the Globe £30 to £40 per annum.

[2] Fleay, *op. cit.*, p. 249. The yearly rental must have included not only the playhouse and its equipment, but the playbooks, apparel, properties, etc., belonging to the Children. These were on July 26, 1608, divided up among the sharers, Kirkham, Rastell, Kendall, and Evans.

Revels. But, unfortunately, they had not learned wisdom from their recent experience, and in the very following year we find them again in serious trouble. John Day's *Isle of Guls*, acted in February, 1606, gave great offense to the Court. Sir Edward Hoby, in a letter to Sir Thomas Edwards,[1] writes: "At this time was much speech of a play in the Blackfriars, where, in the *Isle of Guls*, from the highest to the lowest, all men's parts were acted of two diverse nations. As I understand, sundry were committed to Bridewell." [2]

The Children, however, were soon allowed to resume playing, and they continued for a time without mishap. But in the early spring of 1608 they committed the most serious offense of all by acting Chapman's *Conspiracy and Tragedy of Charles, Duke of Byron*. The French Ambassador took umbrage at the uncomplimentary representation of the contemporary French Court, and had an order made forbidding them to act the play. But the Children, "voyant toute la Cour dehors, ne laisserent de la faire, et non seulement cela, mais y introduiserent la Reine et Madame de Ver-

---

[1] Birch, *Court and Times of James the First*, I, 60; quoted by E. K. Chambers, in *Modern Language Review*, IV, 158.

[2] Possibly an aftermath of the King's displeasure is to be found in the cancellation of Giles's long-standing commission to take up boys for the Chapel, and the issuance of a new commission to him, November 7, 1606, with the distinct proviso that "none of the said choristers or children of the Chapel so to be taken by force of this commission shall be used or employed as commedians or stage players." (The Malone Society's *Collections*, I, 357.)

THE SECOND BLACKFRIARS

neuil, traitant celle-ci fort mal de paroles, et lui donnant un soufflet." Whereupon the French Ambassador made special complaint to Salisbury, who ordered the arrest of the author and the actors. "Toutefois il ne s'en trouva que trois, qui aussi-tôt furent menés à la prison où ils sont encore; mais le principal, qui est le compositeur, échapa."[1] The Ambassador observes also that a few days before the Children of the Revels had given offense by a play on King James: "Un jour ou deux avant, ils avoient dépêché leur Roi, sa mine d'Ecosse, et tous ses Favoris d'une étrange sorte; car aprés lui avoir fait dépiter le Ciel sur le vol d'un oisseau, et fait battre un Gentilhomme pour avoir rompu ses chiens, ils le dépeignoient ivre pour le moins une fois le jour."[2] As a result of these two offenses, coming as a climax to a long series of such offenses, the King was "extrêmement irrité contre ces

---

[1] From the report of the French Ambassador, M. de la Boderie, to M. de Puisieux at Paris, *Ambassades de Monsieur de la Boderie en Angleterre*, 1750, III, 196; quoted by E. K. Chambers in *Modern Language Review*, IV, 158.

[2] The name of this play is not known; probably the King was satirized in a comic scene foisted upon an otherwise innocent piece. Mr. Wallace, in *The Century Magazine* (September, 1910, p. 747), says: "From a document I have found in France the Blackfriars boys now satirized the King's efforts to raise money, made local jokes on the recent discovery of his silver mine in Scotland, brought him on the stage as drunk, and showed such to be his condition at least three times a day, caricatured him in his favorite pastime of hawking, and represented him as swearing and cursing at a gentleman for losing a bird." I do not know what document Mr. Wallace has found; the French document quoted above has been known for a long time.

marauds-là," and gave order for their immediate suppression. This marked the end of the child-actors at Blackfriars.

Naturally Kirkham, Rastell, and Kendall, since there was "no profit made of the said house, but a continual rent of forty pounds to be paid for the same," became sick of their bargain with Evans. An additional reason for their wishing to withdraw finally from the enterprise was the rapid increase of the plague, which about July 25 closed all playhouses. So Kirkham, "at or about the 26 of July, 1608, caused the apparrels, properties, and goods belonging to the copartners, sharers, and masters" to be divided. Kirkham and his associates took away their portions, and "quit the place," the one-time manager using to Evans some unkind words: "said he would deal no more with it, 'for,' quod he, 'it is a base thing,' or used words to such or very like effect." [1] Evans, thus deserted by Kirkham, Rastell, and Kendall, regarded the organization of the Blackfriars as dissolved; he "delivered up their commission which he had under the Great Seal authorizing them to play, and discharged diverse of the partners and poets."

Robert Keysar, however, the old manager, laid plans to keep the Children together, and continue them as a troupe after the cessation of the plague. For a while, we are told, he maintained them at his own expense, "in hope to have enjoyed his said

[1] Fleay, *op. cit.*, pp. 221–22.

THE SECOND BLACKFRIARS 223

bargain ... upon the ceasing of the general sickness."[1] And he expected, by virtue of the share he had purchased from John Marston, to be able to use the Blackfriars Playhouse for his purpose.

In the meanwhile Evans began negotiations with Burbage for the surrender of the lease: "By reason the said premises lay then and had long lyen void and without use for plays, whereby the same became not only burthensome and unprofitable unto the said Evans, but also ran far into decay for want of reparations ... the said Evans began to treat with the said Richard Burbage about a surrender of the said Evans his said lease."[2] This time Burbage listened to the proposal, for he and his fellow-actors at the Globe "considered that the house would be fit for themselves." So in August, 1608, he agreed to take over the building for the use of the King's Men.

Even after Evans's surrender of the lease, Keysar, it seems, made an effort to keep the Children together. On the following Christmas, 1608–09, we find a record of payment to him for performances at Court, by "The Children of Blackfriars." But soon after this the troupe must have been disbanded. Keysar says that they were "enforced to be dispersed and turned away to the abundant hurt of the said young men";[3] and the Burbages and Heminges declare that the children "were dis-

---
[1] Wallace, *Shakespeare and his London Associates*, pp. 83, 97.
[2] *Ibid.*, p. 87.   [3] *Ibid.*, p. 90.

persed and driven each of them to provide for himself by reason that the plays ceasing in the City of London, either through sickness, or for some other cause, he, the said complainant [Keysar], was no longer able to maintain them together."[1] In the autumn of 1609, however, Keysar assembled the Children again, reorganized them with the assistance of Philip Rosseter, and placed them in Whitefriars Playhouse, recently left vacant by the disruption of the Children of His Majesty's Revels. Their subsequent history will be found related in the chapter dealing with that theatre.

When in August, 1608, Richard Burbage secured from Evans the surrender of the Blackfriars lease, he at once proceeded to organize from the Globe Company a syndicate to operate the building as a playhouse. He admitted to partnership in the new enterprise all of the then sharers in the Globe except Witter and Nichols, outsiders who had secured their interest through marriage with the heirs of Pope and Phillips, and who, therefore, were not entitled to any consideration. In addition, he admitted Henry Evans, doubtless in fulfillment of a condition in the surrender of the lease. The syndicate thus formed was made up of seven equal sharers, as follows: Richard Burbage, Cuthbert Burbage, Henry Evans, William Shakespeare, John Heminges, Henry Condell, and William Slye. These sharers leased the building from Richard

[1] Wallace, *Shakespeare and his London Associates*, p. 97.

THE SECOND BLACKFRIARS 225

Burbage for a period of twenty-one years,[1] at the old rental of £40 per annum, each binding himself to pay annually the sum of £5 14s. 4d.[2] The method of distributing the profits between the sharers (known as "housekeepers") and the actors (known as the "company") was to be the same as that practiced at the Globe.[3]

Soon after this organization was completed, the King's Men moved from the Globe to the Blackfriars. They did not, of course, intend to abandon the Globe. Their plan was to use the Blackfriars as a "winter home," and the Globe as a "summer house."[4] Malone observed from the Herbert Manuscript that "the King's Company usually began to play at the Globe in the month of May";[5] although he failed to state at what time in the autumn they usually moved to the Blackfriars, the evidence points to the first of November.

Such a plan had many advantages. For one thing, it would prevent the pecuniary losses often

[1] Twenty-one years was a very common term for a lease to run; but in this case, no doubt, it was intended that the lease of Blackfriars should last as long as the lease of the Globe, which then had exactly twenty-one years to run.

[2] Shortly after this agreement had been made William Slye died, and his executrix delivered up his share to Richard Burbage "to be cancelled and made void." See the Heminges-Osteler documents printed by Mr. Wallace in the London *Times*, October 4, 1909. In 1611 Burbage let William Osteler have this share.

[3] The method is clearly explained in the documents of 1635 printed by Halliwell-Phillipps, in *Outlines*, I, 312.

[4] See Wright, *Historia Histrionica*, Hazlitt's Dodsley, xv, 406.

[5] Malone, *Variorum*, III, 71.

caused by a severe winter. In the *Poetaster* (1601), Jonson makes Histrio, representing the Globe Players, say: "O, it will get us a huge deal of money, and we have need on 't, for this winter has made us all poorer than so many starved snakes; nobody comes at us."[1] This could not be said of the King's Men after they moved to the Blackfriars. Edward Kirkham, a man experienced in theatrical finances, offered to prove to the court in 1612 that the King's Men "got, and as yet doth, more in one winter in the said great hall by a thousand pounds than they were used to get on the Bankside."[2]

Kirkham's testimony as to the popularity of the King's Men in their winter home is borne out by a petition to the city authorities made by "the constables and other officers and inhabitants of Blackfriars" in January, 1619. They declared that to the playhouse "there is daily such resort of people, and such multitudes of coaches (whereof many are hackney-coaches, bringing people of all sorts), that sometimes all our streets cannot contain them, but that they clog up Ludgate also, in such sort that both they endanger the one the other, break down stalls, throw down men's goods from their shops, and the inhabitants there cannot come to their houses, nor bring in their necessary provisions of

---

[1] Act III, scene iv. Cf. also Webster's Preface to *The White Devil*, acted at the Red Bull about 1610.
[2] Fleay, *A Chronicle History of the London Stage*, p. 248.

THE SECOND BLACKFRIARS 227

beer, wood, coal, or hay, nor the tradesmen or shop-keepers utter their wares, nor the passenger go to the common water stairs without danger of their lives and limbs." "These inconveniences" were said to last "every day in the winter time from one or two of the clock till six at night." [1]

As a result of this petition the London Common Council ordered, January 21, 1619, that "the said playhouses be suppressed, and that the players shall from thenceforth forbear and desist from playing in that house." [2] But the players had at Court many influential friends, and these apparently came to their rescue. The order of the Common Council was not put into effect; and so far as we know the only result of this agitation was that King James on March 27 issued to his actors a new patent specifically giving them — described as his "well-beloved servants" — the right henceforth to play unmolested in Blackfriars. The new clause in the patent runs: "as well within their two their now usual houses called the Globe, within our County of Surrey, and their private house situate in the precinct of the Blackfriars, within our city of London." [3] At the accession of King Charles I, the patent was renewed, June 24, 1625, with the same clause regarding the use of Blackfriars.[4]

In 1631, however, the agitation was renewed,

[1] The Malone Society's *Collections*, I, 91.
[2] Halliwell-Phillipps, *Outlines*, I, 311.
[3] The Malone Society's *Collections*, I, 281.   [4] *Ibid.*, I, 282.

this time in the form of a petition from the churchwardens and constables of the precinct of Blackfriars to William Laud, then Bishop of London. The document gives such eloquent testimony to the popularity of the playhouse that I have inserted it below in full:

To the Right Honorable and Right Reverend Father in God, William, Lord Bishop of London, one of His Majesty's Honorable Privy Council. The humble petition of the churchwardens and constables of Blackfriars, on the behalf of the whole Parish, showing that by reason of a playhouse, exceedingly frequented, in the precinct of the said Blackfriars, the inhabitants there suffer many grievances upon the inconveniences hereunto annexed, and many other.

May it therefore please your Lordship to take the said grievances into your honorable consideration for the redressing thereof. And for the reviving the order, which hath been heretofore made by the Lords of the Council, and the Lord Mayor and the Court of Aldermen, for the removal of them. And they shall, according to their duties, ever pray for your Lordship.

> Reasons and Inconveniences Inducing the Inhabitants of Blackfriars, London, to Become Humble Suitors to Your Lordship for Removing the Playhouse in the Said Blackfriars:

1. The shopkeepers in divers places suffer much, being hindered by the great recourse to the plays (especially of coaches) from selling their commodities, and having their wares many times broken and beaten off their stalls.

2. The recourse of coaches is many times so great that the inhabitants cannot in an afternoon take in

any provision of beer, coals, wood, or hay, the streets being known to be so exceeding straight and narrow.

3. The passage through Ludgate to the water [i.e., Water Lane] is many times stopped up, people in their ordinary going much endangered, quarrels and bloodshed many times occasioned, and many disorderly people towards night gathered thither, under pretense of attending and waiting for those at the plays.

4. If there should happen any misfortune of fire, there is not likely any present order could possibly be taken, for the disorder and number of the coaches, since there could be no speedy passage made for quenching the fire, to the endangering of the parish and city.

5. Christenings and burials, which usually are in the afternoon, are many times disturbed, and persons endangered in that part, which is the greatest part of the parish.

6. Persons of honor and quality that dwell in the parish are restrained by the number of coaches from going out, or coming home in seasonable time, to the prejudice of their occasions. And some persons of honor have left, and others have refused houses for this very inconvenience, to the prejudice and loss of the parish.

7. The Lords of the Council in former times have by order directed that there shall be but two playhouses tolerated, and those *without the city*, the one at the Bankside, the other near Golding Lane (which these players still have and use all summer), which the Lords did signify by their letters to the Lord Mayor; and in performance thereof the Lord Mayor and the Court of Aldermen did give order that they should forbear to play any longer there, which the players

promised to the Lord Chief Justice of the Common Pleas (while he was Recorder of London) to observe, entreating only a little time to provide themselves elsewhere.[1]

Bishop Laud endorsed the petition with his own hand "To the Coun. Table," and in all probability he submitted it to the consideration of the Privy Council. If so, the Council took no action.

But in 1633, as a result of further complaints about the crowding of coaches, the Privy Council appointed a committee to estimate the value of the Blackfriars Theatre and "the buildings thereunto belonging," with the idea of removing the playhouse and paying the owners therefor. The committee reported that "the players demanded £21,000. The commissioners [Sir Henry Spiller, Sir William Beecher, and Laurence Whitaker] valued it at near £3000. The Parishioners offered towards the removing of them £100."[2] Obviously the plan of removal was not feasible, if indeed the Privy Council seriously contemplated such action. The only result of this second agitation was the

[1] Collier, *History of English Dramatic Poetry* (1879), I, 455.
[2] The *Calendar of State Papers, Domestic, 1633*, p. 293. The report of the commissioners in full, as printed by Collier in *New Facts* (1835), p. 27, and again in *History of English Dramatic Poetry* (1879), I, 477, is not above suspicion, although Mr. E. K. Chambers is inclined to think it genuine. According to this document the actors estimated the property to be worth £21,990, but the committee thought that the actors might be persuaded to accept £2900 13s. 4d.

THE SECOND BLACKFRIARS 231

issuance on November 20 of special instructions to coachmen: "If any persons, men or women, of what condition soever, repair to the aforesaid playhouse in coach, as soon as they are gone out of their coaches, the coachmen shall depart thence and not return till the end of the play."[1] Garrard, in a letter to the Lord Deputy dated January 9, 1633, says: "Here hath been an order of the Lords of the Council hung up in a table near Paul's and the Blackfriars to command all that resort to the playhouse there to send away their coaches, and to disperse abroad in Paul's Churchyard, Carter Lane, the Conduit in Fleet Street, and other places, and not to return to fetch their company, but they must trot afoot to find their coaches. 'T was kept very strictly for two or three weeks, but now I think it is disordered again."[2] The truth is that certain distinguished patrons of the theatre did not care "to trot afoot to find their coaches," and so made complaint at Court. As a result it was ordered, at a sitting of the Council, December 29, 1633 (the King being present): "Upon information this day given to the Board of the discommodity that diverse persons of great quality, especially Ladies and Gentlewomen, did receive in going to the playhouse of Blackfriars by reason that no coaches may stand ... the Board ... think fit to explain the said order in such manner that as many

---

[1] The Malone Society's *Collections*, I, 99; 387.
[2] *The Earl of Strafforde's Letters* (Dublin, 1740), I, 175.

coaches as may stand within the Blackfriars Gate may enter and stay there." [1]

All this agitation about coaches implies a fashionable and wealthy patronage of the Blackfriars. An interesting glimpse of high society at the theatre is given in a letter written by Garrard, January 25, 1636: "A little pique happened betwixt the Duke of Lenox and the Lord Chamberlain about a box at a new play in the Blackfriars, of which the Duke had got the key, which, if it had come to be debated betwixt them, as it was once intended, some heat or perhaps other inconvenience might have happened." [2] The Queen herself also sometimes went thither. Herbert records, without any comment, her presence there on the 13 of May, 1634.[3] It has been generally assumed that she attended a regular afternoon performance; but this, I am sure, was not the case. The Queen engaged the entire building for the private entertainment of herself and her specially invited guests, and the performance was at night. In a bill presented by the King's Men for plays acted before the members of the royal family during the year 1636 occurs the entry: "The 5th of May, at the Blackfryers, for the Queene and the Prince Elector . . . . . . *Alfonso.*" Again, in a similar bill for the year 1638 (see the bill on page 404) is the entry: "At the Blackfryers, the 23 of Aprill,

---

[1] The Malone Society's *Collections*, I, 388.
[2] *The Earl of Strafforde's Letters* (Dublin, 1740), I, 511.
[3] The Herbert MS., Malone, *Variorum*, III, 167.

THE SECOND BLACKFRIARS 233

for the Queene ...... *The Unfortunate Lovers.*" The fact that the actors did not record the loss of their "day" at their house, and made their charge accordingly, shows that the plays were given at night and did not interfere with the usual afternoon performances before the public.

The King's Men continued to occupy the Blackfriars as their winter home until the closing of the theatres in 1642. Thereafter the building must have stood empty for a number of years. In 1653 Sir Aston Cokaine, in a poem prefixed to Richard Brome's *Plays*, looked forward prophetically to the happy day when

> Black, and White Friars too, shall flourish again.

But the prophecy was not to be fulfilled; for although Whitefriars (i.e., Salisbury Court) did flourish as a Restoration playhouse, the more famous Blackfriars had ceased to exist before acting was allowed again. The manuscript note in the Phillipps copy of Stow's *Annals* (1631) informs us that "the Blackfriars players' playhouse in Blackfriars, London, which had stood many years, was pulled down to the ground on Monday the 6 day of August, 1655, and tenements built in the room." [1]

[1] See *The Academy*, 1882, xxii, 314. Exactly the same fate had overtaken the Globe ten years earlier.

CHAPTER XII
THE GLOBE

AS related more fully in the chapter on "The Theatre," when Cuthbert and Richard Burbage discovered that Gyles Alleyn not only refused to renew the lease for the land on which their playhouse stood, but was actually planning to seize the building and devote it to his private uses, they took immediate steps to thwart him. And in doing so they evolved a new and admirable scheme of theatrical management. They planned to bring together into a syndicate or stock-company some of the best actors of the day, and allow these actors to share in the ownership of the building. Hitherto playhouses had been erected merely as pecuniary investments by profit-seeking business men, — Burbage,[1] Brayne, Lanman, Henslowe, Cholmley, Langley, — and had been conducted in the interests of the proprietors rather than of the actors.[2] As a result, these proprietors had long reaped an unduly rich harvest from the efforts of the players,

---

[1] That even James Burbage is to be put in this class cannot be disputed.

[2] Cuthbert Burbage in 1635 says: "The players that lived in those first times had only the profits arising from the doors, but now the players receive all the comings-in at the doors to themselves and half the galleries from the housekeepers." (Halliwell-Phillipps, *Outlines*, I, 317.)

RICHARD BURBAGE
(Reproduced by permission from a painting in the Dulwich Picture Gallery; photograph by Emery Walker, Ltd.)

taking all or a large share of the income from the galleries. The new scheme was designed to remedy these faults.

For participation in this scheme the Burbages selected the following men: William Shakespeare, not only a successful actor, but a poet who had already made his reputation as a writer of plays, and who gave promise of greater attainments; John Heminges, a good actor and an exceptionally shrewd man of business, who until his death managed the pecuniary affairs of the company with distinguished success; Augustine Phillips and Thomas Pope, both ranked with the best actors of the day;[1] and William Kempe, the greatest comedian since Tarleton, described in 1600 as "a player in interludes, and partly the Queen's Majesty's jester." When to this group we add Richard Burbage himself, the Roscius of his age, we have an organization of business, histrionic, and poetic ability that could not be surpassed. It was carefully planned, and it deserved the remarkable success which it attained. The superiority of the Globe Company over all others was acknowledged in the days of James and Charles, and to-day stands out as one of the most impressive facts in the history of the early drama.

[1] See, for example, Thomas Heywood's *Apology for Actors* (1612). In enumerating the greatest actors of England he says: "Gabriel, Singer, Pope, Phillips, Sly — all the right I can do them is but this, that though they be dead, their deserts yet live in the remembrance of many."

According to the original plan there were to be ten shares in the new enterprise, the Burbage brothers holding between them one-half the stock, or two and a half shares each, and the five actors holding the other half, or one share each. All the expenses of leasing a site, erecting a building, and subsequently operating the building as a playhouse, and likewise all the profits to accrue therefrom, were to be divided among the sharers according to their several holdings.

This organization, it should be understood, merely concerned the ownership of the building. Its members stood in the relation of landlords to the players, and were known by the technical name of "housekeepers." Wholly distinct was the organization of the players, known as the "company." The company, too, was divided into shares for the purpose of distributing its profits. The "housekeepers," in return for providing the building, received one-half of the income from the galleries; the company, for entertaining the public, received the other half of the income from the galleries, plus the takings at the doors. Those actors who were also "housekeepers" shared twice in the profits of the playhouse; and it was a part of the plan of the "housekeepers" to admit actors to be sharers in the building as soon as they attained eminence, or otherwise made their permanent connection with the playhouse desirable. Thus the two organizations, though entirely distinct, were interlocking.

THE GLOBE 237

Such a scheme had many advantages. In the first place, it prevented the company from shifting from one playhouse to another, as was frequently the case with other troupes. In the second place, it guaranteed both the excellence and the permanency of the company. Too often good companies were dissolved by the desertion of a few important members; as every student of the drama knows, the constant reorganization of troupes is one of the most exasperating features of Elizabethan theatrical history. In the third place, the plan, like all profit-sharing schemes, tended to elicit from each member of the organization his best powers. The opportunity offered to a young actor ultimately to be admitted as a sharer in the ownership of the building was a constant source of inspiration,[1] and the power to admit at any time a new sharer enabled the company to recruit from other troupes brilliant actors when such appeared; as, for example, William Osteler and Nathaniel Field, who had attained fame with the Children at Blackfriars and elsewhere. Finally, the plan brought the actors together in a close bond of friendship that lasted for life. Heminges was loved and trusted by them all. Shakespeare was admired and revered; three

---

[1] "The petitioners have a long time with much patience expected to be admitted sharers in the playhouses of the Globe and the Blackfriars, whereby they might reap some better fruit of their labour than hitherto they have done, and be encouraged to proceed therein with cheerfulness." (The Young Players' Petition, 1635, printed by Halliwell-Phillipps, *Outlines*, I, 312.)

members of the troupe seem to have named their sons for him. Indeed, there is nothing more inspiring in a close study of all the documents relating to the Globe than the mutual loyalty and devotion of the original sharers. The publication of Shakespeare's plays by Heminges and Condell is merely one out of many expressions of this splendid comradeship.

The plan of organization having been evolved, and the original members having been selected, the first question presenting itself was, Where should the new playhouse be erected? Burbage, Heminges, and the rest — including Shakespeare — probably gave the question much thought. Their experience in Holywell had not been pleasant; the precinct of Blackfriars, they now well realized, was out of the question; so they turned their eyes to the Bankside. That section had recently become the theatrical centre of London. There were situated the Rose, the Swan, and the Bear Garden, and thither each day thousands of persons flocked in search of entertainment. Clearly the Bankside was best suited to their purpose. Near the fine old church of St. Mary Overies, and not far from the Rose and the Bear Garden, they found a plot of land that met their approval. Its owner, Sir Nicholas Brend, was willing to lease it for a long term of years, and at a very reasonable rate. They made a verbal contract with Brend, according to which the lease was to begin on December 25, 1598.

WILLIAM SHAKESPEARE

Shakespeare seems to have been equally with Burbage a leader in erecting the Globe. In 1599 the building is officially described as "vna domo de novo edificata . . . in occupacione Willielmi Shakespeare et aliorum."

THE GLOBE

Three days later, on December 28, Richard and Cuthbert Burbage, having secured the services of the carpenter, Peter Street, and his workmen, tore down the old Theatre and transported the timber and other materials to this new site across the river; and shortly after the Globe began to lift itself above the houses of the Bankside — a handsome theatre surpassing anything then known to London playgoers.

In the meantime the lawyers had drawn up the lease, and this was formally signed on February 21, 1599. The company had arranged a "tripartite lease," the three parties being Sir Nicholas Brend, the Burbage brothers, and the five actors.[1] To the Burbages Sir Nicholas leased one-half of the property at a yearly rental of £7 5s.; and to the five actors, he leased the other half, at the same rate. Thus the total rent paid for the land was £14 10s. The lease was to run for a period of thirty-one years.

The five actors, not satisfied with tying up the property in the "tripartite lease," proceeded at once to arrange their holdings in the form of a "joint tenancy." This they accomplished by the following device:

William Shakespeare, Augustine Phillips, Thomas Pope, John Heminges, and William Kempe did

---

[1] Exact information about the lease and the organization of the company is derived from the Heminges-Osteler and the Witter-Heminges documents, both discovered and printed by Mr. Wallace. And with these one should compare the article by the same author in the London *Times*, April 30, May 1, 1914.

shortly after grant and assign all the said moiety of and in the said gardens and grounds unto William Levison and Thomas Savage, who regranted and reassigned to every one of them severally a fifth part of the said moiety of the said gardens and grounds.[1]

The object of the "joint tenancy" was to prevent any member of the organization from disposing of his share to an outsider. Legally at the death of a member his share passed into the possession of the other members, so that the last survivor would receive the whole. In reality, however, the members used the "joint tenancy" merely to control the disposition of the shares, and they always allowed the heirs-at-law to receive the share of a deceased member.

The wisdom of this arrangement was quickly shown, for "about the time of the building of said playhouse and galleries, or shortly after," William Kempe decided to withdraw from the enterprise. He had to dispose of his share to the other parties in the "joint tenancy," Shakespeare, Heminges, Phillips, and Pope, who at once divided it equally among themselves, and again went through the process necessary to place that share in "joint tenancy." After the retirement of Kempe, the organization, it will be observed, consisted of six men, and the shares were eight in number, owned

[1] Wallace, *Shakespeare and his London Associates*, p. 53. Shakespeare's leadership in the erection of the Globe is indicated in several documents; for example, the post-mortem inquisition of the estate of Sir Thomas Brend, May 16, 1599.

THE GLOBE

as follows: Richard Burbage and Cuthbert Burbage, each two shares, Shakespeare, Heminges, Phillips, and Pope, each one share.

The tract of land on which the new playhouse was to be erected is minutely described in the lease [1] as follows:

All that parcel of ground just recently before enclosed and made into four separate garden plots, recently in the tenure and occupation of Thomas Burt and Isbrand Morris, diers, and Lactantius Roper, salter, citizen of London, containing in length from east to west two hundred and twenty feet in assize or thereabouts, lying and adjoining upon a way or lane there on one [the south] side, and abutting upon a piece of land called The Park [2] upon the north, and upon a garden then or recently in the tenure or occupation of one John Cornishe toward the west, and upon another garden plot then or recently in the tenure or occupation of one John Knowles toward the east, with all the houses, buildings, structures, ways, easements, commodities, and appurtenances thereunto belonging . . . And also all that parcel of land just recently before enclosed and made into three sep-

---

[1] The lease is incorporated in the Heminges-Osteler documents, which Mr. Wallace has translated from the Anglicized Latin. The original Latin text may be found in Martin, *The Site of the Globe Playhouse of Shakespeare*, pp. 161-62. Since, however, that text is faultily reproduced, I quote Mr. Wallace's translation.

[2] What is meant by "The Park" is a matter of dispute. Some contend that the Park of the Bishop of Winchester is meant; it may be, however, that some small estate is referred to. In support of the latter contention, one might cite Collier's *Memoirs of Edward Alleyn*, p. 91. Part of the document printed by Collier may have been tampered with, but there is no reason to suspect the two references to "The Parke."

arate garden plots, whereof two of the same [were] recently in the tenure or occupation of John Roberts, carpenter, and another recently in the occupation of

THE PARK
(AN ESTATE?)

	GARDEN	GARDEN	GARDEN	GARDEN	
[GARDEN OF JOHN CORNISH]	THESE FOUR GARDENS LATELY IN THE TENURE AND OCCUPATION OF "THOMAS BURT, ISBRAND MORRIS, AND LACTANTIUS RODES."				[GARDEN OF JOHN KNOWLES]

A WAY OR LANE

	GARDEN	GARDEN	GARDEN	
[GARDEN OF JOHN BURGRAM]	THESE TWO GARDENS "LATELY IN THE TENURE OR OCCUPATION OF JOHN ROBERTS"	"LATE IN THE OCCUPATION OF" THOMAS DITCHER.	[GARDEN OF WILLIAM SELLERS]

MAIDEN LANE

A PLAN OF THE GLOBE PROPERTY

Based on the lease and on other documents and references to the property.

one Thomas Ditcher, citizen and merchant tailor of London ... containing in length from east to west by estimation one hundred fifty and six feet of assize or thereabouts, and in breadth from the north to the south one hundred feet of assize by estimation or thereabouts, lying and adjoining upon the other side of the way or lane aforesaid, and abutting upon a garden plot there then or recently just before in the occupation of William Sellers toward the east, and

THE GLOBE

upon one other garden plot there, then or recently just before, in the tenure of John Burgram, sadler, toward the west, and upon a lane there called Maiden Lane towards the south, with all the houses . . .

This document clearly states that the Globe property was situated to the north of Maiden Lane, and consequently near the river. Virtually all the contemporary maps of London show the Globe as so situated. Mr. Wallace has produced some very specific evidence to support the document cited above, and he claims to have additional evidence as yet unpublished. On the other hand, there is at least some evidence to indicate that the Globe was situated to the south of Maiden Lane.[1]

For the purposes of this book it is sufficient to know that the Globe was "situate in Maiden Lane"; whether on the north side or the south side is of less importance. More important is the nature of the site. Strype, in his edition of Stow's *Survey*, gives this description: "Maiden Lane, a long straggling place, with ditches on each side, the passage to the houses being over little bridges, with little garden plots before them, especially on the north side, which is best both for houses and inhabitants." In Maiden Lane, near one of these ditches or "sewers," the Globe was erected; and like the other houses there situated, it was approached over a bridge.[2] In February, 1606, the

---

[1] For the discussions of the subject, see the Bibliography.
[2] This was probably not the only means of approach.

Sewer Commission ordered that "the owners of the playhouse called the Globe, in Maid Lane, shall before the 20 day of April next pull up and take clean out of the sewer the props or posts which stand under their bridge on the north side of Maid Lane."[1] The ground on which the building was erected was marshy, and the foundations were made by driving piles deep into the soil. Ben Jonson tersely writes:[2]

> The Globe, the glory of the Bank . . . Flanked with a ditch, and forced out of a marish.

Into the construction of the new playhouse went the timber and other materials secured from the old Theatre; but much new material, of course, had to be added. It is a mistake to believe that the Globe was merely the old "Theatre" newly set up on the Bankside, and perhaps strengthened here and there. When it was completed, it was regarded as the last word in theatrical architecture. Dekker seems to have had the Globe in mind in the following passage: "How wonderfully is the world altered! and no marvel, for it has lyein sick almost five thousand years: so that it is no more like the old *Theater du munde*, than old Paris Garden is like the King's garden at Paris. What an excellent workman therefore were he, that could cast the *Globe* of it into a new mould."[3] In 1600 Henslowe

---

[1] Wallace, in the London *Times*, April 30, 1914, p. 10; *Notes and Queries* (xi series), xi, 448.

[2] *An Execration upon Vulcan.*

[3] *The Guls Hornbook*, published in 1609, but written earlier.

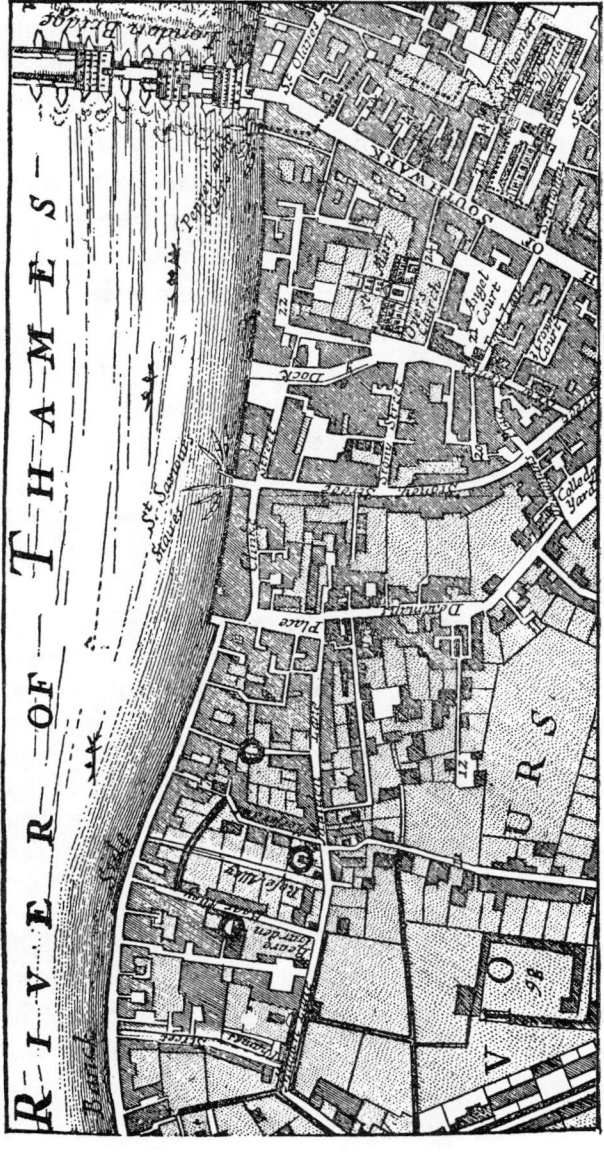

THE SITES OF THE BEAR GARDEN, THE ROSE, AND THE GLOBE
Marked by the author on a plan of the Bankside printed in Strype's *Survey of London*, 1720.

and Alleyn used the Globe as the model of their new and splendid Fortune. They sought, indeed, to show some originality by making their playhouse square instead of round; but this, the one instance in which they departed from the Globe, was a mistake; and when the Fortune was rebuilt in 1623 it was made circular in shape.

A few quotations from the Fortune contract will throw some light upon the Globe:

With such-like stairs, conveyances, and divisions [to the galleries], without and within, as are made and contrived in and to the late-erected playhouse ... called the Globe.

And the said stage to be in all other proportions contrived and fashioned like unto the stage of the said playhouse called the Globe.

And the said house, and other things before mentioned to be made and done, to be in all other contrivations, conveyances, fashions, thing, and things, effected, finished and done according to the manner and fashion of the said house called the Globe, saving only that all the principal and main posts ... shall be square and wrought pilasterwise, with carved proportions called satyrs to be placed and set on the top of every of the said posts.

What kind of columns were used in the Globe and how they were ornamented, we do not know, but presumably they were round. Jonson, in *Every Man Out of His Humour*, presented on the occasion of, or shortly after, the opening of the Globe in 1599, says of one of his characters: "A

THE BEAR GARDEN, THE ROSE, AND THE FIRST GLOBE

Compare this view of the Bankside with the preceding map. (From an equestrian portrait of King James I, by Delaram. The city is represented as it was when James came to the throne in 1603.)

THE GLOBE

well-timbered fellow! he would have made a good column an he had been thought on when the house was abuilding."[1] That Jonson thought well of the new playhouse is revealed in several places; he speaks with some enthusiasm of "this fair-fitted Globe,"[2] and in the passage already quoted he calls it "the glory of the Bank."

In shape the building was unquestionably polygonal or circular, most probably polygonal on the outside and circular within. Mr. E. K. Chambers thinks it possible that it was square;[3] but there is abundant evidence to show that it was not. The very name, Globe, would hardly be suitable to a square building; Jonson describes the interior as a "round";[4] the ballad on the burning of the house refers to the roof as being "round as a tailor's clew"; and the New Globe, which certainly was not square, was erected on the old foundation.[5] The frame, we know, was of timber, and the roof

[1] *Jonson's Works*, ed. Cunningham, I, 71.
[2] In the first quarto edition of *Every Man Out of His Humour*.
[3] *The Stage of the Globe*, p. 356.
[4] Induction to *Every Man Out of His Humour* (ed. Cunningham, I, 66).
[5] I have not space to discuss the question further. The foreign traveler who visited a Bankside theatre, probably the Globe, on July 3, 1600, described it as "Theatrum ad morem antiquorum Romanorum constructum ex lignis" (London *Times*, April 11, 1914). Thomas Heywood, in his *Apology for Actors* (1612), describing the Roman playhouses, says: "After these they composed others, but differing in form from the theatre or amphitheatre, and every such was called *Circus*, the frame *globe*-like and merely round." The evidence is cumulative, and almost inexhaustible.

of thatch. In front of the main door was suspended a sign of Hercules bearing the globe upon his shoulders,[1] under which was written, says Malone, the old motto, *Totus mundus agit histrionem.*[2]

The earliest representation of the building is probably to be found in the Delaram *View of London* (opposite page 246), set in the background of an engraving of King James on horseback. This view, which presents the city as it was in 1603 when James came to the throne, shows the Bear Garden at the left, polygonal in shape, the Rose in the centre, circular in shape, and the Globe at the right, polygonal in shape. It is again represented in Visscher's magnificent *View of London,* which, though printed in 1616, presents the city as it was several years earlier (see page 253). The Merian *View* of 1638 (opposite page 256) is copied from Visscher, and the *View* in Howell's *Londinopolis* (1657) is merely a slavish copy of Merian; these two views, therefore, so far as the Globe is concerned, have no special value.[3]

The cost of the finished building is not exactly known. Mr. Wallace observes that it was erected

[1] See *Hamlet,* II, ii, 378.   [2] Malone, *Variorum,* III, 67.
[3] The circular playhouse in Delaram's *View* is commonly accepted as a representation of the First Globe, but without reason. The evidence which establishes the identity of the several playhouses pictured in the various maps of the Bankside comes from a careful study of the Bear Garden, the Hope, the Rose, the First Globe, the Second Globe, and their sites, together with a study of all the maps and views of London, considered separately and in relation to one another. Such evidence is too complicated to be given here in full, but it is quite conclusive.

THE FIRST GLOBE

From an old drawing in an extra-illustrated copy of Pennant's *London* now in the British Museum. Apparently the drawing is based on Visscher's *View*.

THE GLOBE

"at an original cost, according to a later statement, of £600, but upon better evidence approximately £400." [1] I am not aware of the "better evidence" to which Mr. Wallace refers,[2] nor do I know whether the estimate of £400 includes the timber and materials of the old Theatre furnished by the Burbages. If the Theatre of 1576 cost nearly £700, and the second Globe cost £1400, the sum of £400 seems too small.

Nor do we know exactly when the Globe was finished and opened to the public. On May 16, 1599, a post-mortem inquisition of the estate of Sir Thomas Brend, father of Sir Nicholas, was taken. Among his other properties in Southwark was listed the Globe playhouse, described as "vna domo de novo edificata . . . in occupacione Willielmi Shakespeare et aliorum." [3] From this statement Mr. Wallace infers that the Globe was finished and opened before May 16, 1599. Though this is possible, the words used seem hardly to warrant the conclusion. However, we may feel sure that the actors, the Lord Chamberlain's Men, had moved into the building before the end of the summer.

Almost at once they rose to the position of leadership in the drama, for both Shakespeare and Burbage were now at the height of their powers. It is true that in 1601 the popularity of the Chil-

[1] The London *Times*, October 2, 1909.
[2] Possibly he gives this evidence in his *The Children of the Chapel at Blackfriars*, p. 29, note 4.
[3] Wallace, in the London *Times*, May 1, 1914.

dren at Blackfriars, and the subsequent "War of the Theatres" interfered somewhat with their success; but the interference was temporary, and from this time on until the closing of the playhouses in 1642, the supremacy of the Globe players was never really challenged. When James came to the throne, he recognized this supremacy by taking them under his royal patronage. On May 19, 1603, he issued to them a patent to play as the King's Men [1] — an honor that was as well deserved as it was signal.

In the autumn of 1608 the proprietors of the Globe acquired the Blackfriars Theatre for the use of their company during the severe winter months. This splendid building, situated in the very heart of the city, was entirely roofed in, and could be comfortably heated in cold weather. Henceforth the open-air Globe was used only during the pleasant season of the year; that is, according to the evidence of the Herbert Manuscript, from about the first of May until the first of November.

On June 29, 1613, the Globe caught fire during the performance of a play, and was burned to the ground — the first disaster of the sort recorded in English theatrical history. The event aroused great interest in London, and as a result we have numerous accounts of the catastrophe supplying us with full details. We learn that on a warm "sunneshine" afternoon the large building was "filled

---

[1] Printed in The Malone Society *Collections*, 1, 264.

THE GLOBE

with people" — among whom were Ben Jonson, John Taylor (the Water-Poet), and Sir Henry Wotton — to witness a new play by William Shakespeare and John Fletcher, called *All is True*, or, as we now know it, *Henry VIII*, produced with unusual magnificence. Upon the entrance of the King in the fourth scene of the first act, two cannon were discharged in a royal salute. One of the cannon hurled a bit of its wadding upon the roof and set fire to the thatch; but persons in the audience were so interested in the play that for a time they paid no attention to the fire overhead. As a result they were soon fleeing for their lives; and within "one short hour" nothing was left of the "stately" Globe.

I quote below some of the more interesting contemporary accounts of this notable event. Howes, the chronicler, thus records the fact in his continuation of Stow's *Annals:*

> Upon St. Peter's Day last, the playhouse or theatre called the Globe, upon the Bankside, near London, by negligent discharge of a peal of ordnance, close to the south side thereof, the thatch took fire, and the wind suddenly dispersed the flames round about, and in a very short space the whole building was quite consumed; and no man hurt: the house being filled with people to behold the play, *viz.* of Henry the Eight.[1]

Sir Henry Wotton, in a letter to a friend, gives the following gossipy account:

[1] Howes's continuation of Stow's *Annals* (1631), p. 1003.

Now to let matters of state sleep. I will entertain you at the present with what happened this week at the Bankside. The King's Players had a new play, called *All is True*, representing some principal pieces of the reign of Henry the Eighth, which was set forth with many extraordinary circumstances of pomp and majesty, even to the matting of the stage; the Knights of the Order with their Georges and Garter, the guards with their embroidered coats, and the like — sufficient in truth within awhile to make greatness very familiar, if not ridiculous. Now King Henry, making a masque at the Cardinal Wolsey's house, and certain cannons being shot off at his entry, some of the paper or other stuff wherewith one of them was stopped, did light on the thatch, where being thought at first but an idle smoke, and their eyes more attentive to the show, it kindled inwardly, and ran round like a train, consuming within less than an hour the whole house to the very ground. This was the fatal period of that virtuous fabrick; wherein yet nothing did perish but wood and straw, and a few forsaken cloaks; only one man had his breeches set on fire, that would perhaps have broiled him, if he had not, by the benefit of a provident wit, put it out with bottle ale.[1]

John Chamberlain, writing to Sir Ralph Winwood, July 8, 1613, refers to the accident thus:

The burning of the Globe or playhouse on the Bankside on St. Peter's Day cannot escape you; which fell out by a peal of chambers (that I know not upon what occasion were to be used in the play), the tampin or stopple of one of them lighting in the thatch that cover'd the house, burn'd it down to the

---

[1] *Reliquiæ Wottonianæ* (ed. 1672), p. 425.

THE FIRST GLOBE

From Visscher's *View of London*, published in 1616, but representing the city as it was several years earlier.

ground in less than two hours, with a dwelling house adjoining; and it was a great marvel and fair grace of God that the people had so little harm, having but two narrow doors to get out.[1]

[1] Ralph Winwood, *Memorials of Affairs of State* (ed. 1725), III, 469.

254 SHAKESPEAREAN PLAYHOUSES

The Reverend Thomas Lorkin writes from London to Sir Thomas Puckering under the date of June 30, 1613:

No longer since than yesterday, while Burbage's company were acting at the Globe the play of *Henry VIII*, and there shooting off certain chambers in way of triumph, the fire catched and fastened upon the thatch of the house, and there burned so furiously, as it consumed the whole house, all in less than two hours, the people having enough to do to save themselves.[1]

A contemporary ballad [2] gives a vivid and amusing account of the disaster:

> *A Sonnet upon the Pitiful Burning of the Globe Playhouse in London*
>
> Now sit thee down, Melpomene,
> Wrapt in a sea-coal robe,
> And tell the dolefull tragedy
> That late was played at Globe;
> For no man that can sing and say
> Was scared on St. Peter's day.
>   *Oh sorrow, pitiful sorrow, and yet all this is true.*[3]
>
> All you that please to understand,
> Come listen to my story;
> To see Death with his raking brand
> Mongst such an auditory;

---

[1] Printed in Birch, *The Court and Times of James the First* (1849), I, 251.

[2] Printed by Haslewood in *The Gentleman's Magazine* (1816), from an old manuscript volume of poems. Printed also by Halliwell-Phillipps (*Outlines*, I, 310) "from a manuscript of the early part of the seventeenth century of unquestionable authenticity." Perhaps it is the same as the "Doleful Ballad" entered in the Stationers' Register, 1613. I follow Halliwell-Phillipps's text, but omit the last three stanzas.

[3] Punning on the title *All is True*.

Regarding neither Cardinall's might,
Nor yet the rugged face of Henry the eight.
  Oh sorrow, etc.

This fearful fire began above,
A wonder strange and *true*,
And to the stage-house did remove,
As round as taylor's clew,
And burnt down both beam and snagg,
And did not spare the silken flagg.
  Oh sorrow, etc.

Out run the Knights, out run the lords,
And there was great ado;
Some lost their hats, and some their swords;
Then out run Burbage, too.
The reprobates, though drunk on Monday,
Prayd for the fool and Henry Condy.
  Oh sorrow, etc.

The periwigs and drum-heads fry
Like to a butter firkin;
A woeful burning did betide
To many a good buff jerkin.
Then with swolen eyes, like drunken Flemminges
Distressed stood old stuttering Heminges.
  Oh sorrow, etc.

Ben Jonson, who saw the disaster, left us the following brief account:

   The Globe, the glory of the Bank,
Which, though it were the fort of the whole parish,
Flanked with a ditch, and forced out of a marsh,
I saw with two poor chambers taken in,
And razed ere thought could urge this might have been!
See the world's ruins! nothing but the piles
Left — and wit since to cover it with tiles.[1]

---
[1] *An Execration upon Vulcan.*

The players were not seriously inconvenienced, for they could shift to their other house, the Blackfriars, in the city. The owners of the building, however, suffered a not inconsiderable pecuniary loss. For a time they hesitated about rebuilding, one cause of their hesitation being the short term that their lease of the ground had to run. Possibly a second cause was a doubt as to the ownership of the ground, arising from certain transactions recorded below. In October, 1600, Sir Nicholas Brend had been forced to transfer the Globe estate, with other adjacent property, to Sir Matthew Brown and John Collett as security for a debt of £2500; and a few days after he died. Since the son and heir, Matthew Brend, was a child less than two years old, an uncle, Sir John Bodley, was appointed trustee. In 1608 Bodley, by unfair means, it seems, purchased from Collett the Globe property, and thus became the landlord of the actors. But young Matthew Brend was still under age, and Bodley's title to the property was not regarded as above suspicion.[1]

Four months after the burning of the Globe, on October 26, 1613, Sir John Bodley granted the proprietors of the building a renewal of the lease with an extension of the term until December 25, 1635.[2] But a lease from Bodley alone, in view of

[1] These interesting facts were revealed by Mr. Wallace in the London *Times*, April 30 and May 1, 1914.
[2] Did he increase the amount of the rental to £25 per annum? The rent paid for the Blackfriars was £40 per annum; in 1635 the

MERIAN'S VIEW OF LONDON

A section from Merian's *View*, showing the Bankside playhouses. This *View*, printed in Ludvig Gottfried's *Neuwe Archontologia Cosmica* (Frankfurt am Mayn, 1638), represents London as it was about the year 1612, and was mainly based on Visscher's *View*, with some additions from other sources.

THE GLOBE

the facts just indicated, was not deemed sufficient; so on February 14, 1614, Heminges, the two Burbages, and Condell visited the country-seat of the Brends, and secured the signature of the young Matthew Brend, and of his mother as guardian, to a lease of the Globe site with a term ending on December 25, 1644.

Protected by these two leases, the Globe sharers felt secure; and they went forward apace with the erection of their new playhouse. They made an assessment of "£50 or £60" upon each share.[1] Since at this time there were fourteen shares, the amount thus raised was £700 or £840. This would probably be enough to erect a building as large and as well equipped as the old Globe. But the proprietors determined upon a larger and a very much handsomer building. As Howes, the continuer of Stow's *Annals*, writes, "it was new builded in far fairer manner than before"; or as John Taylor, the Water-Poet, puts it:

> As gold is better that's in fire tried,
> So is the Bankside *Globe* that late was burn'd. [2]

Naturally the cost of rebuilding exceeded the original estimate. Heminges tells us that on one share, or one-fourteenth, he was required to pay for "the re-edifying about the sum of £120." [3]

---

young actors state that the housekeepers paid for both playhouses "not above £65."
[1] Wallace, *Shakespeare and his London Associates*, p. 60.
[2] *Works* (1630), p. 31; The Spenser Society reprint, p. 515.
[3] Wallace, *Shakespeare and his London Associates*, p. 61.

This would indicate a total cost of "about" £1680. Heminges should know, for he was the business manager of the organization; and his truthfulness cannot be questioned. Since, however, the adjective "about," especially when multiplied by fourteen, leaves a generous margin of uncertainty, it is gratifying to have a specific statement from one of the sharers in 1635 that the owners had "been at the charge of £1400 in building of the said house upon the burning down of the former." [1] Heminges tells us that "he found that the re-edifying of the said playhouse would be a very great charge," and that he so "doubted what benefit would arise thereby" that he actually gave away half of one share "to Henry Condell, *gratis*." [2] But his fears were unfounded. We learn from Witter that after the rebuilding of the Globe the "yearly value" of a share was greater "by much" than it had been before.[3]

[1] Halliwell-Phillipps, *Outlines*, I, 316. This evidence seems to me unimpeachable. I should add, however, that Mr. Wallace considers the estimate "excessive," and says that he has "other contemporary documents showing the cost was far less than £1400." (The London *Times*, October 2, 1909.)

[2] Wallace, *Shakespeare and his London Associates*, p. 61. There is, I think, no truth in the statement made by the inaccurate annotator of the Phillipps copy of Stow's *Annals*, that the Globe was built "at the great charge of King James and many noblemen and others." (See *The Academy*, October 28, 1882, p. 314.) The Witter-Heminges documents sufficiently disprove that. We may well believe, however, that the King and his noblemen were interested in the new building, and encouraged the actors in many ways.

[3] Wallace, *Shakespeare and his London Associates*, p. 70.

THE GLOBE

The New Globe, like its predecessor, was built of timber,[1] and on the same site — indeed the carpenters made use of the old foundation, which seems not to have been seriously injured. In a "return" of 1634, preserved at St. Saviour's, we read: "The Globe playhouse, near Maid Lane, built by the company of players, with a dwelling house thereto adjoining, built with timber, about 20 years past, upon an old foundation."[2] In spite of the use made of the old foundation, the new structure was unquestionably larger than the First Globe; Marmion, in the Prologue to *Holland's Leaguer*, acted at Salisbury Court in 1634, speaks of "the vastness of the Globe," and Shirley, in the Prologue to *Rosania*, applies the adjective "vast" to the building. Moreover, the builders had "the wit," as Jonson tells us, "to cover it with tiles." John Taylor, the Water-Poet, writes:

> For where before it had a thatched hide,
> Now to a stately theatre is turn'd.

The Second Globe is represented, but unsatisfactorily, in Hollar's *View of London*, dated 1647 (opposite page 260). It should be noted that the artist was in banishment from 1643 (at which

---

[1] I see no reason to accept Mr. Wallace's suggestion (*The Children of the Chapel at Blackfriars*, p. 34, note 7) that "it seems questionable, but not unlikely, that the timber framework was brick-veneered and plastered over." Mr. Wallace mistakenly accepts Wilkinson's view of the second Fortune as genuine.

[2] Rendle, *Bankside*, p. XVII.

time the Globe was still standing) until 1652, and hence, in drawing certain buildings, especially those not reproduced in earlier views of London, he may have had to rely upon his memory. This would explain the general vagueness of his representation of the Globe.

The construction was not hurried, for the players had Blackfriars as a home. Under normal conditions they did not move from the city to the Bankside until some time in May; and shortly after that date, in the early summer of 1614, the New Globe was ready for them. John Chamberlain writes to Mrs. Alice Carleton on June 30, 1614:

> I have not seen your sister Williams since I came to town, though I have been there twice. The first time she was at a neighbor's house at cards, and the next she was gone to the New Globe to a play. Indeed, I hear much speech of this new playhouse, which is said to be the fairest that ever was in England.[1]

With this New Globe Shakespeare had little to do, for his career as a playwright had been run, and probably he had already retired from acting. Time, indeed, was beginning to thin out the little band of friends who had initiated and made famous the Globe organization. Thomas Pope had died in 1603, Augustine Phillips in 1605, William Slye in 1608, and, just a few months after the opening of the new playhouse, William Osteler, who had been

---

[1] Birch, *The Court and Times of James the First*, 1, 329; quoted by Wallace, *The Children of the Chapel at Blackfriars*, p. 35.

THE SECOND GLOBE
From Hollar's *View of London* (1647).

admitted to the partnership in 1611. He had begun his career as a child-actor at Blackfriars, had later joined the King's Men, and had married Heminges's daughter Thomasine.

A more serious blow to the company, however, fell in April, 1616, when Shakespeare himself died. To the world he had been "the applause, delight, the wonder" of the stage; but to the members of the Globe Company he had been for many years a "friend and fellow." Only Burbage and Heminges (described in 1614 as "old Heminges"), now remained of the original venturers. And Burbage passed away on March 13, 1619:

> He's gone! and with him what a world are dead
> Which he reviv'd — to be revived so
> No more. Young Hamlet, old Hieronimo,
> Kind Lear, the grieved Moor, and more beside
> That lived in him have now for ever died! [1]

Many elegies in a similar vein were written celebrating his wonderful powers as an actor; yet the tribute that perhaps affects us most deals with him merely as a man. The Earl of Pembroke, writing to the Ambassador to Germany, gives the court news about the mighty ones of the kingdom: "My Lord of Lenox made a great supper to the French Ambassador this night here, and even now all the company are at a play; which I, being tender-

---

[1] From a folio MS. in the Huth Library, printed by J. P. Collier in *The History of English Dramatic Poetry* (1879), i, 411, and by various others.

hearted, could not endure to see so soon after the loss of my old acquaintance Burbage." [1]

In 1623 Heminges and Condell, with great "care and paine," collected and published the plays of Shakespeare, "onely to keep the memory of so worthy a Friend and Fellow alive"; and shortly after, they too died, Condell in 1627 and Heminges in 1630.

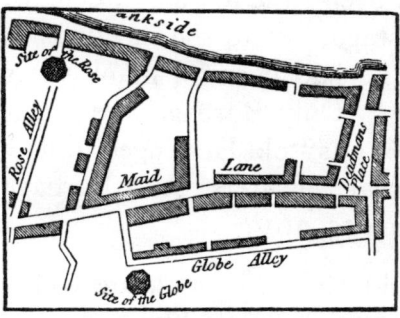

THE TRADITIONAL SITE OF THE GLOBE

From Wilkinson's *Theatrum Illustrata* (1825). This site is still advocated by some scholars. Compare page 245.

After the passing of this group of men, whose names are so familiar to us, the history of the playhouse seems less important, and may be chronicled briefly.

When young Matthew Brend came of age he recovered possession of the Globe property by a decree of the Court of Wards. Apparently he accepted the lease executed by his uncle and guardian, Bodley, by which the actors were to remain in possession of the Globe until December 25, 1635; but in 1633 he sought to cancel the lease he himself had executed as a minor, by which the actors were to remain in possession until 1644. His purpose in

---

[1] Printed by Mrs. Stopes, *Burbage and Shakespeare's Stage*, p. 117, with many other interesting references to the great actor.

THE GLOBE

thus seeking to gain possession of the Globe was to lease it to other actors at a material increase in his profits.[1] Naturally the owners of the Globe were alarmed, and they brought suit in the Court of Requests. In 1635, one of the sharers, John Shanks, declares that he "is without any hope to renew" the lease; and he refers thus to the suit against Brend: "When your suppliant purchased his parts [in 1634] he had no certainty thereof more than for one year in the Globe, and there was a chargeable suit then pending in the Court of Requests between Sir Mathew Brend, Knight, and the lessees of the Globe and their assigns, for the adding of nine years to their lease in consideration that their predecessors had formerly been at the charge of £1400 in building of the said house."[2] The lessees ultimately won their contention, and thus secured the right to occupy the Globe until December 25, 1644 — a term which, as it happened, was quite long enough, for the Puritans closed all playhouses in 1642.

What disposition, if any, the sharers made of the Globe between 1642 and 1644 we do not know. But before the lease expired, it seems, Brend demolished the playhouse and erected tenements on

---

[1] Wallace, "Shakespeare and the Globe," in the London *Times*, April 30 and May 1, 1914.
[2] The Petition of the Young Actors, printed by Halliwell-Phillipps, *Outlines*, I, 312. Mrs. Stopes, in *Burbage and Shakespeare's Stage*, p. 129, refers to a record of the suit mentioned by Shanks, dated February 6, 1634.

its site. In the manuscript notes to the Phillipps copy of Stow's *Annals*, we find the statement that the Globe was "pulled down to the ground by Sir Mathew Brend, on Monday the 15 of April, 1644, to make tenements in the room of it";[1] and the statement is verified by a mortgage, executed in 1706, between Elizabeth, the surviving daughter and heir of Thomas Brend, and one William James, citizen of London. The mortgage concerns "all those messuages or tenements . . . most of which . . . were erected and built where the late playhouse called the Globe stood, and upon the ground thereunto belonging."[2]

After this the history of the property becomes obscure. Mrs. Thrale (later Mrs. Piozzi), the friend of Samuel Johnson, whose residence was near by in Deadman's Place, thought that she saw certain "remains of the Globe" discovered by workmen in the employ of her husband:[3] "For a long time, then, — or I thought it such, — my fate was bound up with the old Globe Theatre, upon the Bankside, Southwark; the alley it had occupied having been purchased and [the tenements] thrown down by Mr. Thrale to make an opening before the windows of our dwelling-house. When it lay desolate in a black heap of rubbish, my mother one day in a

---

[1] Printed in *The Academy*, October 28, 1882, p. 314. Should we read the date as 1644/5?

[2] William Martin, *The Site of the Globe*, p. 171.

[3] Printed in *The Builder*, March 26, 1910, from the Conway MSS. in Mrs. Thrale's handwriting.

THE GLOBE

joke called it the Ruins of Palmyra; and after that they had laid it down in a grass-plot Palmyra was the name it went by. . . . But there were really curious remains of the old Globe Playhouse, which though hexagonal in form without, was round within." In spite of serious difficulties in this narrative it is possible that the workmen, in digging the ground preparatory to laying out the garden, uncovered the foundation of the Globe, which, it will be recalled, was formed of piles driven deep into the soil, and so well made that it resisted the fire of 1613.[1]

At the present time the site of the Globe is covered by the extensive brewery of Messrs. Barclay, Perkins, and Company. Upon one of the walls of the brewery, on the south side of Park Street, which was formerly Maiden Lane, has been placed a bronze memorial tablet[2] showing in relief the Bankside, with what is intended to be the Globe Playhouse conspicuously displayed in the foreground. This is a circular building designed after the circular playhouse in the Speed-Hondius *View of London*, and represents, as I have tried to show, not the Globe, but the Rose. At the left side of

[1] For later discoveries of supposed Globe relics, all very doubtful, see the London *Times*, October 8, 1909; George Hubbard, *The Site of the Globe Theatre;* and William Martin, *The Site of the Globe*, p. 201.

[2] The tablet was designed by Dr. William Martin and executed by Professor Lanteri. For photographs of it and of the place in which it is erected, see *The London Illustrated News*, October 9, 1909, CXXXV, 500.

the tablet is a bust of the poet modeled after the Droeshout portrait. At the right is the simple inscription:

> HERE STOOD THE GLOBE PLAYHOUSE OF
> SHAKESPEARE

Yet it is very doubtful whether the Globe really stood there. Mr. Wallace has produced good evidence to show that the building was on the north side of Park Street near the river; and in the course of the present study I have found that site generally confirmed.

CHAPTER XIII
THE FORTUNE

THE erection of the Globe on the Bankside within a few hundred yards of the Rose was hardly gratifying to the Admiral's Men. Not only did it put them in close competition with the excellent Burbage-Shakespeare organization, but it caused their playhouse (now nearly a quarter of a century old, and said to be in a state of "dangerous decay") to suffer in comparison with the new and far handsomer Globe, "the glory of the Bank." Accordingly, before the Globe had been in operation much more than half a year, Henslowe and Alleyn decided to move to another section of London, and to erect there a playhouse that should surpass the Globe both in size and in magnificence. To the authorities, however, they gave as reasons for abandoning the Rose, first, "the dangerous decay" of the building, and secondly, "for that the same standeth very noisome for resort of people in the winter time."

The new playhouse was undertaken by Henslowe and Alleyn jointly, although the exact arrangement between them is not now clear. Alleyn seems to have advanced the money and to have held the titles of ownership; but on April 4, 1601, he leased to Henslowe a moiety (or one-half interest) in the playhouse and other properties connected with it for a period of twenty-four years at an annual rental of £8 — a sum far below the real value of the moiety.[1]

Whatever the details of the arrangement between the two partners, the main outlines of their procedure are clear. On December 22, 1599, Alleyn purchased for £240 a thirty-three-year lease [2] of a plot of ground situated to the north of the city, in the Parish of St. Giles without Cripplegate. This plot of ground, we are told, stood "very tolerable, near unto the Fields, and so far distant and remote from any person or place of account as that none can be annoyed thereby"; [3] and yet, as the Earl of Nottingham wrote, it was "very convenient for the ease of people." [4]

The property thus acquired lay between Golding Lane and Whitecross Street, two parallel thoroughfares running north and south. There were tenements on the edge of the property facing

[1] Greg, *Henslowe Papers*, p. 25; Wallace, *Three London Theatres*, p. 53. Later, Alleyn rented to the actors the playhouse alone for £200 per annum. In the document, Alleyn *v.* William Henslowe, published by Mr. Wallace in *Three London Theatres*, p. 52, it is revealed that this annual rental of £8 was canceled by Alleyn's rental of a house from Henslowe on the Bankside; hence no actual payments by Henslowe appear in the Henslowe-Alleyn papers.

[2] Later, by a series of negotiations ending in 1610, Alleyn secured the freehold of the property. The total cost to him was £800. See Greg, *Henslowe Papers*, pp. 14, 17, 108.

[3] *Ibid.*, p. 50.   [4] *Ibid.*, p. 49; cf. p. 51.

THE FORTUNE 269

Whitecross Street, tenements on the edge facing Golding Lane, and an open space between. Alleyn and Henslowe planned to erect their new playhouse in this open space "between Whitecross Street and Golding Lane," and to make "a way leading to it" from Golding Lane. The ground set aside for the playhouse is described as "containing in length from east to west one hundred twenty and seven feet and a half, a little more or less, and in breadth, from north to south, one hundred twenty and nine feet, a little more or less." [1]

The lease of this property having been consummated on December 22, 1599, on January 8, 1600, Henslowe and Alleyn signed a contract with the carpenter, Peter Street (who had recently gained valuable experience in building the Globe), to erect the new playhouse. The contract called for the completion of the building by July 25, 1600, provided, however, the workmen were "not by any authority restrained."

The latter clause may indicate that Peter Street anticipated difficulties. If so, he was not mistaken, for when early in January his workmen began to assemble material for the erection of the building, the authorities, especially those of the Parish of St. Giles, promptly interfered. Alleyn thereupon appealed to the patron of the troupe, the Earl of

---

[1] Collier, *The Alleyn Papers*, p. 98. For a slightly different measurement of the plot see Collier, *Memoirs of Edward Alleyn*, p. 167.

Nottingham, the Lord Admiral. On January 12, 1600, Nottingham issued a warrant to the officers of the county "to permit and suffer my said servant [Edward Alleyn] to proceed in the effecting and furnishing of the said new house, without any your let or molestation toward him or any of his workmen." [1] This warrant, however, seems not to have prevented the authorities of St. Giles from continuing their restraint. Alleyn was then forced to play his trump card — through his great patron to secure from the Privy Council itself a warrant for the construction of the building. First, however, by offering "to give a very liberal portion of money weekly" towards the relief of "the poor in the parish of St. Giles," he persuaded many of the inhabitants to sign a document addressed to the Privy Council, in which they not only gave their full consent to the erection of the playhouse, but actually urged "that the same might proceed." [2] This document he placed in the hands of Nottingham to use in influencing the Council. The effort was successful. On April 8 the Council issued a warrant "to the Justices of the Peace of the County of Middlesex, especially of St. Giles without Cripplegate, and to all others whom it shall concern," that they should permit Henslowe and Alleyn "to proceed in the effecting and finishing of the same new house." [3]

[1] Greg, *Henslowe Papers*, p. 49.
[2] *Ibid.*, p. 50.   [3] *Ibid.*, p. 51.

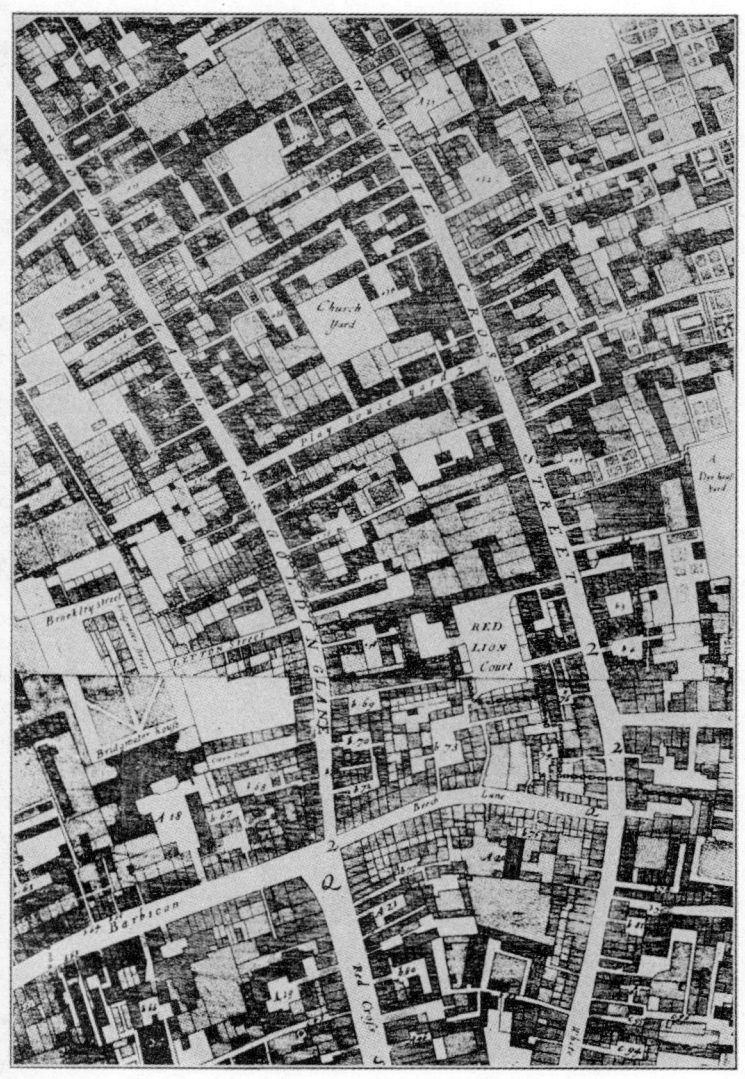

THE SITE OF THE FORTUNE PLAYHOUSE
The site of the Fortune is marked by Playhouse Yard, connecting Golden Lane and Whitecross Street. (From Ogilby and Morgan's *Map of London*, 1677.)

THE FORTUNE

This warrant, of course, put an end to all interference by local authorities. But as the playhouse reared itself high above the walls of the city to the north, the Puritans were aroused to action. They made this the occasion for a most violent attack on actors and theatres in general, and on the Fortune in particular. With this attack the city authorities, for reasons of their own, heartily sympathized, but they had no jurisdiction over the Parish of St. Giles, or over the other localities in which playhouses were situated. Since the Privy Council had specially authorized the erection of the Fortune, the Lord Mayor shifted the attack to that body, and himself dispatched an urgent request to the Lords for reformation. In response to all this agitation the Lords of the Privy Council on June 22, 1600, issued the following order:

Whereas divers complaints have heretofore been made unto the Lords and other of Her Majesty's Privy Council of the manifold abuses and disorders that have grown and do continue by occasion of many houses erected and employed in and about London for common stage-plays; and now very lately by reason of some complaint exhibited by sundry persons against the building of the like house in or near Golding Lane . . . the Lords and the rest of Her Majesty's Privy Council with one and full consent have ordered in manner and form as follows. First, that there shall be about the city two houses, and no more, allowed to serve for the use of the common stage-plays; of the which houses, one [the Globe] shall be in Surrey, in that place which is commonly called the Bankside or thereabouts, and the other [the Fortune] in Middlesex. Secondly, . . . it is likewise ordered that the two several companies of players assigned unto the two houses allowed may play each of them in their several houses twice a week and no oftener; and especially that they shall refrain to play on the Sabbath day . . . and that they shall forbear altogether in the time of Lent.

The first part of this order, limiting the playhouses and companies to two, was merely a repetition of the order of 1598.[1] It meant that the Lords of the Privy Council formally licensed the Admiral's and the Lord Chamberlain's Companies to play in London (of course the Lords might, when they saw fit, license other companies for specific periods). The second part of the order, limiting the number of performances, was more serious, for no troupe could afford to act only twice a week. The order if carried out would mean the ruin of the Fortune and the Globe Companies. But it was not carried out. The actors, as we learn from Henslowe's *Diary*, did not restrict themselves to two plays a week. Why, then, did the Lords issue this order, and why was it not put into effect? A study of the clever way in which Alleyn, Nottingham, and the Privy Council overcame the opposition of the puritanical officers of St. Giles who were interfering with the erection of the Fortune will suggest the explanation. The Lords were making a shrewd move to quiet the noisy enemies of the drama. They did

[1] See page 174.

THE FORTUNE 273

not intend that the Admiral's and the Chamberlain's Men should be driven out of existence; they were merely meeting fanaticism with craft.

Alleyn and Henslowe must have understood this, — possibly they learned it directly from their patron Nottingham, — for they proceeded with the erection of their expensive building. The work, however, had been so seriously delayed by the restraints of the local authorities that the foundations were not completed until May 8.[1] On that day carpenters were brought from Windsor, and set to the task of erecting the frame. Since the materials had been accumulating on the site since January 17, the work of erection must have proceeded rapidly. The daily progress of this work is marked in Henslowe's *Diary* by the dinners of Henslowe with the contractor, Peter Street. On August 8, these dinners ceased, so that on that date, or shortly after, we may assume, the building proper was finished.[2]

For erecting the building Street received £440. But this did not include the painting of the woodwork (which, if we may judge from De Witt's description of the Swan, must have been costly), or the equipment of the stage. We learn from Alleyn's memoranda that the final cost of the playhouse was £520.[3] Hence, after Street's work of

---

[1] Greg, *Henslowe Papers*, p. 10.
[2] Greg, *Henslowe's Diary*, I, 158–59.
[3] Greg, *Henslowe Papers*, p. 108.

erection was finished in August, the entire building had to be painted, and the stage properly equipped with curtains, hangings, machines, etc. This must have occupied at least two months. From Henslowe's *Diary* it appears that the playhouse was first used about the end of November or the early part of December, 1600.[1]

The original contract of Henslowe and Alleyn with Peter Street for the erection of the Fortune, preserved among the papers at Dulwich College, supplies us with some very exact details of the size and shape of the building. Although the document is long, and is couched in the legal verbiage of the day, it will repay careful study. For the convenience of the reader I quote below its main specifications:[2]

Foundation. A good, sure, and strong foundation, of piles, brick, lime, and sand, both without and within, to be wrought one foot of assize at the least above the ground.

Frame. The frame of the said house to be set square, and to contain fourscore foot of lawful assize every way square without, and fifty-five foot of like assize square every way within.

Materials. And shall also make all the said frame in every point for scantlings larger and bigger in assize than the scantlings of the said new-erected house called the Globe.

Exterior. To be sufficiently enclosed without with lath, lime, and hair.

---

[1] Greg, *Henslowe's Diary*, I, 124.
[2] For the full document see Greg, *Henslowe Papers*, p. 4.

THE FORTUNE

Stairs. With such like stairs, conveyances, and divisions, without and within, as are made and contrived in and to the late erected playhouse . . . called the Globe. . . . And the staircases thereof to be sufficiently enclosed without with lath, lime, and hair.

Height of galleries. And the said frame to contain three stories in height; the first, or lower story to contain twelve foot of lawful assize in height; the second story eleven foot of lawful assize in height; and the third, or upper story, to contain nine foot of lawful assize in height.

Breadth of galleries. All which stories shall contain twelve foot of lawful assize in breadth throughout. Besides a jutty forward in either of the said two upper stories of ten inches of lawful assize.

Protection of lowest gallery. The lower story of the said frame withinside . . . [to be] paled in below with good, strong, and sufficient new oaken boards. . . . And the said lower story to be also laid over and fenced with strong iron pikes.

Divisions of galleries. With four convenient divisions for gentlemen's rooms, and other sufficient and convenient divisions for two-penny rooms. . . . And the gentlemen's rooms and two-penny rooms to be ceiled with lath, lime, and hair.

Seats. With necessary seats to be placed and set, as well in those rooms as throughout all the rest of the galleries.

Stage. With a stage and tiring-house to be made, erected, and set up within the said frame; with a shadow or cover over the said stage. Which stage shall be placed and set (as also the staircases of the said frame) in such sort as is prefigured in a plot thereof drawn. [The plot has been lost.] And which stage shall contain in length forty and three foot of lawful assize, and in breadth to extend to the middle of the yard of the said house. The same stage to be paled in below with good, strong, and sufficient new oaken boards.... And the said stage to be in all other proportions contrived and fashioned like unto the stage of the said playhouse called the Globe.... And the said ... stage ... to be covered with tile, and to have a sufficient gutter of lead to carry and convey the water from the covering of the said stage to fall backwards.

Tiring-house. With convenient windows and lights, glazed, to the said tiring-house.

Flooring. And all the floors of the said galleries, stories, and stage to be boarded with good and sufficient new deal boards, of the whole thickness where need shall be.

Columns. All the principal and main posts of the said frame and stage forward shall be square, and wrought pilaster-wise, with carved proportions called satyrs to be placed and set on the top of every of the said posts.

Roof. And the said frame, stage, and staircases to be covered with tile.

Miscellaneous. To be in all other contrivations, conveyances, fashions, thing and things, effected, finished, and done, according to the manner and fashion of the said house called the Globe.

It is rather unfortunate for us that the building was to be in so many respects a copy of the Globe, for that deprives us of further detailed specifications; and it is unfortunate, too, that the plan or drawing showing the arrangement of the stage was not preserved with the rest of the document. Yet we are able to derive much exact information from

THE FORTUNE

the contract; and with this information, at least two modern architects have made reconstructions of the building.[1]

No representation of the exterior of the Fortune has come down to us. In the so-called Ryther *Map of London*, there is, to be sure, what seems to be a crude representation of the playhouse (see page 278); but if this is really intended for the Fortune, it does little more than mark the location. Yet one can readily picture in his imagination the playhouse — a plastered structure, eighty feet square and approximately forty feet high,[2] with small windows marking the galleries, a turret and flagpole surmounting the red-tiled roof, and over the main entrance a sign representing Dame Fortune:

> I'le rather stand here,
> Like a statue in the fore-front of your house,
> For ever, like the picture of Dame Fortune
> Before the Fortune Playhouse.[3]

---

[1] See the Bibliography. A model of the Fortune by Mr. W. H. Godfrey is preserved in the Dramatic Museum of Columbia University in New York City, and a duplicate is in the Museum of European Culture at the University of Illinois. For a description of the model see the *Architect and Builders' Journal* (London), August 16, 1911.

[2] The three galleries (twelve, eleven, and nine feet, respectively) were thirty-two feet in height; but to this must be added the elevation of the first gallery above the yard, the space occupied by the ceiling and flooring of the several galleries, and, finally, the roof.

[3] Thomas Heywood, *The English Traveller* (1633), ed. Pearson, IV, 84. We do not know when the play was written, but the reference is probably to the New Fortune, built in 1623. Heywood generally uses "picture" in the sense of "statue."

278 SHAKESPEAREAN PLAYHOUSES

Nor is there any pictorial representation of the interior of the playhouse. In the absence of such, I offer the reader a verbal picture of the interior as

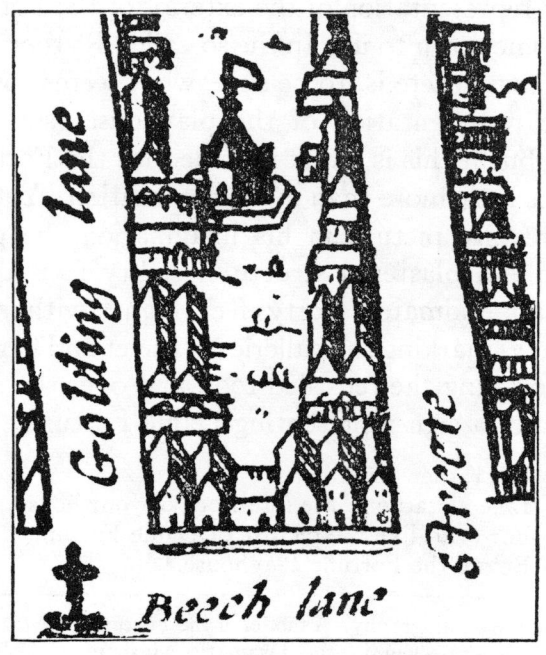

THE FORTUNE PLAYHOUSE (?)

The curious structure with the flag may be intended to mark the site of the Fortune. (From the so-called Ryther *Map of London*, drawn about 1630–40.)

seen from the stage during the performance of a play. In Middleton and Dekker's *The Roaring Girl*, acted at the Fortune, Sir Alexander shows to his friends his magnificent house. Advancing to the middle of the stage, and pointing out over the building, he asks them how they like it:

THE FORTUNE

Goshawk. I like the prospect best.
Laxton.   See how 't is furnished!
Sir Davy. A very fair sweet room.
Sir Alex.   Sir Davy Dapper,
The furniture that doth adorn this room
Cost many a fair grey groat ere it came here;
But good things are most cheap when they're most **dear.**
Nay, when you look into my galleries,
How bravely they're trimm'd up, you all shall **swear**
You're highly pleas'd to see what's set down there:
Stories of men and women, mix'd together,
Fair ones with foul, like sunshine in wet weather;
Within one square a thousand heads are laid,
So close that all of heads the room seems made;
As many faces there, fill'd with blithe looks
Shew like the promising titles of new books
Writ merrily, the readers being their own eyes,
Which seem to move and to give plaudities;
And here and there, whilst with obsequious ears
Throng'd heaps do listen, a cut-purse thrusts and leers
With hawk's eyes for his prey; I need not shew him;
By a hanging, villainous look yourselves may know him,
The face is drawn so rarely: then, sir, below,
The very floor, as 't were, waves to and fro,
And, like a floating island, seems to move
Upon a sea bound in with shores above.
All. These sights are excellent! [1]

A closer view of this audience — "men and women, mix'd together, fair ones with foul" — is furnished by one of the letters of Orazio Busino,[2]

[1] *The Roaring Girl*, I, i. Pointed out by M. W. Sampson, *Modern Language Notes*, June, 1915.

[2] "Diaries and Despatches of the Venetian Embassy at the Court of King James I, in the Years 1617, 1618. Translated by Rawdon Brown." (*The Quarterly Review*, CII, 416.) It is true that the notice of this letter in *The Calendar of State Papers, Venetian*, xv, 67, makes no mention of the Fortune; but the writer in *The*

the chaplain of the Venetian Embassy, who visited the Fortune playhouse shortly after his arrival in London in 1617:

The other day, therefore, they determined on taking me to one of the many theatres where plays are performed, and we saw a tragedy, which diverted me very little, especially as I cannot understand a word of English, though some little amusement may be derived from gazing at the very costly dresses of the actors, and from the various interludes of instrumental music and dancing and singing; but the best treat was to see such a crowd of nobility so very well arrayed that they looked like so many princes, listening as silently and soberly as possible. These theatres are frequented by a number of respectable and handsome ladies, who come freely and seat themselves among the men without the slightest hesitation. On the evening in question his Excellency [the Venetian Ambassador] and the Secretary were pleased to play me a trick by placing me amongst a bevy of young women. Scarcely was I seated ere a very elegant dame, but in a mask, came and placed herself beside me. . . . She asked me for my address, both in French and English; and on my turning a deaf ear, she determined to honour me by showing me some fine diamonds on her fingers, repeatedly taking off no fewer than three gloves, which were worn one over the other. . . . This lady's bodice was of yellow satin richly embroidered, her petticoat of gold tissue with stripes, her robe of red velvet with a raised pile, lined with yellow muslin, with broad stripes of pure gold. She wore an apron

Quarterly Review, who had before him the entire manuscript, states positively that the Fortune was the playhouse visited. I have not been able to examine the manuscript itself, which is preserved in Venice.

THE FORTUNE

of point lace of various patterns; her head-tire was highly perfumed, and the collar of white satin beneath the delicately-wrought ruff struck me as extremely pretty.

That the players were prepared to entertain distinguished visitors both during the performance and after is shown by a letter from John Chamberlain, July 21, 1621, to Sir Dudley Carleton. "The Spanish Ambassador," he writes, "is grown so affable and familiar, that on Monday, with his whole train, he went to a common play at the Fortune in Golding Lane; and the players (not to be overcome with courtesy) made him a banquet, when the play was done, in the garden adjoining."[1]

Upon its completion the new building was occupied by the Admiral's Men, for whom it had been erected. This troupe of players, long famous under the leadership of Edward Alleyn, was now one of the two companies authorized by the Privy Council, and the chief rival of the Chamberlain's Men at the Globe. Henslowe was managing their affairs, and numerous poets were writing plays for them. They continued to act at the Fortune under the name, "The Admiral's Men," until May 5, 1603, when, as Henslowe put it, they "left off play now at the King's coming."[2]

After a short interruption on account of the plague, during a part of which time they traveled

---

[1] Nichols, *The Progresses of King James*, IV, 67.
[2] Greg, *Henslowe's Diary*, I, 174.

in the provinces, the Admiral's Men were taken under the patronage of the youthful Henry, Prince of Wales, and in the early spring of 1604 they resumed playing at the Fortune under their new name, "The Prince's Servants."

For a time all went well. But from July, 1607, until December, 1609, the plague was severe in London, and acting was seriously interrupted. During this long period of hardship for the players, Henslowe and Alleyn seem to have made an attempt to hold the troupe together by admitting its chief members to a partnership in the building, just as the Burbages had formerly admitted their chief players to a partnership in the Globe. At this time there were in the troupe eight sharers, or chief actors.[1] Henslowe and Alleyn, it seems, proposed to allot to these eight actors one-fourth of the Fortune property. In other words, according to this scheme, there were to be thirty-two sharers in the new Fortune organization, Alleyn and Henslowe together holding three-fourths of the stock, or twelve shares each, and the eight actors together holding one-fourth of the stock, or one share each. A document was actually drawn up by Henslowe and Alleyn, with the name of the leader of the Fortune troupe, Thomas Downton, inserted;[2] but since the document was not executed, the scheme,

---

[1] See the Company's Patent of 1606, in The Malone Society's *Collections*, I, 268.
[2] Greg, *Henslowe Papers*, p. 13.

EDWARD ALLEYN
(Reproduced by permission from a painting in the Dulwich Picture Gallery; photograph by Emery Walker, Ltd.)

THE FORTUNE

it is to be presumed, was unsuccessful — at least, we hear nothing further about it.[1]

On November 6, 1612, the death of the young Prince of Wales left the company without a "service." On January 4, 1613, however, a new patent was issued to the players, placing them under the protection of the Palsgrave, or Elector Palatine, after which date they are known as "The Palsgrave's Men."

On January 9, 1616, Henslowe, so long associated with the company and the Fortune, died; and a year later his widow, Agnes, followed him. As a result the entire Fortune property passed into the hands of Alleyn. But Alleyn, apparently, did not care to be worried with the management of the playhouse; so on October 31, 1618, he leased it to the Palsgrave's Men for a period of thirty-one years, at an annual rental of £200 and two rundlets of wine at Christmas.[2]

On April 24, 1620, Alleyn executed a deed of grant of lands by which he transferred the Fortune, along with various other properties, to Dulwich College.[3] But he retained during his lifetime the whole of the revenues therefrom, and he specifically reserved to himself the right to grant leases for

---

[1] For an ordinance concerning "lewd jiggs" at the Fortune in 1612, see *Middlesex County Records*, II, 83.

[2] Greg, *Henslowe Papers*, p. 27; Young, *The History of Dulwich College*, II, 260.

[3] The deed is printed by Young, *op. cit.*, I, 50. The Fortune property, I believe, is still a part of the endowment of the college.

any length of years. The transference of the title, therefore, in no way affected the playhouse, and Alleyn continued to manage the property as he had been accustomed to do in the past.

His services in this capacity were soon needed, for on December 9, 1621, the Fortune was burned to the ground. Alleyn records the event in his *Diary* thus: "*Memorandum.* This night at 12 of the clock the Fortune was burnt." In a less laconic fashion John Chamberlain writes to Sir Dudley Carleton: "On Sunday night here was a great fire at the Fortune in Golding-Lane, the fairest playhouse in this town. It was quite burnt down in two hours, and all their apparel and playbooks lost, whereby those poor companions are quite undone."[1]

The "poor companions" thus referred to were, of course, the players, who lost not only their stock of apparel, playbooks, and stage furniture, but also their lease, which assured them of a home. Alleyn, however, was quite able and ready to reconstruct the building for them; and we find him on May 20, 1621, already organizing a syndicate to finance "a new playhouse" which "there is intended to be erected and set up." The stock of the new enterprise he divided into twelve equal shares, which he disposed of, as the custom was, in the form of whole

---

[1] Birch, *The Court and Times of James the First*, II, 280. Howes, in his continuation of Stow's *Annals* (1631), p. 1004, attributes the fire to "negligence of a candle," but gives no details.

THE FORTUNE

and half shares, reserving for himself only one share.[1] The plot of ground on which the old playhouse stood he leased to the several sharers for a period of fifty-one years at an annual rental of £10 13s. 10d. a share, with the express condition that the building to be erected thereon should never be used for any purpose other than the acting of stageplays. The sharers then proceeded to the task of constructing their playhouse. It was proposed to make the new building larger [2] and handsomer than the old one, and to build it of brick [3] with a tiled roof — possibly an attempt at fireproof construction. It was decided, also, to abandon the square shape in favor of the older and more logical circular shape. Wright, in his *Historia Histrionica*, describes the New Fortune as "a large, round, brick building,"[4] and Howes assures us that it was "farre fairer" than the old playhouse.[5] We do not know how much the building cost. At the outset each

---

[1] Greg, *Henslowe Papers*, pp. 28–30; 112. The names of the sharers are not inspiring: Thomas Sparks, merchant tailor; William Gwalter, innholder; John Fisher, barber-surgeon; Thomas Wigpitt, bricklayer; etc.

[2] Prynne, *Histriomastix*, Epistle Dedicatory.

[3] The writer of the manuscript notes in the Phillipps copy of Stow's *Annals* (see *The Academy*, October 28, 1882, p. 314), who is not trustworthy, says that the Fortune was burned down in 1618, and "built again with brick work on the outside," from which Mr. Wallace assumed that he meant that the building was merely brick-veneered. If the writer meant this he was in error. See the report of the commission appointed by Dulwich College to examine the building (Greg, *Henslowe Papers*, p. 95).

[4] Hazlitt's Dodsley, xv, 408.   [5] Stow, *Annals*, 1631.

sharer was assessed £83 6s. 8d. towards the cost of construction,[1] which would produce exactly £1000; but the first assessment was not necessarily all that the sharers were called upon to pay. For example, when the Globe was rebuilt each sharer was at first assessed "£50 or £60," but before the building was finished each had paid more than £100. So the Fortune may well have cost more than the original estimate of £1000. In 1656 two expert assessors appointed by the authorities of Dulwich College to examine the playhouse declared that "the said building did in our opinions cost building about two thousand pound."[2] This estimate is probably not far wrong. The playhouse was completed in June or July of 1623, and was again occupied by the Palsgrave's Men.[3]

On November 25, 1626, Edward Alleyn died, and the Fortune property came into the full possession of Dulwich College. This, however, did not in any way affect the syndicate of the Fortune housekeepers, who held from Alleyn a lease of the property until 1672. According to the terms of this lease each of the twelve sharers had to pay a yearly

[1] Greg, *Henslowe Papers*, p. 29. Half-shares were £41 13s. 4d., which Murray (*English Dramatic Companies*) confuses with whole shares.
[2] Greg, *Henslowe Papers*, p. 95. This estimate was made after the interior of the building had been "pulled down," and hence refers merely to the cost of erection.
[3] For an account of "a dangerous and great riot committed in Whitecross Street at the Fortune Playhouse" in May, 1626, see Jeaffreson, *Middlesex County Records*, III, 161–63.

THE FORTUNE

rental of £10 13s. 10d.; this rental now merely went to the College instead of to Alleyn.

In 1631 the Palsgrave's Men seem to have fallen on hard times; at any rate, they had to give up the Fortune, and the playhouse was taken over, about December, by the King's Revels, who had been playing at the small private playhouse of Salisbury Court.[1] The Palsgrave's Men were reorganized, taken under the patronage of the infant Prince Charles, and placed in the Salisbury Court Playhouse just vacated by the King's Revels.

In 1635 there was a general shifting of houses on the part of the London companies. The King's Revels left the Fortune and returned to their old quarters at Salisbury Court; the Prince Charles's Men, who had been at Salisbury Court, moved to the Red Bull; and the Red Bull Company transferred itself to the Fortune.

The stay of the Red Bull Company at the Fortune was not happy. Towards the end of 1635 the plague was seriously interfering with their performance of plays;[2] and on May 10, 1636, the Privy Council closed all theatres, and kept them closed, except for a few days, until October 2, 1637.[3] This long inhibition not only impoverished the actors and drove them into the country, but came

---

[1] For details of this move see the chapter on the Salisbury Court Playhouse.
[2] Young, *The History of Dulwich College*, I, 114.
[3] The Malone Society's *Collections*, I, 391, 392; Malone, *Variorum*, III, 239.

near ruining the lessees of the Fortune, who, having no revenue from the playhouse, could not make their quarterly payments to the College. On September 4, 1637, the Court of Assistants at Dulwich noted that the lessees were behind in their rent to the extent of £132 12s. 11d.; "and," the court adds, "there will be a quarter's rent more at Michaelmas next [i.e., in twenty-five days], which is doubted will be also unpaid, amounting to £33 1s. 4d." [1] The excuse of the lessees for their failure to pay was the "restraint from playing." [2]

This "restraint" was removed on October 2, 1637, and the players resumed their performances at the Fortune. But in the early summer of 1639 they fell victims to another bit of ill luck even more serious than their long inhibition. In a letter of Edmond Rossingham, dated May 8, 1639, we read: "Thursday last the players of the Fortune were fined £1000 for setting up an altar, a bason, and two candlesticks, and bowing down before it upon the stage; and although they allege it was an old play revived, and an altar to the heathen gods, yet it was apparent that this play was revived on purpose in contempt of the ceremonies of the Church." [3]

[1] Young, *The History of Dulwich College*, I, 114.
[2] The College appealed to the Lord Keeper, who on January 26 ordered the payment of the sum. But two years later, February, 1640, we find the College again petitioning the Lord Keeper to order the lessees of the Fortune property to pay an arrearage of £104 14s. 5d. See Collier, *The Alleyn Papers*, pp. 95-98.
[3] Printed in *The Calendar of State Papers, Domestic, 1639*, p. 140.

THE FORTUNE

During the Easter period, 1640, the players returned to their old quarters at the Red Bull. After their unhappy experiences at the Fortune they were apparently glad to occupy again their former home. The event is celebrated in a Prologue entitled *Upon the Removing of the Late Fortune Players to the Bull*, written by John Tatham, and printed in *Fancies Theatre* (1640): [1]

> Here, gentlemen, our anchor's fixt; and we
> Disdaining *Fortune's* mutability,
> Expect your kind acceptance.

The writer then hurls some uncomplimentary remarks at the Fortune, observing complacently: "We have ne'er an actor here has mouth enough to tear language by the ears." It is true that during these later years the Fortune had fallen into ill repute with persons of good taste. But so had the Red Bull, and the actors there had no right to throw stones. Apparently the large numbers that could be accommodated in the great public theatres, and the quality of the audience attracted by the low price of admission, made noise and rant inevitable.[2] As chief sinners in this respect the Fortune and the Red Bull are usually mentioned together.

Upon the departure of the Red Bull Company, the Prince Charles's Men (originally the Admiral's,

---

[1] The Prologue is printed in full by Malone, *Variorum*, III, 79.
[2] Not even the Globe was entirely free from this; see the Prologue to *The Doubtful Heir*.

and later the Palsgrave's Men), who had been occupying the Red Bull, came to the Fortune.[1] Thus after an absence of nearly nine years, the old company (though sadly altered in personnel), for which the Fortune had been built, returned to its home to remain there until the end.

On September 2, 1642, the Long Parliament passed an ordinance suppressing all stage-plays; but for a time the actors at the Fortune seem to have continued their performances. In the fifth number of *The Weekly Account*, September 27–October 4, 1643, we find among other entries: "The players' misfortune at the Fortune in Golding Lane, their players' clothes being seized upon in the time of a play by authority from the Parliament." [2] This, doubtless, led to the closing of the playhouse.

After the Fortune was thus closed, the lessees were in a predicament. By a specific clause in their lease they were prevented from using the building for any purpose other than the acting of stage-plays, and now Parliament by a specific ordinance had forbidden the acting of stage-plays. Hence the lessees, some of whom were poor persons, being unable to make any profit from the building, refused to pay any rent. The College entered suit against them, and exhausted all legal means to make them pay, but without success.[3]

[1] Malone, *Variorum*, III, 79.
[2] *The Calendar of State Papers, Domestic, 1643*, p. 564.
[3] For an interesting comment on the situation, especially in the year 1649, see *Notes and Queries* (series x), I, 85.

THE FORTUNE

When the ordinance prohibiting plays expired in January, 1648, the actors promptly reopened the Fortune, and we learn from *The Kingdom's Weekly Intelligencer* that on January 27 no fewer than one hundred and twenty coaches were crowded about the building. But on February 9 Parliament passed a new and even more stringent ordinance against dramatic performances, placing penalties not only upon the players, but also upon the spectators. This for ever put an end to acting at the Fortune.

In 1649 the arrears of the lessees having reached the sum of £974 5s. 8d., the authorities of the College took formal possession of the playhouse.

From certain manuscript notes [1] entered in the Phillipps copy of Stow's *Annals* (1631), we learn that "a company of soldiers, set on by the sectaries of these sad times, on Saturday, the 24 day of March, 1649," sacked the Salisbury Court Playhouse, the Phœnix, and the Fortune. The note states that the Fortune was "pulled down on the inside by the soldiers"; that is, the stage and the seats were dismantled [2] so as to render the building unusable for dramatic purposes.

In the following year, 1650, the inhabitants of the Parish of St. Giles "represent that they are poor, and unable to build a place of worship for themselves, but think it would be convenient if that large building commonly known by the name

---

[1] Printed in *The Academy*, October 28, 1882, p. 314.
[2] See *The Journals of the House of Commons*, July 26, 1648.

of the Fortune Playhouse might be allotted and set apart for that purpose." The request was not granted.[1]

By July, 1656, the condition of the old playhouse was such that the Masters and Wardens of the College appointed two experts to view the building and make recommendations. They reported "that by reason the lead hath been taken from the said building, the tiling not secured, and the foundation of the said playhouse not kept in good repair, great part of the said playhouse is fallen to the ground, the timber thereof much decayed and rotten, and the brick walls so rent and torn that the whole structure is in no condition capable of repair, but in great danger of falling, to the hazard of passengers' lives"; and they add: "The charge for demolishing the same will be chargeable and dangerous. Upon these considerations our opinion is that the said materials may not be more worth than eighty pound." [2]

The authorities of Dulwich took no action on this report. However, on March 5, 1660, they ordered that the property be leased, making a casual reference to the playhouse as "at present so ruinous that part thereof is already fallen down, and the rest will suddenly follow." Accordingly, they inserted in the *Mercurius Politicus* of February 14–21, 1661, the following advertisement: "The For-

[1] Warner, *Catalogue*, xxxi; Greg, *Henslowe's Diary*, ii, 65.
[2] The entire report is printed in Greg, *Henslowe Papers*, p. 95.

THE FORTUNE

tune Playhouse, situate between Whitecross Street and Golding Lane, in the parish of St. Giles, Cripplegate, with the ground thereto belonging, is to be let to be built upon." [1]

No one seems to have cared to lease the property; so on March 16, following, the materials of the building were sold to one William Beaven for the sum of £75; [2] and in the records of the College, March 4, 1662, we read that "the said playhouse ... is since totally demolished." [3]

[1] Discovered by Stevens, and printed in Malone, *Variorum*, III, 55, note 5. Mr. W. J. Lawrence, *Archiv für das Studium der Neueren Sprachen und Literaturen* (1914), p. 314, says that the date of this advertisement is 1660. But the same advertisement is reprinted by H. R. Plomer in *Notes and Queries* (series x), VI, 107, from *The Kingdom's Intelligencer* of March 18, 1661.

[2] Young, *The History of Dulwich College*, II, 265.

[3] Collier, *The Alleyn Papers*, p. 101. I am aware of the fact that there are references to later incidents at the Fortune (for example, the statement that it was visited by officers in November, 1682, in an attempt to suppress secret conventicles that had long been held there), but in view of the unimpeachable documentary evidence cited above (in 1662 the College authorities again refer to it as "the late ruinous and now demolished Fortune playhouse"), we must regard these later references either as inaccurate, or as referring to another building later erected in the same neighborhood. The so-called picture of the Fortune, printed in Wilkinson's *Londina Illustrata*, and often reproduced by modern scholars, cannot possibly be that of the playhouse erected by Alleyn. For an interesting surmise as to the history of this later building see W. J. Lawrence, *Restoration Stage Nurseries*, in *Archiv für das Studium der Neueren Sprachen und Literaturen* (1914), p. 301.

CHAPTER XIV
THE RED BULL

THE builder of the Red Bull Playhouse[1] was "one Aaron Holland, yeoman," of whom we know little more than that he "was utterly unlearned and illiterate, not being able to read."[2] He had leased "for many years" from Anne Beddingfield, "wife and administratrix of the goods and chattles of Christopher Beddingfield, deceased," a small plot of land, known by the name of "The Red Bull." This plot of land, which contained one house, was situated "at the upper end of St. John's Street" in the Parish of St. James, Clerkenwell, the exact location being marked by "Red Bull Yard" in Ogilby and Morgan's *Map of London*, printed in 1677. The property was not much more distant from the heart of the city than the Fortune property, and since it could be easily reached through St. John's Gate, it was quite as well situated for dramatic purposes as was the Fortune.

In or before 1605 [3] Holland erected on this plot

---

[1] This playhouse is not to be confused with the famous Bull Tavern in Bishopsgate Street, for many years used as a theatre.

[2] These statements are based upon the Woodford *v.* Holland documents, first discovered by Collier, later by Greenstreet, and finally printed in full by Wallace, *Three London Theatres*.

[3] Sir Sidney Lee (*A Life of William Shakespeare*, p. 60) says that the Red Bull was "built about 1600." He gives no evidence,

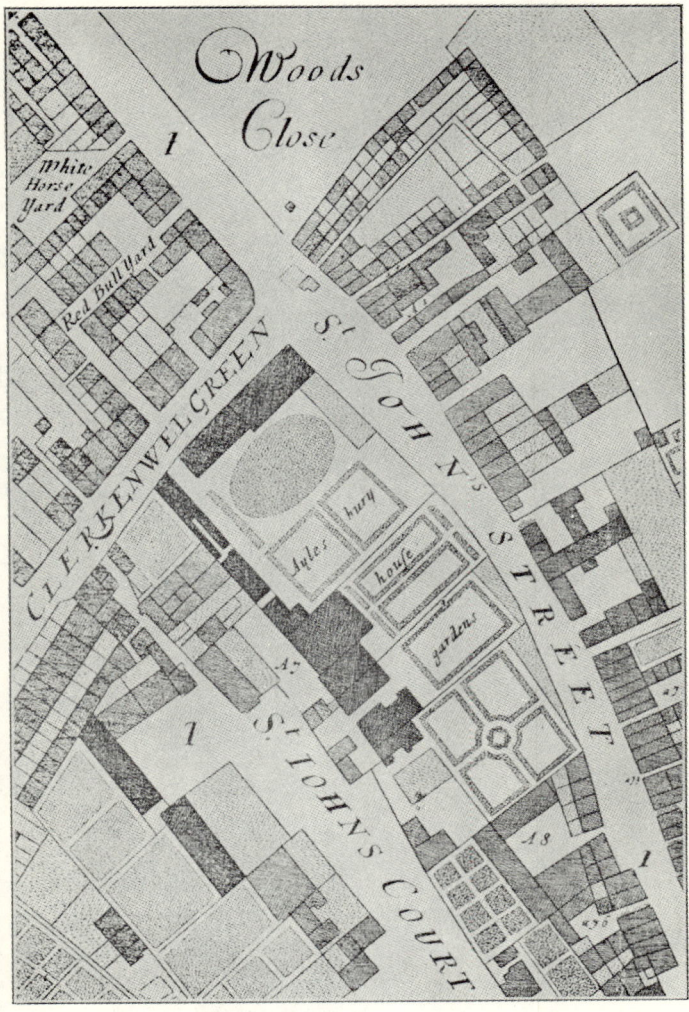

THE SITE OF THE RED BULL PLAYHOUSE
The site is indicated by Red Bull Yard. (From Ogilby and Morgan's *Map of London*, 1677.)

of ground "a playhouse for acting and setting forth plays, comedies, and tragedies." We may suspect that he did this at the instigation of the Earl of Worcester's Men, who had just been taken under the patronage of the Queen, and had been selected by the Privy Council as one of three companies to be "allowed." The warrant of the Privy Council, April 9, 1604, orders the Lord Mayor to "permit and suffer the three companies of players to the King, Queen, and Prince publickly to exercise their plays in their several and usual houses for that purpose, and no other, viz. the Globe, situate in Maiden Lane on the Bankside in the county of Surrey, the Fortune in Golding Lane, and the Curtain, in Holywell." [1] Among these three companies, as Dekker tells us, there was much rivalry.[2] No doubt the Queen's Men, forced to occupy the old Curtain Playhouse, suffered by comparison with the King's Men at the handsome Globe, and the Prince's Men at the new and magnificent Fortune; and this, I suspect, furnished the immediate cause for the erection of the Red Bull. In a draft of a license to the Queen's Men, made late in 1603 or early in 1604, the fact is disclosed that the actors, of whom

and the statement seems to be merely a repetition from earlier and unauthoritative writers.

[1] The original warrant is preserved at Dulwich, and printed by Greg, *Henslowe Papers*, p. 61. Cf. also Dasent, *Acts of the Privy Council*, XXXII, 511.

[2] *Raven's Almanack* (1609); Dekker's *Works* (ed. Grosart), IV, 210.

Thomas Greene was the leader, were contemplating a new playhouse. The company was licensed to use any "playhouse not used by others, by the said Thomas Greene elected, *or by him hereafter to be built.*" [1] Whether or no Greene and his fellows had some understanding with Holland, we cannot say. But in 1605 we find Holland disposing of one share in the new playhouse to Thomas Swynnerton, a member of Queen Anne's Troupe; and he may at the same time have disposed of other shares to other members, for his transaction with Swynnerton comes to our notice only through a subsequent lawsuit. The words used in the documents connected with the suit clearly suggest that the playhouse was completed at the time of the purchase. From the fact that Holland granted "a seventh part of the said playhouse and galleries, with a gatherer's place thereto belonging or appertaining, unto the said Thomas Swynnerton for diverse years," [2] it appears that the ownership of the playhouse had been divided into seven shares, some of which, according to custom, may have been subdivided into half-shares.

The name of the playhouse, as in the case of the Rose and the Curtain, was taken from the name of the estate on which it was erected. Of the building we have no pictorial representation; the picture in Kirkman's *The Wits* (1672), so often reproduced by

---

[1] The Malone Society's *Collections*, I, 265.
[2] Wallace, *Three London Theatres*, p. 18.

THE RED BULL

scholars as "The Interior of the Red Bull," has nothing whatever to do with that building. The Kirkman picture shows a small enclosed room, with a narrow stage illuminated by chandeliers and footlights; the Red Bull, on the contrary, was a large, open-air building, with its stage illuminated by the sun. It is thus described in Wright's *Historia Histrionica* (1699): "The Globe, Fortune, and Bull were large houses, and lay partly open to the weather." [1] Before its door was displayed a sign on which was painted a red bull; hence the playhouse is sometimes referred to simply as "at the sign of the Red Bull."

The building, as I have indicated, seems to have been completed in or before 1605; but exactly when the Queen's Men moved thither from the Curtain is not clear. The patent issued to the company on April 15, 1609, gives them license to play "within their now usual houses, called the Red Bull in Clerkenwell, and the Curtain in Holywell." [2] Since they would hardly make use of two big public playhouses at the same time, we might suspect that they were then arranging for the transfer. Moreover, Heath, in his *Epigrams*, printed in 1610 but probably written a year or two earlier, refers to the three important public playhouses of the day as the Globe, the Fortune, and the Curtain. Yet, that the

[1] Hazlitt's Dodsley, xv, 408. If the Kirkham picture represents the interior of any playhouse, it more likely represents the Cockpit, which was standing at the time of the Restoration.
[2] The Malone Society's *Collections*, i, 270.

Queen's Men were playing regularly at the Red Bull in 1609 is clear from Dekker's *Raven's Almanack*,[1] and they may have been playing there at intervals after 1605.

Dekker, in the pamphlet just mentioned, predicted "a deadly war" between the Globe, the Fortune, and the Red Bull. And he had good reasons for believing that the Queen's Men could successfully compete with the two other companies, for it numbered among its players some of the best actors of the day. The leader of the troupe was Thomas Greene, now chiefly known for the amusing comedy named, after him, *Greene's Tu Quoque*, but then known to all Londoners as the cleverest comedian since Tarleton and Kempe:

Scat. Yes, faith, brother, if it please you; let's go see a play at the Globe.
But. I care not; any whither, so the clown have a part; for, i' faith, I am nobody without a fool.
Gera. Why, then, we'll go to the Red Bull; they say Green's a good clown.[2]

The chief playwright for the troupe was the learned and industrious Thomas Heywood, who, like Shakespeare, was also an actor and full sharer in his

---

[1] Dekker's *Works* (ed. Grosart), IV, 210–11. I cannot understand why Murray (*English Dramatic Companies*, I, 152–53) and others say that Dekker refers to the Fortune, the Globe, and the Curtain. His puns are clear: "*Fortune* must favour some ... the *whole world* must stick to others ... and a third faction must fight like *Bulls*."

[2] *Greene's Tu Quoque*, Hazlitt's Dodsley, XI, 240. In May, 1610, there was "a notable outrage at the Playhouse called the Red Bull"; see *Middlesex County Records*, II, 64–65.

company. Charles Lamb, who was an ardent admirer of Heywood's plays, enthusiastically styled him "a prose Shakespeare"; and Wordsworth, with hardly less enthusiasm, declared him to have been "a great man."

In 1612 Thomas Greene died, and the leadership of the troupe was taken over by Christopher Beeston, a man well known in the theatrical life of the time. Late in February, 1617, Beeston transferred the Queen's Men to his new playhouse in Drury Lane, the Cockpit; in little more than a week the sacking of the Cockpit drove them back to their old quarters, where they remained until the following June. But even after this they seem not to have abandoned the Red Bull entirely.

Edward Alleyn, in his *Account Book*, writes: "Oct. 1, 1617, I came to London in the coach and went to the Red Bull"; and again under the date of October 3: "I went to the Red Bull, and received for *The Younger Brother* but £3 6s. 4d."[1] What these two passages mean it is hard to say, for they constitute the only references to the Red Bull in all the Alleyn papers; but they do not necessarily imply, as some have thought, that Alleyn was part owner of the playhouse; possibly he was merely selling to the Red Bull Company the manuscript of an old play.[2]

[1] Malone, *Variorum*, III, 223; Young, *The History of Dulwich College*, II, 51; Warner, *Catalogue*, p. 165; Collier, *Memoirs of Edward Alleyn*, p. 107.
[2] The play is not otherwise known; a play with this title, however, was entered on the Stationers' Register in 1653.

At the death of Queen Anne, March 2, 1619, the company was deprived of its "service," and after attending her funeral on May 13, was dissolved. Christopher Beeston joined Prince Charles's Men, and established that troupe at the Cockpit;[1] the other leading members of Queen Anne's Men seem to have continued at the Red Bull under the simple title "The Red Bull Company."

In April, 1622, a feltmaker's apprentice named John Gill,[2] while seated on the Red Bull stage, was accidentally injured by a sword in the hands of one of the actors, Richard Baxter. A few days later Gill called upon his fellow-apprentices to help him secure damages. In the forenoon he sent the following letter, now somewhat defaced by time, to Baxter:

> Mr. Blackster [sic]. So it is that upon Monday last it . . . to be upon your stage, intending no hurt to any one, where I was grievously wounded in the head, as may appear; and in the surgeon's hands, who is to have xs. for the cure; and in the meantime my Master to give me maintenance . . . [to my] great loss and hindrance; and therefore in kindness I desire you to give me satisfaction, seeing I was wounded by your own hand . . . weapon. If you refuse, then look to yourself and avoid the danger which shall this day ensue upon your company and house. For . . . as you can, for I am a feltmaker's prentice, and have made it known to at least one hundred and forty of our . . . who are all here present, ready to take revenge upon

---

[1] For details of this change, and of the quarrels that followed, see the chapter on the Cockpit.

[2] The name is also given, incorrectly, as Richard Gill.

THE RED BULL

you unless willingly you will give present satisfaction. Consider there . . . think fitting. And as you have a care for your own safeties, so let me have answer forthwith.[1]

Baxter turned the letter over to the authorities of Middlesex (hence its preservation), who took steps to guard the playhouse and actors. The only result was that prentices "to the number of one hundred persons on the said day riotously assembled at Clerkenwell, to the terror and disquiet of persons dwelling there."

On July 8, 1622, the Red Bull Company secured a license "to bring up children in the quality and exercise of playing comedies, histories, interludes, morals, pastorals, stage-plays and such like . . . to be called by the name of the Children of the Revels."[2] The Children of the Revels occupied the Red Bull until the summer of the following year, 1623, when they were dissolved. The last reference to them is in the Herbert Manuscript under the date of May 10, 1623.[3]

In August, 1623, we find the Red Bull occupied by Prince Charles's Men,[4] who, after the dissolution of the Revels Company, had moved thither from the less desirable Curtain.

Two years later, in 1625, Prince Charles became King, and took under his patronage his father's

[1] Jeaffreson, *Middlesex County Records*, II, 165–66; 175–76.
[2] Malone, *Variorum*, III, 62; The Malone Society's *Collections*, I, 284.
[3] Chalmers, *Supplemental Apology*, p. 213. [4] *Ibid.*, pp. 213–14.

troupe, the King's Men. Some of the members of the Prince Charles Troupe were transferred to the King's Men, and the rest constituted a nucleus about which a new company was organized, known simply as "The Red Bull Company."

About this time, it seems, the playhouse was rebuilt and enlarged. The Fortune had been destroyed by fire in 1621, and had just been rebuilt in a larger and handsomer form. In 1625 one W. C., in *London's Lamentation for her Sins*, writes: "Yet even then, Oh Lord, were the theatres magnified and enlarged."[1] This doubtless refers to the rebuilding of the Fortune and the Red Bull. Prynne specifically states in his *Histriomastix* (1633) that the Fortune and Red Bull had been "lately reedified [and] enlarged." But nothing further is known of the "re-edification and enlargement" of the Red Bull.

After its enlargement the playhouse seems to have acquired a reputation for noise and vulgarity. Carew, in 1630, speaks of it as a place where "noise prevails" and a "drowth of wit," and yet as always crowded with people while the better playhouses stood empty. In *The Careless Shepherdess*, acted at Salisbury Court, we read:

> And I will hasten to the money-box,
> And take my shilling out again;
> I'll go to the Bull, or Fortune, and there see
> A play for two-pence, and a jig to boot.[2]

---

[1] Quoted by Collier, *The History of English Dramatic Poetry* (1879), III, 121.
[2] Malone, *Variorum*, III, 70.

THE RED BULL

In 1638, a writer of verses prefixed to Randolph's *Poems* speaks of the "base plots" acted with great applause at the Red Bull.[1] James Wright informs us, in his *Historia Histrionica*, that the Red Bull and the Fortune were "mostly frequented by citizens and the meaner sort of people."[2] And Edmund Gayton, in his *Pleasant Notes*, wittily remarks: "I have heard that the poets of the Fortune and Red Bull had always a mouth-measure for their actors (who were terrible tear-throats) and made their lines proportionable to their compass, which were sesquipedales, a foot and a half."[3] Probably the ill repute of the large public playhouses at this time was chiefly due to the rise of private playhouses in the city.

In 1635 the Red Bull Company moved to the Fortune, and Prince Charles's Men occupied the Red Bull.

Five years later, at Easter, 1640, Prince Charles's Men moved back to the Fortune, and the Red Bull Company returned to its old home. In a prologue written to celebrate the event,[4] the members of the company declared:

> Here, gentlemen, our anchor's fix't.

This proved true, for the company remained at the

---

[1] Randolph's *Works* (ed. Hazlitt), p. 504.
[2] Hazlitt's Dodsley, xv, 407.
[3] *Pleasant Notes on Don Quixote*, p. 24.
[4] J. Tatham, *Fancies Theatre*. For a fuller discussion of the shifting of companies in 1635 and 1640 see the chapter on "The Fortune."

Red Bull until Parliament passed the ordinance of 1642 closing the playhouses and forbidding all dramatic performances. The ordinance, which was to hold good during the continuance of the civil war, was renewed in 1647, with January 1, 1648, set as the date of its expiration. Through some oversight a new ordinance was not immediately passed, and the actors were prompt to take advantage of the fact. They threw open the playhouses, and the Londoners flocked in great crowds to hear plays again. At the Red Bull, so we learn from the newspaper called *Perfect Occurrences*, was given a performance of Beaumont and Fletcher's *Wit Without Money*.

But on February 9, 1648, Parliament made up for its oversight by passing an exceptionally severe ordinance against dramatic exhibitions, directing that actors be publicly flogged, and that each spectator be fined the sum of five shillings.

During the dark years that followed, the Red Bull, in spite of this ordinance, was occasionally used by venturous actors. James Wright, in his *Historia Histrionica*, tells us that upon the outbreak of the war the various London actors had gone "into the King's army, and, like good men and true, served their old master, though in a different, yet more honourable capacity. Robinson was killed at the taking of a place (I think Basing House) by Harrison . . . Mohun was a captain . . . Hart was cornet of the same troop, and Shatterel

THE RED BULL

quartermaster. Allen, of the Cockpit, was a major. ... The rest either lost or exposed their lives for their king." [1] He concludes the narrative by saying that when the wars were over, those actors who were left alive gathered to London, "and for a subsistence endeavoured to revive their old trade privately." They organized themselves into a company in 1648 and attempted "to act some plays with as much caution and privacy as could be at the Cockpit"; but after three or four days they were stopped by soldiers. Thereafter, on special occasions "they used to bribe the officer who commanded the guard at Whitehall, and were thereupon connived at to act for a few days at the Red Bull, but were sometimes, notwithstanding, disturbed by soldiers." [2] To such clandestine performances Kirkman refers in his Preface to *The Wits, or Sport upon Sport* (1672): "I have seen the Red Bull Playhouse, which was a large one, so full that as many went back for want of room as had entered; and as meanly as you may now think of these drolls, they were then acted by the best comedians then and now in being." Not, however, without occasional trouble. In Whitelocke's *Memorials*, p. 435, we read: "20 Dec., 1649. Some stage-players in St. John's Street were apprehended by troopers, their clothes taken away, and themselves carried to prison"; again, in *The Perfect Account*, December 27–January 3, 1654–1655: "Dec.

---

[1] Hazlitt's Dodsley, xv, 409.   [2] *Ibid.*, 409–10.

30, 1654. — This day the players at the Red Bull, being gotten into all their borrowed gallantry and ready to act, were by some of the soldiery despoiled of all their bravery; but the soldiery carried themselves very civilly towards the audience." [1] In the *Weekly Intelligencer*, September 11–18, 1655, we find recorded still another sad experience for the actors: "Friday, September 11, 1655. — This day proved tragicall to the players at the Red Bull; their acting being against the Act of Parliament, the soldiers secured the persons of some of them who were upon the stage, and in the tiring-house they seized also upon their clothes in which they acted, a great part whereof was very rich." [2]

On this occasion, however, the soldiers, instead of carrying themselves "very civilly" towards the audience, undertook to exact from each of the spectators the fine of five shillings. The ordinance of Parliament, passed February 9, 1648, read: "And it is hereby further ordered and ordained, that every person or persons which shall be present and a spectator at such stage-play or interlude, hereby prohibited, shall for every time he shall be present, forfeit and pay the sum of five shillings to the use of the poor of the parish." [3] But the spectators did not submit to this fine without a struggle. Jeremiah Banks wrote to Williamson on September 16,

[1] Cited by C. H. Firth, in *Notes and Queries*, August 18, 1888, series VII, vol. VI, p. 122.
[2] *Ibid.*
[3] Hazlitt, *The English Drama and Stage*, p. 69.

THE RED BULL

1655: "At the playhouse this week many were put to rout by the soldiers and had broken crowns; the corporal would have been entrapped had he not been vigilant."[1] And in the *Weekly Intelligencer*, September 11–18, we read: "It never fared worse with the spectators than at this present, for those who had monies paid their five shillings apiece; those who had none, to satisfy their forfeits, did leave their cloaks behind them. The Tragedy of the spectators was the Comedy of the soldiers. There was abundance of the female sex, who, not able to pay five shillings, did leave some gage or other behind them, insomuch that although the next day after the Fair was expected to be a new fair of hoods, of aprons, and of scarfs; all which, their poverty being made known, and after some check for their trespass, were civilly again restored to the owners."[2]

At the period of the Restoration the Red Bull was among the first playhouses to reopen. John Downes, in his *Roscius Anglicanus*, writes: "The scattered remnant of several of these houses, upon King Charles' Restoration, framed a company, who acted again at the Bull."[3] Apparently the company

---

[1] *The Calendar of State Papers, Domestic, 1655*, p. 336.

[2] For a further account of this episode see *Mercurius Fumigosus*, No. 69.

[3] Cf. Wright, *Histrio Histrionica*, p. 412; and for the general history of the actors at the Red Bull during this period see the Herbert records in Halliwell-Phillipps, *A Collection of Ancient Documents*.

was brought together by the famous old Elizabethan actor, Anthony Turner. From the *Middlesex County Records* (III, 279) we learn that at first the players were interrupted by the authorities:

12 May, 1659. — Recognizances, taken before Ra: Hall, esq. J. P., of William Wintershall and Henry Eaton, both of Clerkenwell, gentlemen, in the sum of fifty pounds each; "Upon condition that Antony Turner shall personally appear at the next Quarter Sessions of the Peace to be holden at Hicks Hall for the said County of Middlesex; for the unlawful maintaining of stage-plays and interludes at the Red Bull in St. John's Street, which house he affirms that they hire of the parishioners of Clerkenwell at the rate of twenty shillings a day over and above what they have agreed to pay towards the relief of their poor and repairing their highways, and in the meantime to be of good behaviour and not to depart the Court without license. — Ra: Hall." Also similar Recognizances, taken on the same day, before the same J. P., of the same William Wintershall and Henry Eaton, gentlemen, in the same sum of fifty pounds each; for the appearance of Edward Shatterall at the next. Q. S. P. for Middlesex at Hicks Hall, "to answer for the unlawful maintaining of stage-plays and interludes at the Red Bull in St. John's Street &c." S. P. R., 17, May, 1659.

Later, it seems, they secured a license from the authorities, and thenceforth acted without interruption. Samuel Pepys made plans "to go to the Red Bull Playhouse" with Mrs. Pierce and her husband on August 3, 1660, but was prevented by

THE RED BULL

business. An account of his visit there on March 23, 1661, is thus given in his *Diary:*

All the morning at home putting papers in order; dined at home, and then out to the Red Bull (where I had not been since plays came up again), but coming too soon I went out again and walked up and down the Charterhouse Yard and Aldersgate Street. At last came back again and went in, where I was led by a seaman that knew me, but is here as a servant, up to the tiring-room, where strange the confusion and disorder that there is among them in fitting themselves, especially here, where the clothes are very poor and the actors but common fellows. At last into the pit, where I think there was not above ten more than myself, and not one hundred in the whole house. And the play, which is called *All's Lost by Lust*, poorly done; and with so much disorder, among others, that in the musique-room, the boy that was to sing a song not singing it right, his master fell about his ears and beat him so, that it put the whole house in an uproar.

The actors, however, did not remain long at the Red Bull. They built for themselves a new theatre in Drury Lane, whither they moved on April 8, 1663;[1] and after this the old playhouse was deserted. In Davenant's *The Play-House to Be Let* (1663), I, i, we read:

> Tell 'em the Red Bull stands empty for fencers:[2]
> There are no tenants in it but old spiders.

---

[1] After November 8, 1660, they acted also in Gibbon's Tennis Court in Clare Market, which they had fitted up as a theatre; see Halliwell-Phillipps, *A Collection of Ancient Documents*, p. 34.

[2] See Pepys' *Diary*, April 25, 1664.

CHAPTER XV

WHITEFRIARS

THE district of Whitefriars, lying just outside the city wall to the west, and extending from Fleet Street to the Thames, was once in the possession of the order of White Friars, and the site of an important monastery; but in Elizabeth's time the church had disappeared, most of the ancient buildings had been dismantled, and in their place, as Stow tells us, were "many fair houses builded, lodgings for noblemen and others." Since at the dissolution of the monasteries the property had come into the possession of the Crown, it was not under the jurisdiction of the London Common Council—a fact which made Whitefriars, like Blackfriars, a desirable refuge for players seeking to escape the hostility of the city authorities.[1] One might naturally expect the appearance of playing here at an early date, but the evidence is slight.[2]

[1] Whitefriars passed under city control in 1608 by grant of King James I, but certain rights remained, notably that of sanctuary. This has been celebrated in Shadwell's play, *The Squire of Alsatia*, and in Scott's romance, *The Fortunes of Nigel*.

[2] Prynne, in *Histriomastix* (1633), p. 491, quotes a passage from Richard Reulidge's *Monster Lately Found Out and Discovered* (1628), in which there is a reference to a playhouse as existing in Whitefriars "not long after" 1580. By "playhouse" Reulidge possibly meant an inn used for acting; but the whole passage, written by a Puritan after the lapse of nearly half a century, is

WHITEFRIARS

The first appearance of a regular playhouse in Whitefriars dates from the early years of King James's reign. With our present knowledge we cannot fix the date exactly, yet we can feel reasonably certain that it was not long before 1607 — probably about 1605.

The chief spirit in the organization of the new playhouse seems to have been the poet Michael Drayton, who had secured a patent from King James to "erect" a company of child actors, to be known as "The Children of His Majesty's Revels." [1] Obviously his hope was to make the Children of His Majesty's Revels at Whitefriars rival the successful Children of Her Majesty's Revels at Blackfriars. In this ambitious enterprise he associated with himself a wealthy London merchant, Thomas Woodford, whom we know as having been interested in various theatrical investments.[2] These two men leased from Lord Buckhurst for a

---

open to grave suspicion, especially in its details. Again Richard Flecknoe, in *A Short Discourse of the English Stage* (1664), states that the Children of the Chapel Royal acted in Whitefriars. But that he confused the word "Whitefriars" with "Blackfriars" is shown by the rest of his statement.

[1] Fleay, Murray, and others are wrong in assuming that this troupe was merely a continuation of the Paul's Boys. So far as I can discover, there is no official record of the patent issued to Drayton; but that such a patent was issued is clear from the lawsuits of 1609, printed by Greenstreet in *The New Shakspere Society's Transactions* (1887–90), p. 269.

[2] He was part proprietor of the Red Bull. In the case of Witter v. Heminges and Condell he was examined as a witness (see Wallace, *Shakespeare and his London Associates*, p. 74), but what connection, if any, he had with the Globe does not appear.

short period of time a building described as a "mansion house" formerly a part of the Whitefriars monastery: "the rooms of which are thirteen in number, three below, and ten above; that is to say, the great hall, the kitchen by the yard, and a cellar, with all the rooms from the Master of the Revells' office as the same are now severed and divided."[1] The "great hall" here mentioned, once the refectory of the monks, was made into the playhouse. Its "great" size may be inferred from the fact that there were ten rooms "above"; and its general excellence may be inferred from the fact that it was leased at £50 per annum, whereas Blackfriars, in a more desirable location and fully equipped as a theatre, was rented for only £40.

From an early seventeenth-century survey of the Whitefriars property (see the opposite page), we are able to place the building very exactly. The part of the monastery used as a playhouse — the Frater — was the southern cloister, marked in the plan, "My Lords Cloyster." The "kitchen by the yard" mentioned in the document just quoted is clearly represented in the survey by the "Scullere." The size of the playhouse is hard to ascertain, but it was approximately thirty-five feet in width and eighty-five feet in length.[2] In the London of to-

[1] Greenstreet, *The New Shakspere Society's Transactions* (1887–90), p. 275.
[2] The stipple walls, in the original survey colored gray, were of stone; the thinner walls of the adjoining "tenements," in the original colored red, were of brick.

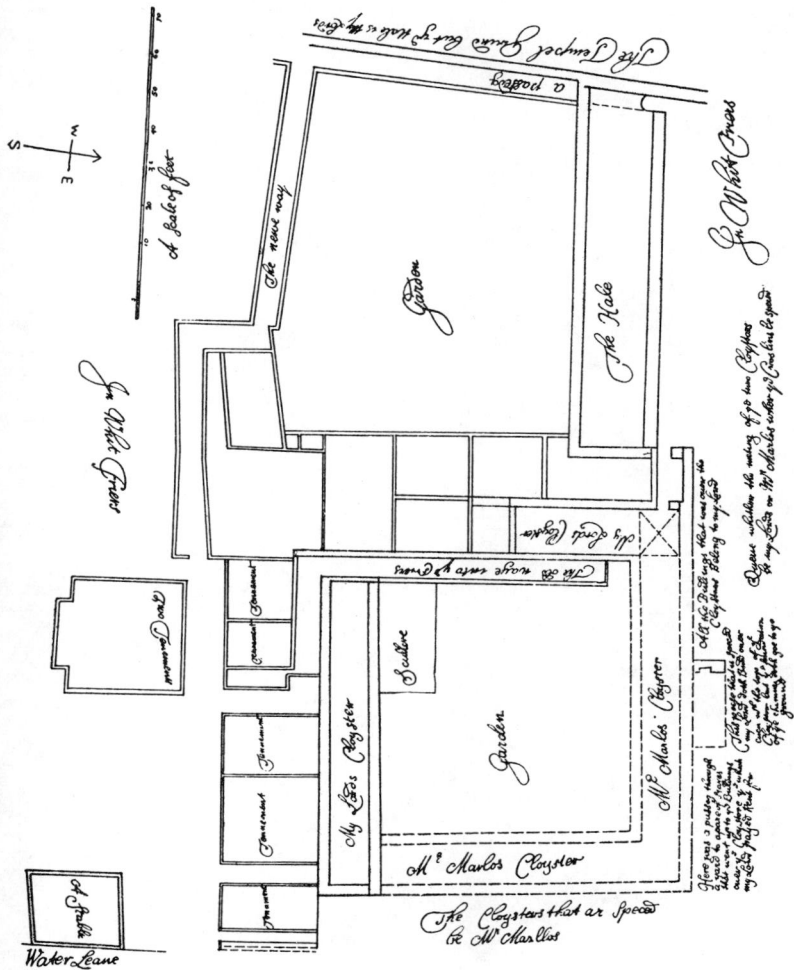

A PLAN OF WHITEFRIARS

A portion of an early seventeenth-century survey of the Whitefriars property. The playhouse adjoined the "Scullere" on the south. (This survey was discovered in the Print Room of the British Museum by Mr. A. W. Clapham, and reproduced in *The Journal of the British Archæological Association*, 1910.)

day it extended roughly from Bouverie Street to Ashen-tree Court, and lay just north of George Yard.

Of the career of the Children under the joint management of Drayton and Woodford we know almost nothing. But in March, 1608, a new management assumed charge of the troupe, and from this point on the history of the playhouse is reasonably clear.

The original lease of the building, it seems, expired on March 5, 1608. But before the expiration — in the latter part of 1607 or in the early part of 1608 — Drayton and Woodford secured a new lease on the property for six years, eight months, and twenty days, or until December 25 (one of the four regular feasts of the year), 1614. In February, 1608, after having secured this renewal of the lease, Thomas Woodford suddenly determined to retire from the enterprise; and he sold his moiety to one David Lording Barry,[1] author of the play *Ram Alley*. Barry and Drayton at once made plans to divide the property into six shares, so as to distribute the expenses and the risks as well as the hoped-for profits. Barry induced his friend, George

---

[1] By a stupid error often called Lodowick Barry. For an explanation of the error see an article by the present writer in *Modern Philology*, April, 1912, ix, 567. Mr. W. J. Lawrence has recently shown (*Studies in Philology*, University of North Carolina, April, 1917) that David Barry was the eldest son of the ninth Viscount Buttevant, and was called "Lording" by courtesy. At the time he became interested in the Whitefriars Playhouse he was twenty-two years old. He died in 1610.

Androwes, to purchase one share, and hence the lawsuit from which we derive most of our knowledge of the playhouse. From this suit I quote below the more significant part relating to the new organization:

> Humbly complaining, sheweth unto your honorable lordship, your daily orator, George Androwes, of London, silkweaver, that whereas one Lordinge Barry, about February which was in the year of our Lord 1607 [i.e., 1608], pretending himself to be lawfully possessed of one moiety of a messuage or mansion house, parcel of the late dissolved monastery called the Whitefriars, in Fleet Street, in the suburbs of London, by and under a lease made thereof, about March then next following, from the right honorable Robert, Lord Buckhurst, unto one Michael Drayton and Thomas Woodford, for the term of six years, eight months, and twenty days then following, for and under the yearly rent of fifty pounds reserved thereupon; the moiety of which said lease and premisses, by mean assignment from the said Thomas Woodford, was lawfully settled in the said Lordinge Barry, as he did pretend, together with the moiety of diverse play-books, apparel, and other furnitures and necessaries used and employed in and about the said messuage and the Children of the Revels,[1] there being, in making and setting forth plays, shows, and interludes, and such like. And the said Lordinge Barry . . . being desirous to join others with him in the interest of the same, who might be contributory to such future charges as should arise in setting forth of plays and shows there, did thereupon . . . solicit

[1] At this time the Children of Blackfriars had lost their patent, so that the Children at Whitefriars were the only Revels troupe.

MICHAEL DRAYTON
(From a painting in the National Portrait Gallery, London: photograph copyrighted by Emery Walker, Ltd.)

and persuade your orator to take from the said Barry an assignment of a sixth part of the messuage, premisses, and profits aforesaid.

This passage gives us an interesting glimpse of Drayton and Barry in their efforts to organize a syndicate for exploiting the Children of His Majesty's Revels. They induced several other persons to buy half-shares; and then they engaged, as manager of the Children, Martin Slaiter,[1] a well-known and thoroughly experienced actor. For his services as manager, Slaiter was to receive one whole share in the organization, and lodgings for himself and his family of ten in the building. The syndicate thus formed was made up of four whole-sharers, Michael Drayton, Lordinge Barry, George Androwes, and Martin Slaiter, and four half-sharers, William Trevell, William Cooke, Edward Sibthorpe, and John Mason.[2]

The "great hall" had, of course, already been fitted up for the acting of plays, and the new lessees did not at first contemplate any expenditure on the building. Later, however, — if we can believe Androwes, — they spent a not inconsiderable sum for improvements. The Children already had certain plays, and to these were added some new ones. Among the plays in their repertoire were Day's *Humour Out of Breath*, Middleton's *Family of Love*,

[1] Also spelled Slater, Slaughter, Slather, Slawghter. Henslowe often refers to him as "Martin."
[2] Mr. Wallace (*The Century Magazine*, 1910, LXXX, 511) incorrectly says that Whitefriars was held by "six equal sharers."

Armin's *The Two Maids of Moreclacke*, Sharpham's *Cupid's Whirligig*, Markham and Machin's *The Dumb Knight*, Barry's *Ram Alley*, and Mason's *The Turk*. The last two writers were sharers, and it seems likely that Drayton, also a sharer and experienced as a dramatist, contributed some plays towards the stock of the company.

The new organization, with bright prospects for success, was launched in March, 1608. Almost at once, however, it began to suffer from ill luck. In April the Children at Blackfriars, by their performance of *Byron*, caused King James to close all playhouses in London. How long he kept them closed we do not know, but we find the lessees of Whitefriars joining with the three other London companies in seeking to have the inhibition raised. As the French Ambassador informed his Government: "Pour lever cette défense, quatres autres compagnies, qui y sont encore, offrent déjà cent mille francs, lesquels pourront bien leur en ordonner la permission." [1]

Even if this inhibition was shortly raised, the Whitefriars organization was not much better off, for in July the plague set in with unusual violence, and acting was seriously if not wholly interrupted for the next twelve months and more. As a result, the profits from the theatre did not come up to the

---

[1] Letter of M. De La Boderie, the French Ambassador to England; quoted by E. K. Chambers, *Modern Language Review*, IV, 159.

"fair and false flattering speeches" which at the outset Barry had made to prospective investors, and this led to bad feeling among the sharers.

The company at Blackfriars, of course, was suffering in a similar way. On August 8, 1608, their playhouse was surrendered to the owner, Richard Burbage, and the Children being thus left without a home were dispersed. Early in 1609, probably in February, Robert Keysar (the manager of the Blackfriars troupe), Philip Rosseter, and others secured the lease of the Whitefriars Playhouse from Drayton and the rest of the discontented sharers, and reassembled there the Children of Blackfriars. What became of the Whitefriars troupe we do not know; but it is highly likely that the new organization took over the better actors from Drayton's company. At any rate, we do not hear again of the Children of His Majesty's Revels.

When Keysar and this new troupe of child-actors moved into Whitefriars, Slaiter and his family of ten were expelled from the building. This led to a lawsuit, and explains much in the legal documents printed by Greenstreet. Slaiter complained with no little feeling that he had been "riotously, willfully, violently, and unlawfully, contrary to the said articles and pretended agreement [by which he had been not only engaged as a manager, but also guaranteed a home for the period of "all the term of years in the lease"], put and kept out of his said rooms of habitation for him, this defendant, and his family, and all other his means of livelihood, thereby leaving this defendant and his whole family, being ten in number, to the world to seek for bread and other means to live by." [1]

The new Whitefriars troupe acted five plays at Court during the winter of 1609–10. Payments therefor were made to Robert Keysar, and the company was referred to merely as "The Children of the Whitefriars." But on January 4, 1610, the company secured a royal patent authorizing the use of the title "The Children of the Queen's Revels." [2] The patent was granted to Robert Daborne, Philip Rosseter, John Tarbock, Richard Jones, and Robert Browne; but Keysar, though not named in the grant, was still one of the important sharers. [3]

The troupe well deserved the patronage of the Queen. Keysar described the Blackfriars Children whom he had reorganized as "a company of the most expert and skillful actors within the realm of England, to the number of eighteen or twenty persons, all or most of them, trained up in that service in the reign of the late Queen Elizabeth for ten years together." [4] And to these, as I have pointed out, it seems likely that the best members of the bankrupt Children of His Majesty's Revels had

---

[1] Greenstreet, *The New Shakspere Society's Transactions* (1887–90), p. 283.
[2] Printed in The Malone Society's *Collections*, I, 271.
[3] See Keysar *v.* Burbage *et al.*, printed by Mr. Wallace, in his *Shakespeare and his London Associates*, pp. 80 ff.
[4] *Ibid.*, p. 90.

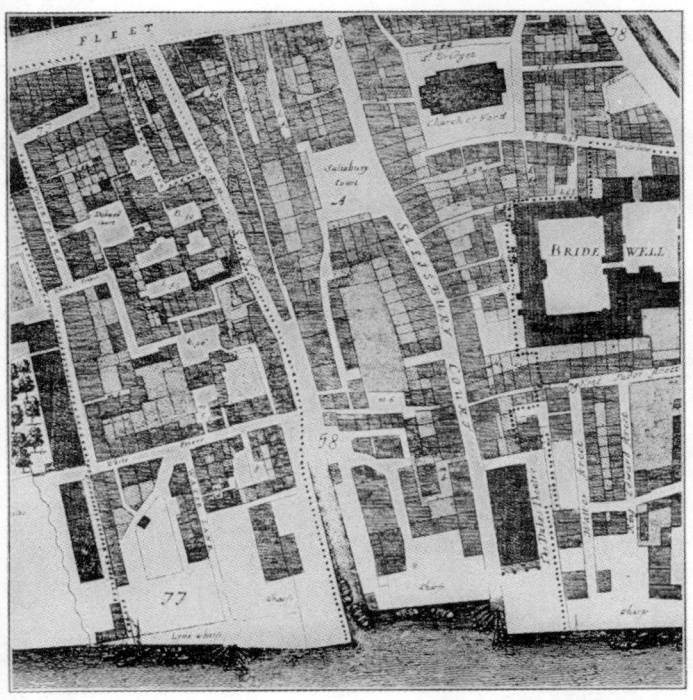

THE SITES OF THE WHITEFRIARS AND THE SALISBURY COURT
PLAYHOUSES

The Whitefriars Playhouse was just north of "K. 46"; the Salisbury Court Playhouse was just south of the court of that name. (From Ogilby and Morgan's *Map of London*, 1677.)

WHITEFRIARS

been added. The chief actor of the new organization was Nathaniel Field, whose histrionic ability placed him beside Edward Alleyn and Richard Burbage. One of the first plays he was called upon to act in his new theatre was Jonson's brilliant comedy, *Epicœne*, in which he took the leading rôle.

The idea then occurred to Rosseter to secure a monopoly on child-acting and on private playhouses. The Children of His Majesty's Revels had ceased to exist. The Blackfriars Playhouse had been closed by royal command, and its lease had been surrendered to its owner, Richard Burbage. The only rival to the Children at Whitefriars was the troupe of Paul's Boys acting in their singing-school behind the Cathedral. How Rosseter attempted to buy them off is thus recorded by Richard Burbage and John Heminges:

There being, as these defendants verily think, but only three private playhouses in the city of London, the one of which being in the Blackfriars and in the hands of these defendants or of their assigns, one other being in the Whitefriars in the hands or occupation of the said complainant himself [Keysar], his partners [Rosseter, *et al.*], or assigns, and the third near St. Paul's Church, then being in the hands of one Mr. Pierce, but then unused for a playhouse. One Mr. Rosseter, a partner of the said complainant [Keysar] dealt for and compounded with the said Mr. Pierce [Master of the Paul's Boys] to the only benefit of him, the said Rosseter, the now complainant [Keysar], the rest of their partners and company, and without the privity, knowledge, or consent of these defendants [the King's Company], or any of them, and that thereby they, the said complainant [Keysar] and the said Rosseter and their partners and company might advance their gains and profit to be had and made in their said house in Whitefriars, that there might be a cessation of playing and plays to be acted in the said house near St. Paul's Church aforesaid, for which the said Rosseter compounded with the said Pierce to give him, the said Pierce, twenty pounds per annum.[1]

By this means Rosseter disposed of the competition of the Paul's Boys. But, although he secured a monopoly on child-acting, he failed to secure a monopoly on private playhouses, for shortly after he had sealed this bargain with Pierce, the powerful King's Men opened up at Blackfriars. Rosseter promptly requested them to pay half the "dead rent" to Pierce, which they good-naturedly agreed to do.

In 1613 Whitefriars was rented by certain London apprentices for the performance "at night" of Robert Taylor's *The Hog Hath Lost His Pearl*. The episode is narrated by Sir Henry Wotton in a letter to Sir Edmund Bacon:

On Sunday last, at night, and no longer, some sixteen apprentices (of what sort you shall guess by the rest of the story) having secretly learnt a new play without book,[2] entitled *The Hog Hath Lost His Pearl*,

[1] Wallace, *Shakespeare and his London Associates*, p. 95.
[2] Miss Gildersleeve, in her valuable *Government Regulation of the Elizabethan Drama*, p. 112, says: "Just what is the meaning of 'a new Play without Book' no one seems to have conjec-

WHITEFRIARS

took up the Whitefriars for their theatre, and having invited thither (as it should seem) rather their mistresses than their masters, who were all to enter *per buletini* for a note of distinction from ordinary comedians. Towards the end of the play the sheriffs (who by chance had heard of it) came in (as they say) and carried some six or seven of them to perform the last act at Bridewell. The rest are fled. Now it is strange to hear how sharp-witted the city is, for they will needs have Sir John Swinerton, the Lord Mayor, be meant by the Hog, and the late Lord Treasurer by the Pearl.[1]

Apparently the Children of the Queen's Revels continued successfully at Whitefriars until March, 1613. On that date Rosseter agreed with Henslowe to join the Revels with the Lady Elizabeth's Men then acting at the Swan. The new organization, following the example of the King's Men, used Whitefriars as a winter, and the Swan as a summer, house. Thus for a time at least Whitefriars came under the management of Henslowe.

Rosseter's lease of the building was to expire in the following year. He seems to have made plans — possibly with the assistance of Henslowe — to erect in Whitefriars a more suitable playhouse for the newly organized company; at least that is a plausible interpretation of the following curious entry in Sir George Buc's Office Book: "July 13,

tured." And she develops the theory that "it refers to the absence of a licensed play-book," etc. The phrase "to learn without book" meant simply "to memorize."

[1] *Reliquiæ Wottonianæ* (ed. 1672), p. 402. The letter is dated merely 1612–13. In connection with the play one should study *The Hector of Germany*, 1615.

1613, for a license to erect a new playhouse in Whitefriars, &c. £20." [1] But the new playhouse thus projected never was built, doubtless because of strong local opposition. Instead, Henslowe erected for the company a public playhouse on the Bankside, known as "The Hope."

In March, 1614, at the expiration of one year, Rosseter withdrew from his partnership with Henslowe. On December 25, 1614, his lease of the Whitefriars expired, and he was apparently unable to renew it. Thereupon he attempted to fit up a private playhouse in the district of Blackfriars, and on June 3, 1615, he actually secured a royal license to do so. But in this effort, too, he was foiled.[2]

After this we hear little or nothing of the Whitefriars Playhouse. Yet the building may occasionally have been used for dramatic purposes. Cunningham says: "The case of Trevill *v.* Woodford, in the Court of Requests, informs us that plays were performed at the Whitefriars Theatre as late as 1621; Sir Anthony Ashley, the then landlord of the house, entering the theatre in that year, and turning the players out of doors, on pretense that half a year's rent was yet unpaid to him."[3] I have not

[1] Malone, *Variorum*, III, 52.
[2] See the chapter on "Rosseter's Blackfriars." The documents concerned in this venture are printed in The Malone Society's *Collections*, I, 277.
[3] *The Shakespeare Society's Papers*, IV, 90. The document printed by Collier in *New Facts Regarding the Life of Shakespeare* (1835), p. 44, as from a manuscript in his possession, is, I think, an obvious forgery.

been able to examine this document. Neither Fleay nor Murray has found any trace of a company at Whitefriars after Rosseter's departure; hence for all practical purposes we may regard the Whitefriars Playhouse as having come to the end of its career in 1614.

CHAPTER XVI

THE HOPE

ON August 29, 1611, Henslowe became manager of the Lady Elizabeth's Men. Having agreed among other things to furnish them with a playhouse,[1] and no longer being in possession of the Rose, he rented the old Swan and maintained them there throughout the year 1612.

In March of the following year, 1613, he entered into a partnership with Philip Rosseter (the manager of the private playhouse of Whitefriars), and "joined" the Lady Elizabeth's Men with Rosseter's excellent troupe of the Queen's Revels. Apparently the intention of Henslowe and Rosseter was to form a company strong enough to compete on equal terms with the King's Men. In imitation of the King's Men, who used the Globe as a summer and the Blackfriars as a winter home, the newly amalgamated company was to use the Swan and the Whitefriars.[2] And the chief actor of the

---

[1] The agreement has been lost, but for a probably similar agreement, made with the actor Nathaniel Field, see Greg, *Henslowe Papers*, p. 23.

[2] Daborne writes to Henslowe on June 5, 1613: "The company told me you were expected there yesterday to conclude about their coming over ... my own play which shall be ready before they come over." This, I suspect, refers to the moving of the company to the Swan for the summer. (See Greg, *Henslowe Pa-*

THE HOPE

troupe, corresponding to Richard Burbage of the King's Men, was to be Nathaniel Field, then at the height of his powers:

> *Cokes.* Which is your Burbage now?
> *Leatherhead.* What mean you by that, sir?
> *Cokes.* Your best actor, your Field.
> *Littlewit.* Good, i' faith! you are even with me, sir.[1]

Among their playwrights were Ben Jonson, Philip Massinger, John Fletcher, and Robert Daborne, not to mention Field, who in addition to acting wrote excellent plays.

If it was the purpose of Henslowe and Rosseter to compete with the Globe Company in a winter as well as in a summer house, that purpose was endangered by the fact that Rosseter's lease of his private theatre expired within a year and a half, and could not be renewed. Rosseter and Henslowe, as pointed out in the preceding chapter, seem to have attempted to erect in Whitefriars a winter home for their troupe; so, at least, I have interpreted the curious entry in Sir George Buc's Office Book: "July 13, 1613, for a license to erect a new playhouse in the Whitefriars, &c. £20."[2] The attempt, however, was foiled, probably by the strong opposition of the inhabitants of the district.

---

pers, p. 72.) That Henslowe was manager of a "private" house in 1613 is revealed by another letter from Daborne, dated December 9, 1613. (See Greg, *ibid.*, p. 79.)

[1] *Bartholomew Fair*, v, iii. The part of Littlewit was presumably taken by Field himself.

[2] Malone, *Variorum*, III, 52.

Shortly after this, Henslowe made plans to provide the company with a new and better public playhouse on the Bankside, more conveniently situated than the Swan. The old Bear Garden was beginning to show signs of decay, and, doubtless, would soon have to be rebuilt. This suggested to Henslowe the idea of tearing down that ancient structure and erecting in its place a larger and handsomer building to serve both for the performance of plays and for the baiting of animals. To this plan Jacob Meade, Henslowe's partner in the ownership of the Bear Garden, agreed.

Accordingly, on August 29, 1613, Henslowe and Meade signed a contract with a carpenter named Katherens to pull down the Bear Garden and erect in its place a new structure. The original contract, preserved among the Henslowe Papers, is one of the most valuable documents we have relating to the early theatres. It is too long and verbose for insertion here, but I give below a summary of its contents.[1] Katherens agreed:

1. To "pull down" the Bear Garden and "the stable wherein the bulls and horses" had been kept; and "near or upon the said place where the said game-place did heretofore stand," to "newly erect, build, and set up" a "playhouse, fit and convenient in all things both for players to play in, and for the game of bears and bulls to be baited in."

[1] The contract is printed in full in Greg, *Henslowe Papers*, p. 19.

THE HOPE PLAYHOUSE, OR SECOND BEAR GARDEN
From Hollar's *View of London* (1647).

THE HOPE

2. "To build the same of such large compass, form, wideness, and height as the playhouse called the Swan."

3. To provide for the building "a good sure, and sufficient foundation of bricks . . . thirteen inches at the least above the ground."

4. To make three galleries: "the inner principal posts of the first story to be twelve feet in height, and ten inches square; in the middle story . . . eight inches square; in the upper story . . . seven inches square." [1]

5. To "make two boxes in the lowermost story, fit and decent for gentlemen to sit in," and in the rest of the galleries "partitions between the rooms as they are in the said playhouse called the Swan."

6. To construct "a stage, to be carried and taken away, and to stand upon tressels, good, substantial, and sufficient for the carrying and bearing of such a stage."

7. To "build the heavens all over the said stage, to be borne or carried without any posts or supporters to be fixed or set upon the said stage."

8. To equip the stage with "a fit and convenient tyre-house."

9. To "build two staircases without and adjoining to the said playhouse . . . of such largeness and

---

[1] The height is given for the first story only. We may assume that the middle and uppermost stories were of diminishing heights. as in the case of the Fortune Playhouse, in which the galleries were respectively twelve, eleven, and nine feet in height.

height as the staircases of the said playhouse called the Swan."

10. "To new build, erect, and set up the said bull-house and stable . . . of that largeness and fitness as shall be sufficient to keep and hold six bulls and three horses."

11. "To new tyle with English tyles all the upper roof of the said playhouse . . . and stable."

12. To have the playhouse finished "upon or before the last day of November," 1613.

For all this Katherens was to receive the sum of £360; but since Henslowe and Meade supplied a large share of the lumber and other materials, the total cost of the building may be estimated as not less than £600.

When completed, the new playhouse was appropriately christened "The Hope."

It has been generally assumed that a picture of the Hope is given in Visscher's *View of London*, published in 1616; but this, I think, is exceedingly doubtful. In drawing the Bankside, Visscher rather slavishly copied the Agas map of 1560, inserting a few new buildings, — notably the playhouses, — and it is virtually certain that he represented the "Bear Garden" (so he distinctly calls it) and the Globe as they were before their reconstruction.[1]

---

[1] The Merian *View of London*, published in 1638 at Frankfort-am-Main, is merely a copy of the Visscher view with the addition of certain details from another and earlier view not yet identi-

THE HOPE

The first representation of the Hope is to be found in Hollar's splendid *View of London* published in 1647 (see page 326). At this time the building, which had for many years been devoted wholly to the royal sports of bull- and bear-baiting, was still standing. It is hard to believe that an artist who so carefully represented the famous edifices of the city should have greatly erred in drawing the "Bear Baiting House," — a structure more curious than they, and quite as famous.

Hollar represents the Hope as circular. According to the contract Katherens was "to build the same of such large compass, form, wideness, and height as the playhouse called the Swan." Whether the word "form" was intended to apply to the exterior of the building we do not know. The Swan was decahedral; Visscher represents the "Bear Garden" as octagonal (which is correct for the Bear Garden that preceded the Hope). But since the exterior was of lime and plaster, and a decahedral form had no advantage, Katherens may well have constructed a circular building as Hollar indicates. Perhaps it is significant in this connection that John Taylor, the Water-Poet, in his *Bull, Bear, and Horse*, refers to the Hope as a "sweet, rotuntious college." Significant also, perhaps, is the

fied. It has no independent value. The *View of London* printed in Howell's *Londinopolis* (1657), is merely a slavish copy of the Merian view. Visscher's representation of the Bear Garden does not differ in any essential way from the representation in Hondius's *View* of 1610. For a fuller discussion see pages 126, 146, 248.

clause in the contract by which Katherens was required to "build the heavens all over the stage," for this exactly describes the heavens as drawn by Hollar. I see no reason to doubt that in the *View* of 1647 we have a reasonably faithful representation of the Hope.

The Hope was probably opened shortly after November 30, 1613, the date at which Katherens had bound himself to have the building "fully finished," and it was occupied, of course, by the Henslowe and Rosseter troupe of actors. The arrangement of the movable stage enabled Henslowe and Meade to use the building also for animal-baiting. According to the contract with the actors, the latter were to "lie still one day in fourteen" for the baiting.[1] This may not have been a serious interruption for the players; but the presence of the stable, the bear dens, and the kennels for the dogs must have rendered the playhouse far from pleasant to the audiences. Ben Jonson, in the Induction to his *Bartholomew Fair*, acted at the Hope in October, 1614, remarks: "And though the Fair be not kept in the same region that some here perhaps would have it, yet think that therein the author hath observed a special decorum, the

---

[1] Greg, *Henslowe Papers*, p. 88; cf. p. 125, where animal-baiting is said to be used "one day of every four days" — a possible error for "fourteen days." In the manuscript notes to the Phillipps copy of Stow's *Survey* (1631), we are told that baiting was used at the Hope on Tuesdays and Thursdays; but the anonymous commentator is very inaccurate.

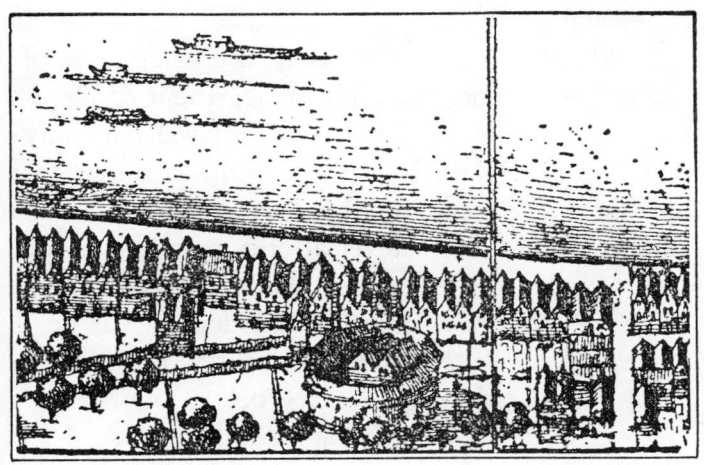

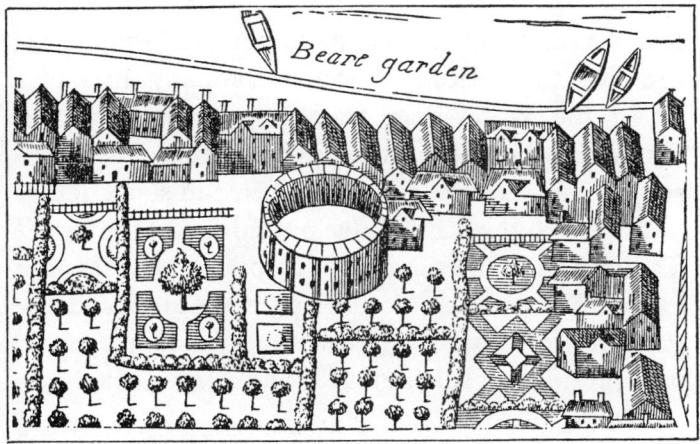

THE HOPE PLAYHOUSE, OR SECOND BEAR GARDEN

The upper view is from Hollar's Post-conflagration map in the Crace Collection of the British Museum; the lower view is from Faithorne's Map of London (1658).

place being as dirty as Smithfield, and as stinking every whit."[1]

In March, 1614, — that is, at the completion of one full year under the joint management of Henslowe and Rosseter, — the amalgamated company was "broken," and Rosseter withdrew, selling his interest in the company's apparel to Henslowe and Meade for £63. The latter at once reorganized the actors under the patent of the Lady Elizabeth's Men, and continued them at the Hope.[2] The general excellence of the troupe thus formed is referred to by John Taylor, the Water-Poet, in the lines:

> And such a company (I'll boldly say)
> That better (nor the like) e'er play'd a play.[3]

But this encomium may have been in large measure due to gratitude, for the company had just saved the Water-Poet from a very embarrassing situation. The amusing episode which gave occasion to this deserves to be chronicled in some detail.

With "a thousand bills posted over the city" Taylor had advertised to the public that at the Hope Playhouse on October 7, 1614, he would engage in a contest of wit with one William Fennor, who proudly styled himself "The King's Majesty's

[1] The Rose Playhouse was likewise affected. Dekker, in *Satiromastix*, III, iv, says: "'Th'ast a breath as sweet as the Rose that grows by the Bear Garden."

[2] Greg, *Henslowe Papers*, p. 87. The articles of agreement between Henslowe and Meade and the company, are printed by Greg on page 23.

[3] *Works*, Folio of 1630; The Spenser Society's reprint, p. 307.

THE HOPE

Riming Poet."[1] On the appointed day the house was "fill'd with a great audience" that had paid extra money to hear the contest between two such well-known extemporal wits. But Fennor did not appear. The result may best be told by Taylor himself:

> I then stept out, their angers to appease;
> But they all raging, like tempestuous seas,
> Cry'd out, their expectations were defeated,
> And how they all were cony-catch'd and cheated.
> Some laught, some swore, some star'd and stamp'd and curst,
> And in confusèd humors all out burst.
> I (as I could) did stand the desp'rate shock,
> And bid the brunt of many dang'rous knock.
> For now the stinkards, in their ireful wraths,
> Bepelted me with lome, with stones, with laths.
> One madly sits like bottle-ale and hisses;
> Another throws a stone, and 'cause he misses,
> He yawnes and bawles, . . .
> Some run to th' door to get again their coin . . .
> One valiantly stepped upon the stage,
> And would tear down the hangings in his rage . . .
> What I endur'd upon that earthly hell
> My tongue or pen cannot describe it well.[2]

At this point the actors came to his rescue and presented a play that mollified the audience. Taylor had to content himself with a printed justification. The bitter invective of Taylor against Fen-

---

[1] Fennor is not to be confused (as is commonly done) with Vennar (see p. 177). Such wit-contests were popular; Fennor had recently challenged Kendall, on the Fortune Stage.

[2] John Taylor's *Works*, Folio of 1630, p. 142; The Spenser Society's reprint, p. 304.

nor, Fennor's reply, and Taylor's several answers are to be found in the folio edition of the Water-Poet's works. The episode doubtless furnished much amusement to the city.

Some three weeks after this event, on October 31, 1614, the Lady Elizabeth's Men produced with great success Jonson's *Bartholomew Fair;* and on November 1 they were called upon to give the play at Court. But the career of the company was in the main unhappy. Henslowe managed their affairs on the theory that "should these fellows come out of my debt, I should have no rule with them."[1] Accordingly in three years he "broke" and again reorganized them no fewer than five times.

At last, in February, 1615, he not only "broke" the company, but severed his connection with them for ever. He turned the hired men over to other troupes, and sold the stock of apparel "to strangers" for £400. The indignant actors, in June, 1615, drew up "Articles of Grievance" in which they charged Henslowe with having extorted from the company by unjust means the sum of £567; and also "Articles of Oppression" in which they accused him of various dishonorable practices in his dealings with them.[2]

Shortly after severing his connection with the Lady Elizabeth's Men, Henslowe, in March, 1615, seems to have taken over Prince Charles's Men, who, it appears, had been acting at the Swan. To

---

[1] Greg, *Henslowe Papers*, p. 89.   [2] *Ibid.*, pp. 86, 89.

THE HOPE

this new company — the "strangers" referred to, I think — he had already transferred some of the hirelings, and had sold the Hope stock of apparel for £400.

Henslowe died early in January of the following year, 1616, and his interest in the theatre passed to Edward Alleyn. On March 20, 1616, Alleyn and Meade engaged Prince Charles's Men to continue at the Hope "according to the former articles of agreement had and made with the said Philip [Henslowe] and Jacob [Meade]." [1] The actors acknowledged themselves indebted to Henslowe "for a stock of apparel used for playing apparel, to the value of £400, heretofore delivered unto them by the said Philip," [2] — the stock formerly used by the Lady Elizabeth's Men; and Alleyn and Meade agreed to accept £200 in full discharge of that debt.[3]

In the winter of 1616–17, Prince Charles's Men quarreled with Meade, who had appropriated an extra day for his bear-baiting. Rosseter had just completed a new private theatre in Porter's Hall,

---

[1] Collier, *Memoirs of Edward Alleyn*, p. 127; Greg, *Henslowe Papers*, p. 91.

[2] Collier, *Memoirs of Edward Alleyn*, p. 127.

[3] My interpretation of the relation of Henslowe to Prince Charles's Men differs from the interpretation given by Fleay and adopted by Greg and others. For the evidence bearing on the case see Fleay, *Stage*, pp. 188, 262; Greg, *Henslowe's Diary*, II, 138; Greg, *Henslowe Papers*, p. 90, note; Chambers, *Modern Language Review*, IV, 165; Cunningham, *Revels*, p. xliv; Wallace, *Englische Studien*, XLIII, 390; Murray, *English Dramatic Companies*.

Blackfriars, and that stood invitingly open. So about February they abandoned the Hope, and wrote a letter of explanation to Edward Alleyn: "I hope you mistake not our removal from the Bankside. We stood the intemperate weather, 'till more intemperate Mr. Meade thrust us over, taking the day from us which by course was ours." [1]

After the company quarreled with Meade and deserted the Hope, there is no evidence that the building was again used for plays. It became associated almost entirely with animal-baiting, fencing, feats of activity, and such-like performances; and gradually the very name "Hope," which was identified with acting, gave way to the earlier designation "Bear Garden." In 1632 the author of *Holland's Leaguer* remarks that "wild beasts and gladiators did most possess it"; and such must have been the chief use of the building down to 1642, when animal-baiting was prohibited by Parliament.[2]

On January 14, 1647, at the disposition of the Church lands, the Hope was sold for £1783 15s.[3]

In certain manuscript notes entered in the Phillipps copy of Stow's *Annals* (1631), we read:

The Hope, on the Bankside, in Southwarke, commonly called the Bear Garden, a playhouse for stage-

---

[1] Greg, *Henslowe Papers*, p. 93. Cf. also the chapter on "Rosseter's Blackfriars."
[2] Collier, *The History of English Dramatic Poetry* (1879), III, 102; Ordish, *Early London Theatres*, p. 237.
[3] Arthur Tiler, *St. Saviour's*, p. 51; Reed's Dodsley, IX, 175.

plays on Mondays, Wednesdays, Fridays, and Saturdays, and for the baiting of Bears on Tuesdays and Thursdays, the stage being made to take up and down when they please. It was built in the year 1610, and now pulled down to make tenements, by Thomas Walker, a petticoat-maker in Cannon Street, on Tuesday, the 25 day of March, 1656. Seven of Mr. Godfrey's bears, by the command of Thomas Pride, then high sheriff of Surrey, were then shot to death on Saturday the 9 day of February, 1655 [i.e. 1656], by a company of soldiers.[1]

The mistakes in the earlier part of this note are obvious, yet the latter part is so circumstantial that we cannot well doubt its general accuracy. The building, however, was not pulled down "to the ground," though its interior may have been converted into tenements.

At the Restoration, when the royal sport of bear-baiting was revived, the Hope was again fitted up as an amphitheatre and opened to the public. The Earl of Manchester, on September 29, 1664, wrote to the city authorities, requesting that the butchers be required, as of old, to provide food for the dogs and bears:

He had been informed by the Master of His Majesty's Game of Bears and Bulls, and others, that the Butchers' Company had formerly caused all their offal in Eastcheap and Newgate Market to be conveyed by the beadle of that Company unto two

---

[1] Printed in *The Academy*, October 28, 1882, p. 314. As to "Mr. Godfrey" see Collier, *The History of English Dramatic Poetry* (1879), III, 102.

barrow houses, conveniently placed on the river side, for the provision and feeding of the King's Game of Bears, which custom had been interrupted in the late troubles when the bears were killed. His Majesty's game being now removed to the usual place on the Bankside, by Order of the Council, he recommended the Court of Aldermen to direct the Master and Wardens of the Butchers' Company to have their offal conveyed as formerly for the feeding of the bears, &c.[1]

For some years the Bear Garden flourished as it had in the days of Elizabeth and James. It was frequently visited by Samuel Pepys, who has left vivid accounts of several performances there. In his *Diary*, August 14, 1666, he writes:

After dinner with my wife and Mercer to the Beargarden; where I have not been, I think, of many years, and saw some good sport of the bull's tossing of the dogs: one into the very boxes. But it is a very rude and nasty pleasure. We had a great many hectors in the same box with us (and one, very fine, went into the pit, and played his dog for a wager, which was a strange sport for a gentleman), where they drank wine, and drank Mercer's health first; which I pledged with my hat off.

John Evelyn, likewise, in his *Diary*, June 16, 1670, records a visit to the Bear Garden:

I went with some friends to the Bear Garden, where was cock-fighting, dog-fighting, bear- and bull-baiting, it being a famous day for all these butcherly sports, or rather barbarous cruelties. The bulls did exceeding

---

[1] *The Remembrancia*, p. 478. Quoted by Ordish, *Early London Theatres*, p. 241.

THE HOPE

well; but the Irish wolf-dog exceeded, which was a tall greyhound, a stately creature indeed, who beat a cruel mastiff. One of the bulls tossed a dog full into a lady's lap as she sat in one of the boxes at a considerable height from the arena. Two poor dogs were killed; and so all ended with the ape on horseback, and I most heartily weary of the rude and dirty pastime, which I had not seen, I think, in twenty years before.

On January 7, 1676, the Spanish Ambassador was entertained at the Bear Garden, as we learn from a warrant, dated March 28, 1676, for the payment of £10 "to James Davies, Esq., Master of His Majesty's Bears, Bulls, and Dogs, for making ready the rooms at the Bear Garden, and baiting of the bears before the Spanish Ambassador, the 7 January last, 1675 [6]."[1]

Rendle[2] quotes from *The Loyal Protestant* an advertisement of an entertainment to be given so late as 1682 "at the Hope on the Bankside, being His Majesty's Bear Garden." And Malcolm writes the following account of the baiting of a horse there in April of the same year:

Notice was given in the papers that on the twelfth of April a horse, of uncommon strength, and between 18 and 19 hands high, would be *baited to death at his Majesty's Bear-Garden* at the Hope on the Bankside, for the amusement of the Morocco ambassador, many of the nobility who knew the horse, and any others who would pay the price of admission. It seems this

---

[1] British Museum Additional MSS. 5750; quoted by Cunningham, *Handbook of London* (1849), I, 67.
[2] *The Antiquarian Magazine and Bibliographer*, VIII, 59.

animal originally belonged to the Earl of Rochester, and being of a ferocious disposition, had killed several of his brethren; for which misdeed he was sold to the Earl of Dorchester; in whose service, committing several similar offenses, he was transferred to the worse than savages who kept the Bear-Garden. On the day appointed several dogs were set upon the vindictive steed, which he destroyed or drove from the arena; at this instant his owners determined to preserve him for a future day's sport, and directed a person to lead him away; but before the horse had reached London Bridge the spectators demanded the fulfilment of the promise of baiting him to death, and began to destroy the building: to conclude, the poor beast was brought back, and other dogs set upon him, without effect, when he was stabbed to death with a sword.[1]

This is the last reference to the Hope that I have been able to discover. Soon after this date the "royal sport of bulls, bears, and dogs" was moved to Hockley-in-the-hole, Clerkenwell, where, as the advertisements inform us, at "His Majesty's Bear Garden" the baiting of animals was to be frequently seen.[2] Strype, in his *Survey of London*, thus describes Bear Garden Alley on the Bankside:

[1] James Peller Malcolm, *Anecdotes of the Manners and Customs of London from the Roman Invasion to the Year 1700* (London, 1811), p. 425.
[2] The earliest advertisement of the Bear Garden at Hockley-in-the-hole that I have come upon is dated 1700. For a discussion of the sports there see J. P. Malcolm, *Anecdotes of the Manners and Customs of London during the Eighteenth Century* (1808), p. 321; Cunningham, *Handbook of London*, under "Hockley"; W. B. Boulton, *Amusements of Old London*, vol. I, chap. I.

THE HOPE

Bear Alley runs into Maiden Lane. Here is a Glass House; and about the middle is a new-built Court, well inhabited, called Bear Garden Square, so called as built in the place where the *Bear Garden* formerly stood, until removed to the other side of the water: which is more convenient for the butchers, and such like who are taken with such rustic sports as the baiting of bears and bulls.[1]

In the map which he gives of this region (reproduced on page 245) the position of the Hope is clearly marked by the square near the middle of Bear Alley.

---

[1] Ordish (*Early London Theatres*, p. 242) is mistaken in thinking that the old building was converted into a glass house. He says: "The last reference to the Hope shows that it had declined to the point of extinction," and he quotes an advertisement from the *Gazette*, June 18, 1681, as follows: "There is now made at the Bear Garden glass-house, on the Bankside, crown window-glass, much exceeding French glass in all its qualifications, which may be squared into all sizes of sashes for windows, and other uses, and may be had at most glaziers in London." From Strype's *Survey* it is evident that the glass house was in Bear Garden Alley, but not on the site of the old Bear Garden.

CHAPTER XVII

ROSSETER'S BLACKFRIARS, OR PORTER'S HALL

PHILIP ROSSETER, the poet and musician, first appears as a theatrical manager in 1610, when he secured a royal patent for the Children of the Queen's Revels to act at Whitefriars. This company performed there successfully under his management until March, 1613, when, for some unknown reason, he formed a partnership with Philip Henslowe, who was managing the Lady Elizabeth's Men at the Swan. The two companies were combined, and the new organization, under the name of "The Lady Elizabeth's Men," made use of both playhouses, the Swan as a summer and the Whitefriars as a winter home.

As already explained in the preceding chapters, Rosseter's lease on the Whitefriars Playhouse was to expire in 1614, and apparently he was unable to renew the lease.[1] Naturally he and his partner Henslowe were anxious to secure a private play-

[1] Nathaniel Field, the leading actor at Whitefriars, published *A Woman is a Weathercock* in 1612, with the statement to the reader: "If thou hast anything to say to me, thou know'st where to hear of me for a year or two, and no more, I assure thee." Possibly this reflects the failure of the managers to renew the lease; after 1614 Field did not know where he would be acting. But editors have generally regarded it as meaning that Field intended to withdraw from acting.

ROSSETER'S BLACKFRIARS 343

house in the city to serve as a winter home for their troupe, especially since the Swan was poorly situated for winter patronage. This may explain the following entry in Sir George Buc's Office-Book: "July 13, 1613, for a license to erect a new playhouse in Whitefriars &c. £20." [1] The new playhouse, however, was not built. Probably the opposition of the inhabitants of the district led to its prohibition.

At the expiration of one year, in March, 1614, Rosseter withdrew from his partnership with Henslowe, and on the old patent of the Children of the Queen's Revels (which he had retained) organized a new company to travel in the country.

In the following year, 1615, he and certain others, Philip Kingman, Robert Jones, and Ralph Reeve, secured a lease of "diverse buildings, cellars, sollars, chambers, and yards for the building of a playhouse thereupon for the better practising and exercise of the said Children of the Revels; all which premises are situate and being within the precinct of the Blackfriars, near Puddlewharf, in the suburbs of London, called by the name of the Lady Saunders's House, or otherwise Porter's Hall." [2] It was their purpose to convert this hall into a playhouse to rival the near-by Blackfriars; and in accordance with this purpose, on June 3,

---

[1] Malone, *Variorum*, III, 52.
[2] The Malone Society's *Collections*, I, 277. For the location of Puddlewharf see the map of the Blackfriars precinct on page 94.

1615, Rosseter secured a royal license under the Great Seal of England "to erect, build, and set up in and upon the said premises before mentioned one convenient playhouse for the said Children of the Revels, the same playhouse to be used by the Children of the Revels for the time being of the Queene's Majesty, and for the Prince's Players, and for the Lady Elizabeth's Players." [1]

The work of converting Porter's Hall into a playhouse seems to have begun at once. On September 26, 1615, the Privy Council records "that one Rosseter, and others, having obtained license under the Great Seal of England for the building of a playhouse, have pulled down [i.e., stripped the interior of] a great messuage in Puddlewharf, which was sometimes the house of the Lady Saunders, within the precinct of the Blackfriars, and are now erecting a new playhouse in that place." [2]

The city authorities, always hostile to the actors and jealous of any new theatres, made so vigorous a complaint to the Privy Council that the Lords of the Council "thought fit to send for Rosseter." He came, bringing his royal license. This document was carefully "perused by the Lord Chief Justice of England," who succeeded in discovering in the wording of one of its clauses a trivial flaw that would enable the Privy Council, on a technicality, to prohibit the building: "The Lord Chief Justice did deliver to their Lordships that the license

[1] The Malone Society's *Collections*, I, 277. [2] *Ibid.*, p. 373.

granted to the said Rosseter did extend to the building of a playhouse without the liberties of London, and not within the city."[1] Now, in 1608 the liberty of Blackfriars had by a special royal grant been placed within the jurisdiction of the city. Rosseter's license unluckily had described the Lady Saunders's house as being "in the suburbs," though, of course, the description was otherwise specific enough: "all which premises are situate and being within the precinct of the Blackfriars, near Puddlewharf, in the suburbs of London, called by the name of the Lady Saunders's House, or otherwise Porter's Hall."

Since "the inconveniences urged by the Lord Mayor and Aldermen were many," the Lords of the Privy Council decided to take advantage of the flaw discovered by the Lord Chief Justice, and prohibit the erection of the playhouse. Their order, issued September 26, 1615, reads as follows:

> It was this day ordered by their Lordships that there shall be no playhouse erected in that place, and that the Lord Mayor of London shall straightly prohibit the said Rosseter and the rest of the patentees, and their workmen to proceed in the making and converting the said building into a playhouse. And if any of the patentees or their workmen shall proceed in their intended building contrary to this their Lordships' inhibition, that then the Lord Mayor shall commit him or them so offending unto prison and certify their Lordships of their contempt in that behalf.[2]

[1] The Malone Society's *Collections*, I, 373.   [2] *Ibid.*

This order, for the time being, halted work on the new playhouse. The Children of the Revels were forced to spend the next year traveling in the provinces; and the Lady Elizabeth's Men and Prince Charles's Men had to remain on the Bankside and endure the oppressions of Henslowe and later of Meade. Possibly their sufferings at the hands of Meade led them to urge Rosseter to complete at once the much desired house in the city. At any rate, in the winter of 1616, Rosseter, believing himself strongly enough entrenched behind his royal patent, resumed work on converting Porter's Hall into a theatre. The city authorities issued "diverse commandments and prohibitions," but he paid no attention to these, and pushed the work to completion. The building seems to have been ready for the actors about the first of January, 1617. Thereupon the company which had been occupying the Hope deserted that playhouse and "came over" to Rosseter's Blackfriars.[1] In the new playhouse they presented Nathaniel Field's comedy, *Amends for Ladies*, which was printed the following year "as it was acted at the Blackfriars both by the Prince's Servants and the Lady Elizabeth's."

The actors, however, were not allowed to enjoy their new home very long. On January 27, 1617, the Privy Council dispatched the following letter to the Lord Mayor:

[1] See the chapter on "The Hope."

Whereas His Majesty is informed that notwithstanding diverse commandments and prohibitions to the contrary, there be certain persons that go about to set up a playhouse in the Blackfriars near unto His Majesty's Wardrobe, and for that purpose have lately erected and made fit a building, which is almost if not fully finished. You shall understand that His Majesty hath this day expressly signified his pleasure that the same shall be pulled down, so as it be made unfit for any such use; whereof we require your Lordship to take notice and to cause it to be performed accordingly, with all speed, and thereupon to certify us of your proceeding.

There can be no doubt that an order so peremptory, carrying the authority both of the Privy Council and of the King, and requiring an immediate report, was performed "with all speed." After this we hear nothing more of the playhouse in Puddlewharf.[1]

[1] I can find no further reference to the Puddlewharf Theatre either in the *Records* of the Privy Council or in the *Remembrancia* of the City. Collier, however, in his *History of English Dramatic Poetry* (1879), I, 384, says: "The city authorities proceeded immediately to the work, and before three days had elapsed, the Privy Council was duly and formally made acquainted with the fact that Rosseter's theatre had been 'made unfit for any such use' as that for which it had been constructed." Collier fails to cite his authority for the statement; the passage he quotes may be found in the order of the Privy Council printed above.

CHAPTER XVIII

THE PHŒNIX, OR COCKPIT IN DRURY LANE

THE private playhouse opened in Drury Lane [1] in 1617 seems to have been officially named "The Phœnix"; but to the players and the public alike it was more commonly known as "The Cockpit." This implies some earlier connection of the site or of the building with cock-fighting, from time out of mind a favorite sport in England. Stowe writes in his *Survey*: "Cocks of the game are yet cherished by diverse men for their pleasures, much money being laid on their heads, when they fight in pits, whereof some be costly made for that purpose." These pits, it seems, were circular in shape, and if large enough might well be used for dramatic purposes. Shakespeare, in *Henry V* (1599), likens his playhouse to a cockpit:

[1] Its exact position in Drury Lane is indicated by an order of the Privy Council, June 8, 1623, concerning the paving of a street at the rear of the theatre: "Whereas the highway leading along the backside of the Cockpit Playhouse near Lincolns Inn Fields, and the street called Queens Street adjoining to the same, are become very foul," etc. (See The Malone Society *Collections*, I, 383. Queens Street may be readily found in Faithorne's *Map of London*.) Malone (*Variorum*, III, 53) states that "it was situated opposite the Castle Tavern." The site is said to be marked by Pit Court.

THE PHŒNIX

> Can this cockpit hold
> The vasty fields of France? or may we cram
> Within this wooden O the very casques
> That did affright the air at Agincourt?

It is possible, then, that the building was an old cockpit made into a playhouse. Howes,[1] in enumerating the London theatres, says: "Five inns or common hostelries turned into playhouses, one cockpit, St. Paul's singing-school," etc. And Thomas Randolph, in verses prefixed to James Shirley's *Grateful Servant* (printed in 1630 as it was acted "in the private house in Drury Lane"), suggests the same metamorphosis:

> When thy intelligence on the Cockpit stage
> Gives it a soul from her immortal rage,
> I hear the Muse's birds with full delight
> Sing where the birds of Mars were wont to fight.

But in this fantastic conceit Randolph may have been thinking simply of the name of the theatre; possibly he knew nothing of its early history. On the whole it seems more likely that the playhouse was newly erected in 1617 upon the site of an old cockpit. The name "Phœnix" suggests that possibly the old cockpit had been destroyed by fire, and that from its ashes had arisen a new building.[2]

---

[1] Stow's *Annals* (1631), p. 1004.
[2] Some scholars have supposed that the playhouse, when attacked by the apprentices in 1617, was burned, and that the name "Phœnix" was given to the building after its reconstruction. But the building was not burned; it was merely wrecked on the inside by apprentices.

Howes describes the Phœnix as being in 1617 "a new playhouse," [1] and Camden, who is usually accurate in such matters, refers to it in the same year as "nuper erectum." [2]

Of its size and shape all our information comes from James Wright, who in his *Historia Histrionica* [3] tells us that the Cockpit differed in no essential feature from Blackfriars and Salisbury Court, "for they were all three built almost exactly alike for form and bigness." Since we know that Blackfriars and Salisbury Court were small rectangular theatres, the former constructed in a hall forty-six feet broad and sixty-six feet long, the latter erected on a plot of ground forty-two feet broad and one hundred and forty feet long, we are not left entirely ignorant of the shape and the approximate size of the Cockpit.[4] And from Middleton's *Inner Temple Masque* (1618) we learn that it was constructed of brick. Its sign, presumably, was that of a phœnix rising out of flames.

The playhouse was erected and managed by Christopher Beeston,[5] one of the most important

---

[1] Continuation of Stow's *Annals* (1631), p. 1026.

[2] William Camden, *Annals*, under the date of March 4, 1617. Yet Sir Sidney Lee (*A Life of William Shakespeare*, p. 60) says, "built about 1610."

[3] Hazlitt's Dodsley, xv, 408.

[4] Fleay and Lawrence are wrong in supposing that the Cockpit was circular.

[5] *Alias* Christopher Hutchinson. Several actors of the day employed *aliases*: Nicholas Wilkinson, *alias* Tooley; Theophilus Bourne, *alias* Bird; James Dunstan, *alias* Tunstall, etc. Whether

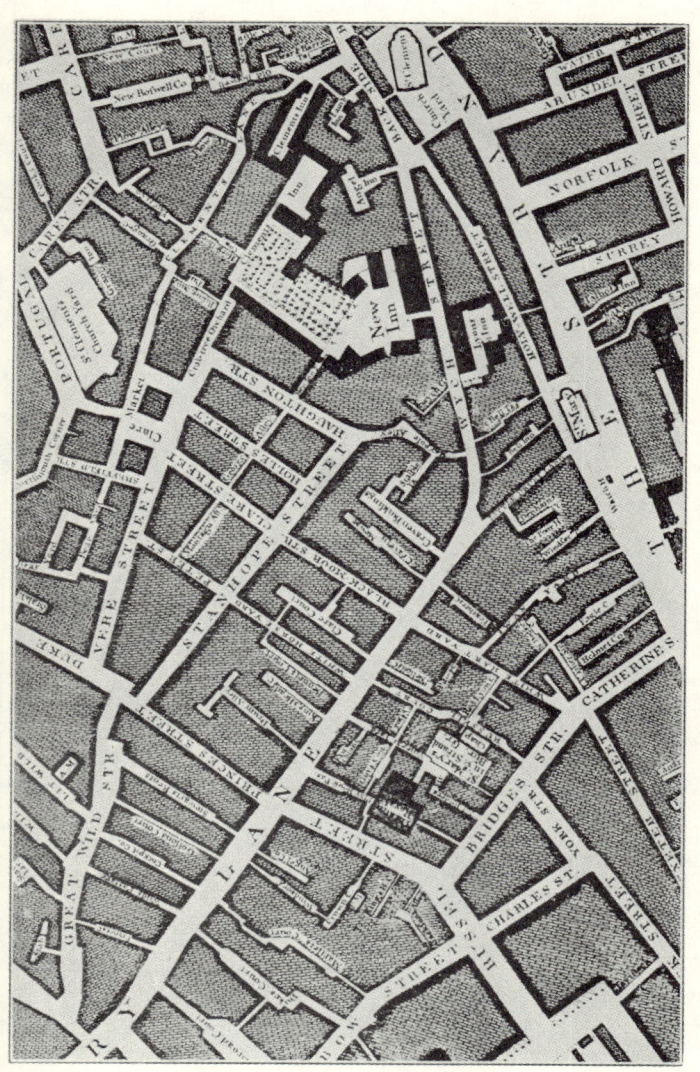

THE SITE OF THE COCKPIT IN DRURY LANE
The site is marked by Cockpit Court. (From Rocque's *Map of London*, 1746.)

THE PHŒNIX 351

actors and theatrical managers of the Elizabethan period. We first hear of him as a member of Shakespeare's troupe. In 1602 he joined Worcester's Company. In 1612 he became the manager of Queen Anne's Company at the Red Bull. He is described at that time as "a thriving man, and one that was of ability and means."[1] He continued as manager of the Queen Anne's Men at the Red Bull until 1617, when he transferred them to his new playhouse in Drury Lane.

The playhouse seems to have been ready to receive the players about the end of February, 1617. We know that they were still performing at the Red Bull as late as February 23;[2] but by March 4 they had certainly moved to the Cockpit.

On the latter date, during the performance of a play, the Cockpit was entered by a mob of disorderly persons, who proceeded to demolish the interior. The occasion for the wrecking of the new playhouse was the Shrove Tuesday saturnalia of

---

Beeston admitted other persons to a share in the building I cannot learn. In a passage quoted by Malone (*Variorum*, III, 121) from the Herbert Manuscript, dated February 20, 1635, there is a reference to "housekeepers," indicating that Beeston had then admitted "sharers" in the proprietorship of the building. And in an order of the Privy Council, May 12, 1637 (The Malone Society's *Collections*, I, 392), we read: "Command the keepers of the playhouse called the Cockpit in Drury Lane, who either live in it or have relation to it, not to permit plays to be acted there till further order."

[1] Wallace, *Three London Theatres*, p. 35.
[2] Wallace, *ibid.*, pp. 32, 46. John Smith was delivering silk and other clothes to the Queen Anne's Men at the Red Bull from 1612 until February 23, 1617.

the London apprentices, who from time immemorial had employed this holiday to pull down houses of ill-fame in the suburbs. That the Cockpit was situated in the neighborhood of such houses cannot be doubted. We may suppose that the mob, fresh from sacking buildings, had crowded into the playhouse in the afternoon, and before the play was over had wrecked that building too.

The event created a great stir at the time. William Camden, in his *Annals*, wrote under the date of March 4, 1617:

> Theatrum ludiorum, nuper erectum in Drury Lane, a furente multitudine diruitur, et apparatus dilaceratur.

Howes, in his continuation of Stow's *Annals*, writes:

> Shrove-Tuesday, the fourth of March, many disordered persons of sundry kinds, amongst whom were very many young boys and lads, that assembled themselves in Lincolnes Inn Field, Finsbury Field, in Ratcliffe, and Stepney Field, where in riotous manner they did beat down the walls and windows of many victualing houses and of all other houses which they suspected to be bawdy houses. And that afternoon they spoiled a new playhouse, and did likewise more hurt in diverse other places.[1]

That several persons were killed, and many injured, is disclosed by a letter from the Privy Council to the Lord Mayor, dated March 5, 1617:

[1] *Annals* (1631), p. 1026.

THE PHŒNIX

It is not unknown unto you what tumultuous outrages were yesterday committed near unto the city of London in diverse places by a rowt of lewd and loose persons, apprentices and others, especially in Lincolns Inn Fields and Drury Lane, where in attempting to pull down a playhouse belonging to the Queen's Majesty's Servants, there were diverse persons slain, and others hurt and wounded, the multitude there assembled being to the number of many thousands, as we are credibly informed.[1]

The Queen's Men returned to the Red Bull and acted there until their ruined playhouse could be repaired. Three months later, on June 3, they again occupied the Cockpit,[2] and continued there until the death of Queen Anne on March 2, 1619.[3] This event led to the dissolution of the company.

[1] The Malone Society's *Collections*, I, 374. Collier, in *The History of English Dramatic Poetry* (1879), I, 386, prints a long ballad on the event; but he does not give its source, and its genuineness has been questioned. The following year threats to pull down the Fortune, the Red Bull, and the Cockpit led to the setting of special watches. See The Malone Society's *Collections*, I, 377.

[2] Greenstreet, Documents, *The New Shakspere Society's Transactions* (1880–86), p. 504.

[3] Mr. Wallace (*Three London Theatres*, p. 29) says that the documents he prints make it "as certain as circumstances unsupported by contemporary declaration can make it, that Queen Anne's company occupied the Red Bull continuously from the time of its erection ... till their dissolution, 1619." His documents make it certain only that Queen Anne's Men occupied the Red Bull until February 23, 1617. Other documents prove that they occupied the Cockpit from 1617 until 1619. (Note the letter of the Privy Council quoted above.) The documents printed by Greenstreet show that Queen Anne's Men moved to the Cockpit on June 3, 1617, and continued there.

For a year or more its members had been "falling at variance and strife amongst themselves," and when the death of the Queen deprived them of a "service," they "separated and divided themselves into other companies." [1] As a result of the quarrels certain members of the company made charges against their former manager, Beeston: "The said Beeston having from the beginning a greater care for his own private gain, and not respecting the good of these defendants and the rest of his fellows and companions, hath in the place and trust aforesaid much enriched himself, and hath of late given over his coat and condition,[2] and separated and divided himself from these defendants, carrying away not only all the furniture and apparel," etc.[3] The charges against Beeston's honesty may be dismissed; but it seems clear that he had withdrawn from his former companions, and was preparing to entertain a new troupe of actors at his playhouse. And Beeston himself tells us, on November 23, 1619, that "after Her Majesty's decease, he entered into the service of the most noble Prince Charles." [4] Thus Prince Charles's Men, after their unfortunate

---

[1] Wallace, *Three London Theatres*, p. 33.
[2] He had joined Prince Charles's Men.
[3] Wallace, *Three London Theatres*, p. 38.
[4] *Ibid.*, p. 40. Fleay, Murray, and others have contended that the Princess Elizabeth's Men came to the Cockpit in 1619, and have denied the accuracy of the title-page of *The Witch of Edmonton* (1658), which declares that play to have been "acted by the Prince's Servants at the Cockpit often." (See Fleay, *A Chronicle History of the London Stage*, p. 299.)

THE PHŒNIX

experiences at the Hope and at Rosseter's Blackfriars, came to Beeston's playhouse, where they remained until 1622. In the spring of that year, however, they moved to the Curtain, and the Princess Elizabeth's Men occupied the Cockpit.[1] Under their tenancy, the playhouse seems to have attained an enviable reputation. Heminges and Condell, in the epistle to the readers, prefixed to the Folio of Shakespeare (1623), bear testimony to this in the following terms: "And though you be a Magistrate of Wit, and sit on the stage at Blackfriars, or the Cockpit, to arraign plays daily." A further indication of their prosperity is to be found in the records of St. Giles's Church; for when in 1623 the parish undertook the erection of a new church building, "the players of the Cockpit," we are informed, contributed the large sum of £20, and the proprietors, represented by Christopher Beeston, gave £19 1s. 5d.[2]

The Princess Elizabeth's Men continued to act at the Cockpit until May, 1625, when all theatres were closed on account of the plague. Beeston made this the occasion to organize a new company called "Queen Henrietta's Men"; and when the theatres were allowed to reopen, about December,

---

[1] Malone, *Variorum*, III, 59.
[2] John Parton, *Some Account of the Hospital and Parish of St. Giles in the Fields*, p. 235. From a parish entry in 1660 we learn that the players had to contribute 2d. to the parish poor for each day that there was acting at the Cockpit. (See *ibid.*, p. 236.)

1625,[1] this new company was in possession of the Cockpit. But the reputation of the playhouse seems not to have been enhanced by the performances of this troupe. In 1629, Lenton, in *The Young Gallant's Whirligig*, writes sneeringly:

> The Cockpit heretofore would serve his wit,
> But now upon the Friars' Stage he'll sit.

And in the following year, 1630, Thomas Carew in verses prefixed to Davenport's *Just Italian*, attacks the Red Bull and the Cockpit as "adulterate" stages where "noise prevails," and "not a tongue of th' untun'd kennel can a line repeat of serious sense." Queen Henrietta's Men probably continued to occupy the building until May 12, 1636, when the theatres were again closed on account of a serious outbreak of the plague. The plague continued for nearly a year and a half, and during this time the company was dissolved.[2]

Before the plague had ceased, early in 1637,

---

[1] In the *Middlesex County Records*, III, 6, we find that on December 6, 1625, because "the drawing of people together to places was a great means of spreading and continuing the infection ... this Court doth prohibit the players of the house at the Cockpit, being next to His Majesty's Court at Whitehall, commanding them to surcease all such their proceedings until His Majesty's pleasure be further signified." Apparently the playhouses in general had been allowed to resume performances; and since by December 24 there had been no deaths from the plague for a week, the special inhibition of the Cockpit Playhouse was soon lifted.

[2] "When Her Majesty's Servants were at the Cockpit, being all at liberty, they dispersed themselves to several companies." (Heton's Patent, 1639, *The Shakespeare Society Papers*, IV, 96.)

THE PHŒNIX 357

"Mr. Beeston was commanded to make a company of boys."[1] In the Office-Book of the Lord Chamberlain we find, under the date of February 21, 1637: "Warrant to swear Mr. Christopher Beeston His Majesty's Servant in the place of Governor of the new company of The King's and Queen's Boys."[2] The first recorded performance by this new company was at Court on February 7, 1637.[3] On February 23, the number of deaths from the plague having diminished, acting was again permitted; but at the expiration of one week, on March 2, the number of deaths having increased, all playhouses were again closed. During this single week the King's and Queen's Boys, we may suppose, acted at the Cockpit.[4]

On May 12, Beeston was arrested and brought before the Privy Council for having allowed his Boys to act a play at the Cockpit during the inhibition.[5] In his apology he explains this as follows: "Petitioner being commanded to erect and prepare a company of young actors for Their Majesties's service, and being desirous to know how they profited by his instructions, invited some

---

[1] Herbert Manuscript, Malone, *Variorum*, III, 240.
[2] Stopes, "Shakespeare's Fellows and Followers," Shakespeare *Jahrbuch*, XLVI, 99. In 1639 Heton applied for a patent as "Governor" of the company at Salisbury Court.
[3] On May 10 Beeston was paid for "two plays acted by the New Company." See Stopes, "Shakespeare's Fellows and Followers," in the Shakespeare *Jahrbuch*, XLVI, 99.
[4] Herbert Manuscript, Malone, *Variorum*, III, 240.
[5] The Malone Society's *Collections*, I, 392.

noblemen and gentlemen to see them act at his house, the Cockpit. For which, since he perceives it is imputed as a fault, he is very sorry, and craves pardon."[1]

On September 17, 1637, "Christopher Beeston, His Majesty's servant, by petition to the Board, showed that he hath many young actors lying unpractised by reason of the restraint occasioned by infection of the plague, whereby they are much disabled to perform their service, and besought that they might have leave to practise. It was ordered that Beeston should be at liberty to practise his actors at Michaelmas next [September 29], if there be no considerable increase of the sickness, nor that there die more than died last week."[2]

On October 2, 1637, the plague having abated, all playhouses were opened, and the King's and Queen's Boys, Herbert tells us, began to play at the Cockpit "the same day."[3] Here, under the popular name of "Beeston's Boys," they enjoyed a long and successful career, which ended only with the prohibition of acting in 1642.

In 1639 Christopher Beeston died, and the position of Governor of the Boys was conferred upon his son, William Beeston, who had long been associated in the management of the company,[4] and who, if we may believe Francis Kirkman, was ad-

[1] *The Calendar of State Papers, Domestic, 1636–1637*, p. 254.
[2] *Ibid.*, *1637*, p. 420.   [3] Malone, *Variorum*, III, 240.
[4] He is referred to as their Governor on August 10, 1639; see Malone, *Variorum*, III, 159.

mirably qualified for the position. In dedicating to him *The Loves and Adventures of Clerico and Lozia*, Kirkman says:

> Divers times in my hearing, to the admiration of the whole company, you have most judiciously discoursed of Poesie: which is the cause I presume to choose you for my patron and protector, who are the happiest interpreter and judge of our English stage-plays this nation ever produced; which the poets and actors of these times cannot (without ingratitude) deny; for I have heard the chief and most ingenious acknowledge their fames and profits essentially sprung from your instruction, judgment, and fancy.

But in spite of all this, William Beeston's career as Governor was of short duration. About the first of May, 1640, he allowed the Boys to act without license a play that gave great offense to the King. Herbert, the Master of the Revels, writes of this play that it "had relation to the passages of the King's journey into the north, and was complained of by His Majesty to me, with command to punish the offenders." [5] In the Office-Book of the Lord Chamberlain, under the date of May 3, 1640, we read:

> Whereas William Beeston and the company of the players of the Cockpit, in Drury Lane, have lately acted a new play without any license from the Master of His Majesty's Revels, and being commanded to forbear playing or acting of the same play by the said Master of the Revels, and commanded likewise to forbear all manner of playing, have notwithstanding,

---

[5] Malone, *Variorum*, III, 241.

in contempt of the authority of the said Master of the Revels, and the power granted unto him under the Great Seal of England, acted the said play, and others, to the prejudice of His Majesty's service, and in contempt of the Office of the Revels, [whereby] he and they and all other companies ever have been and ought to be governed and regulated: These are therefore in His Majesty's name, and signification of his royal pleasure, to command the said William Beeston and the rest of that company of the Cockpit players from henceforth and upon sight hereof, to forbear to act any plays whatsoever until they shall be restored by the said Master of the Revels unto their former liberty. Whereof all parties concernable are to take notice, and conform accordingly, as they and every one of them will answer it at their peril.[1]

Herbert records in his Office-Book:

On Monday the 4 May, 1640, William Beeston was taken by a messenger and committed to the Marshalsea by my Lord Chamberlain's warrant, for playing a play without license. The same day the company at the Cockpit was commanded by my Lord Chamberlain's warrant to forbear playing, for playing when they were forbidden by me, and for other disobedience, and lay still Monday, Tuesday, and Wednesday. On Thursday, at my Lord Chamberlain's entreaty, I gave them their liberty, and upon their petition of submission subscribed by the players, I restored them to their liberty on Thursday.[2]

[1] Collier, *The History of English Dramatic Poetry* (1879), II, 32; Stopes, *op. cit.*, p. 102.
[2] Malone, *Variorum*, III, 241. Herbert did not forget Beeston's insubordination, and in 1660, in issuing to Beeston a license to use the Salisbury Court Playhouse, he inserted clauses to prevent further difficulty of this kind (see *Variorum*, III, 243).

To this period of Beeston's imprisonment I should refer the puzzling Epilogue of Brome's *The Court Beggar:*

There's wit in that now. But this small Poet vents none but his own, and his by whose care and directions this Stage is govern'd, who has for many years, both in his father's days, and since, directed Poets to write and Players to speak, till he trained up these youths here to what they are now. Aye, some of 'em from before they were able to say a grace of two lines long to have more parts in their pates than would fill so many Dry-vats. And to be serious with you, if after all this, by the venomous practice of some, who study nothing more than his destruction, he should fail us, both Poets and Players would be at loss in reputation.

His "destruction" was wrought, nevertheless, for as a result of his indiscretion he was deposed from his position as Governor of the King's and Queen's Company, and William Davenant was appointed in his place. In the Office-Book of the Lord Chamberlain under the date of June 27, 1640,[1] appears the following entry with the heading, "Mr. Davenant Governor of the Cockpit Players":

Whereas in the playhouse or theatre commonly called the Cockpit, in Drury Lane, there are a company of players authorized by me (as Lord Chamberlain to His Majesty) to play or act under the title of The King's and Queen's Servants, and that by reason of some disorders lately amongst them committed

---

[1] Stopes (*op. cit.*) dates this June 5, but Collier, Malone, and Chalmers all give June 27, and Mrs. Stopes is not always quite accurate in such matters.

they are disabled in their service and quality: These are therefore to signify that by the same authority I do authorize and appoint William Davenant, Gent., one of Her Majesty's servants, for me and in my name to take into his government and care the said company of players, to govern, order, and dispose of them for action and presentments, and all their affairs in the said house, as in his discretion shall seem best to conduce to His Majesty's service in that quality. And I do hereby enjoin and command them, all and every of them, that are so authorized to play in the said house under the privilege of His or Her Majesty's Servants, and every one belonging as prentices or servants to those actors to play under the same privilege, that they obey the said Mr. Davenant and follow his orders and directions, as they will answer the contrary; which power and privilege he is to continue and enjoy during that lease which Mrs. Elizabeth Beeston, *alias* Hucheson, hath or doth hold in the said playhouse, provided he be still accountable to me for his care and well ordering the said company.[1]

Under the direction of Davenant the company acted at the Cockpit until the closing of the theatres two years later.

The history of the playhouse during the troubled years that followed is varied. In the churchwarden's account of St. Giles's Parish is found the entry: "1646. Paid and given to the teacher at the Cockpit of the children, 6d."[2] Apparently the old playhouse was then being temporarily used as a school.

[1] Collier, *The History of English Dramatic Poetry* (1879), II, 32, note 1.
[2] John Parton, *Some Account of the Hospital and Parish of St. Giles in the Fields*, p. 235.

THE PHŒNIX

Wright, in his *Historia Histrionica*, tells us that at the outbreak of the civil war most of the actors had joined the royal army and served His Majesty, "though in a different, yet more honorable capacity." Some were killed, many won distinction; and "when the wars were over, and the royalists totally subdued, most of 'em who were left alive gathered to London, and for a subsistence endeavored to revive their old trade privately. They made up one company out of all the scattered members of several, and in the winter before the King's murder, 1648, they ventured to act some plays, with as much caution and privacy as could be, at the Cockpit." John Evelyn records in his *Diary*, under the date of February 5, 1648: "Saw a tragicomedy acted in the Cockpit after there had been none of these diversions for many years during the war." Trouble, however, was brewing for these daring actors. As Wright records: "They continued undisturbed for three or four days, but at last, as they were presenting the tragedy of *The Bloody Brother* (in which Lowin acted Aubery; Taylor, Rollo; Pollard, the Cook; Burt, Latorch; and, I think, Hart, Otto), a party of foot-soldiers beset the house, surprised 'em about the middle of the play, and carried 'em away in their habits, not admitting them to shift, to Hatton House, then a prison, where, having detained them some time, they plundered them of their clothes, and let 'em loose again."[1]

[1] Hazlitt's Dodsley, xv, 409.

In 1649 the interior of the building was sacked, if we may trust the manuscript note entered in the Phillipps copy of Stow's *Annals* (1631): "The playhouse in Salisbury Court, in Fleet Street, was pulled down by a company of soldiers set on by the sectaries of these sad times, on Saturday the 24 day of March, 1649. The Phœnix, in Drury Lane, was pulled down also this day, being Saturday the 24 day of March, 1649, by the same soldiers."[1] In the passage quoted, "pulled-down" merely means that the stage and its equipment, and possibly a part of the galleries and the seats, were wrecked, not that the walls of the building itself were thrown down.

In 1656 Sir William Davenant undertook to create a form of dramatic entertainment which would be tolerated by the authorities. The Lord Protector was known to be a lover of music. Sir William, therefore, applied for permission to give operatic entertainments, "after the manner of the antients," the "story sung in recitative music," and the representation made "by the art of perspective in scenes." To such entertainments, he thought, no one could object. He was wise enough to give his first performances at Rutland House; but in 1658 he moved to the Cockpit, where, says Aubrey, "were acted very well, *stylo recitativo, Sir Francis Drake* and *The Siege of Rhodes* (1st and 2d parts).

---

[1] See *The Academy*, October 28, 1882, p. 314. The soldiers here mentioned also "pulled down on the inside" the Fortune playhouse.

THE PHŒNIX

It did affect the eye and ear extremely. This first brought scenes in fashion in England; before at plays was only a hanging." Thus the Cockpit had the distinction of being the first English playhouse in which scenery was employed, and, one should add, the first English home of the opera.[1]

Later in the same year, 1658, Davenant exhibited at the Cockpit *The Cruelty of the Spaniards in Peru;* but this performance excited the suspicion of the authorities, who on December 23 sent for "the poet and the actors" to explain "by what authority the same is exposed to public view."[2]

"In the year 1659," writes John Downes in his *Roscius Anglicanus,* "General Monk marching then his army out of Scotland to London, Mr. Rhodes, a bookseller, being wardrobe-keeper formerly (as I am informed) to King Charles the First's company of commedians in Blackfriars, getting a license from the then governing state,[3] fitted up a house then for acting, called the *Cockpit*, in Drury Lane, and in a short time completed his company." If this statement is correct, the time must have been early in the year 1659–60, and the company must have attempted at first to play without a proper license. From the *Middlesex*

[1] For a discussion of Davenant's attempts to introduce the opera into England, see W. J. Lawrence, *The Elizabethan Playhouse* (Second Series), pp. 129 ff.

[2] Malone, *Variorum*, III, 93; Collier, *The History of English Dramatic Poetry* (1879), II, 48.

[3] For his troubles with the Master of the Revels see Halliwell-Phillipps, *A Collection of Ancient Documents*, p. 26.

County Records (III, 282), we learn that one of their important actors, Thomas Lilleston, was held under bond for having performed "a public stage-play this present 4th of February [1659–60] in the Cockpit in Drury Lane in the parish of St. Giles-in-the-Fields, contrary to the law in that case made"; and in the Parish Book [1] of St. Giles we find the entry: "1659. Received of Isack Smith, which he received at the Cockpit playhouse of several offenders, by order of the justices, £3 8s. 6d." Shortly after this, it is to be presumed, the company under Rhodes's management secured the "license of the then governing state" mentioned by Downes, and continued thereafter without interruption. The star of this company was Betterton, whose splendid acting at once captivated London. Pepys went often to the theatre, and has left us some interesting notes of his experiences there. On August 18, 1660, he writes:

Captain Ferrers, my Lord's Cornet, comes to us, who after dinner took me and Creed to the Cockpit play, the first that I have had time to see since my coming from sea, *The Loyall Subject*, where one Kinaston, a boy, acted the Duke's sister, but made the loveliest lady that ever I saw in my life, only her voice not very good.

Again on October 11, 1660, he writes:

Here in the Park we met with Mr. Salisbury, who took Mr. Creed and me to the Cockpit to see *The*

---

[1] Parton, *op. cit.*, p. 236.

THE PHŒNIX

Moor of Venice, which was well done. Burt acted the Moor, by the same token a very pretty lady that sat by me called out to see Desdemona smothered.

The subsequent history of the Cockpit falls outside the scope of the present treatise. The reader who desires to trace the part the building played in the Restoration would do well to consult the numerous documents printed by Malone from the Herbert Manuscript.[1]

[1] Malone, *Variorum*, III, 244 ff.

CHAPTER XIX

SALISBURY COURT

THE Salisbury Court Playhouse [1] was projected and built by two men whose very names are unfamiliar to most students of the drama — Richard Gunnell and William Blagrove. Yet Gunnell was a distinguished actor, and was associated with the ownership and management of at least two theatres. Even so early as 1613 his reputation as a player was sufficient to warrant his inclusion as a full sharer in the Palsgrave's Company, then acting at the Fortune. When the Fortune was rebuilt after its destruction by fire in 1621, he purchased one of the twelve shares in the new building, and rose to be manager of the company.[2] In addition to managing the company he also, as we learn from the Herbert Manuscript, supplied the actors with plays. In 1623 he composed *The Hungarian Lion*, obviously a comedy, and in the following year *The Way to Content all*

---

[1] The playhouse discussed in this chapter was officially known as "The Salisbury Court Playhouse," and it should always be referred to by that name. Unfortunately, owing to its situation near the district of Whitefriars, it was sometimes loosely, though incorrectly, called "Whitefriars." Since it had no relation whatever to the theatre formerly in the Manor-House of Whitefriars, a perpetuation of this false nomenclature is highly undesirable.

[2] Malone, *Variorum*, III, 66.

SALISBURY COURT

Women, or How a Man May Please his Wife.[1] Of William Blagrove I can learn little more than that he was Deputy to the Master of the Revels. In this capacity he signed the license for Glapthorne's *Lady Mother*, October 15, 1635; and his name appears several times in the Herbert Manuscript in connection with the payments of various companies.[2] Possibly he was related to Thomas Blagrove who during the reign of Elizabeth was an important member of the Revels Office, and who for a time served as Master of the Revels.

What threw these two men together in a theatrical partnership we do not know. But in the summer of 1629 they decided to build a private playhouse to compete with the successful Blackfriars and Cockpit; and for this purpose they leased from the Earl of Dorset a plot of ground situated to the east of the precinct of Whitefriars. The ground thus leased opened on Salisbury Court; hence the name, "The Salisbury Court Playhouse." In the words of the legal document, the Earl of Dorset "in consideration that Richard Gunnell and William

---

[1] Chalmers's *Supplemental Apology*, pp. 216–17. He may also have been the author of a play called *The Masque*, which Herbert in 1624 licensed: "For the Palsgrave's Company, a new play called *The Masque*." In the list of manuscript plays collected by Warburton we find the title *A Mask*, and the authorship ascribed to R. Govell. Since "R. Govell" is not otherwise heard of, we may reasonably suppose that this was Warburton's reading of "R. Gunell." Gunnell also prefixed a poem to the Works of Captain John Smith, 1626.

[2] Malone, *Variorum*, III, 66, 122, 176, 177.

Blagrove should at their costs and charges erect a playhouse and other buildings at the lower end of Salisbury Court, in the parish of St. Bridges, in the ward of Farringdon Without, did demise to the said Gunnell and Blagrove a piece of ground at the same lower end of Salisbury Court, containing one hundred and forty foot in length and forty-two in breadth... for forty-one years and a half." The lease was signed on July 6, 1629. Nine days later, on July 15, the Earl of Dorset, "in consideration of nine hundred and fifty pounds paid to the said late Earl by John Herne, of Lincoln's Inn, Esquire, did demise to hire the said piece of ground and [the] building [i.e., the playhouse] thereupon to be erected, and the rent reserved upon the said lease made to Gunnell and Blagrove." Herne's lease was for a term of sixty-one years. The effect of this second lease was merely to make Herne, instead of the Earl of Dorset, the landlord of the players.

The plot of ground selected for the playhouse is described with exactness in the lease printed below. The letters inserted in brackets refer to the accompanying diagram (see page 371):

All that soil and ground whereupon the Barn [A], at the lower end of the great back court, or yard of Salisbury Court, now stands; and so much of the soil whereupon the whole south end of the great stable in the said court or yard stands, or contains, from that end of that stable towards the north end thereof sixteen foot of assize, and the whole breadth of the said stable [B]; and all the ground and soil on the east and

SALISBURY COURT

west side of that stable lying directly against the said sixteen foot of ground at the south end thereof between the wall of the great garden belonging to the mansion called Dorset House and the wall that severs

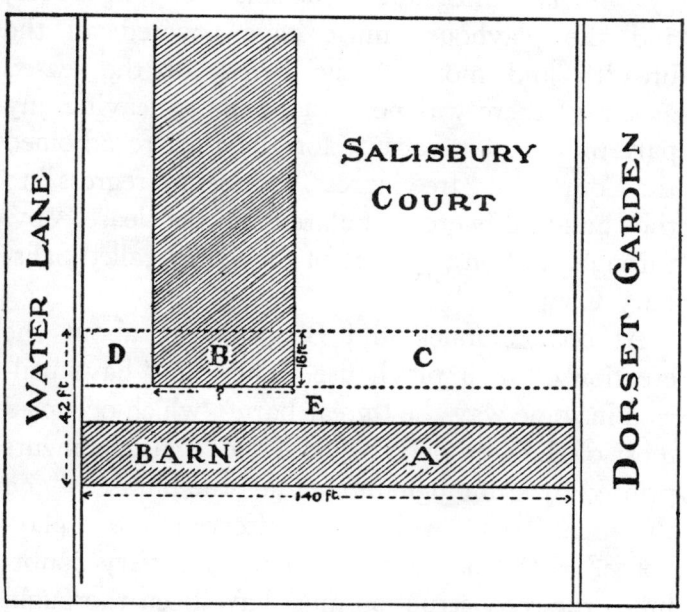

A PLAN OF THE SALISBURY COURT PROPERTY
To illustrate the lease. (Drawn by the author.)

the said Court from the lane called Water Lane [C and D]; and all the ground and soil being between the said walls on the east and west part thereof, and the said barn, stable, and ground on both side the same on the south and north parts thereof [E]. Which said several parcels of soil and ground ... contain, in the whole length ... one hundred and forty foot of assize, and in breadth ... forty and two foot of assize, and lies together at the lower end of the said Court.

This plot, one hundred and forty feet in length by forty-two in breadth, was small for its purpose, and the playhouse must have covered all the breadth and most of the length of the leased ground;[1] there was no actual need of leaving any part of the plot vacant, for the theatre adjoined the Court, and "free ingress, egress, and regress" to the building were stipulated in the lease "by, through, and on any part of the Court called Salisbury Court."

At once Gunnell and Blagrove set about the erection of their playhouse. They may have utilized in some way the "great barn" which occupied most of their property; one of the legal documents printed by Cunningham contains the phrase: "and the great barn, which was afterwards the playhouse."[2] If this be true — I think it very doubtful — the reconstruction must have been thorough, for Howes, in his continuation of Stow's *Annals* (1631), speaks of Salisbury Court as "a new, fair playhouse";[3] and in all respects it seems to have ranked with the best.

[1] The Blackfriars auditorium was sixty-six feet in length and forty-six feet in breadth.
[2] Cunningham, *The Shakespeare Society's Papers*, IV, 104. In his *Handbook for London* Cunningham says that the Salisbury Court Playhouse "was originally the 'barn.'"
[3] *Annals* (1631), p. 1004. In 1633 Prynne (*Histriomastix*) refers to it as a "new theatre erected."

We know very little of the building. But Wright, in his *Historia Histrionica*, informs us that it was "almost exactly like" the two other private houses, the Blackfriars and the Cockpit:

True. The Blackfriars, Cockpit, and Salisbury Court were called private houses, and were very small to what we see now. The Cockpit was standing since the Restoration, and Rhodes' company acted there for some time.
Love. I have seen that.
True. Then you have seen the other two in effect, for they were all three built almost exactly alike for form and bigness.[1]

In spite of what Wright says, however, there is some reason for believing that Salisbury Court was smaller than the other two private houses. The Epilogue to *Totenham Court* refers to it as "my little house"; and the Epistle affixed to the second edition of *Sir Giles Goosecappe* is said to convey the same impression of smallness.[2]

According to Malone, Sir Henry Herbert, the Master of the Revels, was "one of the proprietors" of the house, and held a "ninth share" in the profits.[3] This, however, is not strictly accurate. Sir Henry, by virtue of his power to license playhouses, demanded from each organization of players an

[1] Collier *The History of English Dramatic Literature* (1879), III, 106, thought that Salisbury Court was a round playhouse, basing his opinion on a line in Sharpe's *Noble Stranger* acted at "the private house in Salisbury Court": "Thy Stranger to the Globe-like theatre."
[2] I have not been able to examine this. In the only copy of the second edition accessible to me the Epistle is missing.
[3] Malone, *Variorum*, iii, 178.

annual fee. The King's Men gave him two benefit performances a year; Christopher Beeston, on behalf of the Cockpit in Drury Lane, paid him £60 a year; as for the rest, Herbert tells us that he had "a share paid by the Fortune Players, and a share by the Bull Players, and a share by the Salisbury Court Players."[1] It seems, therefore, that the Salisbury Court organization was divided into eight shares, and that of the profits an extra, or ninth, share was set aside as a fee for the Master of the Revels.

The playhouse was ready for use in all probability in the autumn of 1629; and to occupy it a new company of actors was organized, known as "The King's Revels." The chief members of this company were George Stutville, John Young, William Cartwright, William Wilbraham, and Christopher Goad; Gunnell and Blagrove probably acted as managers. In the books of the Lord Chamberlain we find a warrant for the payment of £30 to William Blagrove "and the rest of his company" for three plays acted by the Children of the Revels, at Whitehall, 1631.[2] The Children continued at Salisbury Court until about December, 1631, when they abandoned the playhouse in favor of the

---

[1] Halliwell-Phillipps, *A Collection of Ancient Documents*, p. 27.

[2] See Mrs. Stopes's extracts from the Lord Chamberlain's books, in the Shakespeare *Jchrbuch* (1910), XLVI, 97. This entry probably led Cunningham to say (*The Shakespeare Society's Papers*, IV, 92) that Blagrove was "Master of the Children of the Revels in the reign of Charles I."

much larger Fortune, surrendered by the Palsgrave's Men.

The Palsgrave's Men, who for many years had occupied the Fortune, seem to have fallen on bad times and to have disbanded. They were reorganized, however, possibly by their old manager, Richard Gunnell, and established in Salisbury Court. The Earl of Dorset, who took a special interest in Salisbury Court, obtained for the troupe a patent to play under the name of the infant Prince Charles, then little more than a year old.[1] The patent bears the date of December 7, 1631; and "The Servants of the High and Mighty Prince Charles" opened at Salisbury Court very soon after [2] with a play by Marmion entitled *Holland's Leaguer*. The Prologue refers to the going of the King's Revels to the Fortune, and the coming of the new troupe to Salisbury Court:

> Gentle spectators, that with graceful eye
> Come to behold the Muses' colony
> New planted in this soil, forsook of late
> By the inhabitants, since made *Fortunate*.

The Prologue closes thus:

> That on our branches now new poets sing;
> And when with joy he shall see this resort
> Phœbus shall not disdain to styl't his *Court*.

But the audiences at Salisbury Court were not large. For six performances of the play, says

---

[1] For Dorset's interest in the matter see Cunningham, *The Shakespeare Society's Papers*, IV, 96.
[2] In December, 1631; see Malone, *Variorum*, III, 178.

Malone, Sir Henry Herbert received "but one pound nineteen shillings, in virtue of the ninth share which he possessed as one of the proprietors of the house." [1]

Of the "new poets" referred to by the Prologue, one, of course, was Marmion himself. Another, I venture to say, was James Shirley, who, as I think, had been engaged to write the company's second play. This was *The Changes*, brought out at Salisbury Court on January 10. The Prologue is full of allusions to the company, its recent misfortunes, and its present attempt to establish itself in its new quarters:

> That Muse, whose song within another sphere [2]
> Hath pleased some, and of the best, whose ear
> Is able to distinguish strains that are
> Clear and Phoebean from the popular
> And sinful dregs of the adulterate brain,
> By me salutes your candour once again;
> And begs this noble favour, that this place,
> And weak performances, may not disgrace
> His fresh Thalia.[3] 'Las, our poet knows
> We have no name; a torrent overflows
> Our little island;[4] miserable we
> Do every day play our own Tragedy.
> But 't is more noble to create than kill,
> He says; and if but with his flame, your will
> Would join, we may obtain some warmth, and prove
> Next them that now do surfeit with your love.

---

[1] Malone, *Variorum*, III, 178.
[2] The Cockpit, for which Shirley had been writing.
[3] Cf. "new poets" of Marmion's Prologue.
[4] An allusion to the smallness of the Salisbury Court Playhouse?

> Encourage our beginning. Nothing grew
> Famous at first. And, gentlemen, if you
> Smile on this barren mountain, soon it will
> Become both fruitful and the Muses hill.

The similarity of this to the Prologue of *Holland's Leaguer* is striking; and the Epilogue is written in the same vein:

> Opinion
> Comes hither but on crutches yet; the sun
> Hath lent no beam to warm us. If this play
> Proceed more fortunate, we shall bless the day
> And love that brought you hither. 'T is in you
> To make a little sprig of laurel grow,
> And spread into a grove.

All scholars who have written on the subject — Collier, Fleay, Greg, Murray, etc. — have contended that the King's Revels Company did not leave Salisbury Court until after January 10, 1632, because Herbert licensed Shirley's *The Changes* on that date,[1] and the title-page of the only edition of *The Changes* states that it was acted at Salisbury Court by His Majesty's Revels. But Herbert records payments for six representations of Marmion's *Leaguer* by Prince Charles's Men at Salisbury Court "in December, 1631."[2] This latter date must be correct, for on January 26 *Holland's Leaguer* was entered on the Stationers' Register "as it hath been lately and often acted with great applause ... at the private house in Salisbury

---

[1] Malone, *Variorum*, III, 232. But Malone was a careless transcriber, and Herbert himself sometimes made errors. Possibly the correct date is January 10, 1631.   [2] *Ibid.*, III, 178.

Court." According to the generally accepted theory, however, the King's Men were still at Salisbury Court, and actually bringing out a new play there so late as January 10. This error has led to much confusion, and to no little difficulty for historians of the stage; for example, Mr. Murray is forced to suppose that two royal patents were granted to Prince Charles's Company.[1] It seems to me likely that the title-page of *The Changes* is incorrect in stating that the play was acted by the King's Revels. The play must have been acted by the new and as yet unpopular Prince Charles's Men, who had occupied Salisbury Court as early as December, and, as Herbert tells us, with poor success. The various dates cited clearly indicate this; and the Prologue and the Epilogue are both wholly unsuited for utterance by the successful Revels Company which had just been "made Fortunate," but are quite in keeping with the condition of the newly organized and struggling Prince Charles's Men, who might naturally ask the public to "encourage our beginning."

Whether Prince Charles's Men ultimately succeeded in winning the favor of the public we do not know. Presumably they did, for at some date before 1635 they moved to the large Red Bull Playhouse. Richard Heton wrote: "And whereas my Lord of Dorset had gotten for a former company at Salisbury Court the Prince's service, they, being

[1] *English Dramatic Companies*, I, 221.

left at liberty, took their opportunity of another house, and left the house in Salisbury Court destitute both of a service and company." [1]

This person, Richard Heton, who describes himself as "one of the Sewers of Her Majesty's Chamber Extraordinary," had now obtained control of Salisbury Court, and had become manager of its affairs.[2] He apparently induced the Company of His Majesty's Revels to leave the Fortune and return to Salisbury Court, for in 1635 they acted there Richard Brome's *The Sparagus Garden*. But their career at Salisbury Court was short; on May 12 of the following year all playhouses were closed by the plague, and acting was not allowed again for nearly a year and a half. During this long period of inactivity, the Company of His Majesty's Revels was largely dispersed.

When at last, on October 2, 1637, the playhouses were allowed to open, Heton found himself with a crippled troupe of actors. Again the Earl of Dorset interested himself in the theatre. Queen Henrietta's Company, which had been at the Cockpit since 1625, having " disperst themselves," Dorset took " care to make up a new company for the

[1] Richard Heton, "Instructions for my Pattent," *The Shakespeare Society's Papers*, IV, 96.
[2] We find a payment to Richard Heton, "for himself and the rest of the company of the players at Salisbury Court," for performing a play before his Majesty at Court, October, 1635. (Chalmers's *Apology*, p. 509.) Exactly when he took charge of Salisbury Court I am unable to learn.

Queen";[1] and he placed this new company under Heton at Salisbury Court. Heton writes: "How much I have done for the upbuilding of this Company, I gave you some particulars of in a petition to my Lord of Dorset." This reorganization of the Queen's Men explains, perhaps, the puzzling entry in Herbert's Office-Book, October 2, 1637: "I disposed of Perkins, Sumner, Sherlock, and Turner, to Salisbury Court, and joyned them with the best of that company."[2] Doubtless Herbert, like Dorset, was anxious for the Queen to have a good troupe of players. This new organization of the Queen's Men continued at Salisbury Court without interruption, it seems, until the closing of the playhouses in 1642.[3]

In 1649 John Herne, son of the John Herne who in 1629 had secured a lease on the property for sixty-one years, made out a deed of sale of the playhouse to William Beeston,[4] for the sum of £600. But the document was not signed. The reason for this is probably revealed in the following passage: "The playhouse in Salisbury Court, in

---

[1] Cunningham, *The Shakespeare Society's Papers*, IV, 96.
[2] Malone, *Variorum*, III, 240.
[3] For certain troubles at Salisbury Court in 1644 and 1648, see Collier, *The History of English Dramatic Poetry* (1879), II, 37, 40, 47.
[4] William Beeston was the son of the famous actor Christopher Beeston, who was once a member of the Lord Chamberlain's Men, later manager of the Fortune, and finally proprietor of the Cockpit. In 1639 William had been appointed manager of the Cockpit Company. (See pages 358 ff.)

SALISBURY COURT

Fleet Street, was pulled down [1] by a company of soldiers set on by the sectaries of these sad times, on Saturday, the 24 day of March, 1649." [2]

Three years later, however, Beeston, through his agent Theophilus Bird, secured the property from Herne at the reduced price of £408: "John Herne, by indenture dated the five and twentieth day of May, 1652, for £408, to him paid by Theophilus Bird, did assign the premises and all his estate therein in trust for the said William Beeston." [3]

Early in 1660 Beeston, anticipating the return of King Charles, and the reëstablishment of the drama, decided to put his building back into condition to serve as a playhouse; and he secured from Herbert, the Master of the Revels, a license to do so.[4] On April 5, 1660, he contracted with two carpenters, Fisher and Silver, "for the rebuilding the premises"; and to secure them he mortgaged the property. The carpenters later swore that they "expended in the same work £329 9s. 4d." [5]

The reconstructed playhouse was opened in 1660, probably as early as June, with a performance

---

[1] That is, stripped of its benches, stage-hangings, and other appliances for dramatic performances.

[2] The manuscript entry in Stow's *Annals*. See *The Academy*, October 28, 1882, p. 314. On the same date the soldiers "pulled down on the inside" also the Phœnix and the Fortune.

[3] Cunningham, *The Shakespeare Society's Papers*, IV, 103.

[4] Printed in Malone, *Variorum*, III, 243, and Halliwell-Phillipps, *A Collection of Ancient Documents*, p. 85. The language clearly indicates that Beeston was to *reconvert* the building into a theatre.

[5] Cunningham, *The Shakespeare Society's Papers*, IV, 103.

of *The Rump*, by Tatham. It was engaged by Sir William Davenant for his company of actors until his "new theatre with scenes" could be erected in Lincoln's Inn Fields.[1] The ubiquitous Pepys often went thither, and in his *Diary* gives us some interesting accounts of the performances he saw there. On March 2, 1661, he witnessed a revival of Thomas Heywood's *Love's Mistress, or The Queen's Masque* before a large audience:

After dinner I went to the Theatre [i.e., Killigrew's playhouse] where I found so few people (which is strange, and the reason I did not know) that I went out again; and so to Salisbury Court, where the house as full as could be; and it seems it was a new play, *The Queen's Masque*, wherein are some good humours: among others a good jeer to the old story of the Siege of Troy, making it to be a common country tale. But above all it was strange to see so little a boy as that was to act Cupid, which is one of the greatest parts in it.

Again, on March 26, he found Salisbury Court crowded:

After dinner Mrs. Pierce and her husband, and I and my wife, to Salisbury Court, where coming late, he and she light of Col. Boone, that made room for them; and I and my wife sat in the pit, and there met with Mr. Lewes and Tom Whitton, and saw *The Bondman*[2] done to admiration.

[1] Malone, *Variorum*, III, 257; Halliwell-Phillipps, *A Collection of Ancient Documents*, p. 27.
[2] By Philip Massinger.

SALISBURY COURT

The history of the playhouse during these years falls outside the scope of this volume. Suffice it to say that before Beeston finished paying the carpenters for their work of reconstruction, the great fire of 1666 swept the building out of existence; as Fisher and Silver declared: "The mortgaged premises by the late dreadful fire in London were totally burned down and consumed." [1]

[1] The subsequent history of Salisbury Court is traced in the legal documents printed by Cunningham. Beeston lost the property, and Fisher and Silver erected nearer the river a handsome new playhouse, known as "The Duke's Theatre," at an estimated cost of £1000.

CHAPTER XX

THE COCKPIT-IN-COURT, OR THEATRE ROYAL AT WHITEHALL

ON birthdays, holidays, and festive occasions in general the sovereigns of England and the members of the royal family were wont to summon the professional actors to present plays at Court. For the accommodation of the players and of the audience, the larger halls at Hampton, Windsor, Greenwich, St. James, Whitehall, or wherever the sovereign happened to be at the time, were specially fitted up, often at great expense. At one end of the hall was erected a temporary stage equipped with a "music-room," "players' houses of canvas," painted properties, and such other things as were necessary to the actors. In the centre of the hall, on an elevated dais, were provided seats for the royal family, and around and behind the dais, stools for the more distinguished guests; a large part of the audience was allowed to stand on platforms raised in tiers at the rear of the room. Since the plays were almost invariably given at night, the stage was illuminated by special "branches" hung on wires overhead, and carrying many lights. In the accounts of the Office of the Revels one may find interesting records of plays presented in this manner, with the miscellaneous items of expense for making the halls ready.

Usually the Court performances, like the masques, were important, almost official occasions, and many guests, including the members of the diplomatic corps, were invited. To provide accommodation for so numerous an audience, a large room was needed. Hampton Court possessed a splendid room for the purpose in the Great Banqueting Hall, one hundred and six feet in length and forty feet in breadth. But the palace at Whitehall for many years had no room of a similar character. For the performance of a masque there in 1559 the Queen erected a temporary "Banqueting House." Again, in 1572, to entertain the Duke of Montmorency, Ambassador from France, she had a large "Banketting House made at Whitehall," covered with canvas and decorated with ivy and flowers gathered fresh from the fields. An account of the structure may be found in the records of the Office of the Revels. Perhaps, however, the most elaborate and substantial of these "banqueting houses" was that erected in 1581, to entertain the ambassadors from France who came to treat of a marriage between Elizabeth and the Duc d'Anjou. The structure is thus described by Holinshed in his *Chronicle:* [1]

This year (against the coming of certain commissioners out of France into England), by Her Majes-

---

[1] Edition of 1808, IV, 434. See also Stow's *Chronicle*, under the year 1581.

ty's appointment, on the sixth and twentieth day of March, in the morning (being Easter Day), a Banqueting House was begun at Westminster, on the south-west side of Her Majesty's palace of Whitehall, made in manner and form of a long square, three hundred thirty and two foot in measure about; thirty principals made of great masts, being forty foot in length apiece, standing upright; between every one of these masts ten foot asunder and more. The walls of this house were closed with canvas, and painted all the outsides of the same most artificially, with a work called rustic, much like stone. This house had two hundred ninety and two lights of glass. The sides within the same house was made with ten heights of degrees for people to stand upon; and in the top of this house was wrought most cunningly upon canvas works of ivy and holly, with pendants made of wicker rods, garnished with bay, rue, and all manner of strange flowers garnished with spangles of gold; as also beautified with hanging toseans made of holly and ivy, with all manner of strange fruits, as pomegranates, oranges, pompions, cucumbers, grapes, carrots, with such other like, spangled with gold, and most richly hanged. Betwixt these works of bays and ivy were great spaces of canvas, which was most cunningly painted, the clouds with stars, the sun and sun-beams, with diverse other coats of sundry sorts belonging to the Queen's Majesty, most richly garnished with gold. There were of all manner of persons working on this house to the number of three hundred seventy and five: two men had mischances, the one broke his leg, and so did the other. This house was made in three weeks and three days, and was ended the eighteenth day of April, and cost one thousand seven hundred forty and four pounds, nineteen shillings, and od mony, as I was credibly informed by the worshipful master Thomas Grave, surveyor unto Her Majesty's works, who served and gave order for the same.

Although built in such a short time, and of such flimsy material, this expensive Banqueting House seems to have been allowed to stand, and to have been used thereafter for masques and plays. Thus, when King James came to the throne, he ordered plays to be given there in November, 1604. We find the following entry in the Treasurer's accounts:

For making ready the Banqueting House at Whitehall for the King's Majesty against the plays, by the space of four days . . . 78s. 7d.

And the accounts of the Revels' Office inform us:

Hallomas Day, being the first of November, a play in the Banqueting House at Whitehall, called *The Moor of Venice*.

Apparently, however, the King was not pleased with the Banqueting House as a place for dramatic performances, for he promptly ordered the Great Hall of the palace — a room approximately ninety feet in length and forty feet in breadth [1] — to be made ready for the next play:

For making ready the Great Chamber at Whitehall for the King's Majesty to see the play, by the space of two days . . . 39s. 4d.

---

[1] This had once already, on Shrove Tuesday, 1604, been used for a play. The situation and ground-plan of the "Great Hall" are clearly shown in Fisher's *Survey* of the palace, made about 1670, and engraved by Vertue, 1747.

The work was completed with dispatch, for on the Sunday following the performance of *Othello* in the Banqueting House, *The Merry Wives of Windsor* was acted in the Great Hall. The next play to be given at Court was also presented in the same room:

On St. Stephen's Night, in the Hall, a play called *Measure for Measure*.

And from this time on the Great Hall was the usual place for Court performances. The abandonment of the Banqueting House was probably due to the facts that the Hall was smaller in size, could be more easily heated in the winter, and was in general better adapted to dramatic performances. Possibly the change was due also to the decayed condition of the old structure and to preparations for its removal. Stow, in his *Annals* under the date of 1607, writes:

The last year the King pulled down the old, rotten, slight-builded Banqueting House at Whitehall, and new-builded the same this year very strong and stately, being every way larger than the first.[1]

This new Banqueting House was completed in the early part of 1608. John Chamberlain writes to Sir Dudley Carleton on January 5, 1608: "The masque goes forward at Court for Twelfth Day, tho' I doubt the New Room will be scant ready."[2] Thereafter the Banqueting House, "every way

[1] Stow's *Annals*, continued by Edmund Howes (1631), p. 891.
[2] John Nichols, *The Progresses of James*, II, 162.

THE COCKPIT-IN-COURT

larger than the first," was regularly used for the presentation of masques. But it was rarely if ever used for plays. Throughout the reign of James, the ordinary place for dramatic performances, as has been observed, was the Great Hall.

On January 12, 1619, as a result of negligence during the preparations for a masque, the Banqueting House caught fire and was burned to the ground. The Reverend Thomas Lorkin writes to Sir Thomas Puckering on January 19, 1619:

> The unhappy accident that chanced at Whitehall last week by fire you cannot but have heard of; but haply not the manner how, which was this. A joiner was appointed to mend some things that were out of order in the device of the masque, which the King meant to have repeated at Shrovetide, who, having kindled a fire upon a false hearth to heat his glue-pot, the force thereof pierced soon, it seems, the single brick, and in a short time that he absented himself upon some occasion, fastened upon the basis, which was of dry deal board, underneath; which suddenly conceiving flame, gave fire to the device of the masque, all of oiled paper, and dry fir, etc. And so, in a moment, disposed itself among the rest of that combustible matter that it was past any man's approach before it was almost discovered. Two hours begun and ended that woful sight.

Inigo Jones, who had dreamed of a magnificent palace at Whitehall, and who had drawn elaborate plans for a royal residence which should surpass anything in Europe, now took charge of building a new Banqueting House as a first step in the realiza-

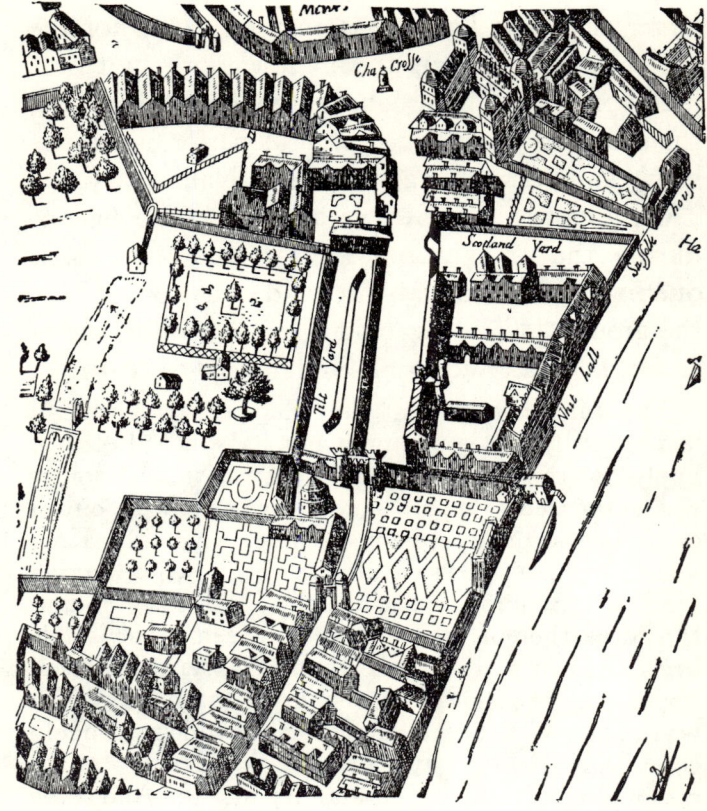

THE COCKPIT

Probably as built by Henry VIII. (From Faithorne's *Map of London*, 1658. The Whitehall district is represented as it was many years earlier; compare Agas's *Map*, 1560).

tion of his scheme. The noble structure which he erected is to-day one of his chief monuments, and the sole relic of the once famous royal palace. It was completed in the spring of 1622; but, as in the case of its predecessor, it was not commonly used

THE COCKPIT-IN-COURT

for dramatic entertainments. Though masques might be given there, the regular place for plays continued to be the Great Hall.

In the meanwhile, however, there had been developed at Court the custom of having small private performances in the Cockpit, in addition to the more elaborate performances in the Great Hall. Since this ultimately led to the establishment of a theatre royal, known as "The Cockpit-in-Court," it will be necessary to trace in some detail the history of that structure.

The palace of Whitehall, anciently called York House, and the home of thirty successive Archbishops of York, was seized by King Henry VIII at the fall of Wolsey and converted into a royal residence.[1] The new proprietor at once made improvements after his own taste, among which were tennis-courts, bowling-alleys, and an amphitheatre for the "royal sport" of cock-fighting. In Stow's description of the palace we read:

> On the right hand be diverse fair tennis courts, bowling alleys, and a Cockpit, all built by King Henry the Eight.

Strype, in his edition of Stow's *Survey* (1720), adds the information that the Cockpit was made "out

---

[1] Shakespeare writes (*Henry VIII*, IV, i, 94-97):
> Sir you
> Must no more call it York-place, that is past;
> For since the Cardinal fell, that title's lost:
> 'Tis now the King's, and called Whitehall.

of certain old tenements."[1] It is pictured in Agas's *Map of London* (1570), and more clearly in Faithorne's *Map* (see page 390), printed in 1658, but apparently representing the city at an earlier date.

During the reign of Elizabeth the Cockpit, so far as I can ascertain, was never used for plays. In the voluminous documents relating to the Office of the Revels there is only one reference to the building: in 1572 flowers were temporarily stored there that were to be used for decking the "Banketting House."

It was during the reign of King James that the Cockpit began to be used for dramatic representations. John Chamberlain writes from London to Sir Ralph Winwood, December 18, 1604: "Here is great provision for Cockpit to entertain him [the King] at home, and of masques and revels against the marriage of Sir Herbert and Lady Susan Vere."[2] Since, however, King James was very fond of cock-fighting, it may be that Chamberlain was referring to that royal entertainment rather than to plays. The small Cockpit was certainly a very unusual place for the formal presentation of plays before His Majesty and the Court.

But the young Prince Henry, whose official residence was in St. James's Palace, often had private or semi-private performances of plays in the Cock-

---

[1] Book VI, page 6.
[2] *Winwood State Papers* (1725), II, 41.

THE COCKPIT-IN-COURT

pit. In the rolls of the expenses of the Prince we find the following records: [1]

For making ready the Cockpit four several times for plays, by the space of four days, in the month of December, 1610, £2 10s. 8d.

For making ready the Cockpit for plays two several times, by the space of four days, in the months of January and February, 1611, 70s. 8d.

For making ready the Cockpit for a play, by the space of two days, in the month of December, 1611, 30s. 4d.

The building obviously, was devoted for the most part to other purposes, and had to be "made ready" for plays at a considerable expense. Nor was the Prince the only one who took advantage of its small amphitheatre. John Chamberlain, in a letter to Sir Dudley Carleton on September 22, 1612, describing the reception accorded to the Count Palatine by the Lady Elizabeth, writes: "On Tuesday she sent to invite him as he sat at supper to a play of her own servants in the Cockpit." [2]

It is clear, then, that at times throughout the reign of James dramatic performances were given in the Cockpit; but the auditorium was small, and the performances must have been of a semi-private nature. The important Court performances, to which many guests were invited, were held in the Great Hall.

---

[1] See Cunningham, *Extracts from the Accounts of the Revels*, pp. xiii–xiv.

[2] John Nichols, *The Progresses of James*, II, 466.

In the reign of the next sovereign, however, a change came about. In the year 1632 or 1633, as well as I am able to judge with the evidence at command, King Charles reconstructed the old Cockpit into a "new theatre at Whitehall," which from henceforth was almost exclusively used for Court performances. The opening of this "new theatre royal" is celebrated by a *Speech* from the pen of Thomas Heywood:

> *A Speech Spoken to Their Two Excellent Majesties at the First Play Play'd by the Queen's Servants in the New Theatre at Whitehall.*
>
> When Greece, the chief priority might claim
> For arts and arms, and held the eminent name
> Of Monarchy, they erected divers places,
> Some to the Muses, others to the Graces,
> Where actors strove, and poets did devise,
> With tongue and pen to please the ears and eyes
> Of Princely auditors. The time was, when
> To hear the rapture of one poet's pen
> A Theatre hath been built.
>
> By the Fates' doom,
> When th' Empire was removed from thence to Rome,
> The Potent Cæsars had their *circi*, and
> Large amphitheatres, in which might stand
> And sit full fourscore thousand, all in view
> And touch of voice. This great Augustus knew,
> Nay Rome its wealth and potency enjoyed,
> Till by the barbarous Goths these were destroy'd.
>
> But may this structure last, and you be seen
> Here a spectator, with your princely Queen,
> In your old age, as in your flourishing prime,
> To outstrip Augustus both in fame and time.

THE COCKPIT-IN-COURT

The exact date of this *Speech* is not given, but it was printed [1] in 1637 along with "The Prologue to the Famous Tragedy of *The Rich Jew of Malta*, as it Was Played Before the King and Queen in His Majesty's Theatre at Whitehall"; and this Prologue Heywood had already published with the play itself in 1633. He dedicated the play to Mr. Thomas Hammon, saying, "I had no better a New-Year's gift to present you with." Apparently, then, the play had been acted at Court shortly before New Year's, 1633; and this sets a forward date to Heywood's *Speech*. Other evidence combines with this to show that "His Majesty's Theatre at Whitehall" was "new" at the Christmas season of 1632–33.

In erecting this, the first "theatre royal," King Charles would naturally call for the aid of the great Court architect Inigo Jones,[2] and by good luck we have preserved for us Jones's original sketches for the little playhouse (see page 396). These were discovered a few years ago by Mr. Hamilton Bell in the Library of Worcester College (where many valuable relics of the great architect are stored), and printed in *The Architectural Record* of New York, March, 1913. Mr. Bell accompanied the plans with

---

[1] See *The Dramatic Works of Thomas Heywood* (1874), VI, 339.
[2] Whether he merely made over the old Cockpit which Henry VIII had constructed "out of certain old tenements," or erected an entirely new building, I have not been able to ascertain. Heywood's *Speech* indicates a "new" and "lasting" structure.

a valuable discussion, but he was unable to discover their purpose. He writes:

We have still no clue as to what purpose this curiously anomalous and most interesting structure was to serve — whether the plan was ever carried out, or whether it remained part of a lordly pleasure-house which its prolific designer planned for the delectation of his own soul.

That the plan actually was carried out, at least in part, is shown by a sketch of the Whitehall buildings made by John Fisher at some date before 1670, and engraved by Vertue in 1747, (see page 398).[1] Here, in the northeast corner of the palace, we find a little theatre, labeled "The Cockpit." Its identity with the building sketched by Inigo Jones is obvious at a glance; even the exterior measurements, which are ascertainable from the scales of feet given on the two plans, are the same.

Mr. Bell describes the plan he discovered as follows:[2]

It represents within a square building, windowed on three sides and on one seemingly attached to another building, an auditorium occupying five sides of an octagon, on the floor of which are shown the benches of a pit, or the steps, five in number, on which they could be set. These are curiously arranged at an angle of forty-five degrees on either side of a central

---

[1] Vertue conservatively dates the survey "about 1680"; but the names of the occupants of the various parts of the palace show that it was drawn before 1670, and nearer 1660 than 1680.

[2] Reprinted here by the kind permission of Mr. Bell and the editors of *The Architectural Record*.

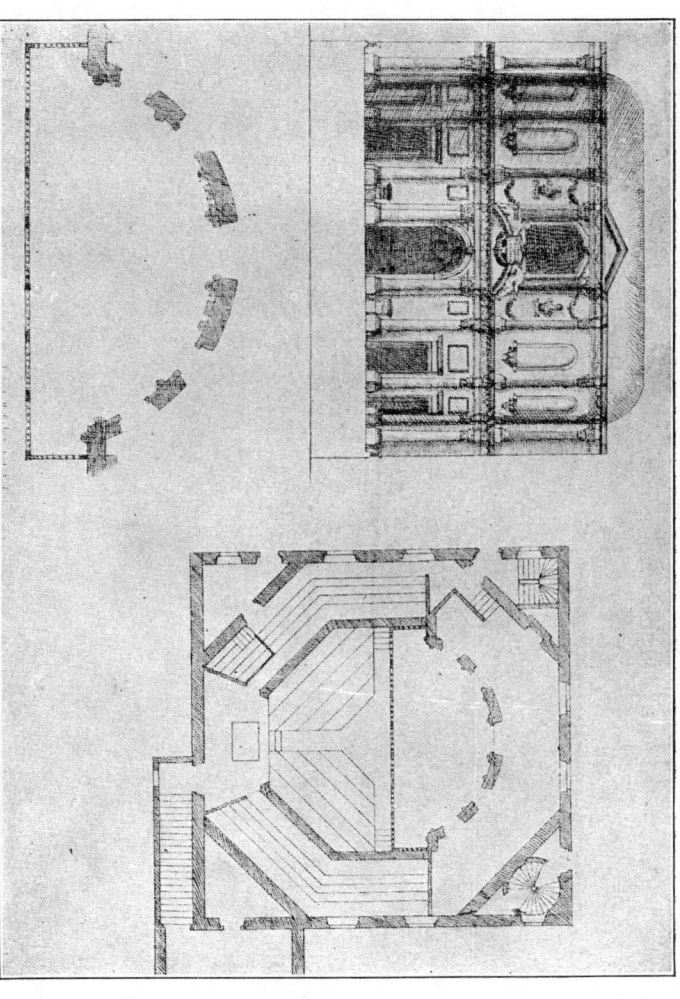

INIGO JONES'S PLANS FOR THE COCKPIT-IN-COURT
Now preserved in the Worcester College Library at Oxford; discovered by Mr. Hamilton Bell, and reproduced in *The Architectural Record*, of New York, 1913

THE COCKPIT-IN-COURT   397

aisle, so that the spectators occupying them could never have directly faced the stage. Surrounding this pit on five sides is a balcony ten feet deep, with, it would seem, two rows of benches on four of its sides; the fifth side in the centre, directly opposite the stage, being partitioned off into a room or box, in the middle of which is indicated a platform about five feet by seven, presumably for the Royal State. Three steps descend from this box to the centre aisle of the pit. To the left of and behind this royal box appears another enclosure or box, partitioned off from the rest of the balcony.

The staircases of access to this auditorium are clearly indicated; one small door at the rear of the *salle* with its own private stairway, communicating with the adjoining building, opens directly into the royal box; as in the Royal Opera House in Berlin to-day.

There is another door, with a triangular lobby, into the rear of the left-hand balcony. Two windows are shown on each side of the house, opening directly into the theatre from the outer air.

The stage runs clear across the width of the pit, about thirty-five feet, projecting in an "apron" or *avant scène* five feet beyond the proscenium wall, and is surrounded on the three outward sides by a low railing of classic design about eighteen inches in height, just as in many Elizabethan playhouses.

If one may trust an elevation of the stage, drawn on the same sheet to twice the scale of the general plan, the stage was four feet six inches above the floor of the pit. This elevation exhibits the surprising feature of a classic façade, Palladian in treatment, on the stage of what so far we have regarded as a late modification of a playhouse of Shakespeare's day. Evidently Inigo Jones contemplated the erection of a permanent architectural *proscenium*, as the ancients called it, of the type, though far more modest, both in scale and ornamentation, of Palladio's Theatro Olimpico at Vicenza, which we know he visited in about 1600, some twenty years after its erection. This *proscenium*, given in plan and elevation, shows a semi-circular structure with a radius of fifteen feet, two stories in height, of the Corinthian or Composite order. In the lower story are five doorways, the centre of which is a large archway flanked by pedestals, on which are inscribed in Greek characters, Melpomene — Thalia; over these and over the smaller doors are tablets.

The second story contains between its lighter engaged columns, over the four side doors, niches with corbels below, destined to carry statues as their inscribed bases indicate. So far as these inscriptions are legible, — the clearest reading "phocles," probably Sophocles, — these were to represent Greek dramatists, most likely Æschylus, Euripides, Sophocles and Aristophanes.

The curved pediment of the central archway runs up into this story and is broken in the middle by a tablet bearing the inscription "Prodesse et Delectare," which is flanked by two reclining genii holding garlands.

Above these are two busts on brackets, Thespis and Epicurus, or possibly Epicharmus. The space directly above this pediment is occupied by a window-like opening five by four feet, the traditional Elizabethan music-room, in all probability, which, Mr. W. J. Lawrence has shown us, occupied this position both in Shakespeare's day and for some time after the Restoration; an arrangement which was revived by Mr. Steele Mackaye in the Madison Square Theatre,

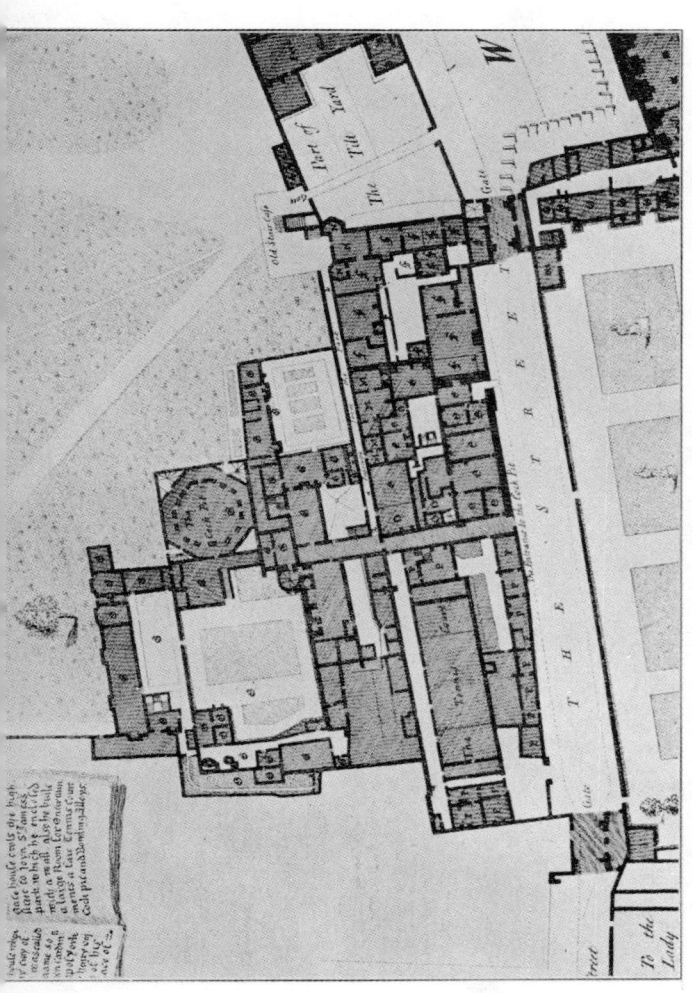

FISHER'S SURVEY OF WHITEHALL SHOWING THE COCKPIT-IN-COURT

A section from Vertue's engraving, 1747, of a survey of Whitehall made by John Fisher, 1660-1670. Compare "The Cockpit" with Inigo Jones's plans.

THE THEATRO OLYMPICO AT VICENZA
Which probably inspired Inigo Jones's plans for the Cockpit-in-Court.

THE COCKPIT-IN-COURT

and originally in the first little Lyceum, New York, both now pulled down. The pyramidal pediment above this opening projects above the upper cornice into a coved ceiling, which would appear from the rendering of the drawing to form an apse above the semi-circular stage. Behind the *proscenium* is a large space with staircases of approach, two windows at the rear, and apparently a fireplace for the comfort of the waiting players. Communication with the front of the house is provided by a door in the proscenium wall opening into the stage door lobby, whence the outside of the building may be reached.

There is no indication of galleries, unless some marks on the angles of the front wall of the balcony may be interpreted without too much license into the footings of piers or posts to carry one; the total interior height shown in the elevation from what I have assumed to be the floor of the pit to the ceiling being only twenty-eight feet, there would hardly have been room for more than one. The only staircases which could have served it are at the rear of the building in the corners behind the stage wall. . . .

The general dimensions would appear to be:

Total width of the auditorium............ 58 ft.
Total width of the pit................... 36 ft.
Total width of the front stage or "apron"... 35 ft.
Total depth of the stage from the railing to the centre of the *proscenium*............ 16 ft.
    The entire building is 58 feet square inside, cut to an octagon of 28 feet each side.
Height from floor to ceiling.............. 28 ft.
Height from stage to ceiling........ about 23 ft. 6 in.
The lower order of the *proscenium*........ 10 ft. 6 in.
The upper order of the *proscenium*........ 9 ft. 6 in.

The scale on the drawing may not be absolutely correct, as measured by it the side doors of the *pro-*

scenium are only five feet high and two feet nine inches wide: this, however, may be an error in the drawing, since we have it on very good authority that Inigo Jones designed without the use of a scale, proportioning his various members by his exquisitely critical eye alone, subsequently adding the dimensions in writing.

I record below some of the references to the Cockpit which I have gathered from the Herbert Manuscript and the Office-Books of the Lord Chamberlain. The earliest payment for plays there, it will be observed, is dated March 16, 1633. Abundant evidence shows that the actors gave their performance in the Cockpit at night without interfering with their regular afternoon performance at their playhouses, and for their pains received the sum of £10. If, however, for any reason they "lost their day" at their house they were paid £20.

1633. March 16. Warrant to pay £270 to John Lowen, Joseph Taylor, and Eilliard Swanston, His Majesty's Comedians, for plays by them acted before His Majesty, viz. — £20 for the rehearsal of one at the Cockpit, by which means they lost their afternoon at their house. . . . [1]

1634. *Bussy d'Amboise* was played by the King's Players on Easter-Monday night, at the Cockpit-in-Court.[2]

---

[1] Lord Chamberlain's Office-Book, C. C. Stopes, "Shakespeare's Fellows and Followers," Shakespeare *Jahrbuch*, XLVI, 96.

[2] Herbert MS., Malone, *Variorum*, III, 237.

THE COCKPIT-IN-COURT

1634. The *Pastorall* was played by the King's Players on Easter-Tuesday night, at the Cockpit-in-Court.[1]

1635. 10 May. A warrant for £30 unto Mons. Josias Floridor, for himself and the rest of the French players for three plays acted by them at the Cockpit.[2]

1635. 10 Decem^r. — A warrant for £100 to the Prince's Comedians, — viz. £60 for three plays acted at Hampton Court, at £20 for each play, in September and October, 1634. And £40 for four plays at Whitehall and [*query* "at"] the Cockpit in January, February, and May following, at £10 for each play.[3]

1636. The first and second part of *Arviragus and Philicia* were acted at the Cockpit before the King and Queen, the Prince, and Prince Elector, the 18 and 19 April, 1636, being Monday and Tuesday in Easter week.[4]

Other similar allusions to performance in the Cockpit might be cited from the Court records. One more will suffice — the most interesting of all, since it shows how frequently the little theatre was employed for the entertainment of the royal family. It is a bill presented by the Blackfriars Company, the King's Men, for Court performances during the year 1637. This bill was discovered and reproduced in facsimile by George R. Wright, F.S.A., in

[1] Herbert MS., Malone, *Variorum*, III, 237.
[2] Lord Chamberlain's Office-Book, Chalmers's *Apology*, p. 508.
[3] *Ibid.*, p. 509.
[4] The Herbert MS., Malone, *Variorum*, III, 238.

The Journal of the British Archæological Association for 1860; but it was wholly misunderstood by its discoverer, who regarded it as drawn up by the company of players that "performed at the Cockpit in Drury Lane." He was indeed somewhat puzzled by the reference to the Blackfriars Playhouse, but met the difficulty by saying: "There can be little doubt that the last-named theatre was lent for the occasion to the Cockpit Company," although he suggests no reason for this strange borrowing of a theatre by a troupe that possessed a house of its own, and much nearer the Court, too. It did not even occur to him, it seems, to inquire how the Cockpit Company secured the plays which we know belonged to Shakespeare's old company. Because of these obvious difficulties scholars have looked upon the document with suspicion, and apparently have treated it as a forgery.[1] But that it is genuine is indicated by the history of "The Cockpit-in-Court" as sketched above, and is proved beyond any question by the fact that the Office-Book of the Lord Chamberlain shows that the bill was paid:

12th March 1638 [9]. — Forasmuch as His Majesty's Servants, the company at the Blackfriars, have by special command, at divers times within the space of this present year 1638, acted 24 plays before His Majesty, six whereof have been performed at Hampton-court and Richmond, by means whereof

[1] Fleay in his elaborate studies of performances at Court ignores it entirely, as do subsequent scholars.

they were not only at the loss of their day at home, but at extraordinary charges by traveling and carriage of their goods, in consideration whereof they are to have £20 apiece for those plays, and £10 apiece for the other 18 acted at Whitehall, which in the whole amounted to the sum of £300. — These are therefore to pray and require you out of His Majesty's treasure in your charge to pay. . . .[1]

A photographic facsimile of this interesting document may be seen in *The Journal of the British Archæological Association*, already referred to; but for the convenience of those who do not read Elizabethan script with ease, I have reproduced it in type facsimile on page 404.

The check-marks at the left were probably made by the clerk in the Chamberlain's office to ascertain how many times the players "lost their day" at their house, and hence were entitled to £20 in payment. For the play given "at the blackfriars the 23 of Aprill for the queene" (presumably the general public was excluded) only the usual £10 was allowed.

With the approach of the civil war, the Cockpit, like the public theatres, suffered an eclipse. Sir Henry Herbert writes: "On Twelfth Night, 1642, the Prince had a play called *The Scornful Lady* at the Cockpit; but the King and Queen were not there, and it was the only play acted at court in the whole Christmas."[2] During the dark days that followed we hear nothing of plays in the Cockpit.

[1] Chalmers, *Apology*, p. 510.
[2] Herbert MS., Malone, *Variorum*, III, 241.

before the king & queene this
yeare of our lord 1638

At the Cocpit the 26th of march.................The lost ladie

At the Cocpit the 27th of march.................Damboyes

At the Cocpit the 3d of Aprill....................Aglaura

At the blackfryers the 23 of Aprill for the queene the vnfortunate lou[ers]

At the Cocpit the 29th of may the princes berthnight......ould Castel

At the Cocpit the last of may agayne the...........vnfortunate louers

At Sumerset-house the 10th of July & our day

— lost at our house mr Carlels play the first part of the pasionate louers

— At Hamton Court the 30th of September........The vnfortunate louer[s]

— At Richmount the 6th of november for the ladie
maries berthnight & the day lost at our house } —The mery divell of Edmonto[n]

At the Cocpit the 8h of november..................The fox

At the Cocpit the 13th of november................Ceaser

At the Cocpit the 15th of november..............The mery wifes of winser

At the Cocpit the 20th of november............The fayre favorett

At the Cocpit the 22th of november...............Chances

At the Cocpit the 27th of november............The Costome of the C[ountry]

At the Cocpit the 29th of november............The northen las

At the Cocpit the 6th of desember............The spanish Curatt

At the Cocpit the 11th of desember agayne.....The fayre favorett

At the Cocpit the 18th of desember m Carlels
play agayne the first part of...............The pasionate louers

At the Cocpit the 20th of desember the 2d part of........The pasionate louers

At the Cocpit the 27 of desember the 2d part agayne of the pasionate louers

— At Richmount the 28 of desember the ladie
Elsabeths berthnight & our day lost at our house } ....The northen las

— At Richmount on newyeares day
and our day lost at our house } ....beggers bush

— At Richmount the 7th of Janeuarye
and our day lost at our house } ....The spanish Cura[tt]

THE COCKPIT-IN-COURT

Later Cromwell himself occupied this section of the palace, and naturally saw to it that no dramatic exhibitions were held there. But at the Restoration "the Prince," now become the King, could have his plays again; and he did not wait long. On November 20, 1660, Edward Gower wrote to Sir Richard Leveson: "Yesternight the King, Queen, Princess, etc., supped at the Duke d'Albemarle's, where they had *The Silent Woman* acted in the Cockpit." [1] From this time on the theatre royal was in constant use for the entertainment of the Court.

Samuel Pepys, as he rose in the world, became a frequent visitor there.[2] In the absence of other descriptions of the building, I subjoin a few of the entries from his *Diary*. Under the date of October 2, 1662, he writes:

At night by coach towards Whitehall, took up Mr. Moore and set him at my Lord's, and myself, hearing that there was a play at the Cockpit (and my Lord Sandwich, who came to town last night, at it), I do go thither, and by very great fortune did follow four or five gentlemen who were carried to a little private door in a wall, and so crept through a narrow place and come into one of the boxes next the King's, but so as I could not see the King or Queen, but many of the fine ladies, who yet are really not so handsome

---

[1] Historical Manuscripts Commission, Fifth Report, p. 200. Pepys, under the date November 20, 1660, gives an anecdote about the King's behavior on this occasion.

[2] He first "got in" on April 20, 1661, "by the favour of one Mr. Bowman." John Evelyn also visited the Cockpit; see his *Diary*, January 16 and February 11, 1662.

generally as I used to take them to be, but that they are finely dressed. Here we saw *The Cardinal*,[1] a tragedy I had never seen before, nor is there any great matter in it. The company that came in with me into the box were all Frenchmen that could speak no English, but Lord! what sport they made to ask a pretty lady that they got among them that understood both French and English to make her tell them what the actors said.

The next time he went to the Cockpit, on November 17, 1662, he did not have to creep in by stealth. He writes:

At Whitehall by appointment, Mr. Crew carried my wife and I to the Cockpit, and we had excellent places, and saw the King, Queen, Duke of Monmouth, his son, and my Lady Castlemaine, and all the fine ladies; and *The Scornful Lady*, well performed. They had done by eleven o'clock.

The fine ladies, as usual, made a deep impression on him, as did the "greatness and gallantry" of the audience. On December 1, 1662, he writes:

This done we broke up, and I to the Cockpit, with much crowding and waiting, where I saw *The Valiant Cid*[2] acted, a play I have read with great delight, but is a most dull thing acted, which I never understood before, there being no pleasure in it, though done by Betterton and by Ianthe,[3] and another fine wench that is come in the room of Roxalana; nor did the King or Queen once smile all the whole play, nor any of the company seem to take any pleasure but what was in the greatness and gallantry of the company.

[1] By James Shirley, licensed 1641.
[2] By Corneille.   [3] Mrs. Betterton.

THE COCKPIT-IN-COURT

THE COCKPIT-IN-COURT

From an engraving by Mazell in Pennant's *London*. Mr. W. L. Spiers, who reproduces this engraving in the *London Topographical Record* (1903), says that it is "undated, but probably copied from a contemporary drawing of the seventeenth century."

Thence ... home, and got thither by 12 o'clock, knocked up my boy, and put myself to bed.

Two entries, from an entirely different source, must suffice for this history of the Cockpit. In the Paper-Office Chalmers discovered a record of the following payments, made in 1667:

To the Keeper of the theatre at Whitehall, £30. To the same for Keeping clean that place, *p. ann.* £6.[1]

[1] Chalmers, *Apology*, p. 530. Cunningham says, in his *Handbook of London*: "I find in the records of the Audit Office a payment of £30 per annum 'to the Keeper of our Playhouse called the Cockpit in St. James Park'"; but he does not state the year in which the payment was made.

And in the Lord Chamberlain's Accounts is preserved the following warrant:

1674, March 27. Warrant to deliver to Monsieur Grabu, or to such as he shall appoint, such of the scenes remaining in the theatre at Whitehall as shall be useful for the French Opera at the theatre in Bridges Street, and the said Monsieur to return them again safely after 14 days' time to the theatre at Whitehall.[1]

What became of the theatre at Whitehall I have not been able to ascertain.[2] Presumably, after the

---

[1] I quote from W. J. Lawrence, *The Elizabethan Playhouse* (First Series), p. 144.

[2] The reasons why the Cockpit at Whitehall has remained so long in obscurity (its history is here attempted for the first time) are obvious. Some scholars have confused it with the public playhouse of the same name, a confusion which persons in the days of Charles avoided by invariably saying "The Cockpit in Drury Lane." Other scholars have confused it with the residential section of Whitehall which bore the same name. During the reign of James several large buildings which had been erected either on the site of the old cockpit of Henry VIII, or around it, were converted into lodgings for members of the royal family or favorites of the King, and were commonly referred to as "the Cockpit." Other scholars have assumed that all plays during the reigns of Elizabeth, James, and Charles were given either in the Banqueting House or in the Great Hall. Finally, still other scholars (e.g., Sir Sidney Lee, in *Shakespeare's England*, 1916) have confused the Cockpit at Whitehall with the Royal Cockpit in St. James's Park. Exactly when the latter was built I have not been able to discover, but it was probably erected near the close of the seventeenth century. It stood at the end of Dartmouth Street, adjacent to Birdcage Walk, but not in the Park itself. John Strype, in his edition of Stow's *Survey* (1720), bk. VI, p. 64, says of Dartmouth Street: "And here is a very fine Cockpit, called the King's Cockpit, well resorted unto." A picture of the building is given by Strype on page 62, and a still better picture may be found in J. T. Smith's *The Antiquities of Westminster*.

THE COCKPIT-IN-COURT

fire of January, 1698, which destroyed the greater part of the palace and drove the royal family to seek quarters elsewhere, the building along with the rest of the Cockpit section was made over into the Privy Council offices.

The Royal Cockpit in Dartmouth Street survived until 1816, when it was torn down. Hogarth, in his famous representation of a cock-fight, shows its interior as circular, and as embellished with the royal coat of arms. Another interesting picture of the interior will be found in Ackermann's *The Microcosm of London* (1808). It is needless to add that this building had nothing whatever to do with the theatre royal of the days of King Charles.

CHAPTER XXI

MISCELLANEOUS

I

WOLF'S THEATRE IN NIGHTINGALE LANE, NEAR EAST SMITHFIELD

IN Jeaffreson's *Middlesex County Records* (1, 260), we find the following entry, dated April 1, 1600:

1 April, 42 Elizabeth. — Recognizance, taken before Sir John Peyton knt., Lieutenant of the Tower of London, and Thomas Fowler, Tobias Woode, Edward Vaghan and Henry Thoresby esqs., Justices of the Peace, of John Wolf, of Eastsmithfield, co. Midd., stationer, in the sum of forty pounds; The condition of the recognizance being "that, whereas the above-bounden John Wolf hath begun to erect and build a playhouse in Nightingale Lane near East Smithfield aforesaid, contrary to Her Majesty's proclamation and orders set down in Her Highness's Court of Starchamber. If therefore the said John Wolf do not proceed any further in building or erecting of the same playhouse, unless he shall procure sufficient warrant from the Rt. Honourable the Lords of Her Majesty's most honourable Privy Council for further . . . then this recognizance to be void, or else to remain in full force."

The only stationer in London named John Wolf was the printer and publisher who at this time had his shop in Pope's Head Alley, Lombard Street. For several reasons he is well known to bibliographers; and his strong personality and tireless energy might easily have led him into the field of the theatre. For many years he was a member of the Fishmongers' Company, to which also, in all probability, his father had belonged. After a ten years' apprenticeship with the eminent printer, John Day, he spent several years abroad "gadding from country to country," but learning the printing trade from the best establishments on the Continent. His longest stay was in Italy, where he was connected with the printing-office of the Giunti, and also, it seems, of Gabriel Giolito. In 1576 he printed two *Rappresentazioni*, "ad instanzia di Giovanni Vuolfio, Inglese." About the year 1579 he established himself in London (where he was dubbed by his fellows "Machiavel"), and began an energetic warfare on the monopolies secured by certain favored printers. The fact that he was for a time "committed to the Clink" failed to deter him. We are told that he "affirmed openly in the Stationers' Hall that it was lawful for all men to print all lawful books, what commandment soever Her Majesty gave to the contrary." And being "admonished that he, being but one, so mean a man, should not presume to contrary Her Highness' government: 'Tush,' said he, 'Luther was but one man, and reformed all the world for religion, and I am *that one man* that must and will reform the government in this trade.'" The courage and energy here revealed characterized his entire life. In 1583 he was admitted a freeman of the Company of Stationers. In 1593 he was elected Printer to the City. In the spring of 1600 he was in serious difficulties with the authorities over the printing of John Hayward's *Life and Raigne of King Henrie IV*, and was forced to spend two weeks in jail. He died in 1601.[1]

If this "John Wolf, stationer," be the man who started to erect a playhouse in East Smithfield, it is to be regretted that we do not know more about the causes which led him into the undertaking.

II

The Projected "Amphitheatre"

In 1620 John Cotton, John Williams, and Thomas Dixon[2] secured from King James a license to build

---

[1] For the life of John Wolf see the following: Edward Arber, *A Transcript of the Stationers' Registers*, especially II, 779–93; *The Calendar of State Papers, Domestic, 1598–1601*, pp. 405, 449, 450; A. Gerber, *All of the Five Fictitious Italian Editions*, etc. (in *Modern Language Notes*, XXII (1907), 2, 129, 201); H. R. Plomer, *An Examination of Some Existing Copies of Hayward's "Life and Raigne of King Henrie IV"* (in *The Library*, N.S., III (1902), 13); R. B. McKerrow, *A Dictionary of Printers and Booksellers . . . 1557–1640;* S. Bongi, *Annali di Gabriel Giolito de' Ferrari*.

[2] Of these men nothing is known; something, however, may be inferred from the following entries in Sir Henry Herbert's Office-Book: "On the 20th August, 1623, a license *gratis*, to John Williams and four others, to make *show* of *an Elephant*, for a year; on the 5th of September to make show of a *live Beaver;* on the 9th of June, 1638, to make show of an outlandish creature, called a *Possum*." (George Chalmers, *Supplemental Apology*, p. 208.)

THE PROJECTED AMPHITHEATRE 413

an amphitheatre [1] "intended principally for martiall exercises, and extraordinary shows and solemnities for ambassadors, and persons of honor and quality," with the power granted to the owners to order "a cessation from other shows and sports, for one day in a month only, upon fourteen days' warning."

But for some reason the King suddenly changed his mind, and on September 29, 1620, he addressed a letter to the Privy Council directing them to cancel the license: [2]

Right trusty and right well-beloved Cousins and Councellors, and right trusty and well-beloved Councellors, we greet you well. Whereas at the humble suit of our servants John Cotton, John Williams, and Thomas Dixon, and in recompence of their services, we have been pleased to license them to build an Amphitheatre, which hath passed our Signet and is stayed at our Privy Seal; and finding therein contained some such words and clauses, as may, in some constructions, seem to give them greater liberty both in point of building and using of exercises than is any way to be permitted, or was ever by us intended, we have thought fit to command and give authority unto you, or any four of you, to cause that already passed to be cancelled, and to give order unto our Solicitor General for the drawing up of a new warrant for our signature to the same parties, according to

---

[1] The place is not indicated, but it was probably outside the city.
[2] See *State Papers, Domestic, 1619–1623*, p. 181. I have quoted the letter from Collier, *The History of English Dramatic Poetry* (1879), I, 408.

such directions and reservations as herewith we send you. Wherein we are more particular, both in the affirmative and the negative, to the end that, as on one side we would have nothing pass us to remain upon record which either for the form might not become us or for the substance might cross our many proclamations (pursued with good success) for buildings, or, on the other side, might give them cause to importune us after they had been at charges; to which end we wish that you call them before you and let them know our pleasure and resolution therein.

Accordingly the license was canceled, and no new license was issued.

In 1626, however, John Williams and Thomas Dixon (what had become of John Cotton we do not know) made an attempt to secure a license from King Charles, then newly come to the throne, to erect an amphitheatre in Lincoln's Inn Fields. Apparently they so worded the proposed grant as to authorize them to present in their amphitheatre not only spectacles, but dramatic performances and animal-baitings as well, with the power to restrain all other places of amusement for one day in each week, on giving two days' warning.

A "bill" to this effect was drawn up and submitted to Thomas Coventry, the Lord Keeper, who examined it hastily, and dispatched it to Lord Conway with the following letter:[1]

My very good Lord, — I have perused this Bill, and do call to mind that about three or four years past

---

[1] Collier, *op. cit.*, 1, 443.

THE PROJECTED AMPHITHEATRE

when I was Attorney General, a patent for an Amphitheatre was in hand to have passed; but upon this sudden, without search of my papers, I cannot give your lordship any account of the true cause wherefore it did not pass, nor whether that and this do vary in substance: neither am I apt upon a sudden to take impertinent exceptions to anything that is to pass, much less to a thing that is recommended by so good a friend. But if upon perusal of my papers which I had while I was Attorney, or upon more serious thoughts, I shall observe anything worthy to be represented to His Majesty, or to the Council, I shall then acquaint your lordship; and in the meantime I would be loath to be the author of a motion to His Majesty to stay it: but if you find His Majesty at fitting leisure, to move him that he will give leave to think of it in this sort as I have written, it may do well; and I assure your lordship, unless I find matter of more consequence than I observe on this sudden, it is not like to be stayed. And so I rest your lordship's very assured to do you service,

THO. COVENTRYE, CH.

CANBURY, 12 *August*, 1626.

Apparently some very influential person was urging the passage of the bill. But the scheme soon evoked the bitter opposition of the various troupes of players, and of the owners of the various theatres and other places of amusement. An echo of the quarrel is found in Marmion's *Holland's Leaguer*, II, iii:

> Twill dead all my device in making matches,
> My plots of architecture, and erecting
> New amphitheatres to draw custom

From playhouses once a week, and so pull
A curse upon my head from the poor scoundrels.[1]

The "poor scoundrels" — i.e., the players — seem to have caused the authorities to examine the bill more closely; and on September 28, 1626, the Lord Keeper sent to Lord Conway a second letter in which he condemned the measure in strong terms:[2]

My Lord, — According to His Majesty's good pleasure, which I received from your lordship, I have considered of the grant desired by John Williams and Thomas Dixon for building an Amphitheatre in Lincoln's Inn Fields; and comparing it with that which was propounded in King James his time, do find much difference between them: for that former was intended principally for martiall exercises, and extraordinary shows, and solemnities for ambassadors and persons of honor and quality, with a cessation from other shows and sports for one day in a month only, upon 14 days' warning: whereas by this new grant I see little probability of anything to be used but common plays, or ordinary sports now used or showed at the Bear Garden or the common playhouses about London, for all sorts of beholders, with a restraint to all other plays and shows for one day in the week upon two days' warning: with liberty to erect their buildings in Lincoln's Inn Fields, where there are too

---

[1] *The Dramatic Works of Shackerley Marmion,* in *Dramatists of the Restoration,* p. 37. Fleay (*A Biographical Chronicle of the English Drama,* II, 66) suggests that the impostors Agurtes and Autolichus are meant to satirize Williams and Dixon respectively.

[2] I quote the letter from Collier, *The History of English Dramatic Poetry* (1879), I, 444.

many buildings already; and which place in the late King's time upon a petition exhibited by the Prince's comedians for setting up a playhouse there, was certified by eleven Justices of Peace under their hands to be very inconvenient. And therefore, not holding this new grant fit to pass, as being no other in effect but to translate the playhouses and Bear Garden from the Bankside to a place much more unfit, I thought fit to give your lordship these reasons for it; wherewithal you may please to acquaint His Majesty, if there shall be cause. And so remain your lordship's very assured friend to do you service,

THO. COVENTRYE.

CANBURY, 28 *Sept.*, 1626.
Lo. CONWAY.

On the letter Lord Conway has written the indorsement: "That it is unfit the grant for the Amphitheatre should passe." And such, no doubt, was the ultimate decision of the Privy Council, for we hear nothing more of the project.

III

OGILBY'S DUBLIN THEATRE

In 1635 a playhouse was opened in Dublin by John Ogilby, — dancing-master, theatrical manager, playwright, scholar, translator, poet, — now best known, perhaps, for the ridicule he inspired in Dryden's *MacFlecknoe* and Pope's *Dunciad*. At the beginning of his versatile career he was a successful London dancing-master, popular with "the nobility and gentry." When Thomas Earl of Strafford was appointed Lord Lieutenant of Ireland, he took Ogilby with him to Dublin, to teach his wife and children the art of dancing, and also to help with the secretarial duties. Under Strafford's patronage, Ogilby was appointed to the post of Master of the Revels for Ireland; and in this capacity he built a small playhouse in Dublin and began to cultivate dramatic representations after the manner of London. Anthony à Wood in *Athenæ Oxonienses,* says:

> He built a little theatre to act plays in, in St. Warburg's street in Dublin, and was then and there valued by all ingenious men for his great industry in promoting morality and ingenuity.[1]

Aubrey writes:

> He had a warrant from the Lord Lieutenant to be Master of the Ceremonies for that kingdom; and built a pretty[2] little theatre in St. Warburgh Street in Dublin.

The history of this "little theatre" is not known in detail. For its actors Ogilby himself wrote at least one play, entitled *The Merchant of Dublin,*[3] and Henry Burnell a tragi-comedy entitled *Landgartha,* printed in 1641 "as it was presented in the

---

[1] Bliss's edition, III, 741.

[2] "Pretty little theatre" is the reading of *MS. Aubr. 7,* folio 20; *MS. Aubr. 8* omits the adjective "pretty." For Aubrey's full account of Ogilby see Andrew Clark's *Brief Lives* (1898), 2 vols.

[3] Aubrey mentions this as having been "written in Dublin, and never printed."

new theatre in Dublin with good applause." But its chief playwright was James Shirley, who came to Dublin in 1636 under the patronage of the Earl of Kildare. For the Irish stage he wrote *The Royal Master*, published in 1638 as "acted in the new theatre in Dublin"; *Rosania, or Love's Victory*, now known as *The Doubtful Heir*, under which title it was later printed; *St. Patrick for Ireland;*[1] and in all probability *The Constant Maid*.[2] The actors, however, had little need to buy original plays, for they were free, no doubt, to take any of the numerous London successes. From Shirley's *Poems* we learn that they were presenting Jonson's *Alchemist*, Middleton's *No Wit*, two of Fletcher's plays, unnamed, and two anonymous plays entitled *The Toy* and *The General;* and we may fairly assume that they honored several of Shirley's early plays in the same way.

The theatre came to a sudden end with the outbreak of the rebellion in 1641. In October the Lords Justices prohibited playing there; and shortly after, we are told, the building was "ruined and spoiled, and a cow-house made of the stage."[3]

[1] Published in 1640 as "the first part," and both the Prologue and the Epilogue speak of a second part; but no second part was printed, and in all probability it never was written.

[2] Never licensed for England; reprinted in 1657 with *St. Patrick for Ireland*.

[3] MS. *Aubr. 7*, folio 20 v. Ogilby's second theatre in Dublin, built after the Restoration, does not fall within the scope of the present work.

IV

The French Players' Temporary Theatre in Drury Lane

In February, 1635, a company of French players, under the leadership of the eminent actor, Josias de Soulas, better known by his stage-name of Floridor,[1] appeared in London, and won such favor at Court that they were ultimately allowed to fit up a house in Drury Lane for a temporary theatre. The history of these players is mainly found in the records of the Master of the Revels and of the Lord Chamberlain. From the former, Malone has preserved the following entries by Herbert:

> On Tuesday night the 17 of February, 1634 [i.e., 1635], a French company of players, being approved of by the Queen at her house two nights before, and commended by Her Majesty to the King, were admitted to the Cockpitt in Whitehall, and there presented the King and Queen with a French comedy called *Melise*,[2] with good approbation: for which play the King gave them ten pounds.
>
> This day being Friday, and the 20 of the same month, the King told me his pleasure, and commanded me to give order that this French company

---

[1] See Frederick Hawkins, *Annals of the French Stage* (1884), I, 148 ff., for the career of this player on the French stage. "Every gift required by the actor," says Hawkins, "was possessed by Floridor."

[2] *La Melise, ou Les Princes Reconnus*, by Du Rocher, first acted in Paris in 1633; see *The Athenæum*, July 11, 1891, p. 73; and cf. ibid., p. 139.

FRENCH PLAYERS' THEATRE

should play the two sermon days in the week during their time of playing in Lent [i.e., Wednesdays and Fridays, on which days during Lent the English companies were not allowed to play], and in the house of Drury Lane [i.e., the Cockpit Playhouse], where the Queen's Players usually play. The King's pleasure I signified to Mr. Beeston [the manager of the Cockpit] the same day, who obeyed readily. The housekeepers are to give them by promise the benefit of their interest [1] for the two days of the first week. They had the benefit of playing on the sermon days, and got two hundred pounds at least; besides many rich clothes were given them. They had freely to themselves the whole week before the week before Easter,[2] which I obtained of the King for them.

The use of the Cockpit in Drury Lane came to an end at Easter, for the Queen's own troupe, under Beeston's management, regularly occupied that building. But the King summoned the French players to act at Court on several occasions. Thus Herbert records:

The 4 April, on Easter Monday,[3] they played the *Trompeur Puny* [4] with better approbation than the other.

---

[1] "Housekeepers" were owners, who always demanded of the players as rental for the building a certain part of each day's takings. The passage quoted means that the housekeepers allowed the French players to receive *all* money taken on the two sermon days of the *first* week, and after that exacted their usual share as rental for the building.

[2] That is, Passion Week, during which time the English companies were never allowed to give performances.

[3] This must be an error, for Easter Monday fell on March 30.

[4] *Le Trompeur Puni, ou Histoire Septentrionale*, by Scuderi.

On Wednesday night, the 16 April,[1] 1635, the French played *Alcimedor* [2] with good approbation.[3]

Clearly these actors were in high favor at Court. Sir Henry, who did not as a rule show any hesitancy in accepting fees, notes in the margin of his book: "The French offered me a present of £10; but I refused it, and did them many other courtesies gratis to render the Queen my mistress an acceptable service." In view of this royal favor, it is not surprising to find that, after they were driven from the Cockpit, they received permission to fit up a temporary playhouse in the manage, or riding-school, of one M. Le Febure, in Drury Lane. The Lord Chamberlain's Office-Book contains the following entry on the subject:

18 April, 1635: His Majesty hath commanded me to signify his royal pleasure that the French comedians (having agreed with Mons. le Febure) may erect a stage, scaffolds, and seats, and all other accommodations which shall be convenient, and act and present interludes and stage plays at his house [and manage [4]] in Drury Lane, during His Majesty's pleasure, without any disturbance, hindrance, or interruption. And this shall be to them, and Mr. le Febure, and to all others, a sufficient discharge, &c.[5]

---

[1] Wednesday was the 15th. [2] *Alcimedon*, by Duryer.
[3] Malone, *Variorum*, III, 121, note.
[4] This clause I insert from Mrs. Stopes's notes on the Lord Chamberlain's records, in the Shakespeare *Jahrbuch*, XLVI, 97.
[5] I have chosen to reproduce the record from Chalmers's *Apology*, p. 506, note *s*, rather than from Mrs. Stopes's apparently less accurate notes in the Shakespeare *Jahrbuch*, XLVI, 97.

FRENCH PLAYERS' THEATRE 423

Apparently the players lost little time in fitting up the building, for we read in Herbert's Office-Book:

A warrant granted to Josias D'Aunay,[1] Hurfries de Lau, and others, for to act plays at a new house in Drury Lane, during pleasure, the 5 May, 1635.

The King was pleased to command my Lord Chamberlain to direct his warrant to Monsieur Le Fevure, to give him a power to contract with the Frenchmen for to build a playhouse in the manage-house, which was done accordingly by my advice and allowance.[2]

In Glapthorne's *The Ladies' Priviledge* is a good-natured allusion to the French Company and their vivacious style of acting:[3]

> *La.* But, Adorni,
> What think you of the French?
> *Ador.* Very airy people, who participate
> More fire than earth; yet generally good,
> And nobly disposition'd, something inclining
> To over-weening fancy. This lady
> Tells my remembrance of a comic scene
> I once saw in their Theatre.
> *Bon.* Add it to
> Your former courtesies, and express it.

Whereupon, according to the stage direction, Adorni "acts furiously."

In the margin of his Office-Book Sir Henry Herbert writes complacently: "These Frenchmen were

---

[1] Should we place a comma after "Josias"? That "Josias Floridor" was the leader of the troupe we know from two separate entries; cf. Chalmers, *Apology*, pp. 508, 509.

[2] Malone, *Variorum*, III, 122, note.

[3] Act II, Scene i. This passage is pointed out by Lawrence, *The Elizabethan Playhouse*, p. 137.

commended unto me by the Queen, and have passed through my hands gratis." This was indeed a rare favor from Herbert; but they did not so easily escape his deputy, William Blagrove, who accepted from them the sum of "three pounds for his pains."

How long the French actors occupied their temporary playhouse in Drury Lane is not clear. In the Lord Chamberlain's book we find an entry showing that they presented a play at Court in December, 1635: "Warrant to pay £10 to Josias Floridor for himself and the rest of the French players for a tragedy by them played before His Majesty Dec. last."[1] The entry is dated January 8, 1636, and, so far as I can discover, this is the last reference to the French players in London. We may suppose that shortly after this they returned to Paris.

V

Davenant's Projected Theatre in Fleet Street

On March 26, 1639, William Davenant, who had succeeded Ben Jonson as Poet Laureate, secured from King Charles a royal patent under the Great Seal of England to erect a playhouse in Fleet Street, to be used not only for regular plays, but also for "musical entertainments" and "scenic representations." Davenant, as we know, was especially inter-

[1] Stopes, *op. cit.*, p. 98, Chalmers, *Apology*, p. 509.

A PROJECTED THEATRE

ested in "the art of perspective in scenes," and also in the Italian *opera musicale*. The royal patent — unusually verbose even for a patent — is printed in full in Rymer's *Fœdera*, xx, 377; I cite below all the essential passages:

[*The Building.*] Know ye, that we, of our especial grace, certain knowledge, and meere motion, and upon the humble petition of our servant William Davenant, gentleman, have given and granted, and by these presents, for us, our heirs, and successors, do give and grant unto the said William Davenant, his heirs, executors, administrators, and assigns, full power, license, and authority ... to frame, new-build, and set up ... a Theatre or Playhouse, with necessary tiring and retiring rooms, and other places convenient, containing in the whole forty yards square at the most,[1] wherein plays, musical entertainments, scenes, or other like presentments may be presented ... so as the outwalls of the said Theatre or Playhouse, tiring or retiring rooms, be made or built of brick or stone, according to the tenor of our proclamations in that behalf.

[*Its Location.*] Upon a parcel of ground lying near unto or behind the Three Kings Ordinary in Fleet Street, in the parishes of Saint Dunstan's in the West, London, or in Saint Bride's, London, or in either of them; or in any other ground in or about that place, or in the whole street aforesaid, already allotted to him for that use, or in any other place that is or hereafter shall be assigned or allotted out to the said

---

[1] The Fortune was only eighty feet square, but the stage projected to the middle of the yard. Davenant probably wished to provide for an alcove stage of sufficient depth to accommodate his "scenes."

William Davenant by our right trusty and right well-beloved cousin and counsellor Thomas, Earl of Arundel and Surrey, Earl Marshall of England, or any other of our commissioners for building for that time being in that behalf.

[*Its Uses.*] And we do hereby, for us, our heirs, and successors, grant to the said William Davenant, his heirs, executors, administrators, and assigns, that it shall and may be lawful to and for him, the said William Davenant, his heirs, executors, administrators, and assigns, from time to time to gather together, entertain, govern, privilege, and keep, such and so many players and persons, to exercise action, musical presentments, scenes, dancing, and the like, as he, the said William Davenant, his heirs, executors, administrators, and assigns shall think fit and approve for the said house; and such persons to permit and continue at and during the pleasure of the said William Davenant, his heirs, executors, administrators, and assigns, from time to time to act plays in such house so to be by him or them erected; and exercise music, musical presentments, scenes, dancing, or other the like, at the same, or other, hours, or times, or after plays are ended,[1] peaceably and quietly, without the impeachment or impediment of any person or persons whatsoever, for the honest recreation of such as shall desire to see the same. And that it shall and may be lawful to and for the said William Davenant, his heirs, executors, administrators, and assigns, to take and receive of such our subjects as shall resort to see or hear any such plays, scenes, and entertainments whatsoever, such sum or sums of

---

[1] That is, he may give his "musical presentments," etc., either at the hours when he was accustomed to give plays, or after his plays are ended. This does not necessarily imply evening entertainments.

A PROJECTED THEATRE 427

money as is, are, or hereafter from time to time shall be accustomed to be given or taken in other playhouses and places for the like plays, scenes, presentments, and entertainments.

The novelty of the scheme and the great size of the proposed building must have alarmed the owners of playhouses. That the established theatrical proprietors were hostile is clearly indicated by the attitude of Richard Heton, one of the Sewers of the Chamber to Queen Henrietta, and at the time manager of the Salisbury Court Playhouse. In September, 1639, he wrote out a document entitled "Instructions for my Patent," in which he advanced reasons why he should receive the sole power to elect the members of the Queen's Company of Players. He observes that under the existing arrangement the company was free to leave the Salisbury Court Playhouse at their pleasure, "as in one year and a half of their being here they have many times threatened"; and he concludes by adding: "and one now of the chief fellows [i.e., sharers of the company], an agent for one [William Davenant] that hath got a grant from the King for the building of a new playhouse which was intended to be in Fleet Street, which no man can judge that a fellow of our Company, and a wellwisher to those that own the house, would ever be an actor in." [1] Doubtless the owners of other houses

[1] Cunningham, *The Whitefriars Theatre*, in *The Shakespeare Society's Papers*, IV, 96.

had the same sentiments, and exercised what influence they possessed against the scheme. But the most serious opposition in all probability came from the citizens and merchants living in the neighborhood. We know how bitterly they complained about the coaches that brought playgoers to the small Blackfriars Theatre, and how strenuously from year to year they sought the expulsion of the King's Men from the precinct.[1] They certainly would not have regarded with complacency the erection in their midst of a still larger theatre.

Whatever the opposition, it was so powerful that on October 2 Davenant was compelled to make an indenture by which he virtually renounced[2] for himself and his heirs for ever the right to build a theatre in Fleet Street, or in any other place "in or near the cities, or suburbs of the cities, of London or Westminster," without further and special permission granted. This document, first printed by Chalmers in his *Supplemental Apology*, is as follows:

This indenture made the second day of October, in the fifteenth year of the reign of our Sovereign Lord Charles, by the grace of God, of England, Scotland, France, and Ireland King, Defender of the Faith, &c. *Anno Domini* 1639. Between the said King's most excellent Majesty of the first part, and William Davenant of London, Gent., of the other

---

[1] See the chapter on the Second Blackfriars.

[2] That he did not actually surrender the patent is shown by the fact that he claimed privileges by virtue of it after the Restoration; see Halliwell-Phillipps, *A Collection of Ancient Documents*, p. 48.

part. Whereas the said King's most excellent Majesty, by His Highness's letters patents under the Great Seal of England bearing date the six and twentieth day of March last past before the date of these presents, did give and grant unto the said William Davenant, his heirs, executors, administrators, and assigns full power, license, and authority that he, they, and every of them, by him and themselves and by all and every such person or persons as he or they shall depute or appoint, and his and their laborers, servants, and workmen, shall and may lawfully, quietly, and peaceably frame, erect, new build, and set up upon a parcel of ground lying near unto or behind the Three Kings Ordinary in Fleet Street in the Parish of St. Dunstan's in the West, London, or in St. Bride's London, or in either of them, or in any other ground in or about that place, or in the whole street aforesaid, already allotted to him for that use, or in any other place that is or hereafter shall be assigned and allotted out to the said William Davenant by the Right Honorable Thomas, Earl of Arundel and Surrey, Earl Marshall of England, or any other His Majesty's Commissioners for Building, for the time being in that behalf, a theatre or playhouse with necessary tiring and retiring rooms and other places convenient, containing in the whole forty yards square at the most, wherein plays, musical entertainments, scenes, or other the like presentments may be presented by and under certain provisors or conditions in the same contained, as in and by the said letters patents, whereunto relation being had more fully and at large, it doth and may appear.

Now this indenture witnesseth, and the said William Davenant doth by these presents declare, His Majesty's intent, meaning at and upon the granting of the said license was and is that he, the said William

Davenant, his heirs, executors, administrators nor assigns should not frame, build, or set up the said theatre or playhouse in any place inconvenient, and that the said parcel of ground lying near unto or behind the Three Kings Ordinary in Fleet Street in the said Parish of St. Dunstan's in the West, London, or in St. Bride's, London, or in either of them, or in any other ground in or about that place, or in the whole street aforesaid, and is sithence found inconvenient and unfit for that purpose, therefore the said William Davenant doth for himself his heirs, executors, administrators, and assigns, and every of them, covenant, promise, and agree to and with our said Sovereign Lord the King, his heirs and successors, that he, the said William Davenant, his heirs, executors, administrators, nor assigns shall not, nor will not, by virtue of the said license and authority to him granted as aforesaid, frame, erect, new build, or set up upon the said parcel of ground in Fleet Street aforesaid, or in any other part of Fleet Street, a theatre or playhouse, nor will not frame, erect, new build, or set up upon any other parcel of ground lying in or near the cities, or suburbs of the cities, of London or Westminster any theatre or playhouse, unless the said place shall be first approved and allowed by warrant under His Majesty's sign manual, or by writing under the hand and seal of the said Right Honorable Thomas, Earl of Arundel and Surrey. In witness whereof to the one part of this indenture the said William Davenant hath set his hand and seal the day and year first above written.

       WILLIAM DAVENANT. L.S.
Signed sealed and delivered
 in the presence of
  Edw. Penruddoks.
  Michael Baker.

Possibly as a recompense for this surrender of his rights, Davenant was made Governor of the King's and Queen's Servants at the Cockpit in June of the following year; and from this time until the suppression of acting in 1642, he expended his energies in managing the affairs of this important playhouse.

BIBLIOGRAPHY

[IN the following list are included the books and articles constituting the main authorities upon which the present study is based. The list is not intended to be an exhaustive bibliography, though from the nature of the case it is fairly complete. For the guidance of scholars the more important titles are marked with asterisks. It will be seen that not all the works are included which are cited in the text, or referred to in footnotes; the list, in fact, is strictly confined to works bearing upon the history of the pre-Restoration playhouses. Considerations of space have led to the omission of a large number of books dealing with the topography of London, and of the counties of Middlesex and Surrey, although a knowledge of these is essential to any thorough study of the playhouses. Furthermore, titles of contemporary plays, pamphlets, and treatises are excluded, except a few of unusual and general value. Finally, discussions of the structure of the early stage, of the manner of dramatic performances in the time of Shakespeare, and of the travels of English actors on the Continent are omitted, except when these contain also material important for the study of the theatres. At the close is appended a select list of early maps and views of London.]

Actors Remonstrance, or Complaint for the Silencing of their Profession. London, 1643. (Reprinted in W. C. Hazlitt's *The English Drama and Stage*, and in E. W. Ashbee's *Facsimile Reprints.*) [1

*ADAMS, J. Q. The Conventual Buildings of Blackfriars, London, and the Playhouses Constructed Therein. (The University of North Carolina *Studies in Philology*, XIV, 64.) [2

—— The Four Pictorial Representations of the Elizabethan Stage. (*The Journal of English and Germanic Philology*, x, 329.) [3

*ADAMS, J. Q. *The Dramatic Records of Sir Henry Herbert, Master of the Revels 1623–1673.* New Haven, 1917. [4

────── Lordinge (*alias* "Lodowick") Barry. (*Modern Philology*, IX, 567. See No. 189.) [5

ALBRECHT, H. A. *Das englische Kindertheater.* Halle, 1883. [6

ARCHER, T. *The Highway of Letters.* London, 1893. (Chap. xv, "Whitefriars and the Playhouses.") [7

ARCHER, W. The Fortune Theatre. (The London *Tribune*, October 12, 1907; reprinted in *New Shakespeariana*, October, 1908, and in the Shakespeare *Jahrbuch*, XLIV, 159. See also Nos. 8, 38, 61, 129.) [8

────── A Sixteenth Century Playhouse. (*The Universal Review*, June, 1888, p. 281. Deals with the De Witt drawing of the Swan.) [9

ARONSTEIN, P. Die Organisation des englischen Schauspiels im Zeitalter Shakespeares. (*Germanisch-Romanische Monatsschrift*, II, 165, 216.) [10

AUDI ALTERAM PARTEM. Cunningham's Extracts from the Revels' Books. (*The Athenæum*, 1911, II, 101, 130, 421; 1912, I, 469, 654; II, 143. See Nos. 80, 179, 180, 183.) [11

BAKER, G. P. The Children of Powles. (*The Harvard Monthly*, May, 1891.) [12

────── *The Development of Shakespeare as a Dramatist.* New York, 1907. [13

BAKER, H. B. *History of the London Stage and its Famous Players.* London and New York, 1904. (A new and rewritten edition of *The London Stage.* 2 vols. London, 1889.) [14

────── *Our Old Actors.* 2 vols. London, 1881. (There was an earlier edition, London, 1878, printed in New York, 1879, with the title, *English Actors from Shakespeare to Macready.*) [15

BAPST, C. G. *Essai sur l'Histoire du Théâtre.* Paris, 1893. [16

BIBLIOGRAPHY 435

BARRETT, C. R. B. *The History of the Society of Apothecaries of London.* London, 1905. [17

BEAR GARDEN AND HOPE. See Nos. 27, 72, 99, 119, 143, 144, 147, 152, 157, 198, 221, 222, 223, 228, 236, 238, 239, 240, 241, 274, 281, 303, 304, 316.

*BELL, H. Contributions to the History of the English Playhouse. (*The Architectural Record*, March and April, 1913.) [18

BELL, W. G. *Fleet Street in Seven Centuries.* London, 1912. (Chap. XIV, "The Whitefriars Playhouses.") [19

BESANT, SIR W. *Mediæval London. London in the Time of the Tudors. London in the Time of the Stuarts.* 4 vols. London, 1903–06. [20

BINZ, G. Deutsche Besucher im Shakespeare'schen London. (*Beilage zur Allgemeinen Zeitung.* München, August, 1902.) [21

——— Londoner Theater und Schauspiele im Jahre 1599. (*Anglia*, XXII, 456.) [22

*BIRCH, T. AND R. F. WILLIAMS. *The Court and Times of James the First.* 2 vols. London, 1849. [23

BLACKFRIARS, FIRST AND SECOND. See Nos. 2, 6, 17, 20, 26, 34, 41, 42, 43, 59, 61, 72, 90, 97, 100, 101, 105, 106, 108, 119, 136, 137, 146, 150, 163, 178, 179, 191, 196, 201, 214, 218, 223, 244, 248, 287, 288, 289, 293, 296, 297, 298.

BLANCH, W. H. *Dulwich College and Edward Alleyn.* London, 1877. [24

BOLINGBROKE, L. G. Pre-Elizabethan Plays and Players in Norfolk. (*Norfolk Archæology*, XI, 336.) [25

BOND, R. W. *The Complete Works of John Lyly.* 3 vols. Oxford, 1902. [26

BOULTON, W. B. *The Amusements of Old London.* 2 vols. London, 1901. [27

*BRAINES, W. W. *Holywell Priory and the Site of the Theatre, Shoreditch.* London, 1915. (Part XLIII of *Indications of Houses of Historical Interest in London*, issued by the London County Council.) [28

BRAND, J. See No. 157.

BRANDES, G. *William Shakespeare.* Translated by William Archer. 2 vols. London, 1898. [29

BRAYLEY, E. W. *Historical and Descriptive Accounts of the Theatres of London.* London, 1826. (Brief notice of the Cockpit in Drury Lane; relates chiefly to Restoration theatres.) [30

BRERETON, J. LE G. De Witt at the Swan. (*A Book of Homage to Shakespeare.* Oxford, 1916, p. 204.) [31

BRUCE, J. Who was "Will, my lord of Leycester's jesting player"? (*The Shakespeare Society's Papers*, I, 88.) [32

BULLEN, G. The Cockpit or Phœnix Theatre in 1660. (*The Athenæum*, May 21, 1881, p. 699.) [33

*BÜLOW, G. VON AND W. POWELL. *Diary of the Journey of Philip Julius, Duke of Stettin-Pomerania, through England in the year 1602.* (*Transactions of the Royal Historical Society*, New Series, VI. See No. 146.) [34

Calendar of State Papers, Domestic Series, 1547–1660. London, 1856–. (See also No. 192.) [35

Calendar of the Patent Rolls. London, 1891–1908. [36

CALMOUR, A. C. *Fact and Fiction about Shakespeare, with Some Account of the Playhouses, Players, and Playwrights of His Period.* Stratford-on-Avon, 1894. [37

A Catalogue of Models and of Stage-Sets in the Dramatic Museum of Columbia University. New York, 1916. (See also Nos. 129, 211.) [38

*CHALMERS, GEORGE. *An Apology for the Believers in the Shakspeare-Papers.* London, 1797. [39

*———— *A Supplemental Apology.* London, 1799. [40

*CHAMBERS, E. K. Commissions for the Chapel. (The Malone Society's *Collections*, I, 357.) [41

*———— Court Performances Before Queen Elizabeth. (*The Modern Language Review*, II, 1.) [42

*———— Court Performances Under James the First. (*Ibid.*, IV, 153.) [43

*———— Dramatic Records from the Lansdowne Manuscripts. (The Malone Society's *Collections*, I, 143.) [44

———— The Elizabethan Lords Chamberlain. (*Ibid.*, I, 31.) [45

CHAMBERS, E. K. [Review of] *Henslowe's Diary*, Edited by Walter W. Greg. (*The Modern Language Review*, IV, 407, 511.) [46
*——— A Jotting by John Aubrey. (The Malone Society's *Collections*, I, 341. Concerns Beeston and the Cockpit in Drury Lane.) [47
——— *The Mediæval Stage.* Oxford, 1903. [48
——— Nathaniel Field and Joseph Taylor. (*The Modern Language Review*, IV, 395.) [49
——— *Notes on the History of the Revels Office under the Tudors.* London, 1906. [50
——— The Stage of the Globe. (*The Works of William Shakespeare.* Stratford-Town Edition. Stratford-on-Avon, 1904–07, X, 351.) [51
——— Two Early Player-Lists. (The Malone Society's *Collections*, I, 348.) [52
——— William Kempe. (*The Modern Language Review*, IV, 88.) [53
*CHAMBERS, E. K. AND W. W. GREG. Dramatic Records from the Privy Council Register, 1603–1642. (The Malone Society's *Collections*, I, 370. For the records prior to 1603 see No. 87. Cf. also No. 260.) [54
*——— Dramatic Records of the City of London. The Remembrancia. (The Malone Society's *Collections*, I, 43. See also No. 224.) [55
*——— Royal Patents for Players. (The Malone Society's *Collections*, I, 260.) [56
CHARLANNE, L. *L'Influence Française en Angleterre au xviie Siecle, Le Théâtre et la Critique.* Paris, 1906. [57
*CHILD, H. The Elizabethan Theatre. (*The Cambridge History of English Literature*, vol. VI, chap. X.) [58
CLAPHAM, A. W. On the Topography of the Dominican Priory of London. (*Archæologia*, LXIII, 57. See also Nos. 2, 61.) [59
*——— The Topography of the Carmelite Priory of London. (*The Journal of the British Archæological Association*, New Series, XVI, 15. See also No. 61.) [60
CLAPHAM, A. W. AND W. H. GODFREY. *Some Famous*

BIBLIOGRAPHY

Buildings and their Story. Westminster, [1913]. (Contains Godfrey's study of the Fortune contract, and, in abbreviated form, the two articles by Clapham noted above, Nos. 59, 60. See also Nos. 8, 38, 116, 129.) [61

CLARK, A. Players or Companies on Tour 1548–1630. (*Notes and Queries*, X Series, XII, 41.) [62

COCKPIT-IN-COURT. See Nos. 18, 80, 81, 82, 83, 89, 99, 180, 181, 182, 183, 184, 197, 228, 250, 253, 305, 313.

COCKPIT-IN-DRURY LANE. See Nos. 4, 30, 33, 47, 72, 88, 91, 99, 119, 138, 139, 142, 147, 159, 197, 223, 227, 228, 303.

*COLLIER, J. P. *The Alleyn Papers.* London. Printed for The Shakespeare Society. 1843. (See No. 161.) [63

—— *The Diary of Philip Henslowe.* London. Printed for The Shakespeare Society, 1845. (See No. 143.) [64

*—— *The History of English Dramatic Poetry.* 3 vols. 1831. Second edition, London, 1879. [65

—— *Lives of the Original Actors.* (See No. 68.) [66

*—— *Memoirs of Edward Alleyn.* London. Printed for The Shakespeare Society, 1841. (See No. 316.) [67

—— *Memoirs of the Principal Actors in the Plays of Shakespeare.* London. Printed for The Shakespeare Society. 1846. (Reprinted with some corrections in No. 65.) [68

—— On Players and Dramatic Performances in the Reign of Edward IV. (*The Shakespeare Society's Papers*, II, 87.) [69

*—— Original History of "The Theatre" in Shoreditch, and Connexion of the Burbadge Family with it. (*Ibid.*, IV, 63.) [70

—— Richard Field, Nathaniel Field, Anthony Munday, and Henry Chettle. (*Ibid.*, IV, 36.) [71

*—— *The Works of Shakespeare*, London, 1844. (Vol. I, p. ccxli, reprints a record of the end of certain early playhouses from "some manuscript notes to a copy of Stowe's *Annales*, by Howes, folio, 1631, in the possession of Mr. Pickering." See No. 119.) [72

CONRAD, H. Robert Greene als Dramatiker. (The Shakespeare *Jahrbuch*, XXIX–XXX, 210.) [73

CORBIN, J. Shakspere his own Stage-Manager. (*The Century Magazine*, LXXXIII, 260.) [74

CREIGHTON, C. *A History of Epidemics in Britain*. 2 vols. Cambridge, 1891–94. [75

CREIZENACH, W. *Geschichte des neueren Dramas*. Vol. IV, Part I, Book viii. Halle, 1909. (English translation by Cécile Hugon, London, 1916.) [76

―――― Die Schauspiele der englischen Komödianten. (*Deutsche National-Litteratur*, XXIII.) [77

CULLEN, C. Puritanism and the Stage. (*Proceedings of the Royal Philosophical Society of Glasgow*, XLIII, 153.) [78

CUNNINGHAM, P. Did General Harrison Kill "Dick Robinson" the Player? (*The Shakespeare Society's Papers*, II, II.) [79

*―――― *Extracts from the Accounts of the Revels at the Court in the Reigns of Queen Elizabeth and King James I.* London. Printed for The Shakespeare Society, 1842. (See Nos. 11, 180, 181, 184.) [80

―――― *A Handbook of London*. 2 vols. London, 1849. (A new edition, "corrected and enlarged," London, 1850. See also No. 305.) [81

―――― *Inigo Jones. A Life of the Architect*. London. Printed for The Shakespeare Society. 1848. [82

―――― Inigo Jones, and his Office under the Crown. (*The Shakespeare Society's Papers*, I, 103.) [83

―――― Plays at Court, Anno 1613. (*Ibid.*, II, 123.) [84

―――― Sir George Buc and the Office of the Revels. (*Ibid.*, IV, 143.) [85

*―――― The Whitefriars Theatre, the Salisbury Court Theatre, and the Duke's Theatre in Dorset Gardens. (*Ibid.*, IV, 89.) [86

CURTAIN. See Nos. 96, 150, 151, 222, 223, 284.

*DASENT, J. R. *Acts of the Privy Council of England*. New Series. London, 1890–. (This contains the Acts to the end of Elizabeth's reign; for those Acts relating to the drama from 1603 to 1642, see No. 54. Cf. No. 260.) [87

Description of the Great Machines of the Descent of Or-

pheus into Hell. Presented by the French Comedians at the Cockpit in Drury Lane. London, 1661. [88

Diaries and Despatches of the Venetian Embassy at the Court of King James I., in the Years 1617, 1618. Translated by Rawdon Brown. (*The Quarterly Review,* CII, 398.) [89

Diary, of the Duke of Stettin-Pomerania. (See Nos. 34, 146.)

DOBELL, B. Newly Discovered Documents. (*The Athenæum,* March 30, 1901, p. 403. Of value for Blackfriars.) [90

*DOWNES, J. *Roscius Anglicanus.* London, 1708. [91

DRAMATICUS. On the Profits of Old Actors. (*The Shakespeare Society's Papers,* I, 21.) [92

——— The Players Who Acted in *The Shoemaker's Holiday,* 1600. (*Ibid.,* IV, 110.) [93

DURAND, W. Y. Notes on Richard Edwards. (*The Journal of Germanic Philology,* IV, 348.) [94

——— *Palæmon and Arcyte, Progne, Marcus Geminus,* and the Theatre in Which They Were Acted, 1566. (*Publications of the Modern Language Association of America,* XX, 502.) [95

ELLIS, H. *The History and Antiquities of the Parish of Saint Leonard, Shoreditch.* London, 1798. [96

ELTON, C. I. *William Shakespeare, His Family and Friends.* London, 1904. (Chap. IV deals with Blackfriars and the Globe.) [97

EVANS, M. B. An Early Type of Stage. (*Modern Philology,* IX, 421.) [98

EVELYN, J. *Diary and Correspondence.* Edited by William Bray and H. B. Wheatley. 4 vols. London, 1906. [99

*FEUILLERAT, A. Blackfriars Records. (The Malone Society's *Collections,* II, I.) [100

——— *John Lyly.* Cambridge, 1910. [101

——— *Le Bureau des Menus-Plaisirs (Office of the Revels) et la Mise en Scène a la Cour D'Élizabeth.* Louvain, 1910. [102

*FEUILLERAT, A. *Documents Relating to the Office of the Revels in the Time of Queen Elizabeth.* Louvain, 1908. [103

——— *Documents Relating to the Revels at Court in the Time of King Edward VI and Queen Mary.* (*The Loseley Manuscripts.*) Louvain, 1914. [104

*——— The Origin of Shakespeare's Blackfriars Theatre. (The Shakespeare *Jahrbuch*, XLVIII, 81.) [105

——— Shakespeare's Blackfriars. (The London *Daily Chronicle*, December 22, 1911.) [106

*FIRTH, C. H. The Suppression of the Drama during the Protectorate and Commonwealth. (*Notes and Queries*, VII Series, VI, 122.) [107

FITZJEFFREY, H. *Notes from Black-fryers.* London, 1620. [108

*FLEAY, F. G. *A Biographical Chronicle of the English Drama, 1559–1642.* 2 vols. London, 1891. [109

——— *A Chronicle History of the Life and Work of William Shakespeare.* London, 1886. [110

*——— *A Chronicle History of the London Stage, 1559–1642.* London, 1890. [111

——— History of the Theatres in London from their First Opening in 1576 to their Closing in 1642. (*Transactions of the Royal Historical Society*, X, 114. Also privately issued.) [112

——— On the Actor Lists, 1578–1642. (*Ibid.*, IX, 44.) [113

——— *A Shakespeare Manual.* London, 1878. [114

FLECKNOE, R. A Short Discourse of the English Stage. (Attached to *Love's Kingdom*, 1664; reprinted in No. 158.) [115

FORESTIER, A. The Fortune Theatre Reconstructed. (*The Illustrated London News*, August 12, 1911, p. 276.) [116

——— Origins of the English Stage (*Ibid.*, CXXXV, 934; CXXXVI, 57, 169, 225, 344, 423.) [117

FORTUNE. See Nos. 8, 24, 38, 46, 61, 63, 64, 67, 72, 89, 116, 119, 120, 126, 129, 143, 144, 161, 190, 211, 223, 231, 234, 235, 239, 303, 304, 316.

Fowell, F. and F. Palmer. *Censorship in England.* London, [1913]. [118

*Furnivall, F. J. The End of Shakespeare's Theatres. (*The Academy*, xxii, 314. Manuscript notes from the Phillipps copy of Stow's *Annals*, 1631. Previously printed by Collier. See No. 72.) [119

────── The Fortune Theatre in 1649. (*Notes and Queries*, x Series, i, 85.) [120

*────── *Harrison's Description of England.* The New Shakspere Society. London, 1877-78. (See No. 154.) [121

G., G. M. *The Stage Censor, an Historical Sketch: 1544-1907.* London, 1908. [122

*Gaedertz, K. T. *Zur Kenntnis der altenglischen Bühne.* Bremen, 1888. (On the De Witt drawing of the Swan. See Nos. 31, 193, 306.) [123

Gaehde, C. *Das Theater; Schauspielhaus und Schauspielkunst vom griechischen Altertum bis auf die Gegenwart.* Leipzig, 1908. [124

Gardner, A. E. The Site of the Globe Playhouse of Shakespeare. (*The Athenæum*, December 5, 1914.) [125

Gayton, E. *Pleasant Notes on Don Quixot.* London, 1654. (The second edition, 1768, is of no value.) [126

Genest, J. *Some Account of the English Stage from the Restoration in 1660 to 1830.* 10 vols. Bath, 1832. [127

*Gildersleeve, V. C. *Government Regulation of the Elizabethan Drama.* New York, 1908. [128

Globe. See Nos. 38, 49, 51, 72, 97, 117, 119, 125, 150, 152, 165, 166, 167, 171, 176, 191, 205, 206, 207, 208, 211, 212, 213, 223, 233, 236, 237, 240, 241, 251, 257, 266, 292, 297, 299, 300, 301.

Godfrey, W. H. An Elizabethan Playhouse. (*The Architectural Review*, London, April, 1908; reprinted in No. 61. See also the *Architect and Builder's Journal*, London, August 16, 1911, and *The Architectural Review*, London, January, 1912, for descriptions of Mr. Godfrey's model of the Fortune. This model is now in the Dramatic Museum at Columbia University, and a duplicate is in the Museum of European Culture at the University of Illinois. See also Nos. 8, 38, 61, 116, 211.) [129

BIBLIOGRAPHY

GOODWIN, A. T. Court Revels in the Reign of Henry VII. (*The Shakespeare Society's Papers*, 1, 47.) [130

GRABO, C. H. Theatres of Elizabeth's London. (*Chautauquan*, November, 1906.) [131

*GRAVES, T. S. *The Court and the London Theatres During the Reign of Elizabeth*. Menasha, Wis., 1913. [132

*———— A Note on the Swan Theatre. (*Modern Philology*, IX, 431. See No. 135.) [133

———— The Shape of the First London Theatre. (*The South Atlantic Quarterly*, July, 1914.) [134

———— Tricks of Elizabethan Showmen. (*Ibid.*, April, 1915. Deals with The Swan. See No. 133.) [135

*GREENSTREET, J. The Blackfriars Playhouse: Its Antecedents. (*The Athenæum*, July 17, 1886, p. 91, January 7, 1888, p. 25.) [136

*———— Blackfriars Theatre in the Time of Shakespeare. (*Ibid.*, April 7, 1888, p. 445; April 21, 1888, p. 509; August 10, 1889, p. 203. These documents are reprinted by Fleay, No. 111.) [137

*———— Documents Relating to the Players at the Red Bull, Clerkenwell, and the Cockpit in Drury Lane, in the Time of James I. (*The New Shakspere Society Transactions*, 1880–86, p. 489. Also in *The Athenæum*, February 21, 1885. Reprinted by Fleay, No. 111.) [138

*———— Drury Lane Theatre in the Reign of James I. (*The Athenæum*, 1885, February 21, p. 258; August 29, p. 282. Reprinted by Fleay, No. 111.) [139

*———— The Red Bull Playhouse in the Reign of James I. (*The Athenæum*, November 28, 1885, p. 709. Reprinted by Fleay, No. 111; and by Wallace, in completer form, No. 303.) [140

*———— The Whitefriars Theatre in the Time of Shakespeare. (*The New Shakspere Society Transactions*, 1887–90, p. 269.) [141

*———— The Will of Thomas Greene, with Particulars as to the Red Bull. (*The Athenæum*, August 29, 1885. Reprinted by Fleay, No. 111.) [142

*GREG, W. W. *Henslowe's Diary*. 2 vols. London, 1904–1908. (See No. 46.) [143

*GREG, W. W. *Henslowe Papers.* London, 1907. [144

———— See also under CHAMBERS, E. K. AND W. W. GREG.

GROTE, W. Das London zur Zeit der Königin Elisabeth in deutscher Beleuchtung. (*Neueren Sprachen*, XIV, 633.) [145

*HAGER, H. Diary of the Journey of Philip Julius, Duke of Stettin-Pomerania, through England in the Year 1602. (*Englische Studien*, XVIII, 315. See No. 34.) [146

*HALLIWELL-PHILLIPPS, J. O. *A Collection of Ancient Documents Respecting the Office of the Master of the Revels, and Other Papers Relating to the Early Theatre.* London, 1870. (Only eleven copies printed. The documents, with others, have been reprinted by Adams in No. 4.) [147

———— Dispute between the Earl of Worcester's Players and the Corporation of Leicester in 1586. (*The Shakespeare Society's Papers*, IV, 145.) [148

———— *Illustrations of the Life of Shakespeare.* London, 1874. (The material of this book has been embodied in No. 150.) [149

*———— *Outlines of the Life of Shakespeare.* 2 vols. The eleventh edition. London, 1907. (The page numbers have not been changed since the seventh edition, 1887.) [150

———— *Tarlton's Jests, and News out of Purgatory.* London. Printed for The Shakespeare Society. 1844. [151

———— *Two Old Theatres. Views of the Globe and Bear Garden.* Privately printed. Brighton. 1884. [152

———— *The Visits of Shakespeare's Company of Actors to the Provincial Cities and Towns of England, Illustrated by Extracts Gathered from Corporate Records.* Privately printed. Brighton, 1887. [153

*HARRISON, WILLIAM. *Harrison's Description of England.* Edited by F. J. Furnivall. The New Shakspere Society, London, 1877–78. (Additions by Mrs. C. C. Stopes, *The Shakespeare Library*, 1908. Edited also by L. Withington, London, 1902.) [154

HASLEWOOD, JOSEPH. *Account of the Old London Theatres.* (*Roxburghe Revels*, Edinburgh, 1837, p. 85. Fifty copies only printed.) [155

BIBLIOGRAPHY 445

HATCHER, O. L. *A Book for Shakespeare Plays and Pageants.* New York, 1916. ("Theatres," p. 133.) [156

HAZLITT, W. C. *Brand's Popular Antiquities of Great Britain. Faiths and Folklore.* 2 vols. London, 1905. [157

*―― *The English Drama and Stage under the Tudor and Stuart Princes, 1543–1664.* Printed for the Roxburghe Library. 1869. [158

HECKETHORN, C. W. *Lincoln's Inn Fields, and the Localities Adjacent.* London, 1896. [159

HENTZNER, P. *Itinerarium Germaniæ; Galliæ; Angliæ; Italiæ.* Nüremberg, 1612. [160

HERBERT, J. F. Additions to "The Alleyn Papers." (*The Shakespeare Society's Papers*, 1, 16. See No. 63.) [161

HEYWOOD, T. *An Apology for Actors.* London, 1612. (London: Reprinted for The Shakespeare Society. 1841.) [162

*HISTORICAL MANUSCRIPTS COMMISSION. *Calendars* and *Reports.* London, 1870–. [163

HITCHCOCK, R. *An Historical View of the Irish Stage.* 2 vols. Dublin, 1788. [164

HOPE. See Bear Garden and Hope.

*HUBBARD, G. On the Exact Site of the Globe Playhouse of Shakespeare. (*Transactions of the London and Middlesex Archæological Society*, New Series, vol. II, part iii, 1912.) [165

*―― The Site of the Globe Theatre of Shakespeare on Bankside as Shown by Maps of the Period. (*Journal of the Royal Institute of British Architects*, London, 1909, Third Series, XVII, 26.) [166

―― The Site of the Globe. (*Notes and Queries*, XII Series, XII, 11, 50, 70, 201, 224.) [167

HUGHSON, D. *An Epitome of the Privileges of London, Including Southwark, as Granted by Royal Charters.* London, 1812. [168

―― *Multum in Parvo. The Privileges of Southwark.* London, [c. 1818]. [169

INGLEBY, C. M. *A Complete View of the Shakespeare*

Controversy. London, 1861. (A discussion of the inaccuracies and forgeries of J. P. Collier.) [170

JACKSON, R. C. *The Site of Shakespeare's Globe Playhouse.* (*The Athenæum,* October 30, 1909, p. 525.) [171

*JEAFFRESON, J. C. *Middlesex County Records.* 4 vols. London, 1886–92. [172

JENKINSON, W. The Early Playhouses and the Drama as Referred to in Tudor and Stuart Literature. (*The Contemporary Review,* CV, 847.) [173

JUSSERAND, J. J. Les Théâtres de Londres au Temps de Shakespeare. (*La Revue de Paris,* VI, 713.) [174

——— *A Literary History of the English People From the Renaissance to the Civil War.* 2 vols. London, 1906–09. (Vol. II, bk. v, chap. v.) [175

K., L. L. Site of the Globe Theatre (*Notes and Queries,* XI Series, X, 290, 335.) [176

*KELLY, W. *Notices Illustrative of the Drama and Other Popular Amusements.* London, 1865. [177

*KEMPE, A. J. *The Loseley Manuscripts.* London, 1836. [178

*LA FÈVRE DE LA BODERIE, ANTOINE. *Ambassades de Monsieur de La Boderie en Angleterre . . . depuis les années 1606 jusq' en 1611.* 5 vols. [Paris], 1750. [179

LAW, E. Cunningham's Extracts from the Revels' Books, 1842. (*The Athenæum,* 1911, vol. II, pp. 297, 324, 388; 1912, vol. I, pp. 390, 469. See Nos. 11, 80, 181, 184.) [180

——— *More About Shakespeare "Forgeries."* London, 1913. (See Nos. 11, 80, 180, 184.) [181

——— Shakespeare at Whitehall. (The London *Times,* October 31, 1910, p. 10.) [182

——— Shakespeare's Christmas, St. Stephen's Day, 1604. (*Ibid.,* December 26, 1910, p. 10.) [183

——— *Some Supposed Shakespeare Forgeries.* London, 1911. (See Nos. 11, 80, 180, 181.) [184

*LAWRENCE, W. J. *The Elizabethan Playhouse and Other Studies.* Stratford-upon-Avon. 1912. Second Series, 1913. (I do not record separately the numerous articles by Mr.

Lawrence which appeared first in periodicals, and which are reprinted in these two volumes.) [185

*LAWRENCE, W. J. The Evolution and Influence of the Elizabethan Playhouse. (The Shakespeare *Jahrbuch*, XLVII, 18.) [186

*―――― A Forgotten Restoration Playhouse. (*Englische Studien*, XXXV, 279.) [187

―――― Ireland's First Theatrical Manager. (*The Weekly Freeman*, St. Patrick's Day Number, March 11, 1916.) [188

*―――― The Mystery of Lodowick Barry. (The University of North Carolina *Studies in Philology*, XIV, 52.) [189

*―――― Restoration Stage Nurseries. (*Archiv für das Studium der Neueren Sprachen und Literaturen*, 1914, p. 301.) [190

LEE, SIR S. *A Life of William Shakespeare*. New York, 1916. (Chap. VI.) [191

**Letters and Papers, Foreign and Domestic, of the Reign of Henry VIII*. London, 1862–1905. (Calendar of State Papers; see No. 35.) [192

LOGEMAN, H. Johannes de Witt's Visit to the Swan Theatre. (*Anglia*, XIX, 117. Cf. *The Academy*, December 26, 1896. See No. 31, 123, 306.) [193

LONDON TOPOGRAPHICAL SOCIETY. *London Topographical Record*. London, 1901–. [194

MAAS, H. *Äussere Geschichte der Englischen Theatertruppen in dem Zeitraum von 1559 bis 1642*. Louvain, 1907. [195

―――― *Die Kindertruppen*. Göttingen, 1901. [196

*MCAFEE, H. *Pepys on the Restoration Stage*. New Haven, 1916. [197

MALCOLM, J. P. *Anecdotes of the Manners and Customs of London during the Eighteenth Century*. London, 1808. [198

―――― *Anecdotes of the Manners and Customs of London from the Roman Invasion to the Year 1700*. London, 1811. [199

*MALONE, E. *The Plays and Poems of William Shakespeare*. 21 vols. London, 1821. (The Variorum edition, edited by Boswell.) [200

MANLY, J. M. The Children of the Chapel Royal and their Masters. (*The Cambridge History of English Literature*, vol. VI, chap. xi.) [201

MANNING, O. AND W. BRAY. *The History and Antiquities of the County of Surrey.* 3 vols. London, 1804–14. [202

MANTZIUS, K. *Engelske Theaterforhold i Shakespearetiden.* Khvn., 1901. (See No. 204.) [203

―――― *A History of Theatrical Art in Ancient and Modern Times.* Authorised Translation by Louise von Cossel. Vol. III, "The Shakespearean Period in England." London, 1904. [204

MARTIN, W. *Shakespeare in London.* (The London *Times*, October 8, 1909, p. 10.) [205

―――― The Site of Shakespeare's Globe Playhouse. (*The Athenæum*, October 9, 1909, p. 425.) [206

―――― The Site of the Globe. (*Notes and Queries*, XI Series, X, 209, XII, 10, 121, 143, 161.) [207

*―――― The Site of the Globe Playhouse of Shakespeare. (*Surrey Archæological Collections*, London, 1910, XXIII, 149. Also separately printed.) [208

MEMBER FROM THE BEGINNING. Accounts of Performances and Revels at Court in the Reign of Henry VIII. (*The Shakespeare Society's Papers*, III, 87.) [209

MEYMOTT, W. J. *The Manor of Old Paris Garden; an Historical Account of Christ Church, Surrey.* London, 1881. (Printed for private circulation. Inaccurate. See *Notes and Queries*, VII Series, III, 241.) [210

MILES, D. H. The Dramatic Museum at Columbia University. (*The American Review of Reviews*, XLVI, 67. Illustrations of models of early playhouses. See No. 38, 129.) [211

MILLS, C. A. Shakespeare and the Globe Theatre. (The London *Times*, April 11, 1914.) [212

Model of the Globe Playhouse. (*The Graphic*, London, LXXXII, 579; *Illustrated London News*, CXXXVI, 423.) [213

MORGAN, A. The Children's Companies. (*Shakesperiana*, IX, 131.) [214

MURRAY, J. T. English Dramatic Companies in the

BIBLIOGRAPHY 449

Towns Outside of London, 1550–1600. (*Modern Philology*, II, 539.) [215

*MURRAY, J. T. *English Dramatic Companies*. 2 vols. London, 1910. [216

N., T. C. The Old Bridge at Newington. (*Notes and Queries*, II Series, XII, 323.) [217

NAIRN, J. A. Boy-Actors under the Tudors and Stuarts. (*Transactions of the Royal Society of Literature*, II Series, XXXII, 11.) [218

*NICHOLS, J. *The Progresses and Public Processions of Queen Elizabeth*. 4 vols. London, 1823. [219

*—— *The Progresses, Processions, and Magnificent Festivities of King James the First*. 4 vols. London, 1828. [220

ONIONS, C. T. *Shakespeare's England*. 2 vols. Oxford, 1916. (Chap. XXIV, "Actors and Acting," by Percy Simpson; chap. XXV, "The Playhouse," by William Archer and W. J. Lawrence; chap. XXVII, section 7, "Bearbaiting, Bull Baiting, and Cockfighting," by Sir Sidney Lee. A popular treatise.) [221

*ORDISH, T. F. *Early London Theatres*. London, 1894. (For an important review, see E. K. Chambers in *The Academy*, August 24, 1895, p. 139.) [222

*—— London Theatres. (*The Antiquary*, XI–XVI. "Theatre and Curtain," XI, 89; "Rose," XI, 212; "Bear Garden," XI, 243; "Globe," XII, 41; "Elizabethan Stage," XII, 193; "Swan," XII, 245; "Blackfriars," XIV, 22, 55, 108; "Fortune," XIV, 205; "Red Bull," XIV, 236, "Cockpit," XV, 93; "Whitefriars," XV, 262; "Salisbury Court," XVI, 244.) [223

*OVERALL, W. H. AND H. C. *Analytical Index to the Series of Records Known as the Remembrancia. Preserved among the Archives of the City of London. 1579–1664.* London, 1878. (See No. 55.) [224

OVEREND, G. H. On the Dispute between George Maller, Glazier and Trainer of Players to Henry VIII, and Thomas Arthur, his Pupil. (*The New Shakspere Society's Transactions*, 1877–79, p. 425.) [225

PAGET, A. H. *The Elizabethan Playhouses.* London, 1891. (Privately printed, 8vo, 14 pp.) [226

*PARTON, J. *Some Account of the Hospital and Parish of St. Giles in the Fields, Middlesex.* London, 1822. (Contains parish records relating to the Cockpit in Drury Lane.) [227

PAUL'S. See Nos. 6, 12, 26, 101, 196, 201, 214, 218, 297.

*PEPYS, S. *The Diary of Samuel Pepys.* Edited by Henry B. Wheatley. 9 vols. London, 1893. [228

PHŒNIX. See Cockpit in Drury Lane.

PINKS, W. J. *The History of Clerkenwell.* Second edition. London, 1880. (The Red Bull Playhouse, p. 190.) [229

Pleadings in Rastell v. Walton, a Theatrical Lawsuit, temp. Henry VIII. (Arber, *An English Garner, Fifteenth Century Prose and Verse*, 1903, p. 305.) [230

PLOMER, H. R. Fortune Playhouse (*Notes and Queries*, X Series, VI, 107.) [231

POLLOCK, A. The Evolution of the Actor. (*The Drama*, August and November, 1915, and November, 1916.) [232

PORTER, C. Playing Hamlet as Shakespeare Staged It in 1601. (*Ibid.*, August and November, 1915.) [233

PRYNNE, W. *Histriomastix.* London, 1633. [234

RANKIN, G. Early London Theatres. (*Notes and Queries*, IV Series, VI, 306; cf. p. 423.) [235

RED BULL. See Nos. 4, 91, 107, 126, 138, 139, 140, 142, 147, 197, 223, 228, 229, 234, 303.

Remembrancia. See Nos. 55, 224.

*RENDLE, W. The Bankside, Southwark, and the Globe Playhouse. (In Furnivall's edition of Harrison's *Description of England*, Part II, Book iii. See No. 121. Deals with the Swan, Bear Garden, Hope, Rose, and Globe.) [236

*—— The Globe Playhouse. (*Walford's Antiquarian*, VIII, 209.) [237

—— Paris Garden and Christ Church, Blackfriars. (*Notes and Queries*, VII Series, III, 241, 343, 442.) [238

—— Philip Henslowe. (*The Genealogist*, IV, 149.) [239

*—— The Playhouses at Bankside in the Time of

Shakespeare. (*The Antiquarian Magazine and Bibliographer*, VII, 207, 274; VIII, 55.) [240

RENDLE, W. *Old Southwark and its People*. London, 1878. [241

——— The Swan Playhouse, Bankside, *circa* 1596. (*Notes and Queries*, VII Series, VI, 221.) [242

*RENDLE, W. AND P. NORMAN. *The Inns of Old Southwark and Their Associations*. London, 1888. [243

Report of the Royal Commission on Historical Manuscripts. London, 1870–. (See No. 163.) [244

RIMBAULT, E. F. *The Old Cheque-Book, or Book of Remembrance, of the Chapel Royal from 1561 to 1744*. (*The Camden Society*, 1872.) [245

——— Who was "*Jack Wilson*" the Singer of Shakespeare's Stage? London, 1846. (Cf. *The Shakespeare Society's Papers*, II, 33.) [246

ROSE. See Nos. 24, 46, 63, 64, 67, 143, 144, 161, 222, 223, 236, 239, 240, 241, 257, 263, 300, 302, 304, 316.

*RYE, W. B. *England as Seen by Foreigners in the Days of Elizabeth and James I*. London, 1865. [247

SALISBURY COURT. See Nos. 4, 7, 19, 72, 86, 91, 99, 119, 147, 197, 223, 228.

SCHELLING, F. E. "An Aery of Children, Little Eyases." (*The Queen's Progress and Other Elizabethan Sketches*, Boston and New York, 1904, chap. v.) [248

——— The Elizabethan Theatre. (*Lippincott's Monthly Magazine*, LXIX, 309.) [249

Shakespeare's England. See No. 221.

SHEPPARD, E. *The Old Royal Palace of Whitehall*. London and New York, 1902. [250

The Site of the Globe Theatre, Bankside. (*The Builder*, March 26, 1910, p. 353.) [251

SMITH, W. H. *Bacon and Shakespeare. An Inquiry Touching Players, Playhouses, and Play-Writers in the Days of Elizabeth*. London, 1857. [252

SPIERS, W. L. An Autograph Plan by Wren. (*The London Topographical Record*, 1903. Concerns Whitehall Palace and the Cockpit.) [253

State Papers. See Nos. 35, 192.
Statutes of the Realm. Record Commission. 9 vols. London, 1810–28. [254

STEPHENSON, H. T. *Shakespeare's London.* New York, 1905. (Chap. XIV, "The Theatres.") [255

—— *The Study of Shakespeare.* New York, 1915. (Chap. III, "The Playhouses.") [256

*STOPES, C. C. *Burbage and Shakespeare's Stage.* London, 1913. [257

—— The Burbages and the Transportation of "The Theatre." (*The Athenæum,* October 16, 1909, p. 470.) [258

—— Burbage's "Theatre." (*The Fortnightly Review,* XCII, 149.) [259

—— Dramatic Records from the Privy Council Register, James I and Charles I. (The Shakespeare *Jahrbuch,* XLVIII, 103. See No. 54.) [260

—— Giles and Christopher Alleyn of Holywell. (*Notes and Queries,* X Series, XII, 341.) [261

—— "The Queen's Players" in 1536. (*The Athenæum,* July 24, 1914.) [262

—— The Rose and the Swan, 1597. (*The Stage,* January 6, 1910. The documents here summarized are printed in full in No. 257 and again in No. 302.) [263

—— *Shakespeare's Environment.* London, 1914. (Chapters on William Hunnis, Burbage's "Theatre," and The Transportation of Burbage's "Theatre.") [264

——* Shakespeare's Fellows and Followers. (The Shakespeare *Jahrbuch,* XLVI, 92.) [265

—— The Site of the Globe. (*Notes and Queries,* XI Series, XI, 447.) [266

—— "The Theatre." (*Archiv für das Studium der Neueren Sprachen und Literaturen,* CXXIV, 129.) [267

—— William Hunnis. (The Shakespeare *Jahrbuch,* XXVII, 200.) [268

—— William Hunnis. (*The Athenæum,* March 31, 1900.) [269

—— *William Hunnis and the Revels of the Chapel Royal.* Louvain, 1910. [270

BIBLIOGRAPHY 453

*STOW, J. *A Survey of London.* Edited by C. L. Kingsford. 2 vols. Oxford, 1908. [271

*———— *A Survey of the Cities of London and Westminster . . . Corrected, Improved, and Very Much Enlarged . . . by John Strype.* 2 vols. London, 1720. [272

*———— *Annales, or A Generall Chronicle of England, Continued by Edmund Howes.* London, 1631. [273

STRUTT, J. *Sports and Pastimes of the People of England.* London, 1801. [274

STRYPE, J. See No. 272.

———— *The Anatomy of Abuses.* Edited by F. J. Furnivall, for The New Shakspere Society. London, 1877–79. (There is an earlier edition by J. P. Collier, 1870.) [275

SWAN. See Nos. 9, 31, 46, 123, 133, 135, 144, 193, 210, 214, 222, 223, 236, 238, 240, 241, 242, 257, 263, 302, 306.

SYMONDS, J. A. *Shakespeare's Predecessors.* London, 1883. (Chap. VIII, "Theatres, Playwrights, Actors, and Playgoers.") [276

THEATRE, BURBAGE'S. See Nos. 28, 70, 96, 134, 150, 151, 222, 223, 257, 258, 259, 261, 264, 267, 277, 290.

The Theater; a Middlesex Sessions Record Touching James Burbage's "Theater." (*The Athenæum,* February 12, 1887, p. 233.) [277

*THOMPSON, E. N. S. *The Controversy between the Puritans and the Stage.* New York, 1903. [278

THORNBURY, G. W. *Shakespeare's England.* 2 vols. London, 1856. (Vol. II, chap. X, "The Theatre.") [279

*THORNDIKE, A. H. *Shakespeare's Theatre.* New York, 1916. (Chap. III, "The Playhouses.") [280

TILER, A. *The History and Antiquities of St. Saviours.* London, 1765. [281

TOMLINS, T. E. A New Document Regarding the Authority of the Master of the Revels. (*The Shakespeare Society's Papers,* III, 1. The document is reprinted in No. 103.) [282

———— The Original Patent for the Nursery of Actors and Actresses in the Reign of Charles II. (*Ibid.,* III, 162.) [283

BIBLIOGRAPHY

*TOMLINS, T. E. Origin of the Curtain Theatre, and Mistakes Regarding It. (*The Shakespeare Society's Papers*, I, 29.) [284

—— Three New Privy Seals for Players in the Time of Shakespeare. (*Ibid.*, IV, 41.) [285

TYSON, W. Heming's Players at Bristol in the Reign of Henry VIII. (*Ibid.*, III, 13.) [286

Victoria History of London. London, 1909. [287

*WALLACE, C. W. *The Children of the Chapel at Blackfriars 1597–1603.* Lincoln [Nebraska], 1908. (Originally printed in *University Studies*, University of Nebraska, 1908.) [288

*—— *The Evolution of the English Drama up to Shakespeare, with a History of the First Blackfriars Theatre.* (*Schriften der Deutschen Shakespeare-Gesellschaft*, Band IV. Berlin, 1912.) [289

*—— *The First London Theatre, Materials for a History.* (*University Studies*, University of Nebraska, vol. XII. Lincoln, Nebraska, 1913.) [290

—— Gervase Markham, Dramatist. (The Shakespeare *Jahrbuch*, XLVI, 345. Cf. J. Q. Adams, in *Modern Philology*, X, 426.) [291

*—— *Globe Theatre Apparel.* [London.] Privately printed, August, 1909. (For the nature of the contents see the London *Times*, November 30, 1909, p. 12; and the Shakespeare *Jahrbuch*, XLVI, 239.) [292

—— *Keysar v. Burbage and Others.* Privately printed, 1910. (These documents are included in the author's *Shakespeare and his London Associates*, No. 297.) [293

—— A London Pageant of Shakespeare's Time. (The London *Times*, March 28, 1913.) [294

—— New Shakespeare Discoveries. (*Harper's Monthly Magazine*, CXX, 489. See No. 297.) [295

—— Old Blackfriars Theatre. (The London *Times*, September 12, 1906; the New York *Evening Post*, September 24, 1906.) [296

*—— Shakespeare and His London Associates as Revealed in Recently Discovered Documents. (*University Studies*, University of Nebraska, X, 261.) [297

WALLACE, C. W. Shakespeare and the Blackfriars Theatre. (*The Century Magazine*, September, 1910. The documents on which this popular article is based may be found in Nos. 289 and 297.) [298

*———— Shakespeare and the Globe. (The London *Times*, October 2 and 4, 1909. Deals with the Osteler-Heminges documents, and the site of the Globe. These documents Mr. Wallace has privately printed in *Advance Sheets from Shakespeare, The Globe, and Blackfriars*, The Shakespeare Head Press, 1909, whence they were printed in the Shakespeare *Jahrbuch*, XLVI, 235.) [299

*———— Shakespeare and the Globe. (The London *Times*, April 30 and May 1, 1914.) [300

———— Shakspere's Money Interest in the Globe Theatre. (*The Century Magazine*, August, 1910. The documents on which this popular article is based may be found in No. 297.) [301

*———— The Swan Theatre and the Earl of Pembroke's Servants. (*Englische Studien*, XLIII, 340. See Nos. 257, 263.) [302

*———— Three London Theatres of Shakespeare's Time. (*University Studies*, University of Nebraska, IX, 287.) [303

*WARNER, G. F. *Catalogue of the Manuscripts and Muniments of Alleyn's College of God's Gift at Dulwich*. [London], 1881. [304

WHEATLEY, H. B. *London, Past and Present. . . . Based upon the Handbook of London by the late Peter Cunningham*. London and New York, 1891. (See No. 81.) [305

*———— On a Contemporary Drawing of the Interior of the Swan Theatre, 1596. (*The New Shakspere Society's Transactions*, 1887–90, p. 213.) [306

WHITEFRIARS. See Nos. 5, 6, 7, 19, 43, 60, 61, 86, 141, 144, 189, 196, 201, 214, 218, 223, 239, 287, 293, 297.

*WILKINSON, R. *Londina Illustrata*. 2 vols. London, 1819–25. (The second volume is entitled *Theatrum Illustrata*.) [307

WILSON, J. D. *Life in Shakespeare's England*. Cambridge, 1911. (Chap. VII, "The Theatre.") [308

*WILSON, J. D. *The Puritan Attack upon the Stage.*
(*The Cambridge History of English Literature*, vol. VI.) [309
*WINWOOD, R. *Memorials of Affairs of State.* 3 vols.
London, 1725. [310
WOOLF, A. H. *Shakespeare and the Old Southwark Playhouses: a Lecture.* London, 1903. (20 pp., 8vo, privately printed.) [311
WOTTON, SIR H. *Reliquiæ Wottonianæ.* London, 1651.
[312
WRIGHT, G. R. *The English Stage in the Year 1638.*
(*The Journal of the British Archæological Association*, XVI, 275; reprinted in the author's *Archæologic and Historic Fragments*, London, 1887.) [313
*WRIGHT, J. *Historia Histrionica*, London, 1699. (Reprinted in Hazlitt's Dodsley, vol. XV.) [314
WRIGHT, T. *Queen Elizabeth and Her Times.* 2 vols.
London, 1838. [315
*YOUNG, W. *The History of Dulwich College, with a Life of the Founder, Edward Alleyn, and an Accurate Transcript of his Diary, 1617–1622.* 2 vols. London, 1889. (Edition limited to 250 copies, privately printed for the author.)
[316

MAPS AND VIEWS OF LONDON

I

CRACE, J. G. *A Catalogue of Maps, Plans, and Views of London, Westminster, and Southwark, Collected and Arranged by Frederick Crace.* London, 1878. (This collection of maps is now in the British Museum. The Catalogue is not always trustworthy.)

GOMME, L. The Story of London Maps. (*The Geographical Journal,* London, 1908, XXXI, 489, 616.)

MARTIN, W. A Study of Early Map-Views of London. (*The Antiquary,* London, 1909, XLV, 337, 406. See also *Home Counties Magazine,* IX.)

II

VAN DEN WYNGAERDE, A. View of London, Westminster, and Southwark. (The original drawing, made about 1530, is now preserved in the Sutherland Collection in the Bodleian Library. A reproduction in three sections will be found in Besant's *London in the Time of the Tudors.*)

BRAUN, G., AND F. HOGENBERGIUS. *Londinum Feracissimi Angliæ Regni Metropolis.* (In *Civitates Orbis Terrarum,* Cologne, 1572. The map is based on an original, now lost, drawn between 1554 and 1558; see Alfred Marks, *The Athenæum,* March 31, 1906.)

AGAS, R. *Civitas Londinum.* (This map, executed about 1570, is based on the same original map, 1554–58, made use of by Braun and Hogenbergius, although Agas has introduced a few changes. The two earliest copies are in Guildhall, London, and in the Pepysian Library at Cambridge. The student should be warned against Vertue's reproduction, often met with. The best reproduction is that by The London Topographical Society, 1905.)

NORDEN, J. *London*. (In *Speculum Britanniæ, an Historical and Chorographical Description of Middlesex. By the Travaile and View of John Norden*. London, 1593. The map was engraved by Pieter Vanden Keere.)

DELARAM, F. View of London. (In the background of an engraving, made about 1603, representing King James on horseback.)

HONDIUS, J. *London*. (A small view of the city set in the large map of "The Kingdome of Great Britaine and Ireland" printed in John Speed's *Theatre of the Empire of Great Britaine*, London, 1611. The plate is dated 1610, but the inset view of London seems to have been based on an earlier view, now lost, representing the city as it was in or before 1605. Apparently the views, in the Delaram portrait of King James, and on the title-pages of Henry Holland's *Herowlogia*, 1620, and Sir Richard Baker's *Chronicle*, 1643, were based also on this lost view.)

VISSCHER, C. J. *London*. (This splendid view was printed in 1616; but it was drawn several years earlier, and represents the city as it was in or before 1613.)

MERIAN, M. *London*. (In J. L. Gottfried's *Neuwe Archontologia Cosmica*, Frankfurt am Mayn, 1638. Based mainly on Visscher's View, but with additions from some other earlier view not yet identified.)

[RYTHER, A.] *The Cittie of London*. (This map, erroneously attributed to Ryther in the Catalogue of the Crace Collection, is often misdated 1604. It was made between 1630 and 1640; see *Notes and Queries*, IV Series, IX, 95; VI Series, XII, 361, 393; VII Series, III, 110, 297, 498.)

HOLLAR, W. View of London. (The View is dated 1647; Hollar was in banishment from England between the years 1643 and 1652. Excellently reproduced by The London Topographical Society, 1907.)

[?HOLLAR, W.] *London*. (In James Howell's *Londinopolis*, London, 1657. This view is a poor copy of Merian's splendid view, 1638. Though generally attributed to Hollar, it is unsigned.)

MAPS AND VIEWS OF LONDON

FAITHORNE, W., AND R. NEWCOURT. *An Exact Delineation of the Cities of London and Westminster, and the Suburbs Thereof.* London, 1658. (Reproduced by The London Topographical Society, 1905.)

PORTER, T. Map of London and Westminster. (About 1660. Probably based on the earlier map, 1630-40, mistakenly ascribed to Ryther. Reproduced by The London Topographical Society, 1898.)

MOORE, J. Map of London, Westminster, and Southwark. (Drawn in 1662. Reproduced by The London Topographical Society, 1912.)

OGILBY, J., AND W. MORGAN. *A Large and Accurate Map of the City of London*, 1677. (Reproduced by The London and Middlesex Archæological Society, 1895, with Ogilby's description of the map, entitled *London Surveyed*.)

MORDEN, R., AND P. LEA. *London &c. Actually Survey'd*, 1682. (Reproduced by The London Topographical Society, 1904.)

ROCQUE, J. *An Exact Survey of the Cities of London and Westminster, the Borough of Southwark... Begun in 1741, Finished in 1745, and published in 1746.* London, 1746. (An excellent reproduction of this large map is now being issued in parts by The London Topographical Society, 1913–.)

INDEX

Abuses, 116.
Admiral-Prince Henry-1 Palsgrave-3 Prince Charles's Company:
  Admiral's Company, 14, 16, 61 n., 72–73, 153–57, 174–75, 176, 267, 269, 272, 281–82, 289–90.
  Prince Henry's Company, 88, 282–83, 295.
  Palsgrave's Company, 283–87, 290, 368, 369 n., 375.
  Prince Charles II's Company, 287, 289–90, 303, 375–79, 401.
Æschylus, 398.
Agas, Ralph, 328, 392.
Aglaura, 404.
Albemarle, George Monck, 1 Duke of, 365, 405.
Albright, V. E., vii.
Alchemist, The, 419.
Alcimedon, 422.
Aldgate, 7, 10.
Alexander and Campaspe, 109, 113.
Alfonso, 232.
Allen, William, 305.
Alleyn, Edward, 57, 72, 85, 86, 133, 140, 150–51, 153, 156, 246, 267–74, 281–87, 299, 319, 335–36.
Alleyn, Gyles, 30–38, 43, 47, 52, 53, 58–65, 84, 182, 190, 199, 234.
Alleyn, Joan Woodward, ix, 151.
Alleyn, John, 57–58, 72, 73.
Alleyn, Sara. See Gyles Alleyn.
All is True, 251–55. See *Henry VIII*.
All's Lost by Lust, 309.
Allyn, Sir William, 81.
Alnwick Castle, 173 n.
Amends for Ladies, 346.
Amphitheatre, the projected, 411–17.
Andronicus, 140, 152.
Androwes, George, 313, 314, 315.
Anjou, Duke of, 385.
Anne of Denmark, Queen of England, 300, 353. Her players, see under Worcester, Children of the Chapel, and Children of Her Majesty's Royal Chamber.
Antonio's Revenge, 112.
Apothecaries, Society of, 191 n.
Architectural Record, The, ix, 395.
Aristophanes, 398.
Armin, Robert, 316.
Arundel and Surrey, Thomas Howard, 2 Earl of, 426, 429, 430.
Arundel's Company, 70, 83.
Arviragus and Philicia, 401.
Ashen-tree Court, 313.
Ashley, Sir Anthony, 322.
Aubrey, John, 78, 364.
Aunay, Josias d', 423.

Bacon, Anthony, 15.
Bacon, Sir Edmund, 320.
Bacon, Francis, 15, 65.
Baker, Michael, 430.
Baker, Sir Richard, 127, 146.
Banks, Jeremiah, 306.
Banks's horse, 13.
Bankside, 28–29, 63, 64, 119 f., 134 f., 142 f., 161 f., 182–83, 185, 238 f., 267, 326 f.
Banqueting-House at Whitehall, 385–89.
Barclay, Perkins, and Company, 265.
Barry, David Lording, 313, 314–15, 316, 317.
Barry, Lodowick. See David Barry.
Bartholomew Fair, 325 n., 330, 334.
Bath, 71.
Baxter, Richard, 300–01.
Bear Alley, 340, 341.
Bear Garden (First), 15, 119–33, 145, 146, 146 n., 159 n., 167, 182, 238, 244, 248, 326, 328, 329, 332 n., 336, 416.
Bear Garden (Second). See Hope Playhouse.

INDEX

Bear Garden Alley, 340, 341.
Bear Garden Glass House, 341 *n*.
Bear Garden Square, 341.
Beaumont, Francis, 116, 304, 404.
Beaven, William, 293.
Beddingfield, Anne, 294.
Beddingfield, Christopher, 294.
Beecher, Sir William, 230.
Beeston, Christopher, 158, 299–300, 350–58, 374, 421.
Beeston, Mrs. Elizabeth, 362.
Beeston, William, 358–61, 380–83.
Beeston's Boys. *See* King's and Queen's Company.
Beggar's Bush, 404.
Bell, Hamilton, ix, 395–400.
Bell Inn, 1–17, 67.
Bell Savage Inn, 1–17.
Bermondsey, Monastery of, 161.
Bethelem, 69.
Betterton, Thomas, 366, 406.
Betterton, Mrs. Thomas, 406 *n*.
Bevis, 133.
Bird, Theophilus, 350 *n*., 381.
Bird, William, 170, 174.
Bishop, Nicholas, 57.
Bishopsgate Street, 7 f., 67.
Black Book, The, 73 *n*.
Blackfriars Playhouse (First), 8, 91–110, 113, 183, 194, 201, 202, 204, 208, 311 *n*.
Blackfriars Playhouse (Second), 59, 74, 86, 93, 98 *n*., 116, 117, 118, 182–233, 250, 256, 260, 261, 311, 312, 317, 319, 320, 324, 343, 350, 355, 356, 365, 369, 372 *n*., 373, 402, 403, 404, 428.
Blackfriars Playhouse (Rosseter's). *See* Rosseter's Blackfriars.
Blagrove, Thomas, 369.
Blagrove, William, 368–72, **374**, 424.
Bloody Brother, The, 363.
Blount, Thomas, 122.
Boar's Head Inn, Eastcheap, 7 *n*.
Boar's Head Inn, Whitechapel, 1–17, 87, 157–58, 159.
Boar's Head Yard, 17.
Bodley, Sir John, 256–57, 262.
Bondman, The, 382.
Bonetti, Rocho, 194–95.
Boone, Colonel, 382.
Bourne, Theophilus, 350 *n*.

Bouverie Street, 313.
Bowes, Sir Jerome, 184.
Bowman (the actor), 405 *n*.
Box, Edward, 160.
Bradshaw, Charles, 192.
Braun, G., and F. Hogenbergius, 122.
Brayne, John, 39–58, 72, 78, 83, 144, 234.
Brayne, Mrs. Margaret, 43, 44 *n*., 54–58.
Brend, Elizabeth, 264.
Brend, Matthew, 257, 262–63.
Brend, Sir Nicholas, 238–39, 249, 256.
Brend, Sir Thomas, 240 *n*., 249.
Brend, Thomas (the younger), 264.
Bridges Street, 408.
Bristol, 172.
Brockenbury, Richard, 35.
Brome, Richard, 233, 361, 379.
Bromvill, Peter, 176.
Brooke. *See* Cobham.
Browker, Hugh, 176–77.
Brown, Sir Matthew, 256.
Brown, Rawdon, 279 *n*.
Browne, Robert, 318.
Bruskett, Thomas, 191, 195.
Bryan, Sir Francis, 184.
Bryan, George, 73.
Buc, Sir George, 321, 325, 343.
Buchell, Arend van, 166.
Buckhurst, Robert, Lord, 311–12, 314.
Bull Inn, 1–17, 67, 294 *n*.
Burbage, Cuthbert, 39 *n*., 40, 45 *n*., 49, 52, 54–65, 74, 84, 198, 199–200, 223, 224, 234–41, 249, 257, 282.
Burbage, James, 11, 27–59, 65, 66, 67, 70–74, 75, 78, 83, 91, 98 *n*., 144, 161, 182–99, 202, 234.
Burbage, Mrs. James, 56, 57, 63.
Burbage, Richard, 40, 57, 61, 62, 63, 73, 74, 84, 111, 117, 140, 198, 199, 200–01, 204, 208 *n*., 215, 218, 223–25, 234–41, 249, 255, 257, 261, 282, 317, 319, 325.
Burghley, William Cecil, Lord, 14, 20, 69.
Burgram, John, 242–43.
Burnell, Henry, 418.
Burt, Nicholas, 363, 367.

INDEX 463

Burt, Thomas, 241-42.
Busino, Orazio, 130, 279.
Bussy D'Ambois, 400, 404.
Buttevant, Viscount, 313 n.
Byron, 220, 316.

C., W., 302.
Cambridge, 67.
Camden, William, 350, 352.
Campaspe, 109, 113.
Campeggio, Cardinal Lorenzo, 186.
Cape, Walter, 55.
Cardinal, The, 406.
Careless Shepherdess, The, 302.
Carew, Thomas, 302, 356.
Carey. *See* Hunsdon.
Carlell, Lodowick, 404.
Carleton, Mrs. Alice, 260.
Carleton, Sir Dudley, 212 n., 281, 284, 388, 393.
Carter, Lane, 231.
Cartwright, William, 374.
Castle, Tavern, 348 n.
Castlemaine, Lady, 406.
Catherine of Aragon, Queen, 186.
Cawarden, Sir Thomas, 96, 184, 186-90, 193.
Challes, 69-70, 83.
Chalmers, George, 137-38, 428.
Chamberlain, John, 212 n., 252, 260, 281, 284, 388, 392, 393.
Chamberlain's Company. *See* Strange-Derby, etc., company.
Chambers, E. K., ix, 44 n., 230 n., 247.
Chambers, George, 206.
Chambers, Richard, 206.
Chances, The, 404.
Changes, The, 376-78.
Chapel Royal, 91 f. *See also* Children of the Chapel.
Chapman, George, 116, 206, 217, 220.
Chappell, John, 206.
Charles I, 227, 231, 301-02, 359, 394, 395, 414, 424. His players, *see* King's and Queen's Company, King's Revels Company, Prince Charles's Company, Strange-Derby, etc., Company.
Charles II, 287, 405. His players, *see under* Admiral.
Chasserau, Peter, 75 n., 79.

Cheeke, Sir John, 96, 184, 190.
Chettle, Henry, 158.
Cheyney, Sir Thomas, the Lord Warden, 184, 188.
Children of Blackfriars. *See* Children of the Chapel, etc.
Children of Her Majesty's (Queen Anne's) Royal Chamber of Bristol, 215 n.
Children of His Majesty's (James I's) Revels (at Whitefriars), 224.
Children of St. Paul's, 91, 108-10, 111-18, 217, 311 n., 319.
Children of the Chapel - 1 Queen's Revels - Revels - Whitefriars - 2 Queen's Revels Company:
  Children of the Chapel (at First Blackfriars), 91-110, 111, 113.
  Children of the Chapel (at Second Blackfriars), 200-15, 237, 249-50.
  1 Children of the Queen's (Anne's) Revels, 215-18, 219, 311.
  Children of the Revels (or of Blackfriars), 218-24, 314 n., 316-17.
  Children of Whitefriars, 318.
  2 Children of the Queen's (Anne's) Revels, 117, 318-21, 324, 342-46.
Children of the Queen's Revels. *See under* Children of the Chapel, etc., and *under* Worcester-Queen, etc.
Children of Whitefriars. *See under* Children of the Chapel, etc.
Children of Windsor Chapel, 91-108, 111, 201.
Cholmley, John, 143-44, 148, 148 n., 234.
Clerkenwell, 78, 88, 301, 294 f.
Clifton, Henry, 205-13.
Clifton, Thomas, 210-13.
Clink, the Liberty of the, 124 f., 135, 142, 145, 161.
Clough, George, 53-54.
Cobham, George Brooke, Lord, 96, 184.
Cobham, Henry Brooke, Lord, 184.
Cobham, William Brooke, Lord, 98, 99, 184, 198, 199, 212 n.
Cockpit-in-Court, 384-409, 420.

INDEX

Cockpit in Dartmouth Street, 408 n.
Cockpit Playhouse in Drury Lane, 291, 297 n., 299, 300, 305, 348–67, 369, 373, 376 n., 381 n., 408 n., 421–22, 431.
Cokaine, Sir Aston, 233.
Colefox, Edwin, 34–35.
Collett, John, 256.
Collier, J. P., vii, 76, 138, 230 n., 322 n., 377, 347 n., 353 n., 373 n.
Columbia University, 277.
Condell, Henry, 224, 238, 255, 257, 258, 262, 355.
Conspiracy and Tragedy of Charles, Duke of Byron, The, 220, 316.
Constant Maid, The, 419.
Conway, Edward, Lord, 414–17.
Cooke, William, 315.
Cooper, Lane, ix.
Corneille, Pierre, 406 n.
Cornishe, John, 241–42.
Cotton, John, 412–14.
Court Beggar, The, 361.
Coventry, Thomas, 414–17.
Cranydge, James, 13.
Creed, John, 366.
Crew, John, 406.
Cromwell, Oliver, 364, 405.
Cross Keys Inn, 1–17, 68.
Cruelty of the Spaniards in Peru, The, 365.
Cunningham, Peter, 322, 372, 374 n., 407 n.
Cupid and Psyche, 113.
Cupid's Whirligig, 316.
Curtain Court, 79, 90.
Curtain Playhouse, 8, 10, 16, 26, 32 n., 46, 47, 61, 62, 69, 70, 72, 75–90, 135, 144 n., 155, 159, 167, 172 n., 174, 182, 200, 295, 296, 297, 298 n., 301, 355.
Curtain Road, 34, 90.
Custom of the Country, The, 404.
Cutwell, 11.
Cynthia's Revels, 209 n.

Daborne, Robert, 318, 324 n., 325.
Dancaster, Thomas, 35.
Daniel, Samuel, 215 n., 216.
Davenant, William, 309, 361–65, 382, 424–31.
Davenant's Projected Theatre, 424–31.
Davenport, Robert, 356.
David, John, 12.
Davies, James, 339.
Day, John (playwright), 158, 220, 315.
Day, John (printer), 411.
Deadman's Place, 264.
Dekker, Thomas, 116, 158, 244, 278, 298, 332 n.
Delaram, F., 128, 146, 248, 248 n.
De Lawne, William, 190.
Derby, Ferdinando Stanley, Earl of, 73, 153.
Derby's Company. *See under* Strange-Derby, etc.
Devonshire, Charles Blount, Earl of, 216 n.
De Witt, Johannes, 46, 77 n., 146 n., 165–68, 273.
Ditcher, Thomas, 242.
Dixon, Thomas, 412–17.
Doctor Faustus, 73.
Dorchester, Evelyn Pierrepont, Marquis of, 340.
Dorset, Edward Sackville, Earl of, 369–70, 375, 378–80.
Dorset House, 371.
Dotridge, Alice, 35.
Doubtful Heir, The, 289, 419.
Downes, John, 307, 365, 366.
Downton, Thomas, 170, 174, 282.
Dragon, John, 34–35.
Drayton, Michael, 311–17.
Droeshout, Martin, 266.
Drury Lane, 309, 348 f., 420 f.
Dryden, John, 417.
Dublin Theatre, 417–19.
Duchy Chamber, 189 f.
Dudley, Robert, *See* Leicester.
Duke, John, 158.
Duke's Theatre, 383 n.
Dulwich College, ix, 133, 144 n., 274, 283, 285 n., 286–93.
Dumb Knight, The, 316.
Dun, 178.
Dunstan, James, 350 n.
Du Rocher, R. M., 420 n.
Duryer, Pierre, 422 n.
Dutch Courtesan, The, 196 n.

Earthquake, 82–83.
Eastcheap, 7 n., 122.
East Smithfield, 410 f.

INDEX 465

Eastward Hoe, 217.
Eaton, Henry, 308.
Elizabeth, Princess (daughter of James I), 393. Her players, *see* Princess Elizabeth's Company.
Elizabeth, Queen of England, 91, 108, 113–14, 158 n., 171, 212 n., 215, 385. Her players, *see* Queen's Company.
Endimion 114.
England's Joy, 177–78.
English Traveller, The, 277.
Epicharmus, 398.
Epicoene, 319, 405.
Epicurus, 398.
Erasmus, Desiderius, 120.
Essex, 44 n.
Essex, Robert Devereux, Earl of, 13, 216.
Euripides, 398.
Evans, Henry, 107, 110, 192–225.
Evelyn, John, 338, 363, 405 n.
Every Man in His Humour, 85.
Every Man out of his Humour, 246, 247 n.

Fair Favourite, The, 404.
Faithorne, W., 348 n., 392.
Falcon Stairs, 164.
Family of Love, The, 315.
Farrant, Anne, 104–10.
Farrant, Richard, 91–110, 183, 200, 201, 202, 203, 204.
Faunte, William, 133.
Fennor, William, 177 n., 332–34.
Ferrers, Captain, 366.
Ferretti, Francesco, 164.
Ferrys, 173.
Feuillerat, A., 101 n., 186.
Field, John, 125.
Field, Nathaniel, 206, 237, 319, 324 n., 325, 342 n., 346.
Finsbury Field, 28–38, 75, 81, 135, 142, 268, 352.
Fisher, Edward, 381, 383.
Fisher, John, 285 n., 387 n., 396.
Fitz-Stephen, William, 120.
Fleay, F. G., 112, 115, 179 n., 201 n., 311 n., 323, 335 n., 350 n., 354 n., 377, 402 n., 416 n.
Flecknoe, Richard, 6, 7, 17, 111, 311 n.
Fleet Street, 231, 314, 424 f.

Fleetwood, William, 20, 46, 69–70, 71.
Fletcher, Dr., 172.
Fletcher, John, 251, 304, 325, 419.
Floridor, Josias, 401, 420–24.
Fortescue, Sir John, 211.
Fortune Playhouse, 45, 85, 88, 156–57, 176, 177 n., 229, 246, 259 n., 267–93, 295, 297, 298, 302, 303, 327 n., 333 n., 353 n., 364 n., 368, 374, 375, 379, 381 n., 425 n.
Fortunes of Nigel, The, 310 n.
Fowler, Thomas, 172, 410.
Fox, The, 404.
Frederick V, Elector Palatine of Palsgrave, 393.
French Ambassador, 113 n., 220–21, 261, 316.
French players, 401, 420–24.
French Players' Theatre, 420–24.
Friar Bacon and Friar Bungay, 150.
Frith, Sir Richard, 96, 190.

Gabriel. *See* Spencer.
Gaedertz, Karl T., 167.
Gardiner, William, 34.
Garrard, G., 231, 232.
Gasquine, Susan, 159 n.
Gayton, Edmund, 303.
Gazette, The, 341 n.
General, The, 419.
George Yard, 313.
Gerschow, Frederic, 197, 208.
Gibbon's Tennis-Court Playhouse, 309 n.
Gildersleeve, Virginia C., 320 n.
Giles, Nathaniel, 201–13, 220 n.
Gill, John, 300.
Gill, Richard, 300 n.
Giolito, Gabriel, 411.
Giunti, 411.
Glapthorne, Henry, 369, 423.
Globe Playhouse, 65, 74, 85, 86, 86 n., 88, 112, 128, 146, 146 n., 155, 156, 159 n., 176, 180, 200, 209, 210, 214 n., 219 n., 223, 224, 227, 229, 233, n., 234–66, 267, 274–76, 282, 286, 289 n., 295, 297, 298, 311 n., 324, 328.
Goad, Christopher, 374.
Godfrey (Master of the Bear Garden), 337.

466 INDEX

Godfrey, W. H., 277 n.
Golding Lane, 88, 268 f.
Goodman, Nicholas, 180–81, 336.
Gosson, Stephen, 11, 47, 113.
Goulston Street, 17.
Govell, R., 369 n.
Gower, Edward, 405.
Grabu, M., 408.
Grace Church Street, 7 f., 67, 68.
Grateful Servant, The, 349.
Grave, Thomas, 387.
Graves, T. S., vii, 47 n., 177 n.
Gray, Lady Anne, 184.
Greene, Robert, 150.
Greene, Thomas, 296, 298–99.
Greene's Tu Quoque, 298.
Greenstreet, J., 317.
Greenwich, 384.
Greg, W. W., ix, 73, 148, 159 n., 179 n., 335 n., 377.
Grigges, John, 48.
Grymes, Thomas, 206.
Guildford, Lady Jane, 184.
Gunnell, Richard, 368–72, 374, 375.
Gwalter, William, 285 n.
Gyles, Thomas, 113–15, 206.

Hall, Ralph, 308.
Hamlet (Pre-Shakespearean), 74, 140.
Hamlet (Shakespeare), 208–10, 212 n., 248 n., 261.
Hammon, Thomas, 395.
Hampton Court, 384, 385, 401, 402, 404.
Harberte, Thomas, 81.
Harington, Sir John, 69.
Harper, Sir George, 184.
Harrison, Joan, 34–35.
Harrison, Thomas (Colonel), 304.
Hart, William, 304, 363.
Harvey, Gabriel, 48.
Hathaway, Richard, 158.
Hatton, Sir Christopher (Vice-Chamberlain), 70.
Hatton House, 363.
Haukins, William, 85.
Hawkins, Alexander, 211, 213, 214, 215.
Hayward, John, 411.
Heath, John, 297.
Hector of Germany, The, 89, 321 n.
Heminges, John, 62, 73, 84, 204, 208 n., 223, 224, 235–41, 255, 257, 258, 261–62, 319, 355.
Heminges, Thomasine, 261.
Henrietta Maria, Queen of England, 232–33, 420–22. Her players, *see* Queen's Company, King's and Queen's Company.
Henry IV, 7 n., 404.
Henry V (not Shakespeare's), 13.
Henry V (Shakespeare), 77 n., 348.
Henry VI, 150.
Henry VIII, 251–55, 391 n.
Henry VIII, 29, 186, 391.
Henry, Prince of Wales, 282–83, 392–93. His players, *see under* Admiral.
Henslowe, Agnes, 283.
Henslowe, Philip, 73, 85, 140, 140 n. 142–60, 161, 166, 174–75, 179, 213 n., 234, 244–46, 267–74, 281–83, 321–22, 324–35, 342–43, 346.
Henslowe, William, 268 n.
Hentzner, Paul, 131, 162.
Herbert, Sir Henry, 89, 225, 232, 250, 301, 307 n., 351 n., 357 n., 358, 359, 360, 360 n., 367, 368, 369, 373, 374, 376, 377, 377 n., 378, 380, 381, 400, 401 n., 403, 412 n., 420–24.
Herbert, Sir Philip, 392.
Herbert, Thomas, 81.
Herne, John, 370, 380.
Herne, John (the younger), 380–81.
Heton, Richard, 356 n., 357 n., 378–80, 427.
Heywood, Thomas, 158, 235 n., 247 n., 277 n., 298–99, 382, 394–95.
Hide, John, 51, 53–55, 70 n.
High Street, Southwark, 121.
Hill, John, 50.
Hoby, Sir Edward, 220.
Hoby, Sir Philip, 184.
Hockley-in-the-hole, Clerkenwell, 340.
Hogarth, William, 409 n.
Hog Hath Lost His Pearl, The, 320.
Holinshed, Raphael, 385.
Holland, Aaron, 294–96.
Holland, Henry, 127, 146.
Hollandia, Dona Britannica, 180.
Holland's Leaguer (Goodman), 180, 336.

INDEX 467

Holland's Leaguer (Marmion), 259, 375, 377, 415.
Hollar, W., 181, 259, 329–30.
Hollywell Lane, 81.
Holywell Priory, 30 f., 75 f., 88, 182, 183.
Honduis, J., 127, 146, 265, 329 n.
Hope Playhouse, 46, 128, 133, 146 n., 166, 179, 180, 248 n., 322, 324–41, 346, 355.
Horton, Joan, 143.
Houghton, John, 129.
Housekeepers, 225, 234 n., 236, 237 n., 351 n., 421 n.
Howard, Charles, the Lord Admiral. *See* Nottingham.
Howell, James, 248, 329 n.
Howes, Edmund, 7, 45 n., 111, 141, 251, 257, 285, 349, 350, 352, 372. *See also* Phillipps.
Humour Out of Breath, 315.
Hungarian Lion, The, 368.
Hunks, Harry, 121.
Hunnis, William, 102–10, 202, 203.
Hunsdon, George Carey, Lord, 184, 189, 198, 199, 212 n., 214.
Hunsdon, Henry Carey, Lord, 14, 68 n., 71, 184.
Hunsdon's Company (not the Strange-Derby, etc. Company), 69–71.
Hunsdon's Company. *See under* Strange-Derby, etc. Company.
Hutchinson, Christopher, 350 n., 362.
Hynde, John, 11.

Ianthe, 406.
Ibotson, Richard, 11.
Inner Temple Masque, The, 350.
Isle of Dogs, The, 84, 154, 170–75.
Isle of Guls, The, 220.
Italian players, 21.

Jack Drum's Entertainment, 115.
James I, 215, 217, 218, 221, 227, 250, 258, 281, 310 n., 316, 387, 392, 413, 416. His players, *see* Children of His Majesty's Revels, King's Revels Company, Strange-Derby, etc. Company.
James, William, 264.

Jeaffreson, J. C., 85, 410.
Jeffes, Anthony, 174 n.
Jeffes, Humphrey, 174 n.
Jerningham, Sir Henry, 184, 189.
Jew, The, 11.
Jew of Malta, The, 140, 150, 395.
Johnson, Henry, 60.
Johnson, Peter, 191–92, 196.
Johnson, Samuel, 264.
Jones, Inigo, 389, 395–400.
Jones, Richard, 168, 174, 318.
Jones, Robert, 343.
Jonson, Ben, 78, 84, 85, 171–73, 174 n., 206, 207, 217, 226, 244, 246, 247, 251, 255, 259, 319, 325, 330, 334, 419, 424.
Joyner, William, 194.
Julius Cæsar, 404.
Just Italian, The, 356.

Katherens, Gilbert, 326–30.
Kempe, Anthony, 189.
Kempe, William, 62, 73, 84, 115, 158, 235–40, 298.
Kelly, William, 17.
Kendall, Richard, 177 n., 333 n.
Kendall, Thomas, 213–22.
Kendall, William, 213 n.
Kenningham, Robert, 41.
Keysar, Robert, 117, 218–19, 222–24, 317–20.
Kiechel, Samuel, 47, 77.
Kildare, Earl of, 419.
Killigrew's playhouse, 382.
Kinaston, Edward, 207, 366.
Kingdom's Weekly Intelligencer, The, 291, 293 n.
King Lear, 261.
King Leir, 153.
Kingman, Philip, 343.
King's and Queen's Company (or Beeston's Boys), 357–62.
King's Company. *See under* Strange-Derby, etc.
King's (James I's) Revels Company, 311–18.
King's (Charles I's) Revels Company, 287, 374, 377–79.
Kingsland Spittle, 89.
Kingston, Lady Mary, 189.
Kingston, Sir William, 184.
Kirkham, Edward, 116, 208 n., 213–22, 226.

INDEX

Kirkman, Francis, 296–97, 305, 358–59.
Knowles, John, 241–42.
Kymbre, 41.
Kynaston, Edward, 207, 366.
Kyrkham, Sir Robert, 184.

Ladies' Priviledge, The, 423.
Lady Elizabeth's Company. *See* Princess Elizabeth's Company.
Lady Mother, The, 369.
La Fèvre de la Boderie, Antoine, 220–22, 316 n.
Lamb, Charles, 299.
Lambarde, William, 15.
Lambeth, 121, 161.
Landgartha, 418.
Laneham, Robert, 128.
Langley, Francis, 161, 170–76, 234.
Lanham, John, 67, 69, 80 n.
Lanman, Henry, 78–82, 83, 86, 87, 144, 234.
Lanteri, Edward, 265 n.
Lau, Hurfries de, 423.
Laud, William, 228–30.
Lawrence, W. J., vii, 48 n., 112, 177 n., 293 n., 313 n., 350 n., 365 n., 398, 408, 423 n.
Leaden Hall, 12.
Lee, Sir Sidney, 124 n., 294 n., 350 n., 408 n.
Le Febure (or Fevure), 422–23.
Leicester, Robert Dudley, Earl of, 106–07.
Leicester's Company, 22, 66, 67, 71, 80 n.
Lennox, James Stuart, 4 Duke of, 232.
Lennox, Ludovick Stuart, 2 Duke of, 261.
Lenton, Francis, 356.
Leveson, Sir Richard, 405.
Levison, William, 240.
Lewes, Thomas, 382.
Lilleston, Thomas, 366.
Lincolns, Inn Fields, 348 n., 352, 382, 414 f.
Lodge, Thomas, 74.
London's Lamentation for her Sins, 302.
Long, Maurice, 81.
Lorkin, Thomas, 254, 389.
Lost Lady, The, 404.

Loves and Adventures of Clerico and Lozia, The, 359.
Love's Mistress, or the Queen's Masque, 382.
Lowin, John, 158, 363, 400.
Loyal Protestant, The, 339.
Loyal Subject, The, 366.
Ludgate, 7 f., 226.
Ludlow, 71.
Luther, Martin, 113 n., 411.
Lyly, John, 109–10, 112, 113–14, 194, 202.

Machiavel, 411.
Machin, Lewis, 316.
Machyn, Henry, 124 n.
Mackaye, Steele, 398.
Madden, Sir Frederick, 130.
Madison Square Theatre, 398.
Maiden Lane, 88, 144, 243 f., 341.
Malcolm, J. P., 339.
Malone, Edmund, vii, 77, 89, 160 n., 225, 248, 367, 373, 375–76, 420.
Manchester, Edward Montagu, Earl of, 122, 337.
Mankind, 2–4.
Manningham, John, 178.
Mantzius, Karl, 48 n.
Markham, Gervais, 316.
Marlowe, Christopher, 73.
Marmion, Shackerley, 259, 375, 376, 377, 415.
Marston, John, 85 n., 112, 115, 116, 196 n., 216, 217–18, 223.
Martin, William, 265 n.
Martin Marprelate Controversy, 114.
Martin's Month's Mind, 10, 69.
Mason, John, 315, 316.
Masque, The, 369 n.
Massinger, Philip, 325, 382 n.
Mathews, John, 14.
Meade, Jacob, 326–36, 346.
Measure for Measure, 388.
Melise, ou Les Princes Reconnus, La, 420.
Mercer, Will, 338.
Merchant of Dublin, The, 418.
Mercurius Fumigosus, 307 n.
Mercurius Politicus, 292.
Meres, Francis, 175 n., 176.
Merian, M., 146 n., 180 n., 248, 328 n.

INDEX 469

Merry, Edward, 192.
Merry Devil of Edmonton, The, 404.
Merry Wives of Windsor, The, 388, 404.
Midas, 112.
Middlesex Street, 17.
Middleton, Thomas, 116, 207, 209 n., 278, 315, 350, 419.
Mohun, Michael, 304.
Monk, General. *See* Albemarle.
Monkaster. *See* Mulcaster.
Montmorency, Duke of, 385.
Moore, Mr. (of Pepy's *Diary*), 405.
Moor Field, 81.
Moor of Venice, The, 367, 387.
More, Sir Christopher, 184.
More, Sir William, 96–110, 113, 184, 189–90, 208.
Morocco Ambassador, 339.
Morris, Isbrand, 241–42.
Motteram, John, 206.
Mountjoy, Lord, 81.
Mulcaster, Richard, 206.
Munday, Anthony, 82.
Murray, J. T., 71, 88, 89 n., 111 n., 286 n., 298 n., 311 n., 323, 354 n., 377, 378.
Myles, Ralph, 57.
Myles, Robert, 28 n., 42, 43, 54–58.

Nash, Thomas, 10 n., 69, 84, 114–15, 154, 171–73.
Neuendorff, B., vii.
Neville, Sir Henry, 95–100, 102 n., 184.
Newgate Market, 122.
Newington Butts Playhouse, 73, 134–41, 151, 154.
New Inn Yard, 34, 79.
Newman, John, 107–08.
Nexara, Duke of, 130.
Nicholas, Basilius, 224.
Nightingale Lane, 410–12.
Noble Stranger, The, 373 n.
Norden, John, 128 n., 145.
Northbrooke, John, 76.
Northern Lass, The, 404.
Northup, Clark S., ix.
Nottingham, Charles Howard, Earl of, 155 n., 268–70, 272–73. His players, *see* Admiral.
No Wit, No Help like a Woman's, 419.

Ogilby, John, 294, 417–19.
Ogilby, John, and William Morgan, 294.
Ogilby's Dublin Theatre, 417–10.
Oldcastle, 404.
Opera, 365, 425.
Ordish, T. F., vii, 48 n., 341 n.
Orlando Furioso, 150.
Osteler, William, 225 n., 237, 260.
Othello, 367, 387, 388.
Oxford, Edward de Vere, Earl of, 16, 108–10, 157, 202.
Oxford's Company, 16, 87 n., 157–59.

Palatine. *See* Frederick V.
Palladio, Andrea, 398.
Pallant, Robert, 158.
Palmyra, 265.
Palsgrave. *See* Frederick V.
Palsgrave's Company. *See under* Admiral.
Pappe with an Hatchet, 112.
Paris, Robert de, 122.
Paris Garden. *See* Bear Garden.
Paris Garden, Manor of, 121 f., 135, 161 f.
Park, The, 241.
Park Street, 265.
Parliament Chamber, 186 f.
Passionate Lovers, The, 404.
Pastorall, The, 401.
Pavy, Salmon (or Salathiel), 206, 207.
Payne, Robert, 215.
Peckam, Edmund, 51–52, 66.
Pembroke, William Herbert, Earl of, 261.
Pembroke and Montgomery, Philip Herbert, Earl of, 232.
Pembroke's Company, 84, 154–55, 157, 170–75.
Penruddoks, Edward, 430.
Pepys, Samuel, 17, 207, 308, 338, 366, 382, 405.
Perfect Account, The, 305.
Perfect Occurrences, 304.
Perkins, Richard, 158, 380.
Perrin, Lady, 184.
Peyton, Sir John, 410.
Phillips, Augustine, 62, 73, 84, 224, 235–41, 260.
Phillipps, Sir Thomas (his copy of

Stow's *Annals*), 233, 258 n., 264, 285 n., 291, 330 n., 336, 364, 381 n.
Philotas, 216.
Phoenix Playhouse. *See* Cockpit Playhouse in Drury Lane.
Pierce, Edward, 116, 117, 319–20.
Pierce, James, 382.
Pierce, Mrs. James, 308, 382.
Pierce the Ploughman's Creed, 196.
Piozzi, Hester Lynch, 264.
Pipe Office, 190 n., 197.
Pit Court, 348 n.
Plague, 12, 15, 20, 23, 24, 67 n., 74 n. 152–53, 159, 215, 222, 223, 224, 281, 282, 287–88, 316, 355, 356, 357, 358, 379.
Playhouse to be Let, 309.
Playhouse Yard, 197.
Plomer, H. R., 293 n.
Poetaster, 1 n., 226.
Pollard, Thomas, 363.
Pope (a scrivener?), 159.
Pope, Alexander, 417.
Pope, Morgan, 159 n.
Pope, Thomas, 62, 73, 84, 86, 159 n., 224, 235–41, 260.
Porter's Hall. *See* Rosseter's Blackfriars Playhouse.
Portynary, Sir John, 184, 193.
Pride, Thomas, 337.
Prince Charles - 2 Red Bull Company:
    Prince Charles I's Company, 17, 88, 89, 179, 300, 301–02, 334–35, 344, 346, 354–55, 417.
    2 Red Bull Company, 301–04.
Prince Charles's (Charles II's) Company. *See under* Admiral, etc.
Prince Henry's Company. *See under* Admiral, etc.
Prince's Arms Inn, 180 n.
Princess Elizabeth's Company, 179, 321, 324, 332–35, 342, 344, 346, 354 n., 355.
Prynne, William, 302, 310 n., 372 n.
Ptolome, 11.
Puckering, Sir Thomas, 254, 389.
Puddlewharf, 343 f.
Puiseux, M. de, 221 n.
Puritans, 6, 18–19, 29, 85, 126, 156.
Pykman, Phillipp, 206.

Queen Anne's Company. *See under* Worcester, etc.
Queen's (Elizabeth's) Company, 12, 13, 66–72, 80 n., 84, 153.
Queen's (Henrietta's) Company, 355–56, 379–80, 394, 421, 427.
Queen's Revels. *See under* Children of the Chapel, etc.
Queen's Street, 348 n.

Raleigh, Sir Walter, 126.
Ram Alley, 313, 316.
Randolph, Thomas, 303, 349.
Rastell, William, 213–22.
Ratcliffe, 352.
Rathgeb, Jacob, 132.
1 Red Bull Company. *See under* Worcester, etc.
2 Red Bull Company. *See under* Prince Charles, etc.
Red Bull Playhouse, 75 n., 88, 89, 219 n., 226 n., 287, 294–309, 311 n., 351, 353, 353 n., 356, 374, 378.
Red Bull Yard, 294.
Redwood, C. W., ix.
Reeve, Ralph, 343.
Rendle, William, 12, 124 n., 143, 178 n., 180 n., 339.
Reulidge, Richard, 8, 310 n.
Revels Office, 94, 96.
Reynolds, G. F., vii.
Rhodes, John, 365, 366.
Richards, Hugh, 36.
Richmond, 402, 404.
Roaring Girl, The, 278.
Roberts, John, 242.
Robinson, James, 205, 213.
Robinson, Richard, 304.
Rochester, John Wilmot, Earl of, 340.
Romeo and Juliet, 85.
Roper, Lactantius, 241–42.
Rosania, 259, 419.
Rose Alley, 144, 160 n.
Rose Playhouse, 16, 16 n., 61 n., 63, 73 n., 75 n., 77 n., 128, 139, 140, 142–60, 167, 168 n., 174, 179, 182, 238, 248, 265, 267, 296, 324, 332 n.
Rosseter, Philip, 117, 118, 224, 317–23, 324–25, 330–32, 335, 342–47.
Rosseter's Blackfriars Playhouse, 322, 336, 342–47, 355.

INDEX

Rossingham, Edmond, 288.
Rowlands, Samuel, 185 n.
Roxalana, 406.
Royal Master, The, 419.
Rump, The, 382.
Russell, Dowager Lady Elizabeth, 199.
Rutland, Edward Manners, Earl of, 36, 36 n., 37.
Rutland House, 364.
Ryther, Augustine, 277.

Sacarson, 121.
Sackful of News, A., 10.
St. Bride's, Parish of, 425 f.
St. Dunstan's, Parish of, 425 f.
St. Giles, Cripplegate, 268 f.
St. Giles in the Fields, 355, 362.
St. James, Palace of, 384, 392.
St. James, Parish of, 294 f.
St. John's Gate, 294.
St. John's Street, 11, 96, 294 f., 305.
St. Mary Overies, 64–65, 168 n., 238.
St. Mildred, Parish of, 143, 159.
St. Patrick for Ireland, 419.
St. Paul's Boys. *See* Children of St. Paul's.
St. Paul's Cathedral, 29 n., 167.
St. Paul's Playhouse, 8, 111–18, 349.
St. Saviours, Parish of, 145, 170, 259.
St. Warburg's Street, Dublin, 418.
Salisbury, Mr. (portrait painter), 366.
Salisbury, Robert Cecil, Earl of, 221.
Salisbury Court Playhouse, 233, 259, 287, 291, 302, 350, 357 n., 360 n., 364, 368–83, 427.
Sampson, M. W., 279 n.
Sandwich, Edward Montagu, Earl of, 405.
Sapho and Phao, 109, 113.
Satiromastix, 332.
Saunders, Lady, 343 f.
Saunders, Sir Thomas, 184.
Savage, Thomas, 240.
Scornful Lady, The, 403, 406.
Scott, Sir Walter, 310 n.
Scuderi, Georges de, 421 n.
Sellers, William, 242.
Shadwell, Thomas, 310 n.
Shakespeare, William, 62, 63, 65, 73, 84, 85, 140, 150, 186, 208–10, 212 n., 224, 235–41, 249, 251, 261–62, 298, 348, 391 n.
Shanks, John, 263.
Sharp, Lewis, 373 n.
Sharpham, Edward, 316.
Shatterel, Edward, 304–05, 308.
Shaw, Robert, 168, 172–74.
Sherlock, William, 380.
Shirley, James, 259, 349, 376, 377, 406 n., 419.
Shoreditch, 30, 78, 185.
Sibthorpe, Edward, 315.
Siege of Rhodes, The, 364.
Silent Woman, The, 319, 405.
Silver, George, 13 n., 194–95.
Silver, Thomas, 381, 383.
Singer, John, 235 n.
Sir Francis Drake, 364.
Sir Giles Goosecappe, 373.
Skevington, Richard, 172.
Skialetheia, 46, 61.
Slaiter, Martin, 315, 317–18.
Slye, William, 224, 225 n., 235 n., 260.
Smallpiece, Thomas, 108.
Smith, Isack, 366.
Smith, John, 351 n.
Smith, Captain John, 369 n.
Smith, Wentworth, 158.
Smith, William, 63.
Smithfield, 332.
Somerset House, 404.
Sophocles, 398.
Soulas, Josias de, 420–24.
Spanish Ambassador, 281, 339.
Spanish Curate, The, 404.
Spanish Tragedy, The, 150, 261.
Sparagus Garden, The, 379.
Sparks, Thomas, 285 n.
Speed, John, 265.
Spencer, Gabriel, 168, 172–74, 235 n.
Spiller, Sir Henry, 230.
Spykes School, 206.
Squire of Alsatia, The, 310 n.
Stanley, Ferdinando, Lord Strange. *See* Derby.
Star of the West, 133.
Steevens, George, 77–78.
Stepney Field, 352.
Stettin-Pomerania, Philip Julius, Duke of, 207, 214–15.
Stevens, John, 183.

INDEX

Stockwood, John, 8, 26, 46, 48.
Stone, George, 121.
Stopes, Charlotte C., 361 n.
Stoughton, Robert, 36.
Stow, John, 124, 136, 166, 348, 388, 391. See also Howes, Phillipps, and Strype.
Strafford, Thomas Wentworth, Earl of, 417–18.
Strange, Lord. See Derby.
Strange - Derby - 1 Chamberlain - Hunsdon - 2 Chamberlain - King James I - King Charles I's Company:
    Strange's Company, 14, 139, 150–54.
    Derby's Company, 73, 87 n., 153.
    1 Chamberlain's Company, 14–15, 150, 153–54.
    Hunsdon's Company, 199, 199 n.
    2 Chamberlain's Company, 16, 61, 61 n., 62, 68 n., 73–74, 84, 85, 150, 154–55, 159 n., 174–75, 176, 200, 209 n., 212 n., 235–38, 249, 267, 272–73, 351.
    King James I's Company, 88, 118, 223–27, 250–62, 295, 320–21, 324, 325, 374.
    King Charles I's Company, 227–33, 262–63, 302, 365, 374, 378, 400, 401, 402.
Street, Peter, 63, 64, 239, 269, 273–74.
Strype, John, 243, 340, 391, 408 n.
Stubbes, Philip, 83, 125.
Stutville, George, 374.
Summer playhouse, 67–68, 225, 250, 321, 324, 325, 342.
Sumner, John, 380.
Sussex's Company, 152.
Swan Inn, 180 n.
Swan Playhouse, 77 n., 84, 154–55, 161–81, 182, 238, 273, 321, 324, 326, 327, 329, 334, 342–43.
Swanston, Eilliard, 400.
Swinerton, Sir John, 321.
Swynnerton, Thomas, 296.

Taming of a Shrew, The, 140.
Tarbock, John, 318.

Tarleton, Richard, 12, 13, 14 n., 67, 69, 72, 72 n., 235, 298.
Tarlton's Jests, 13.
Tarlton's News out of Purgatory, 69, 75.
Tatham, John, 289, 303 n., 382.
Taylor, John (the Water Poet), 251, 257, 259, 329, 332–34.
Taylor, Joseph, 363, 400.
Taylor, Robert, 320.
Theatre Playhouse, 8, 10, 11 n., 15, 26, 27–74, 75, 76, 77, 78, 83, 84, 91, 112, 135, 138, 154, 155, 167, 172 n., 182, 199, 200, 234–35, 239, 244, 249.
Thespis, 398.
Thoresby, Henry, 410.
Thorndike, A. H., vii.
Thrale, Mrs. Henry, 264.
Three Kings Ordinary, 425, 429, 430.
Tilney, Edmund, 66, 85.
Titus Andronicus, 140, 152.
Tomlins, T. E., 76.
Tom Tell Troth's Message, 146.
Tooley, Nicholas, 350 n.
Topclyfe, Richard, 172–73.
Totenham Court, 373.
Toy, The, 419.
Trevell, William, 315.
Trompeur Puni, Le, 421.
Trussell, Alvery, 206.
Tunstall, James, 350 n.
Turk, The, 316.
Turner, 178.
Turner, Anthony, 308, 380.
Turnor, Richard, 50.
Two Maids of Moreclacke, The, 316.

Underwood, John, 86.
Unfortunate Lovers, The, 233, 404.
University of Illinois, 277 n.

Vaghan, Edward, 410.
Valient Cid, The, 406.
Vaughan, Sir William, 125.
Venetian Ambassador, 280.
Vennar, Richard, 177–78, 333 n.
Vere, Lady Susan, 392.
Verneuil, Madame de, 220–21.
Vertue, George, 387 n., 396.
Virgin, performance by a, 74 n.
Visscher, C. J., 127, 128, 146 n.,

INDEX

164-65, 248, 253, 328, 328 n., 329.
Volpone, 404.
Vox Graculi, 89.
Vuolfio, Giovanni. *See* John Wolf.

Walker, Thomas, 337.
Wallace, C. W., ix, 67, 71, 110 n., 115, 117, 140, 148 n., 160 n., 168 n., 170 n., 177 n., 178 n., 179 n., 192 n., 196 n., 197, 197 n., 201 n., 204 n., 208, 212 n., 215 n., 221 n., 243, 248-49, 258 n., 259 n., 266, 285 n., 353 n.
Walsingham, Sir Francis, 110.
Warburton, John, 369 n.
War of the Theatres, 250.
Warwick, Ambrose Dudley, Earl of, 12.
Water Lane, Blackfriars, 98, 102.
Water Lane, Whitefriars, 371.
Way to Content all Women, or How a Man May Please his Wife, 368-69.
Webster, John, 116, 158, 226 n.
Weekly Account, The, 290.
Weekly Intelligencer, The, 306, 307.
Westcott, Sebastian, 113.
Westminster Cathedral, 126, 167.
Westminster School, 206.
What You Will, 112.
Whitaker, Laurence, 230.
White, Thomas, 48, 76.
Whitechapel, 8 n., 17.
Whitechapel Street, 7.
Whitecross Street, 268 f.
White Devil, The, 226 n.
Whitefriars Playhouse, 8, 117, 224, 310-23, 324, 342-43, 368 n.
Whitehall, 356 n., 374, 384 f., 387-91, 403.
White Hart Inn, 1.
Whitelock, Bulstrode, 305.
Whitton, Tom, 382.
Wigpitt, Thomas, 285 n.
Wilbraham, 172.
Wilbraham, William, 374.
Wilkinson, Nicholas, 350 n.
Wilkinson, R., 259 n., 293 n.
Williams, John, 412-17.
Williamson, Joseph, 306.
Wilson, J. D., 76 n.

Wilson, Robert, 12, 176.
Winchester, Bishop of, 119, 134, 241 n.
Windsor, 384. *See also* Children of Windsor Chapel.
Winter playhouse, 67-68, 225, 233, 250, 321, 324, 325, 342.
Wintershall, William, 308.
Winwood, Sir Ralph, 252, 392.
Wirtemberg, Duke of, 132.
Witch of Edmonton, The, 354 n.
Witt, Johannes de, 77 n., 146 n., 165-68, 273.
Witter, John, 224, 258.
Wit Without Money, 304.
Wolf, John, 410-12.
Wolf's Theatre, 410-12.
Wolsey, Cardinal, 186, 252, 391.
Woman is a Weathercock, A, 140, 342 n.
Wood, Anthony à, 418.
Woode, Tobias, 410.
Woodford, Thomas, 311, 313, 314, 322.
Woodman, 193.
Woodward, 142.
Woodward, Agnes, 142-43, 283.
Woodward Joan, ix, 151.
Worcester College, 395.
Worcester-Queen-1 Red Bull-Children of the Revels Company:
  Worcester's Company, 16, 72, 87, 157-59, 295, 351.
  Queen Anne's Company, 16, 87, 88, 158, 295-300, 351, 353.
  1 Red Bull Company, 300-01.
  Children of the Revels, 301.
Wordsworth, William, 299.
Wotton, Sir Henry, 251, 320.
Wright, George R., 401.
Wright, James, 285, 297, 303, 304, 350, 363, 373.
Wyngaerde, A. van den, 124.

Yarmouth, 45 n.
York House, 391.
Young, John, 374.
Younger Brother, The, 299.
Young Gallant's Whirligig, The, 356.

Zanche, Lord, 184.